The Pursuit of Pleasure

The Pursuit of Pleasure

DRUGS AND STIMULANTS IN IRANIAN HISTORY, 1500–1900

Rudi Matthee

PRINCETON UNIVERSITY PRESS

PRINCETON AND OXFORD

Copyright © 2005 by Princeton University Press
Published by Princeton University Press, 41 William Street, Princeton, New Jersey 08540
In the United Kingdom: Princeton University Press, 3 Market Place, Woodstock, Oxfordshire OX20 ISY

All Rights Reserved

Library of Congress Cataloging-in-Publication Data

Matthee, Rudolph P.
  The pursuit of pleasure: drugs and stimulants in Iranian history, 1500–1900 /
Rudi Matthee.
    p. cm.
  Includes bibliographical references and index.
  ISBN 0-691-11855-8 (cloth: alk. paper)
  1. Drug abuse—Iran—History. 2. Drug utilization—Iran—History. 3. Stimulants—Iran—History. I. Title.

HV5840.I7M38 2005
362.29'0955'0903—dc22   2004058688

British Library Cataloging-in-Publication Data is available

This book has been composed in Sabon

Printed on acid-free paper. ∞

pup.princeton.edu

Printed in the United States of America

10 9 8 7 6 5 4 3 2 1

For Ruth

Contents

List of Illustrations

Note on Transliteration

THE ARABIC AND PERSIAN transliteration used in this book follows the Library of Congress system without the diacritical marks. Exceptions are nonroman place names such as Tehran and Herat, and terms such as *jizya* and shari`a, which are spelled without the final *h*. Dates in the text are given according to the Common Era calendar, except when there is a compelling reason to give the (solar) *hijri* date as well. Russian spelling, too, conforms to the Library of Congress system.

Preface

IRANIAN HISTORY has come a long way from its former focus on poetry and religion, bred from a common perception that the immaterial, spiritual aspects of life constitute the country's essence and soul. Whereas the imprint of high culture on Iranian history writing remains strong, rightfully so given the country's glorious achievements, in the last twenty years or so scholars have begun to examine other aspects of Iran's past. This book aims to contribute to that trend. It does so by addressing material culture, a dimension of Iranian history that remains underdeveloped, in dialogue with a range of ideas and behaviors involving taste, pleasure, status, and respectability. Drugs and stimulants form the prism through which I view Iranian society. Far from being simply "luxuries," and thus peripheral to society, they blur the line between "luxuries" and "necessities," and thus become emblems of cultural processes and meaning as well as signifiers of the long-term, evolutionary change that this study seeks to identify.

It is important to set out in advance what this book is not or at least what it does not intend to achieve. It addresses both the pharmacological properties of the substances it examines and their physical appearance and that of their accessories, but it fundamentally wants to be a study of Iranian society and its evolution over time. It only pays limited attention to Sufism, and the nature of the available sources has forced me to focus on elites and urban life more than I would have liked. It is, finally, not my intention to exoticize pre-twentieth-century Iran, to argue or imply that it was inherently different and inexplicable and that its inhabitants were constitutionally given to massive drug consumption. Such an impression would be false if only because no society has arguably been more into drug use than the modern West. It would also be reductionist, because more than half of the material presented here concerns caffeinated beverages and tobacco, which barely qualify as mind-altering. Using a comparative approach, I argue in fact that Iran was not all that different from contemporary societies elsewhere, including European ones, and that whereas many people of all rank and class ingested opium and its derivatives, those who drank wine mostly belonged to the ruling elite.

My encounter with drugs and stimulants in an Iranian context goes back to the year I spent as an exchange student in Iran in 1976–77, when evenings with opium and tea were part of visits with friends to the forests of Gilan. My interest in the topic was revived and assumed an intellectual dimension during my days as a research assistant for

Professor Nikki Keddie at UCLA. In 1990, she was invited to take part in a one-day seminar on drugs and narcotics in world history at the Welcome Institute for Medicine in London, organized by the late Roy Porter. She asked me to do some preliminary work on a paper dealing with the remarkable similarities in the spread and reception of stimulants such as coffee, tea, and cocoa in the early modern period from a comparative perspective. I did and wrote a paper on the topic. Nikki then suggested that I go to London to present the paper as my own work. Out of it came a publication,[1] and further interest in the subject, which resulted in a few more articles dealing with aspects of the introduction and acceptance of coffee and tea in Iranian history, and eventually the idea to expand the material that kept accumulating into a book.[2] I always will be grateful to Nikki Keddie for her generosity in allowing me to take her place in London and for encouraging me to pursue the intriguing topic of drugs and stimulants beyond that initial foray into it.

I owe a debt of gratitude to the colleagues and friends who read all or parts of the book with a critical eye and made helpful suggestions: Drs. Rula Abi Saab, Thomas Allsen, Elena Andreeva, Said Amir Arjomand, Houchang Chehabi, Michael Cook, Alice Hunsberger, Baber Johansen, Manouchehr Kasheff, Leonard Lewisohn, Paul Losensky, Hossein Modarressi, and Ernest Tucker. I heeded most, although not all, of their advice and suggestions. All factual mistakes and questionable interpretations that remain are obviously mine. Manouchehr Kasheff deserves special thanks for generously giving of his time to decipher `Imad al-Din Shirazi's treatise on opium with me. I thank Massumeh Farhad and Abolala Soudavar for allowing me to use images, Stephen Dale for sharing the galleys of his biography of Babur with me, and Parvin Salehi of Tehran for her efficiency in procuring documents. I am appreciative of Holly Schissler of the University of Chicago, Bert Fragner of the Österreichische Akademie der Wissenschaften in Vienna, as well as the organizers of the Columbia University Iran Seminar and those of the History Graduate Studies Seminar at UCLA for inviting me to speak on various aspects of this study. A General University Research Grant from the University of Delaware enabled me to do research abroad, and a year as an NEH Fellow at the Institute for Advanced Study in Princeton made it possible for me to finish much of the writing in a sylvan setting. Thanks to all members of IAS, and especially Patricia Crone and Oleg Grabar, for an exciting year. Any views, findings, conclusions, or recommendations expressed in this book do not necessarily reflect those of the National Endowment for the

---

[1] Matthee, "Exotic Substances."
[2] Matthee, Coffee in Safavid Iran"; and "From Coffee to Tea."

Humanities. Thanks also to my colleagues at the University of Delaware, and especially Carole Haber, for their help and encouragement, and to Angie Hoseth for assisting with the map and the illustrations. The librarians and archivists of the Majlis Library in Tehran, the India Office Library in London, the Archives des Affaires Etrangères in Paris and Nantes, and the Nationaal Archief in The Hague all deserve credit for their efficiency and helpfulness. I am grateful to Silvia Zengueneh di Monteforte for allowing me to take a look at her grandfather's papers during a brief visit to Paris. At Princeton University Press, Brigitta van Rheinberg has been a terrific editor and Alison Kalett and Laura Lawrie have made the production process a breeze.

My family remains my ultimate drug. Ruth's creative and passionate pursuit of her own scholarship continues to inspire me more than I can tell. I dedicate this book to her. Max and Theo energize me with their own boundless, infectious lust for life. Watching them makes me realize how lucky I am and gives me hope for this world. My mother, finally, I can't thank enough for her continued quiet faith in me.

Abbreviations

A&P	Accounts and Papers
BSOAS	Bulletin of the School of Oriental and African Studies
EI^2	Encyclopedia of Islam, 2nd edition
EIr.	Encyclopedia Iranica
IJMES	International Journal of Middle East Studies
Iran	Iran. British Journal of Persian Studies
IS	Iranian Studies
JAOS	Journal of the American Oriental Society
JESHO	Journal of the Economic and Social History of the Orient
JRGS	Journal of the Royal Geographical Society
JWH	Journal of World History
MAS	Modern Asian Studies
MII	Miras-i Islami-yi Iran
MOOI	Moyen Orient et Océan Indien XVIe–XIXe
OMO	Oesterreichische Monatschrift für den Orients
RMM	Revue du Monde Musulman
SI	Studia Islamica
Stud. Ir.	Studia Iranica
TBGS	Transactions of the Bombay Geographical Society
WI	Die Welt des Islams

The Pursuit of Pleasure

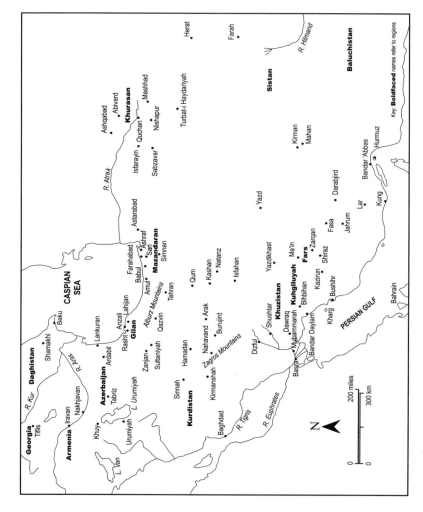

Iran and surrounding area, 1500–1900

THIS BOOK addresses the topic of drugs and stimulants in Iran's history as a dialogue between their status as part of material culture—as concrete, tangible consumables with a physical working—and the array of meanings Iranian's have attached to them over a period of four hundred years, in the belief that such an approach might reveal something significant about Iran—as a society at any given moment in that long period, as a society in process, and as a society interacting with the outside world.

From ancient times until the present-day Islamic Republic, psychoactive agents have influenced Iranian social, political, and economic life in ways that range from the ordinary to the surprising and remarkable. Wine, which may have originated in Iran, was the drink of choice for Iranian elites in premodern times. Its consumption does not seem to have diminished much following the Arab conquest and the introduction of Islam in the seventh century C.E. Far from always being a private affair, inebriation at times diminished military vigor and the quality of political leadership. The wine-soaked defeat Shah Isma'il suffered against the Turks in the battle of Chaldiran in 1514 illustrates this point as vividly as the fact that alcholism shortened the lives of several Safavid rulers.

The same is true for opium, which has been part of the Iranian landscape since Sasanian times and a popular drug since at least the Safavid period. Although people typically took a daily dose that was too small to render them incapable of going about their daily lives, excess did occur, and, as with wine, overindulgence among the ruling elite at times came at the expense of good governance. Most dramatically, the expansion of opium cultivation was a contributing factor to the terrible famine of 1869–72 that may have wiped out one tenth of Iran's population. Tobacco, tremendously popular almost from the moment it entered the country in the sixteenth century, three hundred years later became the centerpiece of a revolt that sparked the Constitutional Revolution, arguably the most far-reaching revolution in Iranian history to this day. Although coffee and tea can lay claim to no such fame, these beverages did not just become popular but also had a substantial part in fashioning new forms of sociability, and tea eventually triumphed as Iran's most popular beverage by far.

This book examines these various intoxicants, the ones that, in the words of a long-time foreign resident of seventeenth-century Iran, provided

Iranians with *damagh*, gave them a "kick," got them into a good mood.[1] By tracing their historical trajectory and the role they have played in Iranian society, it follows examples set by recent scholarship on narcotics and stimulants in other parts of the early modern world. The last two decades have seen a surge in attention to consumption, including the consumption of psychotropic substances, in early modern times. A fair share of the resulting scholarship has been devoted to the study of stimulants such as coffee and tea, which are no longer viewed as mere commodities in the "trade and consumer" revolutions but are now explored as emblems and symbols of religious practice, social relations, or political change. Alcoholic beverages and opiates, too, have begun to attract the attention of historians. Scholars have addressed their function in religious imagery and medical experimentation, examined their acceptance and distribution as indices of social class and status, or focused on governmental reactions to their widespread adoption, which ranged from legal prohibition to fiscal stimulation.[2]

With the exception of the original areas of cultivation, South America for tobacco, Yemen for coffee and China for tea, the non-European world has received short shrift in this recent scholarship.[3] Rudolf Gelpke's broad-ranging book on narcotics in East and West and Franz Rosenthal's more specific study on hashish in medieval Muslim society aside, drugs and stimulants, the context in which they were used and the ritual that surrounded them, have just begun to enter the consciousness of Middle East historians.[4] The ones who have taken the lead in examining this aspect of daily life in the early modern Middle East are scholars of the Ottoman Empire.[5] And coffee has received by far the most attention. The classic study on the subject, Ralph Hattox's book on the culture of its

---

[1]Du Mans, "`Estat de 1660," in Richard, *Raphaël du Mans*, 2:102.

[2]Recent social studies of narcotics and stimulants in the early modern period, mostly in a European context, include, in chronological order, Sandgruber, *Bittersüsse Genüsse* (1986); Daniella Ball, ed., *Kaffee im Spiegel europäischer Trinksitten* (1991); Karl Wassenberg, *Tee in Ostfriesland: Vom religiösen Wundertrank zum profanen Volksgetränk* (1991); Schivelbush, *Tastes of Paradise* (1992); Hans Gros, *Rausch und Realität: Eine Kulturgeschichte der Drogen* (1996); Thomas Hengartner et al., eds. *Genussmittel, Eine Kulturgeschichte* (1999); Courtwright, *Forces of Habit* (2001); Iain Gately, *Tobacco: A Cultural History of How an Exotic Plant Seduced Civilization* (2001); Weinberg and Bealer. *The World of Caffeine* (2001); Jessica Warner, *Craze: Gin and Debauchery in an Age of Reason* (2002). For Russia, see Smith and Christian, *Bread and Salt*; for China, see Dikötter et al., *Narcotic Culture*; For the Middle East, see Desmet-Grégoire and Georgeon, eds., *Cafés d'Orient revisités*.

[3]For Yemen, see Brouwer, *Cauwa ende Comptanten/Cowha and Cash*. For coffee in the Ottoman Empire, see Hattox, *Coffee and Coffeehouses*. A recent study of tea in China is Evans, *Tea in China*.

[4]Rosenthal. *The Herb*; and Gelpke, *Vom Rausch im Orient und Okzident*.

[5]See, for example, Farooqhi, *Subjects of the Sultan*; and Quataert, ed., *Consumption Studies*.

consumption in the Ottoman Empire, has recently been joined by studies of various other, mostly trade-related, aspects of coffee's rise to prominence.[6] The history of tea, by contrast, the most popular beverage in much of the Middle East, remains largely unexamined. Remarkably, the same is true for wine. Peter Heine and, more recently, Kathryn Kueny, have addressed the important topic of alcohol in the Islamic world, but wine remains most readily associated with mystical poetry.[7] With David Fahey, we may wonder why the paradox that many Muslims drink despite their religion's ban on alcohol has not excited the curiosity of researchers more than it has.[8]

Focusing on Iran, the answer to this question, and the more general one concerning the dearth of scholarship on all psychoactive substances, will have to take into account the idealist tradition in the country's history, which is arguably as strong as if not stronger than in the case of Arab lands and the Ottoman Empire. The gravitational force of a culture that has tended to value and validate transcendence and essence over palpable, outer reality, has caused scholars of Iran, Iranians and Westerns alike, to privilege the study of the loftier, more spiritual pursuits of human existence over their interest in life's material aspects, including matters of production and consumption.[9] Add to that the richness of Iran's cultural tradition and the relative poverty of socio-economic documentation for any period prior to the modern age, and one begins to understand why the intoxicating effect of drug taking has agitated scholars mostly as a poetic metaphor.

By sending contradictory signals, the current intellectual climate in the West has been only partially helpful in remedying this situation. Recent trends in scholarship—a broadening of research topics, including socio-economic ones, and a turn to innovative cultural approaches—hold great promise for the field of Middle Eastern studies. Yet, as new vistas have opened up, historians also have faced the anxiety of being branded as "Orientalists," scholars who confuse the study of texts or, worse, texts written by nonnatives, with the study of reality and who use those texts to portray the East as a land of capricious rulers and static societies.

Highlighting alcoholism in court circles and widespread drug use throughout society might not seem the best way to subvert this latter

---

[6]Tuchscherer, ed., *Le commerce du café*

[7]Heine, *Weinstudien*; Kueny, *Rhetoric of Sobriety*. See also Malecka, "The Muslim Bon Vivant." For a study on wine in Persian poetry, see Epinette, "Le thème du vin."

[8]David M. Fahey, "'I'll Drink to That,'" 643.

[9]An exception is the ample attention paid to drugs in Ravandi, *Tarikh-i ijtima`i-yi Iran*, 7:225-99. For tobacco, also see Floor, "The Art of Smoking." Matthee, "Coffee in Safavid Iran," is mostly incorporated into the present study.

image. It is indeed easier to ignore the voluminous firsthand literature on the topic, because it does not readily fit the image of an energetic society poised for modernity, and to argue, by way of justification, that much of this literature was written by uninformed foreign observers. I have chosen not to do so, in part because ignoring the topic evidently does not make it disappear, and in part because I believe that indigenous sources are as "tainted" for being biased as foreign ones—although for different reasons—and that there is therefore no inherent reason to privilege domestic voices over external ones. Indigenous sources may appear as more authentic to the society that produced them, but they also tend to present and represent a particular, elitist, selective version of reality, aside from yielding little information on issues of socioeconomic import. Proximity and intimate familiarity do not necessarily trump the reflective detachment of the eyewitness account by outsiders, especially not if the latter record their impressions and observations without a denigrating or overly moralizing tone, as those visiting Iran prior to the nineteenth century often did.[10] Accounts of foreigners can thus find a place in a carefully constructed narrative that goes beyond societal stasis and dissolute elite behavior.

The issue of stasis can be summarily dismissed. Origins and early patterns invariably gave way to development and change. The very introduction and spread of the stimulants that entered Iran during the Safavid period, tobacco, coffee, and tea, signal a vibrant rather than an atrophying society. Not only was Safavid Iran being incorporated into a new global matrix of commerce and consumption; Iranians played an active role in its very formation by enthusiastically embracing the new consumables and adapting them to their needs and tastes.

It is admittedly more difficult to subvert the image of fainéant, drug-addled elites, but here, too, a more nuanced picture might be gained. The apparent contrast between the hard-working, disciplined early modern West and the languid, pleasure-seeking Orient created and nurtured by centuries of image-making and reiteration, has of late been undermined by a steady stream of studies that have burrowed deeply underneath the exterior of Western rationalism and bourgeois frugality to find rich layers of deviant social and sexual behavior. When dealing with early modern Middle Eastern society, there is no need to follow the tendency of this scholarship to hail such behavior for being subversive

---

[10]This is not to say that these sources are all equal or that the information of even someone like Chardin did not fit into the framework of a seventeenth-century European perspective in which writing about Safavid society and religion was as much about Iran as about the court of the French king or one's position on Catholicism. For such ulterior motives among French travelers to the Middle East and particularly Iran in the seventeenth century, see Carnoy, *Représentations de l'Islam.*

of the prevailing (and oppressive) moral order. To level the playing field, it might be rather more useful neither to follow the "traditional" approach nor to adopt the "new" approach—that is, neither to condemn nor to celebrate and romanticize similar behavior—both of which easily reinforce received notions by identifying drugs with Iranians and their entire culture. To avoid "essentialism" it seems more productive to follow a more functionalist approach by investigating the specific circumstances under which these substances came to play a role in society and how that role changed as circumstances changed.

Specificity, in turn, can be tested and, if need be, challenged through comparison. Tracing Iran's history to the pre-Islamic period takes the burden off Islam as the sole organizing principle of the country's culture and society. Synchronic comparisons, moreover, reveal that in some ways Iran was unique, in others operated in a regional world with which it shared an Islamic cultural idiom, and in yet other ways must be seen as an early modern society that was not that different from faraway countries of a different cultural disposition.[11] It is important to remember in this context that, even as attitudes toward narcotics and stimulants have changed and continue to evolve, as Davenport-Hines says, "absolute sobriety is not a natural or primary human state."[12] Their use is of all time and each society uses its own, but the consumption of legal and illegal substances may be greater in modern times and in the Western world than at any time and in any past society.

The Pursuit of Pleasure, then, seeks to join the literature on Europe with a panoramic, yet detailed study of stimulants that keep you awake, that help improve one's concentration—tobacco, coffee, and tea—and the inebriants, narcotics and hallucinogens that have a mellowing effect—wine, opium, and hashish—in early modern Iranian history along the lines of what scholars such as Schivelbusch and Courtwright have achieved for these consumables in the Western or a larger global context. Its aim is to inspire a wider examination of patterns of consumption and consumerism—consumption on a high level and on the

[11]The tem "early modern" requires some clarification in this context. Following Jack Goldstone's recent observations, I use the term as temporal shorthand for the period 1500 to 1850, or rather 1500 to 1900, without the implication that this period marks Iran's transition to modernity and that the Western example is a useful template for studying it. Despite strong reformist impulses and a number of actual reforms throughout the nineteenth century, the country until the Constitutional Revolution (1906–11) remained largely premodern in its economic structure, its mode of governance, and in general in the relationship between rulers and subjects. The one distinct feature that Iran shared with many other countries in this period is its incorporation into a global network of commercial exchange. See Goldstone, "The Problem of the 'Early Modern' World."

[12]Davenport-Hines, The Pursuit of Oblivion, ix.

basis of particular scales of values—in Middle Eastern history.[13] It looks at these *Genussmittel* (lit. means of enjoyment), to use the evocative German term, with an eye to their material manifestation—their pharmacological properties and the accessories associated with their use—but, more important, views them as a prism refracting a variety of economic, social, and political issues. Drugs and stimulants will be discussed in their commercial context, paying attention to patterns of importation and distribution, but the study's larger objective is to offer a social history of ways in which Iranians have approached drugs and stimulants since 1500, adapting them to their cultural environment or adapting their cultural environment to them. It explores the circumstances under which wine and opium were transmitted from earlier times or, in the case of tobacco, coffee, and tea, newly introduced and disseminated, how they became integrated into people's lives, why people used them, which social groups were most affected by them, how they fashioned new patterns of recreation and sociability, and how, finally, they figured in the ongoing process of negotiation between institutions of authority—the state and the religious establishment—and society.

The book pays particular attention to a few specific questions and themes. The first concerns origins, antecedents, and (outside) influence. A distinction needs to be made here between, on the one hand, opium and especially wine, both psychoactive agents that had been part of Iranian society since ancient times, and the "new" stimulants, coffee, tobacco, and tea, on the other, which were introduced and gained popularity only some four hundred years ago. The use of the former goes back to pre-Islamic times, and even after the Arab invasion much of the merriment surrounding Iranian court life can be traced to inherited, non-Islamic cultural traditions. Banquets attended by rulers engaged in ceremonial drinking and enlivened by music-making and homoerotic dancing betray the influence of pre-Islamic Iranian beliefs and practices, in which the rite of drinking wine—a symbol for liquid gold and flowing fire—substituted for the even more ancient blood libation, and an ambience in which catamites abounded. Safavid society sanctioned the excessive drinking of its rulers with a widespread belief that, as the son of the Shi`i Imam, the shah was exempt from the ban on drinking alcohol. As was true in many part of the world, opiates served as the only effective painkiller as well as a cure-all for a whole array of ailments and diseases, whereas various opium-laced electuaries were a favorite means for the elite to prolong and enhance sexual performance.

Other non-Islamic, external forces were at work as well. Beginning in the eleventh century C.E. an infusion of Central Asian Turco-Mongol

---

[13] Adshead, *Material Culure in Europe and China*, 24.

traditions and customs involving excessive drinking and "loose" morals only reinforced such practices. Both traditions resisted the separation of the "clean" from the "dirty" encouraged by the "civilizing process" of normative Islam. The result was a society rich in paradox and ambiguity, led by a royal court legitimized in Islamic terms yet engaged in sexual revelry, the habitual use of opium, and heavy drinking.

In the sixteenth century, wine and opium were joined by tobacco and coffee, both stimulants that entered Iran as part of the so-called Commercial Revolution—the massive movement of goods and people around the globe that started with the European maritime explorations. As was the case in Europe, Iranians initially appreciated these products as medicinal agents, but they soon became very popular as stimulants consumed in an ambience of leisurely sociability. Tobacco conquered the country and both sexes within decades after its introduction. First adopted in Sufi circles, coffee took longer to find a wider consumer base and only became a common beverage with the introduction of the urban coffeehouse at the turn of the seventeenth century. Tea had long been known in Iran through overland contacts with China, but it, too, came to be accepted as more than a remedy for ailments following the sixteenth-century worldwide expansion of trade.

Modern scholars, enthralled or perhaps distracted by the forces of globalization and the attendant loss of visibility of productive forces in the Western world, have shown a growing fascination with consumption as an end in itself.[14] This book makes a conscious attempt to link consumption to the dynamics of production and distribution, in the belief that a narrow focus on consumption at the expense of a careful consideration of underlying demand *and* supply factors severely distorts reality. A simple diffusionist model rarely accounts for the complexity of the spread of food and drink. In most parts of the world the popularity of coffee, tea, and tobacco was not simply the outcome of availability following Europe's exploration of the seas but, rather, of a complex interplay between supply and demand factors. The lifting of logistical obstacles is surely a precondition for dissemination beyond a tiny elite, but as the popularization of coffee in Europe demonstrates—after the initial introduction by immigrant laborers it took almost a hundred years for the drink to become a commercial success—not a sufficient one.[15] Iran was no different. Matters of geography as much as issues of class and status having to do with outside influence determined the country's

---

[14]Agnew, "Coming Up for Air."

[15]For this argument, made in the case of the consumption of coffee in early modern England, see Smith, "Early Diffusion of Coffee Drinking in England."

eventual preference for tea over coffee. It remains a mystery why the water pipe became the smoking vehicle *par excellence* in Iran and throughout the Middle East, although not in Europe, but one clue might be an "elective affinity" between the age-old usage of hashish and that of newly introduced tobacco.

This study develops two other lines of thought. One of these concerns the discrepancy between the idealized version of life as rhetorically envisioned by the ulama, and life as lived practice, messy, defiant of precise boundaries, resistant to control and discipline. The paradox is addressed here in reference to Safavid Iran, a religiously inspired state that paired piety with prostitution and drug use.

Safavid Iran (1501–1722) began as a tribal formation harking back to Central Asian nomadic models and ended as a sedentary agrarian-based polity centering on an elaborate, mostly nontribal bureaucracy. Shi'ism, its official religion, at first manifested itself as a heterodox and extremist populist creed but in time followed the imperatives of the state by becoming mainstream and scripturalist. The importance and influence of its spokesmen, the Shi'i ulama, grew accordingly. Initially operating on the margins of a tribal society and its semipagan beliefs, the religious leaders soon entered the ranks of the elite through intermarriage and bureaucratic appointment. This newly found status enabled them to put their imprimatur on the state and its ways. One way of doing this was to enjoin believers to lead a life of moral probity and to call on the state to enforce Islamic codes of behavior. The results are seen in periodic restrictions and bans on the movement and activities of non-Muslims, and on state-led attempts to convert unbelievers—Jews and Armenians—to Islam. Their activism included calls for the banishment of conduct and consumption that was deemed un-Islamic—prostitution, drinking, and, in some cases, the consumption of coffee and tobacco, both newly introduced stimulants that generated debate and controversy and that contributed to the emergence of new forms of public life. The ascendance of the clerical estate culminated in the late seventeenth century with the accession of Shah Sultan Husayn (r. 1694–1722) and the incumbency of Muhammad Baqir Majlisi as *shaykh al-islam* of Isfahan, the highest clerical authority of the realm. Pious and weak-willed, the shah reigned under the spell of Majlisi, and, in deference to the latter's uncompromising brand of Shi'i Islam, at the outset of his reign outlawed wine, prostitution, and gambling.

The historical implications of this narrative might seem clear: To the casual observer it is but a short step from (late) Safavid Iran to the Islamic Republic, from Majlisi to Khomeini. Late Safavid Iran indeed seems to prefigure today's Iran in its stern application of Islamic law and the observation of a puritanical morality, at least in the popular imagination of the West.

This book challenges the above image of early modern Iran as a harbinger of the current Islamic Republic. It does not dispute the trajectory of the Safavid state from a steppe polity to a bureaucratic state with ideological underpinnings that became more and more aligned with the tenets of doctrinaire Shi'ism. It does, however, take issue with the notion that, in the process, Safavid society increasingly came to reflect the ideal preached by the zealous; that the clerical estate successfully made everyone conform to the letter of the Islamic holy law. Gender segregation in Safavid Iran was strictly enforced, to the point where the call to prayer was not ordinarily done from the top of a minaret for fear that the muezzin might see women in their enclosed gardens. Yet visitors noted the presence in the capital alone of some ten thousand prostitutes who openly plied their trade.[16] Although the state periodically heeded Islamic strictures, its legal codes were borne out of conflict and challenge and the measures it enacted were often symbolic and rhetorical rather than practical in nature. Their effect was invariably temporary at best. Prostitution continued to thrive. Clerical suspicions of coffee and tobacco did not prevent Iranians from enthusiastically embracing these novelties. The use of opium was widespread, binge drinking remained common among the elite, and even some religious officials liked to imbibe. Royal banquets and receptions habitually included performances by female dancers and young male singers and jugglers, and numerous courtesans were attached to the households of top government officials. Safavid Iran, in sum, reveals itself as a society that mixed the sacred and the profane, where pleasure and proscription were not mutually exclusive, and in which long-standing habits—and economic imperatives—usually won out over moral considerations.

The Pursuit of Pleasure seeks to explain such discrepancies between discourse and practice, between rhetorical virtue and public "vice," as deriving from a complex historical tradition of which formal religion is only one aspect. First, a state that itself heavily engaged in riotous living could do little more than engage in periodic incantations to bridge the gap between normative and actual behavior. Second, although the state derived its legitimacy from religion, always paid lip service to its tenets, and, as said, occasionally heeded its counsel, it was essentially secular in its makeup and will to power. It also was nothing if not pragmatic. Its pragmatism grew out of an accommodationist instinct, a need to engage in "tacit bargaining" with society and its irrepressible urges, but derived

[16]For this, see Matthee, "Prostitutes, Courtesans, and Dancing Girls."

above all from the dilemma that has confronted governments through the ages: the need to choose between principles and profit.[17] As everywhere else, morality in early modern Iran generally foundered on the imperatives of revenue collection, so that Safavid authorities connived at prostitution and smoking in large part because of the tax income these activities generated.

The religious leaders had a role in this as well, but it was not simply that of an oppositional force keen to remind the community of God's commands. Such a picture would be altogether too simplistic, and not just because the ulama failed to bend society to their will. Their ability to curb illicit behavior was limited, to be sure. They faced a recalcitrant society and a state with limited power that was mostly concerned about enforcement to the extent that it served its own interests. But far from being a negative force, vainly exhorting the state to enforce proper religious conduct, the religious authorities had a productive role insofar as they had a stake in the decadence they decried. The existence of bad behavior justified and legitimized their existence and their status in society. By defining themselves against vice, they became vested in it. Inasmuch they all too often engaged in illicit activities themselves, they perpetuated vice by choosing to ignore it or to channel it into acceptable categories. They continued to enjoin the state to live up to its duty of upholding public morality. But because executive power belonged to the state, they were resigned to sporadic enforcement that rarely matched pious intentions. What appears, on the surface, as a dichotomy between norm and reality, on a deeper level turns out to be a dialectic process in which both reproduced each other in an unending creative tension between hedonism and puritanism.

The third and last theme concerns historical continuity and change. Safavid Iran began and ended as a polity in which religion and state were entwined, but the nature of their relationship evolved in accordance with the transformation of society itself from a tribally based disposition centered on a messianic leader to a quasi-bureaucratic, patrimonial enterprise led by a palace-bound shah. The trajectory of wine illustrates this best. Although the tensions inherent in wine were never

[17] For the term "tacit bargaining," see Dale Eickleman, "Foreword: The Religious Public Sphere in Early Muslim Societies," in Hoexter et al., eds., *The Public Sphere in Muslim Societies*, 6.

To what tangled knots of complication and contradiction the dilemma of proscription versus profitability can lead is still vividly illustrated in modern Japan. There tobacco revenue "bankrolls the state" in that it is the largest single moneymaker for the government, so that antismoking measures proposed by the health ministry run up against opposition by the ministry of finance. See Stephanie Strom, "Japan and Tobacco Revenue: Leader Faces Difficult Choice," *New York Times* June 13 (2001), A1, 14.

solved, its place in society changed considerably in the course of the Safavid period. Where Shah Isma`il's orgies had been flamboyant, theatrically visible affairs, Shah Tahmasb repented for his own youthful extravagance by issuing an edict against this and other forms of "sinful and frivolous" behavior. Most subsequent shahs drank and some drank heavily, but they typically wavered between guilt-ridden indulgence and abstention. Wine lost its sacral character to become a profane drink consumed in private, reflecting the evolution of Iranian society from a tribal polity predicated on openness and access to a sedentary state in which the ruler all but absconded into the confines of his palace.

Change naturally did not stop with the demise of the Safavids. The dramatic fall of Isfahan in 1722, although it effectively ended Safavid rule and ushered in a period of turmoil and destitution with significant repercussions for commerce and consumption, did not constitute a decisive break in Iranian history. The Qajar period, 1796–1925, neither picked up Iran's history seamlessly following the chaotic eighteenth century, nor did it represent something radically novel. Iran remained a preindustrial society. Many social practices endured until the late nineteenth century, and in some cases well into more recent times, but some things began to change. For one, beginning with Fath `Ali Shah (r. 1797–1834), Qajar rulers, concerned about their religious credentials, no longer indulged in the type of orgiastic drinking rituals known from the Safavid period. The justification of drinkers changed as well. Whereas in Safavid times those who drank seem to have done so either unselfconsciously or plagued by a guilty conscience, the Qajar period saw the appearance of drinking as a statement, as an act of defiance, as a way to flaunt one's libertinism, to show one's disdain for the clergy and its religious law, in a gesture reminiscent of the Sufis of yesteryear, although largely devoid of alternative religious pretensions.

Under Nasir al-Din Shah (r. 1848–96) the Qajar state also took a series of measures against stimulants and the venues where they were consumed. Recognizing the harmful effect of the rapid spread of opium smoking—as opposed to the traditional eating—at the time, the authorities sought to curb the practice. They also temporarily closed coffeehouses as centers of political agitation and opposition. The impulse behind such measures, moral and political concerns, recalls Safavid times. Yet, religious motives played virtually no role in Qajar intervention and interdiction, not even at the rhetorical level. The real contrast with the Safavid state lies in different challenges facing the state: the concerns of late Qajar rulers were no longer those of those of a premodern loose and latudinarian polity pressured by religious conservatism but those of a centralizing and modernizing state buffeted by political and economic forces beyond its control.

The book follows a thematic approach within a chronological sequence in the presentation of its material. Its opening chapter offers a broad overview of Iran's political, social, and economic history between 1500 and 1900, providing the nonspecialized reader with a background to the themes developed later on. What follows is divided into two parts, one covering the period between 1500 and 1800, the era of Safavid rule and its immediate aftermath, the other the nineteenth century, the Qajar period. Part I contains four chapters and discusses as many stimulants, one per chapter. Part II reexamines each of these, in addition to tea, in a different historical context.

Part I opens with two chapters that explore the Safavid contribution to Iran's rich history of alcohol and, more specifically, wine, the oldest and most ambiguous of the stimulants under consideration. Chapter 2 examines consumption, focusing on the elite, which by all accounts were the only ones who drank, and especially the role of drinking in the changing nature of kingship. Chapter 3 concentrates on the unease alcohol consumption generated in a Muslim environment and explores the causes and circumstances of the bans that were periodically issued against it.

Chapter 4 looks into the history of opium and hashish in Safavid times. Unlike alcohol, opium and cannabis did not carry a religious stigma in premodern Iran; indeed, both qualified as legitimate substitutes for wine. Long eaten rather than smoked, opium especially was well integrated into society, so well in fact that French observers of Safavid society likened its use to that of wine in their home country, arguing that Iranians knew how to deal with it and generally did not succumb to its addictive qualities.

Tobacco, to be considered in chapter 5, switches the focus to the "new" stimulants, the ones that were introduced as part of the commercial revolution. Next to tea, it is probably the most powerful of the stimulants in terms of its cultural adaptability, of its "capacity to acquire meaning beyond its pharmacological properties."[18] This chapter will first investigate the circumstances of tobacco's introduction and popularization, and then turn its attention to the controversy it raised in religious and medical circles.

Chapter 6 examines coffee in the Safavid period. As an import product, the trade in coffee is relatively well documented, and commerce therefore dominates the first part of the chapter. Turning to consumption, the second part discusses coffee's evolution from a medicinal agent to a

---

[18]Gladwell, "Java Man," 76.

recreational beverage, but the focus will be on the coffeehouse as the venue where the various pastimes and practices associated with it became the object of political and religious concern.

Part II of the book explores patterns of continuity and transformation in the period following the rise of the Qajar dynasty at the turn of the nineteenth century, with an eye to changes undergone by the various drugs and stimulants and the venues where they were consumed. Its four chapters are concerned as well with social and political developments in nineteenth-century Iranian society, and especially with its fitful trajectory toward modernization and the policies this entailed.

The first of these, chapter 7, charts the evolution of wine beyond Safavid times and investigates the role of drinking in the continuing evolution of Iranian society from a hard-drinking steppe polity predicated on openness and access, to a sedentary state in which the court reached out for different symbols of legitimacy.

The process of change receives further attention in chapter 8, which documents the evolution of opium and tobacco from popular consumables to substances of national import. When the more invasive habit of smoking rather than ingesting it gained ground in the late nineteenth century, opium lost it relatively unproblematic place in society to become a source of widespread addiction and an array of social ills. It turned into not simply a cash crop but into the country's principal cash crop and in some regions a virtual monoculture, exposing Iran to famine. Tobacco resembled opium in turning into one of the country's most lucrative export items, but political events caused it to follow a different trajectory. The enormous popularity of smoking had long rendered the clerical debate about tobacco's permissibility moot. When the state resolved to hand the production, sale, and distribution of tobacco to foreign interests, the ulama intervened, mobilizing smokers to reject the outside forces that had sullied the nation by acquiring control over it.

Chapter 9 will turn to coffee and tea in the period from the early eighteenth century to the "triumph" of tea in the late nineteenth century. It first discusses the relative popularity of the two drinks in Safavid times and the reasons for the virtual disappearance of coffeehouses in the tumultuous period following the fall of Isfahan in 1722. The chapter then traces the shift in taste from coffee to tea as the favorite beverage of the Iranian people, exploring the role of tea-drinking Russia and England and social circumstances having to do with class and taste that made this transformation possible.

Chapter 10, finally, examines the phenomenon that accompanied the breakthrough of tea, the emergence of the "new" coffeehouse in the second half of the late nineteenth century, which was similar to the traditional *qahvah-khanah* even though it now served tea rather than coffee. This chapter considers the physical shape of these reconstituted establishments as well as their function and their clientele. Its real focus is on the concerns and anxieties they generated, prompting the government at various times to interfere in their operation. These anxieties ranged from a preoccupation with the nation's balance of trade to fears of social unrest, thus representing long-standing Iranian sensibilities.

PART I

Safavid Period

CHAPTER 1

General Overview: Iran between 1500 and 1900

Safavid Iran

The period of the Safavids, the dynasty that took control of Iran in the early sixteenth century, is often considered the beginning of the country's modern history, just as the state they created is sometimes said to mark the genesis of the Iranian nation state. It is, however, anachronistic to call Safavid Iran a modern nation state as, in many ways, Safavid society continued Mongol and Timurid patterns and practices—ranging from its coinage to its administrative institutions. The Safavids consciously built their legitimacy on past tradition. Their historians made an effort to link the genealogy of the dynasty to that of the Shi`i Imams and to associate the greatest of Safavid rulers, Shah `Abbas I (r. 1587–1629), with the great Central Asian conqueror, Timur Lang (d. 1405). Yet, it is true that the Safavids made many original contributions and that in various ways their legacy survives until today. They unified much of Iran under single political control, transforming an essentially tribal nomadic order into a predominantly sedentary society deriving most of its revenue from agriculture and trade. Most important, they introduced a concept of patrimonial kingship combining territorial authority with religious legitimacy that, with modifications, would endure until the twentieth century. The political system that emerged under them had overlapping political and religious boundaries and a core language, Persian, which served as the literary tongue and that in time even began to replace Arabic as the vehicle for religious thought. A number of administrative institutions created during the Safavid period or adapted from earlier times continued to exist well into the subsequent Qajar era. The Safavid period, finally, witnessed the beginning of frequent and sustained diplomatic and commercial interaction between Iran and Europe.

In discussing Iran between 1501 and 1722, several peculiarities of the area and the time are relevant. The first concerns the country's physical environment and its effects. Much of Iran consists of arid, unproductive land. Large parts receive insufficient rainfall to support agriculture but are well suited to pastoral nomadism. Nomads, organized in tribes, in this period comprised as much as one third to one half of the country's population. Second, and related, military power in Iran was usually tribal power, and political power followed suit. Until the twentieth century, all of Iran's ruling dynasties had their origins in tribal ambitions. The nomadic makeup of the state is reflected in an ambulant royal court and the absence of a fixed capital. Safavid Iran knew a succession of capitals and in practice the capital was where the shah and his entourage happened to be. Third, ethnic Turks generally held military and political power in Iran, whereas ethnic Iranians, called Tajiks, were dominant in the areas of administration and culture. The Safavids, as Iranians of Kurdish ancestry and of nontribal background, did not fit this pattern, although the state they set up with the aid of Turkmen tribal forces of Eastern Anatolia closely resembled this division in its makeup. Yet, the Turk versus Tajik division was not impregnable. Over time, many Turks served as bureaucrats, whereas quite a few Tajiks held military posts. Nor should the tension and rivalry created by mutual suspicion and divergent interests between the two groups be exaggerated. Finally, statecraft in premodern Iran combined Islamic traditions of governance, ancient Iranian notions of kingship, and Central Asian, Turco-Mongolian principles of legitimacy and power. In the first, the ruler ruled the religious community as God's trustee; the second was built around the notion of an absolutist monarch governing over his people as a shepherd over his flock, whereas in the third, power and legitimacy resided in the clan, which included women, mothers, daughters, as much as sons and uncles, rather than residing in the person of the ruler. In this, as in other areas, Safavid Iran had much in common with its neighbors, Mughal India and the Ottoman Empire. The absence of primogeniture in the Turco-Mongolian tradition turned every succession into a long struggle for power and thus created much instability (although in Safavid Iran, the older Iranian principle of the oldest son succeeding the father usually prevailed).

Background

The Safavids began in circa 1300 as a mystical order centered in the northwestern town of Ardabil, the hometown and burial place of the order's founder, Shaykh Safi al-Din (1252–1334). Weathering the political storms attending the demise of Mongol rule in Iran and the rise and fall of Timur Lang, the Safavid order continued under the leadership of Safi al-Din's descendants, most notably Junayd (r. 1447–60), and Haydar (r. 1460–88), growing into an ambitious movement inhabiting the interstices of the territory ruled by two tribal dynasties known as Aq-Quyunlu (White Sheep) and Qara-Quyunlu (Black Sheep). Their main supporters were tribal groups known as Qizilbash, Redheads, in reference to the red headgear that they are said to have adopted at the time of Haydar and that, with its twelve gores, symbolized their allegiance to the Safavid ruler and the twelve Shi'i Imams. Despite their collective name, these warriors did not boast a common descent and retained their individual clan affiliation, and the different clans continued to be each other's bitter rivals. The main Qizilbash clans supporting the Safavid cause all migrated from Syria and Anatolia to different parts of Iran, where a clan leader typically was appointed governor once the Safavids conquered the region.

The Qizilbash formed the cavalry elite of the fledgling state and served as the praetorian guard for the shah, but their relationship with the ruler also was the mystical one of the disciple, *murid*, and the Sufi master, *murshid*. Fiercely loyal to their leader and convinced of their own invincibility, they often threw themselves into battle without armor. They also engaged in rituals involving wild drinking parties and, allegedly, cannibalism against enemies. Junayd gathered a following among these mostly Turkmen tribesmen, trained them for military operation, and used them in raids against the Christian inhabitants of the Caucasus.

Much about the early Safavid order remains unclear. One point of uncertainty is the precise nature of their religious beliefs. Originally they harbored Sunni convictions, but at the turn of the fifteenth century they are said to have gravitated toward Shi'ism under the influence of their Turkmen supporters. Originating as it did in a frontier region rife with beliefs mixing Islamic and pre-Islamic, millenarian elements, their belief system long bore little relation to literate Twelver Shi'ism, however, and was filled with Shamanistic and animistic notions that included a belief in reincarnation and the transmigration of souls, as well as the idea of a leader invested with divine attributes.

IRAN IN THE SIXTEENTH CENTURY

It was with Haydar's son, Isma'il, that the Safavids evolved from a messianic movement to a political dynasty led by a shah rather than a shaykh. Under Shah Isma'il, a genealogy was fabricated according to which Safi al-Din descended from the seventh Imam, Musa al-Kazim. Although this did little to make Isma'il care for the official doctrine of the newly established faith, it did mark a fusion between worldly power and faith that would prove to be extremely powerful. Instrumental in this were the Qizilbash, who as loyal devotees received land and who also served as tutors for Safavid princes. Isma'il in 1499 emerged from the Caspian region where he had lived under the protection of a local ruler, and set out to wrest western Iran from the Aq-Quyunlu. In 1501, barely fifteen years of age, he proclaimed himself shah in Tabriz. He also declared Shi`ism the official faith of the realm, thus endowing his new state with a strong ideological basis while giving Iran overlapping political and religious boundaries that with some modifications last until today. By 1510 the entire country with the exception of the northeastern region of Khurasan was in Safavid hands. When in 1510 Isma`il took Khurasan by defeating Muhammad Shibani Khan Uzbeg, the Safavid realm attained the greatest expanse in the dynasty's history.

The main rivals of the Safavids were to be the Ottomans, who as self-declared defenders of Sunni Islam felt threatened by the establishment of a militant Shi`i state on their border. Safavid provocations and pro-Safavid rebellions in Anatolia soon prompted Sultan Selim to march against Iran, in a campaign that culminated in 1514 in the famous battle of Chaldiran, where an Ottoman army equipped with field artillery and hand guns routed Isma`il's troops fighting with bow and arrow. It is famously said that his defeat at Chaldiran broke Isma`il's spirit and that he never led his troops into battle again. Although it is true that the shah henceforth took to hunting, wine drinking, and spending time in the company of young boys, preferring these activities over the management of state affairs, the Safavid army did recover after the shattering defeat and in the following years advanced into northern, Ottoman-held Mesopotamia.

Shah Isma`il died in 1524, to be succeeded by his ten-year-old son Tahmasb. Given his age, it is only natural that real power was initially exercised by a body of Qizilbash regents. Nor, given the divisiveness within Qizilbash ranks and the decreased messianic aura of the shah, is it surprising that his early reign unleashed a tribal power struggle that degenerated into a ten-year civil war among the Qizilbash. Only in the 1530s did Tahmasb emerge victorious from this struggle, determined to consolidate his power by curtailing the unruly tribal forces. Hence, the first appointments of Tajik officials to key positions traditionally reserved for Turks, including military ones. The royal practice of contracting marriages with Georgian and Circassian women dates from this period as well, although for the time being the heirs who gained the throne continued to be the sons of Turkmen mothers.

Shah Tahmasb made great efforts to further implant Shi`ism in his realm, employing religious propagandists whose task it was to vilify Sunnis, chiefly by cursing the first three Sunni caliphs, whom the Shi`is saw as usurpers of the first Shi`i Imam, `Ali. Attempts were made to standardize religious practice around a scriptural urban-based version of the faith as opposed to the folk beliefs of the Qizilbash. To disseminate the Shi`i creed, to shore up his legitimacy as a Shi`i ruler, and to build a religious cadre without ties to any domestic tribal and ethnic factions, the shah invited scholars from Arab lands, most notably Lebanon, to migrate to Iran, in return for land, cash, and high positions. The most prominent of these was `Ali al-Karaki, who would become the supreme cleric of his age.

Having established his person credentials, Shah Tahmasb managed to extend his authority over a number of areas, from the Caspian provinces to Khurasan and Qandahar, which under his father had been buffer regions or vassal states. The Ottomans, meanwhile, conducted three campaigns against Iran during Tahmasb's reign, prompting him in 1548 to move his capital from Tabriz to Qazvin, a city located further in the interior. In 1534–36, Iraq fell to the Ottomans. The third campaign ended in 1555 with the treaty of Amasya, which recognized Ottoman suzerainty over Iraq and eastern Anatolia while leaving Iran in control of Azerbaijan and the southeastern Caucasus.

Georgia, which Shah Tahmasb invaded several times, was never properly subjugated. Yet, the region became important as the source of originally Christian slave soldiers, *ghulams*, captured during raiding expeditions into the region. Initiated by Isma`il, this practice was continued under Tahmasb, the first Safavid ruler to build up these Caucasian recruits as a countervailing force against the overbearing Qizilbash. The males, converted to Islam, were trained as administrators, whereas the women became employed in the royal harem, where their influence would be considerable. This system had similarities to the Ottoman system of slave recruitment in Christian territories.

In a shift that had begun with his father's defeat at Chaldiran, Shah Tahmasb's reign saw a growing focus on the shah's role as the representative of the Hidden Imam. Twelver Shi`ism believes in twelve infallible Imams, `Ali and his descendants, with the last Imam having disappeared as an infant, but still alive and to return in the future as the messianic Mahdi. Whereas Shah Isma`il had represented a primordial semipagan world in which orgiastic ritual involving drinking and wild sexual practices awkwardly mixed with an appeal to Islamic legitimization, Shah Tahmasb inaugurated a phase of greater emphasis on outward religious behavior. A devout and, according to some, melancholy ruler who rarely appeared in public, Tahmasb in 1533–34 experienced a repentance during a pilgrimage to the Shi`i shrine city of Mashhad in Khurasan. He gave up wine and issued bans on taverns and other forms of amusement. Undergoing a definitive transformation in 1544, the shah became fastidious in matters of hygiene and food, and averse to the arts that he had formerly patronized so avidly.

By the time Shah Tahmasb died in 1576, the Safavids had proven their staying power in the face of the powerful Qizilbash, the persistent Ottoman threat, and a weakening ideology. The brief and bloody reign of his son and successor, Isma`il II and that of the weak, purblind Muhammad Khudabandah, invited a resurgence of Qizilbash power and much infighting in their ranks. Iran's neighbors took advantage of the attendant turmoil. The Uzbegs staged incursions into Khurasan in 1578, and in the same year a new round of Safavid-Ottoman warfare erupted that would continue until 1590, causing severe economic disruption in the border lands. Matters would only improve with the coming to power of Shah 'Abbas I in 1587.

Shah 'Abbas I

Shah 'Abbas I is seen universally as the greatest Safavid ruler, the embodiment of the age-old Iranian ideal of the just monarch. Eyewitness observers attest to his justice and generosity, as well as to a relative lack of corruption under him. His reign also marks a crucial phase in the evolution of Safavid Iran from a tribal formation to a (quasi-) bureaucratic state. This is noticeable, for example, in a shift in Safavid historiography from a tribal to a dynastic emphasis. Whereas earlier chronicles offered general histories concerned with universal history built on legitimacy reflecting Turko-Mongol claims, the ones written as of the late sixteenth century revolve more narrowly around the Safavids as Iranian rulers. The state's growing Iranian focus is reflected in the fact that religious works began to be composed in the Persian language and that Persian replaced Arabic on the coinage.

Shah 'Abbas was first and foremost an outstanding strategist, keen to regain the territories that had been lost to outside enemies or internal sedition. Especially against the Ottomans, his strategic brilliance made up for military weakness. This enabled him to recapture Tabriz and also territory taken by Uzbegs and Mughals. Aware that he would not be able to fight on two fronts simultaneously and intent on having his hands free in the east, Shah 'Abbas first concluded a peace with the Ottomans that cost him Azerbaijan and parts of the Caucasus and Iraq. Turning his attention to the Uzbegs, he recaptured Mashhad and Herat and definitively established control over Gilan and Mazandaran. This done, 'Abbas turned to the western front and, having secured the support of the rulers of Georgia through alliances, resumed war with the Ottomans, chasing them out of the northwestern regions as well as Iraq.

Regaining Iran's territory was intimately linked to Shah 'Abbas's main objective: maximizing personal control and centralizing power. 'Abbas ended the practice of appointing the crown prince as governor of Khurasan and other sons to various provincial governorates under the tutelage of Qizilbash guardians; instead, in order to forestall rebellion and premature claims to the throne, he killed one of his sons and blinded two more. Following Ottoman precedent, he also locked his grandchildren up in the harem, thereby starting a trend that would shield the ruler against premature challenges to his power but also deprive future rulers of valuable experience.

Most important, Shah `Abbas embarked on a number of internal reforms designed to break the power of the Qizilbash tribes. Intent on creating substitute military and administrative elites only answerable to him, he raised the profile of the *ghulam* institution, infusing their ranks with thousands of Armenians, Georgians, and Circassians taken captive during a series of brutal wars in the Caucasus. He appointed *ghulam*s to high positions in the military, where they served to counterbalance the Qizilbash, and also gave them greater administrative power. Major, centrally located provinces such as Qazvin, Isfahan, and Yazd, as well as the silk-producing regions of Gilan and Mazandaran, were converted to crown land, with their revenue accruing to the royal coffers, and *ghulam*s were appointed as governors. The most prominent of these was the Armenian Allah Virdi Khan, who received control over Fars province. Only border regions, such as Georgia, Kurdistan, and Khuzistan, where the Safavids had to negotiate for power with local and external forces, remained semiautonomous, governed by so-called *valis*, who were often local rulers.

Shah `Abbas was a great builder. He often spent winters in Mazandaran, where he had the towns of Ashraf and Farahabad constructed. His most celebrated measure is the embellishment of Isfahan, which in the 1590s became the new Safavid capital, far away from the exposed western frontier. The focus of Isfahan's urban design was a new commercial and administrative area centering on a magnificent central square known as the *maydan-i naqsh-i jahan*. Isfahan at this time became a large, cosmopolitan city mixing people of many nationalities who congregated in its bazaars and socialized in its coffeehouses. On holidays and following royal campaigns the square and the main bazaar would be lit with thousands of lamps, symbolizing the ruler's illumination of the world, and spectacle sports such as polo and wolf baiting would be held. The city also became a center of art and philosophy.

Shah `Abbas is especially known for his encouragement of commerce, which became an important source of royal revenue. He reestablished road security and had a great many caravanserais constructed throughout his realm. In 1619 the shah monopolized the export of silk for the crown, thus enhancing the income the royal treasury derived from Iran's most profitable export product. To harness the commercial skills of his Armenian subjects, he resettled a large number of them from the town of Julfa, in the border area with the Ottoman Empire, to a suburb of his new capital, which was named New Julfa. Offered trading privileges, especially in the export trade in silk, the Armenians turned into a commercial gentry in the service of the crown and the country's most active long-distance merchants. Some of the Julfan merchant houses became fabulously rich, exporting silk to the Ottoman ports of Aleppo and Izmir, and returning with large amounts of cloth and cash.

Shah `Abbas was the first Safavid ruler to establish control over the Persian Gulf coast, an area with strong ties to the Indian Ocean and long ruled by independent, mostly Arab dynasties. His reasons for engaging with the region included a desire for territorial conquest and commercial objectives—a desire to eliminate Portuguese control over the port of Hurmuz and to find ways around Ottoman territory in commercial dealings with the outside world. With the assistance of the English, he managed to oust the Portuguese from Hurmuz in 1622, after which he transferred its activities to a newly founded port on the mainland called, after himself, Bandar `Abbas.

Shah `Abbas's forays into the Persian Gulf region were part of a larger diplomatic and commercial project that opened Iran to the wider world in unprecedented ways. Shah `Abbas intensified Safavid contacts with European rulers in an effort to find Western allies against his Ottoman adversaries. He dispatched numerous embassies to Europe and Russia, and he similarly welcomed various Western trading nations, most notably the English and Dutch East India Companies, who during his reign made their appearance in Iran, intent on capturing a share of the country's silk trade, and established a presence in Bandar `Abbas as well as in Isfahan, Kirman, and Shiraz. He granted the English half of Bandar `Abbas's toll receipts in return for their assistance in expelling the Portuguese from Hurmuz, and offered the Dutch the right to engage in toll-free trade in exchange for a contractual obligation to take an annual volume of six hundred bales of silk.

Other Europeans who came to Iran in great numbers in this period included representatives of Christian monastic orders. Shah `Abbas welcomed the Augustinians and Carmelites, among others, and allowed them to establish convents in his realm. Long ascribed to the shah's natural affection for Christians, this policy in fact was largely informed by political considerations: the missionaries served as liaisons with major Christian countries such as Spain, France and the Papacy, and mostly hailed from countries with which the shah hoped to build alliances in his struggle against the Ottomans.

The Later Period

Shah `Abbas had no direct male successor when he died in early 1629, and was succeeded by his grandson Safi. Shah Safi, the first of the Safavid rulers to have spent his youth in the confines of the harem, came to the throne in an atmosphere of discord and rebellion, with provincial forces attempting to regain autonomy. The most dramatic manifestation of this was a messianic uprising in Gilan, which combined religious expectations with fiscal grievances. The shah managed to quell the revolt, but he remained weak and dependent on court forces until in 1631–33 he asserted himself by eliminating many state officials, among them the powerful khan of Fars and the de facto ruler over most of southern Iran, Imam Quli Khan, son and successor of Allah Virdi Khan. The massacre marked the end of a system where by the extended Safavid family held corporate power and inaugurated a phase in which the shah became the sole ruler surrounded by his palace entourage consisting of women, eunuchs, and *ghulam*s.

Under Safi the trend toward great power for the *ghulam*s continued, as did the drive to convert state domain to crown land. The revenue this generated was, however, not necessarily applied to the army. Shah Safi himself was of the old warrior type, but a emergence of a pacifist camp, headed by the women and harem eunuchs, and continuing antagonism between the Qizilbash and the *ghulam*s resulted in diminished military expenditure and thus contributed to a weakening of Iran's fighting spirit. This was seen in the Ottoman success in recapturing Iraq, and the subsequent peace accord of Zuhab, concluded in 1639, which by and large reaffirmed the boundaries stipulated by the treaty of Amasya and definitively established peace between the Safavids and the Ottomans.

Shah Safi died in 1642, aged thirty-one and exhausted from excessive drinking. The reign of his son and successor, Shah `Abbas II, has been called the Indian Summer of the Safavid era, in reference to his success in recapturing Qandahar and the favorable conditions foreign observers detected in his realm. Mounting the throne at age ten, Shah `Abbas II escaped a long childhood dependence on the forces that dominated the harem. Three years later, he asserted his independence by sanctioning a Qizilbash conspiracy against his octogenarian grand vizier, Mirza Muhammad "Saru" (blond) Taqi, who, in league with the shah's mother, had wielded great power since his appointment by Shah Safi in 1633. After the vizier's assassination, the ruler resolved to have the conspirators removed as well. `Abbas II subsequently grew into a forceful ruler with a reputation for justice, and his reign was mostly a period of stability and peace.

Shah `Abbas II's reign witnessed a continuation of many long-standing trends. One, which followed the growing prominence of clerical forces, was a shift from tolerance for expressions of popular religiosity to a growing emphasis on a strict interpretation of the faith. A manifestation of this was the launching in 1645 of an officially sanctioned morality campaign directed against brothels and wine taverns. This period also saw an outpouring of clerical writings against popular Sufism, with its connotations of antinomian behavior. Yet this did not prevent many ulama from adhering to high-minded and philosophical mysticism. Shah `Abbas II himself similarly paid his respects to the representatives of various Sufi orders.

Part of the same development was growing friction in the relationship between religion and state. The Safavids never resolved the tension between a religious hierarchy that was in theory only beholden to the Hidden Imam and a state built around ancient Iranian notions of divine kingship. In the period of Shah `Abbas II, we hear of high-ranking ulama who openly declared the rule of the shah illegitimate and called for direct clerical governance. Not too much should be made of this, for it was certainly not a general tendency, and the ulama, convinced of the need for a monarch as the patrimonial head of the body-politic, overwhelmingly acquiesced in the status quo, whereby the state wielded ultimate power and the religious leaders saw themselves as moral guardians while serving in a variety of bureaucratic offices. This division of labor is also visible in the judicial system. Religious law and customary law existed side by side. `Urf, common law, prevailed over the shari`a, though, especially in criminal cases, and most people are said to have favored government courts over qadi courts. Worldly power, in sum, usually trumped religious authority, even as the shah's status as Sufi patron diminished.

In 1666 Abbas II died and was succeeded by Shah Safi II. After a year on the throne that was marked by epidemics and famine, he was re-crowned as Sulayman. Myriad signs of economic retrenchment, most strikingly reflected in a fall in agricultural output, growing numbers of commercial bankruptcies, and a deteriorating currency, became visible during Sulayman's rule. A stagnating influx of precious metal from the Ottoman Empire, although very much related to European conditions, reflected the poor state of Iran's economy as well, and led to the closing of numerous mints in this period. It is not true, as is often claimed, that the government failed to respond to these conditions, and it is therefore not quite proper to speak of unchecked decline. Safavid authorities other than the shah were well aware of the lamentable state of affairs, and Shaykh `Ali Khan, Sulayman's energetic grand vizier, made great efforts to remedy the situation. But such efforts foundered on structural economic weakness, endemic corruption, and a lack of royal support.

Shah Sultan Husayn, Sulayman's son, was not the most logical successor to the throne when his father died in 1694. Instrumental in the choice of the new king were the palace eunuchs, who preferred a malleable ruler to an independent one, and the new shah's maternal grand-aunt, Maryam

Bigum, who would wield a great deal of power throughout her grand-nephew's reign. The increased power of eunuchs and women followed the growing centrality of a royal household that had become a fixed place and that had more than doubled in size since the late 1500s. Beginning with Shah Sulayman, the eunuchs of the royal harem were the ones who wielded effective power, taking over the shah's task of balancing competing interests among state courtiers. The important place of women in political life has been documented for the sixteenth century, but the phenomenon was even more pronounced in the later Safavid period, even if, following the shift from corporate to individual legitimacy, it was now the queen mother rather than royal sisters and daughters who wielded power and influence.

The changed position of the sovereign under Sulyaman and Sultan Husayn shows how, by this time, the Safavid polity, once driven by millenarian energy, had lost its ideological direction. Their predecessors had been roving warriors, forever vigilant in patrolling their realm to pacify unruly tribes and withstand external enemies. In keeping with nomadic, Central Asian tradition, the early shahs also had been highly visible and approachable and, in the case of Shah `Abbas, even informal in their governing style. The Safavids never completely lost that mobility and even later shahs continued to prefer the open space of the steppe to the confinement of the city, frequently residing outside the city, in the extra-mural garden. But Sulayman and Sultan Husayn reigned as stationary monarchs who, aside from occasional hunting parties, preferred to live ensconced in or near the capital and invisible to all but the most intimate of courtiers.

The pious and impressionable Sultan Husayn, who had seen little more of the world than the harem walls when he came to power, quickly fell under the spell of the ulama, and more particularly of Muhammad Baqir Majlisi, a prolific scholar and the most prominent cleric of his time. At Majlisi's behest, the shah's enthronement was accompanied by an official ban on alcohol and other activities deemed contrary to Islam. Sufis bore the brunt of persecution instigated by Majlisi, but Iran's Sunni non-Muslim inhabitants suffered as well.

Shah Sultan Husayn's accession was soon followed by multiple insurrections around the country. The army, always a scourge on the local population, began to plunder villages located on its marching routes. Road security lapsed and caravans suffered attack close to the gates of Isfahan. After 1715, matters further deteriorated. While Lezghi tribesmen raided Safavid lands in the Caucasus, the Omani Arabs took Bahrain in the Persian Gulf. Revolts broke out in Kurdistan and Luristan as well as in Khurasan, where the Abdali Afghans seized Herat and Mashhad. The reaction from Isfahan typifies the disarray in a court crippled by factionalism and venality. Under pressure from Maryam Bigum the shah organized a military campaign, but problems with the recruitment and payment of soldiers doomed the effort, and even the shah's decision to have the gold from Shi'i shrines struck into coins failed to yield the requisite funds.

The decisive blow was to come from the east and began in 1701, when Gurgin Khan, the governor of Qandahar, used his Georgian troops to brutally suppress a local insurrection. The rebellion by the local Ghalzai population this provoked ended with their leader, Mir Ways, being captured and sent to Isfahan. There, he managed to turn the shah against Gurgin Khan. Released, Mir Ways murdered Gurgin Khan on his return to Qandahar, after which he established himself as an autonomous ruler.

The end followed soon after the invasion of Iranian territory by Mahmud Ghalzai, Mir Ways's successor, in 1721. The Afghans moved on and in March 1722 won a confrontation with a hastily assembled Safavid army at Gulnabad, near Isfahan. Unable to breach Isfahan's city walls, they resorted to a blockade. After a six-month siege during which Prince Tahmasb, the shah's third son, was spirited out of the city, starvation brought the city down, and Sultan Husayn submitted to Mahmud, conferring on him the title of shah. Upon the news of the fall, Tahmasb proclaimed himself shah in Qazvin.

As the Safavid regime crumbled, both the Ottomans and the Russians cast covetous eyes on its northern region. Peter the Great used the death of some Russian merchants in Iran and appeals from Gilan for protection against the Afghans as a pretext to invade the Caspian provinces. The Ottomans, in turn, captured Georgia and Kirmanshah and in 1725 took Ganja and Tabriz.

AFTER THE FALL OF ISFAHAN

The demise of Safavid rule set off a long period of chaos and political disarray that lasted until the emergence of Nadir Shah, a military adventurer who reunified most of Iran. Depicted in contemporary chronicles as the restorer of the Safavid dynasty, this last of the great Asian conquerors in reality was a warlord of humble descent whose costly campaigns and extortionate rule mark a grim and ruinous episode for the country. Born in Khurasan, Nadir began his exploits in 1723 as a military officer in the service of Tahmasb, projecting himself as the restorer of the Safavid dynasty. Numerous campaigns against rebel forces around the country followed. In 1729 Nadir managed to inflict a decisive defeat on the Afghan forces at the Battle of Mihmandust. Having seized Isfahan from Ashraf, Mahmud's successor, Nadir allowed Tahmasb to be enthroned as the new shah. He then reopened hostilities with the Ottomans, eventually forcing them to retreat to the borders of 1639, led a campaign to pacify the south, during which he built Iran's first navy, and retook parts of the Caucasus from the Russians. In the process, he had Tahmasb deposed for incompetence and installed the latter's infant son as the new shah while appointing himself regent. Soon, Nadir's power base had become so strong that he could afford to give up the pretense of serving a Safavid heir. In 1736 he crowned himself the legitimate ruler of Iran. On the same occasion, he proposed that Twelver Shi'ism be recognized as a legitimate fifth school of Islam. Some scholars have seen this as an attempt to return Iran to Sunnism, and some as an effort to ease tensions between Afghans and Qizilbash, to appease the Ottomans or to distinguish himself from the Shi'i Safavids. The long-term effect of Nadir's actual indifference to religious issues was a split between the state and the clergy and the growing autonomy of the latter.

Nadir next subdued Qandahar and, having regained all of Iran's territory, moved on toward India, land of legendary wealth. His sack of Delhi was marked by massacres and widespread looting, which included the fabled Peacock Throne. Further campaigns followed, to Transoxania, Daghistan, and against the Ottomans in Mesopotamia, until in 1746 a final peace treaty was concluded that recognized the accord of Zuhab. The costs more than offset the Indian windfall and devolved on Iran's hapless population in the form of crushing exactions, so that revolts now broke out all over the country. Always cruel, Nadir in his later years also exhibited signs of mental imbalance, and engaged in erratic torture and massacres as punishment for rebellion. In 1747 he was finally murdered by a group of conspirators led by his nephew Ali-quli Khan, who subsequently mounted the throne under the name `Adil Shah.

`Adil Shah failed to restore peace and stability in Iran. Within a year of his accession he was deposed and blinded by his brother, Ibrahim, who in turn was defeated and murdered by the followers of Shahrukh, Nadir's grandson and the sole survivor of the massacre that had followed the events of 1747. Shahrukh, in turn, was shortly succeeded by yet another scion of the Safavids, Mir Sayyid Muhammad, a grandson of Sultan Husayn, who in 1749 was enthroned as Shah Sulayman II. In the east power fell to the Abdali chief Ahmad Khan, who, crowned Durr-i Durran, became the founder of the Durrani dynasty and of modern Afghanistan.

The real struggle for the legacy of Nadir took place in the central and western parts of the country. Contenders for power were tribal leaders such as the Bakhtiyari chief `Ali Mardan Khan, and the Zands, a subgroup of the Lurs, whose leader, Karim Khan, managed to establish control over a large area east of Kirmanshah. Assisted by various regional rulers, he next marched on Isfahan. This brought him into conflict with `Ali Mardan Khan, who had expansionist ambitions of his own. After a protracted conflict between the two, Karim Khan in the early 1750s managed to assume sole power, ruling, like others before him, in name of a nominal Safavid monarch. In 1765, after years of campaigning, he entered Shiraz, which became his capital.

Pragmatic, Karim Khan never crowned himself shah, thus avoiding the charge of having usurped a Safavid prerogative. Instead, he preferred to call himself *vakil al-ri`aya*, viceroy of the people. He is known to this day as a benevolent ruler whose justice lured many back to Iran and especially to Shiraz, which under him became a thriving commercial center endowed with new bazaars, mosques, and gardens. His encouragement of trade prompted the Dutch and English to relocate their ailing operations from Bandar `Abbas toward the upper Gulf, where Bushihr became the main port.

THE QAJAR PERIOD

Karim Khan's death in 1779 was followed by renewed chaos in the country as well as the quick rise to prominence of the Qajars, who in Safavid times had been a minor clan with a northern base. Their new leader, Agha Muhammad, hostage to Karim Khan during his lifetime, managed to escape to Shiraz after the *vakil*'s death, to unleash a reign of terror until he had extended his power to all of Iran. In 1796 he declared himself shah, thus inaugurating the Qajar dynasty.

The record of the Qajars, who would remain in power until 1925, is decidedly mixed. They were the first dynasty to unify Iran after almost a century of political turmoil and economic decline. By choosing Tehran, located close to their pasture grounds, as their new capital, they moved the center of power back to the north. But their hold over the country long remained weak. Lacking a modern army, they were unable to stand up to Russian and British military aggression. But by playing them off against each other, they successfully balanced both powers, and thus preserved Iran's (nominal) sovereignty. But the Qajars showed far less energy in modernizing their country than did contemporary rulers of the Ottoman Empire and Egypt. This was in part a combined function of continued tribal strength, comparative isolation from Europe—until the Suez Canal shortened the trip, it would take almost six months to reach Iran by ship and the road through Russia was long and arduous as well—and a forbidding Iranian physical environment in the form of high mountain ranges, large and fearsome deserts, and a small productive base. A more important factor in Iran's relative backwardness was the poor quality of Qajar leadership and the relative strength of a conservative clergy opposed to most innovations. Contributing to this weakness was a lack of religious legitimacy, which forced the Qajars to be much more accommodating to the ulama that the Safavids had been. The religious leaders, in turn, had emerged from the chaos of the eighteenth century strengthened, having filled a long power vacuum and responding to the need for guidance among a rudderless populace.

Agha Muhammad Khan was murdered in 1797 and was succeeded by his nephew Baba Khan, who, taking the name of Fath `Ali Shah, ruled until 1834. Fath `Ali Shah was known for his lavish lifestyle and his numerous offspring, but he was also very pious and under him the clerical estate enjoyed great prestige and came to benefit from extensive government patronage. Hostility toward Sufism, a clerical concern inherited from the Safavid period, flared up and led to a wave of persecution. Its main instigator, the prominent cleric Aqa Muhammad `Ali Bihbahani, whose nickname was *sufikush*, Sufi-killer, persuaded Fath `Ali Shah to expel all Sufis from Tehran. This persecution broke the connection between Sufism and the common people and resulted in Sufism's becoming mostly an upper-class phenomenon.

Until the Qajar period, foreigners had played a role of limited importance in Iran. Both Western merchants and European missionaries were only marginally successful in their bid for influence at the royal court, and even the maritime companies lacked the military power to act beyond the coastal area. This began to change after 1800s, when Iran was drawn into the orbit of Russian-British rivalry. Russia, taking advantage of Iran's glaring weakness, intensified its territorial aggression, whereas the British, who saw Iran as an extension of their Indian domains, sought to keep the country from falling under Russian control.

Initially, this led to a complicated diplomatic game involving shifting Iranian alliances directed either against Russia or Napoleon, who had his own designs on Iran as a gateway to India. But Iran suffered territorial loss as well. Russia and Iran fought two wars between 1800 and 1828. Iran lost both and, with the Treaties of Gulistan (1813) and Turkomanchai (1828), Russia annexed a significant portion of its territory in the Caucasus. Russia also forced Iran to open up to foreign trade by making it sign a commercial treaty favorable to Russian merchants. Trade between the two countries expanded and a great volume of European goods began to be transported into Iran via Trabzon and the Russian Black Sea ports. By mid-century, half of European imports into Iran came via Trabzon. Beginning in the 1830s, many foreign trade representatives, mostly Greeks and Armenian and Georgian

Russian subjects, took up residence in Iran's northern cities. Iran, in turn, saw an exodus of people going to Russia in pursuit of trade and employment or, in the case of Armenians, of a more congenial religious environment.

Defeats by the Russians made Iran's leaders painfully aware of the country's military weakness and led the most forward-looking among them, `Abbas Mirza, Fath `Ali Khan's son and governor of Azerbaijan, to push for reform. Priority was given to military reform, and soon European experts were engaged to train Iranians in the art of modern warfare. At the same time the first Iranian students went to Europe for practical training in the military sciences. Tabriz, the gateway for the introduction of Western ideas, was also the site of Iran's first printing press.

The premature death of `Abbas Mirza in 1823 ended this first experiment. Not until the middle of the century, under Nasir al-Din Shah (1848–96), would reform be resumed. This time its driving force was Mirza Taqi Khan, also known as Amir Kabir, the shah's grand vizier and confidant. Amir Kabir again sent students to Europe and under his auspices the first nonreligious institute of higher learning, called *Dar al-funun*, was established in Iran. The instructors initially were all European. But this phase, too, fizzled when Amir Kabir died, strangled in his bathtub at the order of the shah who had been persuaded by Amir Kabir's rivals that he posed a threat to the throne.

Mirza Aga Khan Nuri became Nasir al-Din's new grand vizier, but he was dismissed in 1858, and until 1871 the shah ruled without a chief minister. Tehran underwent significant urban renewal in this period. The telegraph reached Iran, allowing the government to increase its control over the country. Because of the rising number and influence of foreigners, new ideas also gained ground. But the next real reform cycle only began in 1871, following the shah's trip to Iraq—his first abroad—where he witnessed some of the fruits of Ottoman modernization, and coinciding with the appointment of Mirza Husayn Khan, first as minister of justice, then as grand vizier. Under him, some legal and administrative reforms were undertaken, involving a regularization of the judiciary, a greater role for secular courts, and the establishment of government departments. The first of the shah's three trips to Europe in 1873 brought more change, most notably the engagement of Austrian experts and advisers for police and postal services. Yet, ultimately the results were disappointing, and the momentum was interrupted by the dismissal of Mirza Husayn Khan at the instigation of Anis al-Dawlah, the shah's favorite wife. Especially in later years, Nasir al-Din Shah showed himself hesitant to engage in substantive reform, apprehensive of clerical reaction, fearing that his power and authority might be undermined, and ultimately lacking in vision. Least of all was the shah inclined to follow the advice of Iranians who returned from Europe and the Ottoman Empire to advocate the need for more radical political change along European lines. Despite growing censorship, intellectuals such as Malkum Khan, Mirza Yusuf Khan Mustashar al-Dawlah, and `Abd al-Rahim Talibuf who preached the need for constitutionalism and the rule of law, nonetheless prepared the ground for such change.

The ulama were overwhelmingly against Western-inspired reform, which they associated with unbelief and the undermining of Iran as a Shi`i nation. They had suffered a temporary setback under Fath `Ali Shah's successor, Muhammad Shah (1834–48), whose mystical inclinations were reinforced by his controlling, Sufi-minded tutor, Hajji Mirza Aqasi. But weak secular rule and their financial independence from the state continued to give them much power in provincial centers, in some of which they ran urban rackets assisted by *lutis*, thugs. Although the ulama remained quite willing to associate themselves with the royal court, they also capitalized on their role as cultural spokesmen at a time of royal ineptitude to mobilize the masses against the growing foreign influence in the country. They also gained in organizational strength. In the 1700s, their perennial debate over the nature of authority in the absence of a living Imam had given prominence to a theory that stated the need for a living source of religious authority, the *mujtahid*. A growing acceptance of this theory prepared the ground for the establishment of a clerical hierarchy in the nineteenth century, and, more particularly, for the emergence of one or a few supreme clerics with the title of *marja` al-taqlid*, source of emulation.

The power of the ulama at this time is visible in their reaction to the emergence of the messianic Babi movement, founded by Sayyid `Ali Muhammad Shirazi, who in 1844 proclaimed himself the Bab—the gate through which God speaks to humankind. Originally a movement among young seminarians, Babism originally did not preach a total break with Islam; it was, rather, an outgrowth of Shaykhism, a current in Shi`i Islam that was heavily influenced by the rational philosophical tradition in Iran that preached the need for a living intermediary between the Imam and humanity (and that influenced mainstream clerical thinking as well). At the instigation of the clergy the Bab was executed and, following several popular revolts, his followers were ruthlessly persecuted. Many followers of the Bab became radical opponents of the later Qajars and reform advocates. In the 1860s, a Babi leader claimed to be a new prophet with a new scripture, founding the Bahai religion, which focused on an ecumenical and liberal message.

Resistance to foreign influence grew, meanwhile, and not just among the ulama. Merchants took the lead in protests against competition in the form of growing imports of cheaply manufactured Western goods that drove out Iranian products. This became particularly acute after 1841, when the British joined the Russians in achieving lower tariffs for their merchants with the signing of the Anglo-Persian Commercial Treaty. Another contentious issue was Herat, which had been lost to Iran as part of the emergence of Afghanistan. Iran's attempts to regain the city in 1835 had led to a brief war with the British who saw Herat as a possible corridor for a Russian drive toward India and were determined to keep it in their own sphere of influence. Following a second confrontation in the 1850s, the British forced Nasir al-Din Shah to withdraw from Herat and to give up on his Afghan aspirations.

The Herat imbroglio led to a temporary upswing of French influence at the Qajar court but could not stop the growing power of the British, especially after the Suez Canal helped open up Iran to contact with the outside world. As the British increased their political influence, their merchants came to dominate in the upper part of the Persian Gulf, distributing their wares to Muhammarah (modern Khurramshahr) on the Shatt al-`Arab, and later via the Karun River, which in the 1880s was opened up for navigation as far as Ahvaz.

Foreign control over Iran's resources reached a new level of intensity with the concessions that the shah began to award to Westerners in exchange for loans. Resistance was especially strong against the far-reaching Reuter concession of 1872, which brought Iran's mines, irrigation works, and the construction of future canals, roads, and telegraphs and factories under the control of a foreign national. Opposed by the Russians and Russophile Iranians, it also was resisted by intellectuals arguing from nationalist motives, and ulama who resented the shah for selling out Iran to infidel forces.

The 1870 saw growing misery in Iran, with the outbreak of a devastating famine following years of drought and exacerbated by the conversion of cereals to cash crops such as opium. Insecurity remained high. Until the late nineteenth century, the Qajars were unable to prevent Turkmen tribes from Central Asia from engaging in slave raids that took them deep into Khurasan. The situation was exacerbated by the machinations and corrupt practices of Mirza `Ali Asghar Amin al-Sultan, who in the 1890s was not just prime minister but also in control of the mint and customs. An opportunist and one of many who, mainly concerned with their own fortunes, were willing to sell their service to the highest bidder, he first served British interests, and later became a Russophile. The British capitalized on this by making separate agreements with local rulers, especially in the south. The Russians typically did the same in the north.

Government inaction and growing corruption caused popular resentment to grow steadily. It was the clergy who channeled this resentment by giving it ideological articulation. The first major outburst came in 1891, when the shah awarded control over Iran's tobacco production to a British subject. This move galvanized widespread popular discontent and sparked a major protest movement, first among merchants in Fars, Iran's main tobacco-growing region, who saw their livelihood threatened, and soon by the clerics, who excoriated this concession for putting infidels in control of Iranian tobacco. When Hajji Mirza Hasan Shirazi, a leading *mujtahid*, issued a *fatwa* declaring smoking contrary to Islam, a general boycott of tobacco ensued, forcing the shah to rescind the concession. Nasir al-Din Shah failed to regain legitimacy and in 1896 fell victim to the bullet of an assassin.

The Tobacco Protest proved to be dress rehearsal for an even more significant and far-reaching movement, the Constitutional Revolution of 1905–11, which brought together a disparate group comprising intellectuals, merchants and ulama united in their deep frustration with the misrule of the Qajars, now represented by the weak and spendthrift Muzaffar al-Din Shah (r. 1896–1906), and outrage over the government's continued willingness to sell the country to foreign interests. The movement erupted as an outcry over the hiring of Belgian customs officials, and initially took the form of thousands of merchants, mullahs, and ordinary people taking sanctuary, *bast*, in Tehran's main mosque. Because the British seemed sympathetic to their cause, their legation later became a main refuge for protesters as well, although British sympathy ended after the 1907 Anglo-Russian entente dividing Iran into spheres of influence. A demand for justice, always an integral part of Iranian political culture, became the movement's rallying cry, and soon a clamor arose for a "house of justice," a parliament. Only the intellectuals and some of the more progressive ulama, most notably Muhammad Tabataba'i and `Abdullah Bihbihani, understood the term for what it was, a legislative body engaged in the crafting of manmade laws. The shah gave in to the creation of a representative assembly, or *majlis*, and in late 1906, on his deathbed, signed the Fundamental Law, the first part of a written constitution. A supplementary law was adopted in the following year. Introducing a constitutional monarchy, the new constitution limited the right of the shah to engage in foreign deals and also promised equal treatment for Iranians of all religions.

By this time a significant opposition had formed against the experiment. The new shah, Muhammad `Ali Shah, took the lead in this, and, in collusion with the country's reactionary forces and the Russians, in 1908 staged a successful coup against the *majlis*. A combination of progressive forces centered in Tabriz and opposition from the southern Bakhtiari tribe came to the rescue of the parliament. In the chaotic period that followed, the *majlis* was temporarily dissolved as a result of Russian aggression. The constitution endured, however. It had introduced the idea of limited government and mass political participation through political parties, and as such radically changed Iran's political culture.

CHAPTER 2

Wine in Safavid Iran I: Between Excess and Abstention

ساقی بیار باده که ماه صیام رفت

Cup-bearer, bring on the wine, for the month of fasting is past

Hafiz

بسیاری از ملوک و سلاطین را وسیلهٔ هلاک شراب بوده

Wine has been the means of death for many kings and rulers

Mulla Muhammad Baqir Sabzavari,
Rawzat al-anwar-i `Abbasi

INTRODUCTION: HISTORICAL ANTECEDENTS

An Iranian legend holds that the mythical King Jamshid was the first to experiment with the fermentation of grape juice. He tried the liquid that resulted, thought the taste acid and took it for poison. One of his wives, who suffered from terrible headaches, ingested the liquid to put herself out of her misery. Yet, instead of killing her, the drink put her to sleep and cured her. Overjoyed by this result, King Jamshid ordered greater quantities to be prepared and had it called "happy poison," *zahr-i khush*.

The historical record seems to validate the legend of Jamshid for it points to Iran as one of the world's first regions where wine was cultivated and consumed. Jars from 5400 to 5000 B.C.E. containing deposits that likely are remnants of wine have been found at Hajji Firuz Tepe in the northern Zagros Mountains.[1] More specific information comes from the Achaemenid period. The modern Persian word for wine, *may*, is related to the Avestan word *madu*, which means intoxication.[2] Elamite tablets found at Persepolis refer to wine rations for functionaries and courtesans, and we know that wine flowed freely at the banquets of the elite. Herodotus claimed that the Iranians were fond of wine and that their king drank a variety that was especially reserved for him. According

---

[1] McGovern, *Ancient Wine*, 64–68.
[2] Gignoux, "Matériaux pour une histoire du vin," 37.

to Strabo, referring to the Parthians, Iranians often deliberated on the gravest issues in a state of drunkenness.[3] A few centuries later, the Sasanian banquet, *bazm*, revolved around wine and music-making.

Various accessories related to Iranian wine drinking, such as the wine bull, the wine boat, the wine horn, and the wine leg or the elephant's leg, go back to pre-Islamic times. The wine bull in particular seems to refer to the ancient libation ritual of slaughtering a bull. This rite may have been abolished at the time of Zoroaster's prophecy, but the symbolism lived on in the celebration of wine substituting for blood and being drunk in a bull-shaped vessel.[4] Blood and wine also come together in life-giving rituals in ancient Near Eastern mythology that involve ritual dismemberment, and sacrificing grapes by severing them from the vine continued to be a theme in Persian literature long into the Islamic period.[5] Substituting wine for blood, Zoroastrianism retained the concept of wine as light, of wine symbolizing the liquid gold and flowing fire of the radiant sun, and the metaphor of drinking wine at dawn represented the conjunction of the new moon and the sun. By drinking wine, the king was honored as the "master of the conjunction," *sahibqiran*, an epithet for Iranian rulers since ancient times.[6]

The coming of Islam to Iran signaled change as much as continuity in the consumption of wine and the rituals surrounding it. At first glance, the abundance of wine drinking and the openness of the practice in many parts of the Middle East, including Iran, stand in stark contrast to Islam's fierce condemnation of alcohol. On closer inspection, however, the case is far more ambiguous. It is true that Islam considers alcohol an abomination and that in Sura V:90–91 the Koran explicitly prohibits wine, *khamr*, threatening offenders with eternal punishment. One also might say that on the ontological level, in the realm of the ideal, these conditions do not apply. Thus, the promised pleasures of paradise include rivers of wine, albeit of the uninebriating kind.[7] In the earthly realm, matters are different. Yet, here, too, the Koran (IV:43) suggests that not intoxication is the problem, but intoxication in so far as it clouds the mind and interferes with being a good Muslim, and inasmuch as it precludes the execution of proper ritual.[8]

---

[3]Ibid., 38–39; and Briant, *Histoire de l'Empire perse*, 304.

[4]See Melikian-Chirvani, "Les taureaux à vin"; idem, "The Wine Bull"; idem, "From the Royal Boat"; and idem, "The Iranian Wine Leg."

[5]For this, see Hanaway, "Blood and Wine," 30–31.

[6]Melikian-Chirvani, "The Iranian Bazm," 95.

[7]Mcauliffe, "Wines of Earth and Paradise"; and the discussion in Hattox, *Coffee and Coffeehouses*, 46ff.

[8]Kueny, *Rhetoric of Sobriety*.

The aggregate of Koranic references to alcohol suggests that Islam does not reject alcohol unconditionally and categorically, as it does with pork, carrion, and blood. More than wine's intrinsic properties, it was the drinking habits of his companions that caused the Prophet to move against it. The Koran allows one to trace his progressively more negative stance vis-à-vis drinking. Sura XVI:66 confers a positive meaning on wine by hailing it as good nourishment and as one of God's special signs to the community of true believers. Muhammad's initial warning against the misuse of wine is reflected in Sura II:219, which insists that wine's tendency to lead to sin is greater than its usefulness. As people paid no heed to this rebuke, a new revelation came down in the form of Sura IV:46, which forbade the faithful to attend prayer drunk. An outright call to avoidance only appeared in Sura V:90–91.[9] In sum, rather than flatly condemning it as a substance, the Koran approaches alcohol sequentially, referring to its various aspects, differentiating between levels of existence and circumstance without making an effort to reconcile these.

The Prophet's direct successors, the caliphs Abu Bakr and ʿUmar, instituted a penalty of forty and eighty lashes, respectively, for imbibers. But following the establishment of a Muslim state beyond the confines of the Arabian Peninsula, religious exegetes long argued over what separated fermented from nonfermented drinks, and whether wine really counted as a proscribed drink if it was made from other than fermented grapes. Keen to bring the world under the rule of transparent principles, they turned the ambiguities surrounding alcohol into straightforward precepts, so that over time the distinction between drinking and abstemiousness became a fixed line. The Islamic injunction to "command right and forbid wrong" thus came to include a formal ban on alcohol. Yet enough loopholes were left for those intent on finding them to engage in casuistic arguments in order to justify their drinking habits.

Throughout, older cultural patterns, in which wine was either a symbol in religious liturgy or a social lubricant, endured, and nowhere more so than in the Iranian cultural realm—which includes the milieu of Baghdad under the ʿAbbasid caliphs, the classical period of Islam. Periodic outbursts of religious zeal notwithstanding, wine was ubiquitous in elite circles, serving as the mainstay of the *majlis*, the convivial gathering of the ruler and his boon companions, which often included poets, singers, and dancers.[10] Some rulers encouraged the consumption of wine because of the tax revenue it generated.[11] Wine retained its time-honored medical status, with

[9]Wensinck, "Khamr," 994.
[10]Brookshaw, "Palaces, Pavilions," 200–1.
[11]Heine, *Weinstudien*, 47, 64–65.

none less than the famous physician Abu Bakr Muhammad b. Zakariya al-Razi (865–925) claiming that a moderate intake benefits one's health.[12] Wine and literature were inextricably intertwined. Persian poetry from the Islamic period is replete with wine imagery, ambiguously referring to metaphysical drunkenness or to the tangible pleasures of the bacchanal. Throughout time, wine has been one of the most frequently used and semantically rich images for the Persian poet, who used it metaphorically, its limpid radiance to symbolize the illumination the Sufi attains, its intoxicating capacity to denote the delirious bond of love between the mystic and the divine or to symbolize his defiance of orthodox rigidity. Frequent allusions to the *jam-i Jam*, Jamshid's chalice, referring to the alleged introduction of the wine libation ritual by Jamshid, directly connect the Islamic-Iranian mystical tradition to pre-Islamic themes and patterns. Other metaphors used to great effect in mystical verse include the drinking tavern, managed by the Magian elder, and located in the ruins, outside of the city, beyond the pale of civilization, as well as the *saqi*, the youthful handsome wine server who represents the poet's beloved.[13] The references to wine in Persian mystical and worldly poetry are too numerous, the shades and nuances of the symbolism that surrounds it too rich, to be analyzed or even summarized here. Suffice it to point to the justification for wine in poetry and life as expressed in the words of the eleventh-century poet Farrukhi: "Although wine is forbidden, I believe that it becomes licit for lovers when spring arrives. God gives us His blessings as we drink. Come and don't regret it."[14]

Beyond the symbolic connotations, the abundance of poetic references to wine points to the fact that Sufis engaged in actual wine consumption as well. Excessive drinking was indeed a hallmark of the more antinomian groups among them. Most prominently represented in Khurasan, they engaged in social deviance as a token of their direct line to God. Drinking wine was a means for them to achieve ecstasy, but also part of their exhibitionist practices. Such heterodox tendencies continued to be strongly represented on the Iranian plateau and in Anatolia, where the libation ritual involving wine remained part of various millennial cults.[15] Especially noteworthy in this regard are the Qalandars, nonconformist, anarchic Sufis, mostly Iranians, even those who operated in Egypt and Syria as of the thirteenth century. Dressed in woolen sacks and going around with shaved heads, the mostly itinerant and mendicant Qalandars took delight

---

[12]See Waines, "Al-Balkhi on the Nature of Forbidden Drink."

[13]Some of these are discussed in Yarshater, "Wine-Drinking in Persian Poetry."

[14]Quoted in Ruymbeke, "Le vin, interdiction et licence," 174.

[15]An example is the early ninth-century Babak in Azerbaijan.

in shocking orthodox Muslims with their visits to brothels, taverns, and gambling houses.[16]

The ambiguity that surrounds wine in the cultural tradition of Islamic Iran is manifest as well in the advisory manuals on manners knows as *adab* literature. The *Qabusnamah*, written by the Ghaznavid vassal Kaykavus as a guide for his son, is a case in point. Kaykavus, who spent years as the boon companion of Sultan Mawdud Ghaznavi (r. 1041?–48), devotes an entire chapter to wine. Wine, he argues, is *haram*, but that status only obtains on Fridays and Saturdays. On all other days consuming it is permissible, an activity for which one can repent before God. Besides, Kaykavus observes, a young man will find it difficult to withstand his friends' peer pressure. Telling him not to touch alcohol would therefore be futile. Kaykavus sensibly concludes that, although abstaining altogether earns one divine approval and shields one from the blame of others, it is best not to drink too much, it is preferable to drink at night, and it is important to keep the result of overindulgence, inebriation, within the four walls of one's home.[17]

I. Outside Influence: Central Asia and the Caucasus

The reference to the Ghaznavids, a Turkic dynasty ruling eastern Iran in the tenth and eleventh century, points to Central Asia as a cultural realm whose habits and tastes influenced the use of alcohol in Islamic Iran following the influx of Turkic peoples from beyond the Oxus River. The noted Ghaznavid historian Bayhaqi portrays both Mahmud and Mas`ud, the dynasty's two leading rulers, as heavy drinkers.[18] In the twelfth century wine taverns, their doors marked with a little flag, operated in the open.[19] Of the people of Inner Asia especially the Mongols were known for a lifestyle that, by embracing prostitution and prodigious drinking, flew in the face of Islamic precepts. All travelers who spent time with the Mongols commented on the frequent celebrations in which both men and women engaged in high-volume drinking. John of Plano Carpini even asserted that drunkenness was considered honorable among them. Both Persian and Chinese sources describe Ögödei, Chingiss Khan's third son and designated heir (r. 1229–41), as a tippler

---

[16]Sohrweide, "Der Sieg der Safaviden," 102; Karamustafa, *God's Unruly Friends*, 33, 44, 54–55; and Ja`fariyan, *Safaviyah dar `arsah-i din*, 2:773.

[17]For an analysis of the topic of wine in the *Qabusnamah*, see Fouchécour, *Moralia*, 190–91.

[18]See Ravandi, *Tarikh-i ijtima`i-yi Iran*, 7:268–69.

[19]Goushegir, "Forme et évolution," 244–45.

who died of alcoholism.[20] Originally, fermented mare's milk, *qumis*, was the only alcoholic drink available to the Mongols, but as they conquered sedentary societies they became acquainted with other, stronger varieties as well. This included wine, which, unlike *qumis*, could be stored for long periods of time. The Mongols thus engaged in more intense drinking precisely at the time when they grew estranged from their nomadic way of life and took to greater idleness.[21] In Iran, taverns and brothels flourished under Mongol (Il-Khanid) rule (1256–1336), their business intertwined to the point where the two were often indistinguishable. Public drunkenness in urban areas had a negative effect on law and order, with drunks harassing people in bazaars and getting into brawls that caused injuries and even fatalities. The devout, scandalized at these outrages, frequently complained but their objections were little heeded until the reign of Ghazan Khan (1295–1304), the first Il-Khanid ruler to convert to Islam.[22]

Heavy drinking continued to be common among later dynasties with roots in Central Asia, among them the Ottomans as well as the Timurids and their successors. Various kinds of debauchery, including heavy drinking, are associated with the early Ottoman sultans, beginning with Bayazid I (r. 1389–1402).[23] The Central Asian warlord Timur Lang considered the *bazm* an essential part of the rite of kingship and is said to have died of an overdose of arak.[24] Sultan Babur (1483–1530), founder of the Indian Mughals, the direct descendants of the Timurids, carried on the tradition of compulsive drinking, consuming wine, *boza*, a beer made from rice, millet, or barley, and arak, until shortly before the end of his life.[25]

A final conduit is formed by the habits and customs prevailing in the Christian territories adjacent and at times subjected to the various dynasties that ruled Iran. Recent research has established that winemaking in the Georgian Caucasus goes back eight thousand years.[26] In Georgia and Armenia, alcohol was an integral part of life and liturgy, and especially the

---

[20]Morgan, *The Mongols*. 114.

[21]Smith, "Dietary Decadence," 39–42; and Ruotsala, *Europeans and Mongols*, 120–21. As the name *araki*, from the Arabic `*araq*, indicates, a particular kind of fermented mare's milk consumed by the Mongols may have been the outcome of a distillation process that was initially introduced from west Asia and that they brought back when they invaded Iran and established their rule over the country in the thirteenth century. See Allsen, "Ever Closer Encounters," 13–14.

[22]Gronke, *Derwische im Vorhof der Macht*, 75–76.

[23]Lowry, "Impropriety and Impiety."

[24]Ravandi, *Tarikh-i ijtima`i-yi Iran*, 7:283.

[25]Malecka, "The Muslim Bon Vivant," 310–27; Dale, *Garden of the Eight Paradises*, 144, 181–83, 300–1, 346.

[26]McGovern, *Ancient Wine*, 24.

Georgians were known to be inveterate drinkers. A story from the Safavid period offers us a glimpse of the cross-cultural traffic in drinking habits that must have taken place. The people inhabiting Mingrelia, the western part of Georgia, greatly esteemed those who could hold their liquor. At the time of the Iranian Shah Safi (1629–42), the story goes, someone in Georgia by the name of Scedan Cilaze was so renowned for this that the Safavid ruler asked King Dadran to send him to Isfahan. This man tested himself against some of Iran's hardiest drinkers and invariably won in the contests held at court. The king himself challenged him and died in the process, after which the Georgian champion returned to his country, rich and famous. The story may be apocryphal—alcoholism contributed to Shah Safi's death but no other source links his demise to a drinking contest—but it does make the point of Georgian habits spreading to Iran.[27]

The issue of Georgians and Armenians takes us to the Safavid period. With their lands gradually falling under Safavid control, large numbers of Georgians began to be imported into Iran as slave soldiers, *ghulams*, where as of the mid-sixteenth century they came to play a steadily growing and ultimately preeminent role in the administration—and in the case of the women, in the harems of the shah and the ruling elite.[28] Armenians were brought to Iran in large numbers as well, most notably in 1604, when Shah 'Abbas I deported thousands of them to his new capital Isfahan, settling them in a newly constructed suburb called New Julfa. Although they all had been made to convert to Islam, especially the Georgians were known to wear their new religion but lightly. There can be little doubt that their natural penchant to drink alcohol infiltrated Iranian society and above all court culture. Georgia's fiscal status within the Safavid polity reflects this. Taxed in kind during the Safavid period, Georgia every six months was made to furnish the royal wine cellar with about twenty cases of wine of ten bottles each, each bottle containing more than three pints or about 1½ liters.[29] There were many *ghulams* among those who drank. The role of the royal harem, the private sanctum of the royal palace where, beginning with Shah 'Abbas I's successor, Safavid rulers grew up surrounded by mostly Georgian women, cannot be ignored either. It is quite likely that the fondness for wine displayed by many rulers originated in this environment.

[27]Lamberti, "Relation de la Colchide ou Mengrellie," in Thévenot, *Relation de divers voyages curieux*, 35–36.

[28]The Safavid chronicler Iskandar Beg Turkaman (Munshi) insisted that during 'Abbas I's 1616 expedition into Georgia alone some 130,000 Georgians were captured and taken to Iran, and Kaempfer in the 1680s claimed that 20,000 of Isfahan's inhabitants were of Georgian, Circassian or Daghistani background. See Turkaman, *Tarikh-i 'alam-ara-yi 'Abbasi*, 900–1; Kaempfer, *Am Hofe des persischen Grosskönigs*, 204.

[29]Chardin, *Voyages*, 9:360–61.

II. The Safavid Period: Alcohol in Society

Iranian wine was considered quite good by no less an authority than the Frenchman Chardin, our best outside source on Safavid Iran, who called the wines of Shiraz and Georgia excellent.[30] The wine with the best reputation, that of Shiraz, was reserved for the shah, the court and other high officials, and each year some twelve hundred liters were sent to the shah's wine cellar.[31] Yet, only some one third of the Shiraz harvest was turned into wine for domestic consumption; much of it went into the making of syrup and a great deal was also exported. The German physician Kaempfer found the taste of Shiraz wine to be between that of French burgundy and champagne. He called its effect remarkable, as a moderate intake produced a wonderful alacrity and enhanced the appetite, and insisted that, although excessive consumption roused passions and generated rage, it did not cause hangovers.[32] Another region that produced prized wines was Georgia. Its *vali* (governor) supervised the viticulture in his region and, as said, each year sent about three hundred liters to the royal court as a tax.[33] Wine grapes were cultivated in many other parts of the country as well, ranging from Armenia to Qazvin and from Isfahan to Yazd.[34] Yazd produced a lesser but still delicate wine, which was transported to Lar, where it was consumed by the Jewish population, and to Hurmuz, whence it was exported to India.[35] At times, such export may have taken place illegally, as Iranian wine was "smuggled to Lahore, in bottles, packed in cases under the name of rose-water."[36] White wine from Isfahan enjoyed a low reputation for being cold on the stomach and sending fumes to the head.[37]

French wines, Chardin claimed, were more delicate than Iranian ones, but then delicacy was not what Iranians wanted from their wines: they were only interested in strength and body, and tended to drink it undiluted, at times spicing it with additives like hempseed and chalk for enhanced aroma and intoxicating power, or with *nux vomica* (Persian: *kuchulah*), a strychnine-containing seed, against hangovers. To get drunk was the purpose, and if a wine didn't achieve this state fast enough, the consumer would ask: "What kind of wine is this? It has no

---

[30]Ibid., 360.
[31]Ibid., 361; Tavernier, *Les six voyages*, 1:420.
[32]Kaempfer, *Reisetagebücher*, 106.
[33]Chardin, *Voyages*, 9:360.
[34]Tavernier, *Les six voyages*, 1:419.
[35]Ibid., 420; Bernier, *Travels in the Mogul Empire*, 253.
[36]Teixeira, *Travels*, 197.
[37]Tavernier, *Les six voyages*, 1:420–21.

kick (*damagh nadarah*)."[38] Iranian rulers only consumed Iranian wine. European visitors presented them with wines from Spain, France, and the Rhineland, but none of those appealed to them as much as Iranian varieties.[39] Indeed, when the topic of wine came up during a dinner conversation between Shah `Abbas I and the Spanish envoy Don Garcia de Silva y Figueroa, the former complained that, because Spanish wine was very strong, it caused a headache.[40]

Iranian wine was kept not in barrels but in earthenware vessels that were varnished or smeared with the fat of the sheep tail on the inside to prevent the clay from tainting the wine, and covered with wooden lids. These pots were stored in caves. Conserving the wine did not require special measures; it was enough to cover the mounts of the amphorae with cloth in order to prevent insects and impurities from entering.[41] Thus stored, the wine could be kept for long periods, but generally was not for fear that a valuable deposit might get lost to a bout of Muslim antiliquor rage.[42]

Despite the religious ban on alcohol, many upper-class Iranians drank, to while away boredom, to get heated and to gain good spirits, in Chardin's words.[43] Those who went abroad to visit Christian lands often consumed alcohol as if liberated from the moral restrictions at home. Husayn `Ali Beg, Shah `Abbas I's envoy to Spain and Portugal and the Papacy, was noted for his drinking during his travels outside Iran.[44] Musa Beg, who visited the Netherlands as Safavid envoy in 1626–27, too, established a reputation for bibulousness during his time abroad.[45] Not even religious leaders were immune to the lure of alcohol. Mirza `Abd al-Husayn, the *shaykh al-islam* of Urdubad in Azerbaijan in the reign of Shah Sulayman (1666–94), is said to have become a drunk in his later years.[46] Tavernier tells the story of a "rich mullah" he met near Kirman, who invited him to his home and gave him some excellent wine to drink.[47] Those who had performed the pilgrimage to Mecca

[38]Chardin, *Voyages*, 3:218; 4:69–70.

[39]Chardin, *Voyages*, 3:73; 9:360. The Russians, too, offered Shah `Abbas I wine as a gift. Thus ambassador Tiufiakin brought 200 *vedro*, circa 2,000 liters, of wine with him on his mission to Iran in 1597. See Bushev, *Istoriia posol'stv, 1586–1612 gg.*, 271.

[40]Silva y Figueroa, *Comentarios*, 2:104.

[41]Kaempfer, *Reisetagebücher*, 106.

[42]Chardin, *Voyages*, 4:70–72.

[43]Ibid., 69–70.

[44]Alonso, "Embajadores de Persia," 155; Lefèvre, "Su un ambasciata persiana," 369–70.

[45]Dunlop, ed., *Bronnen*, 207, Visnich, Isfahan to Heren XVII, 1 Oct. 1626.

[46]Zak`aria of Agulis, *Journals*, 149.

[47]Tavernier, *Les six voyages*, 1:115

would abstain for the rest of their lives, but otherwise few people of rank seem to have had any scruples about drinking.[48]

All indications are that alcohol consumption was not common among ordinary people—who drank little more than water.[49] Mystics were the exception. It is clear that the numerous references to wine in Safavid Sufi poetry are not simply rhetorical in nature but reflect reality and practice. Sam Mirza's *Tuhfah-i Sami*, which covers the early Safavid period, abounds in references to a milieu in which heavy drinking and homosexuality were commonplace. The author treats his readers to an array of love-addicted poets who roamed cemeteries at night in search of love, of sodden libertines who drank day and night, to the point where they were no longer able to distinguish day from night.[50] Mawlana Abdal Isfahani, a druggist turned poet, is said to have been spurned by a lover, after which he set his shop on fire, left town and ended up wandering around as a dervish covered in rags. He eventually was locked up in a hospital for three months, but to no avail. Released, he first wandered around Isfahan for three years, destitute, and next moved to Tabriz, where he spent another five years haunting the Armenian wine taverns, until he finally repented.[51] The same source provides details about Baba Fighani (d. 1519), an early Safavid poet from Shiraz who was known to be an "alcoholic with a great appetite for wine" who "spent all his time in taverns." Fighani's poems are replete with references to wine.[52] A number of so-called *saqi-namah*s, wine poems of mystical content and collected in the *Tazkirah-i maykhanah*, the Compendium of the Wine Tavern, also have come to us from the hand of early Safavid poets.[53]

Muslims might drink, but the manufacturing and sale for wine was the bailiwick of non-Muslims, Armenian, and Jews. Wine was made everywhere in Iran except in places where no one was allowed to drink it, such as in areas where no Christians, Jews, or Zoroastrians resided.[54] In Isfahan, the Safavid capital after 1590, Armenians living in the suburb of New Julfa were engaged in wine making. In Shiraz, it was manufactured by the local Jewish population, which numbered some six hundred families. Their poverty did not prevent local governors from taxing them heavily for this privilege. Writing in the 1660s, Tavernier estimated the total production of the Shiraz region in a good year to be

[48]Ibid., 1:561.

[49]Della Valle, *Viaggi*, 1:688.

[50]Sam Mirza Safavi, *Tuhfah-i Sami*, 109, 267, 282, 283, 298.

[51]Ibid., 212–14.

[52]Ibid., 176. For the poetic references, see Losensky, *Welcoming Fighānī*, passim.

[53]Qazvini, *Tazkirah-i maykhanah*, 126, 140ff.

[54]Chardin, *Voyages*, 4:70–72.

Feast of the dervishes, ca. 1615, attributed to Afzal. Courtesy of Abolala Soudavar.

more than 200,000 *man*, equaling some 580,000 liters.[55] The shah at this time allowed four foreign nations, the Portuguese, the English, the Dutch, and the French, to produce wine as well in Shiraz, 12,000 *man* in the case of the first three, and 14,000 *man* in the case of the French. The English, the Dutch, and the French had their own representatives in town. The Portuguese, by contrast, operated out of Kung on the Persian Gulf, held by them as of 1649, and had an Armenian middleman transport their wine from Shiraz to the coast, from where it was sent to their factories throughout Asia.[56] The wine was carried in flasks that were so well packed in straw that they rarely broke.[57] Iran exported its wine in small quantities to various ports in India. According to a Dutch report, in the 1715–16 trading season, 625 cases were transported on indigenous ships.[58]

Wine was by far the most prevalent alcoholic beverage in Safavid Iran, but not the only one. Arak, imported from Russia, was common in court circles. Some public bathhouses may have served it to their customers.[59] Date-brandy, distilled by Jews, was especially widespread in the *Garmsir*, the hot Persian Gulf littoral.[60] In Bandar `Abbas brawls involving brandy-drinking European sailors and the shah's subjects each year claimed two to three lives. This prompted the Dutch East India Company in 1647 to seek a royal decree forbidding the Jews from distilling and selling liquor in town. It is not know if such a decree was ever issued.[61]

III. Alcohol at the Royal Court

Almost all of the available information about alcohol consumption in Safavid times concerns members of the royal court, reflecting not just superior documentation but also an incontrovertibly high incidence of drinking among them. The Iranian *bazm*, held in conjunction with warfare, *razm*, became a mainstay and remained virtually unchanged from Sasanian times until the days of Mahmud of Ghazna in the eleventh century, and as such is frequently celebrated as a three-day feast in Iran's

[55]Tavernier, *Les six voyages*, 1:734.

[56]Ibid.; and Bembo, "Viaggio e giornale," 216.

[57]Tavernier, *Les six voyages*, 1:734.

[58]NA, VOC 1886, List of foreign ships mooring at Bandar `Abbas, 13 April 1715–15, February 1716, fols. 401–4.

[59]Fryer, *A New Account*, 3:33–34.

[60]Teixeira, *Travels*, 197; Mandelslo, *Morgenländische Reyse-Beschreibung*, 19; and Aubin, "Le royaume d'Ormuz," 151. For arak in Kirman, see Mashizi (Bardsiri), *Tazkirah-i Safaviyah-i Kirman*, 439–40.

[61]NA, VOC 1162, Instruction Geleynssen de Jongh for Bastinck and Verburgh, 20 Feb. 1647, fol. 241v; idem in VOC 1165, fol. 287v.

national epic, Firdawsi's *Shahnamah*.[62] The *razm u bazm* tradition was further transmitted to the period of the Safavids in Iran and the Mughals in India.[63] As with Iranian rulers before and after them, for the Safavids the fight enabled the king to display his ability to confront powerful enemies and his valor and tenacity on the battlefield, whereas the open-air feasting that preceded and followed it showed his capacity to enjoy life's pleasures. The sources are replete with stories about such banquets.[64] Early Safavid annalistic accounts in particular offer many examples of the *bazm*, combining copious wine drinking, dance, and music-making, as well, at the court and especially among the Qizilbash, the tribal warriors whose fighting spirit enabled the Safavids to expand far and wide across Iran.[65] Such depictions are in fact a topos in Iranian annalistic literature, a standard ingredient of a genre that marked the beginning of each year with a florid narrative of nature's reawakening and whose very raison d'être was its focus on the life and career of the ruler and his warrior entourage. The Persian sources rarely dwell on the part sexuality played in these festivities, and if they do, they tend to use generic terms like *lahv va la'ib*, lust and play. We know that the *bazm* involved sex with females but, in keeping with a long tradition of sodomy in Iranian culture and in light of the occasional reference in the sources, it is equally clear that especially sex with young boys who served as cup-bearers and dancers formed an integral part of such festivities.[66]

The references are particularly numerous for Shah Isma'il I (r. 1501–24), who famously ordered the skull of his vanquished Uzbek enemy, Muhammad Shibani Khan, to be cast in gold and inlaid with jewels so as to serve as a royal drinking vessel.[67] The sources attest to Isma'il's binge drinking as early as 1503, two years after his public appearance at the age of fourteen, and continue to give examples until 1524, the year of his death. Festivities that included copious wine consumption were typically held following a campaign.[68] But they might precede combat as well. A well-known story has it that on the eve of the

---

[62]Melikian-Chirvani, "The Iranian Bazm," 97ff.

[63]Aubin, "L'avènement des Safavides," points to an Iranian tradition that goes back to Achaemenid times, and a Turco-Mongol custom that is rooted in Central Asia as the double origin for the *bazm* as it was held in Safavid times.

[64]See De Bruijn, *Of Piety and Poetry*, 157–60.

[65]For examples, see Aubin, "L'avènement des Safavides," 48. Writing long after the Qizilbash had lost their central position in the Safavid polity, Della Valle insisted that wine was especially prevalent during military campaigns and among the Qizilbash. See Della Valle, *Viaggi*, 1:688.

[66]For a discussion of this aspect, see Aubin, "L'avènement des Safavides," 52ff.

[67]Junabadi, *Rawzat al-Safaviyah*, 241.

[68]Anon., *Travels of a Merchant in Persia*, 201; and Junabadi, *Rawzat al-Safaviyah*, 227.

battle of Chaldiran of 1514 against the Ottomans, the shah and his Qizilbash commanders indulged in a *bazm* that left them utterly drunk and that contributed to their being routed the next day.[69] Rather than sobering up after this costly lesson, Shah Isma'il is said to have taken to drinking with a vengeance, giving up on his ambition to conquer the world and neglecting the affairs of state. The Safavid chronicler Qazi Ahmad, in an apparent effort to exonerate the shah, claims that it was his vizier Mirza Shah Husayn Isfahani who enticed Isma'il to spend the last ten years of his life pursuing the pleasures of sex and alcohol.[70] With several other chroniclers, Qazi Ahmad attributes the shah's early death to his overindulgence. Shah Isma'il, they claim, spent so much of his time with women and wine that it sapped his strength, until his body gave out and he expired.[71] We have the eyewitness report of the Portuguese traveler António Tenreiro to confirm that the shah indeed drank until his death in 1524.[72]

All subsequent Safavid shahs drank and some regularly drank in excess. Shah Tahmasb appears to be the exception, but he, too, was given to alcohol before publicly foreswearing it. The Persian chroniclers offer no information on Tahmasb's early drinking, preferring instead to focus on his repentance and the lifelong abstemiousness that followed it.[73] He is likely to have enjoyed the rather jovial social life of Herat, where he served as governor before ascending the throne.[74] Tenreiro observed how in 1524, the ten-year-old Tahmasb, fresh on the throne, "drank like his father under the sound of numerous musical instruments."[75]

Shah Tahmasb famously ceased to drink after proclaiming his Edict of Sincere Repentance in 1532–33. All sources agree that Tahmasb never touched a drop of wine again until his death in 1576. His reign proved to be an anomaly, however. The next ruler, Shah Isma'il II (r. 1576–77), whose reign marked a temporary revival of Qizilbash influence, revoked the ban on drinking that his father had instituted, although his own reputation lay more in the prodigious use of opiates than in alcohol abuse. His successor, Shah Muhammad Khudabandah (r. 1577–87), is said to have spent most of his time in the company of his wives and concubines.

---

[69]Bacqué-Grammont, *Les Ottomans, les Safavides,* 47; and Aubin, "L'avènement des Safavides," 47.

[70]Sam Mirza Safavi, *Tuhfah-i Sami,* 11; Qazi Ahmad, *Khulasat al-tavarikh,* 154.

[71]Khurshah, *Tarikh-i ilchi-yi Nizam Shah,* 79; and Junabadi, *Rawzat al-Safaviyah,* 358, who claims that "the constant drinking reduced the shah's appetite to the point where the mere smell of food vexed him."

[72]Tenreiro, "Itinerário," 37–38.

[73]Parsadust, *Shah Tahmasb,* 609.

[74]Qazi Ahmad, *Khulasat al-tavarikh,* 168.

[75]Tenreiro, "Itinerário," 36.

His supposed piety did not keep him from consuming alcohol. His lifestyle—a function, according to one chronicler, of having grown up in the joyous, exhilarating ambience of Herat[76]—and the fact that it caused him to pay little attention to the affairs of state prompted Junabadi to insert the following verse in his chronicle:

مساقات و رنج و تعب بردن است   ایالت نه بازی و می خوردن است

شود بی گمان کار ملکش خراب   چو خسرو کند میل مستی و خواب

سر و کار عالم بود با نظام   اگر شاه آگاه باشد مدام

Governance is not play and drinking wine.	It is endurance and labor and hardship.
When the ruler pursues drunkenness and sleep,	without doubt his realm goes to ruin.
When the shah is constantly attentive,	the affairs of the world are in order.[77]

Even Shah 'Abbas I (r. 1587–1629), who is known to have abhorred addictive substances and who more than once targeted them with prohibitive measures, liked to imbibe. Contemporary Persian chronicles state that 'Abbas often spent his time enjoying wine, music and dance, and from their references to his feasting during campaigns or as part of urban festivals it can be deduced that the *razm u bazm* tradition was alive and well during his reign. So fond was the shah of wine that he ordered one of the renowned physicians of the time, Qazi bin Kashif al-Din Muhammad, to compose a treatise for him on the benefits and effects of wine and the etiquette of consuming it. Written in accessible language, the *Jam-i jahan-namah-i 'Abbasi* bears the date of 1028/1619. Its author at first expresses doubt about the permissibility of ingesting wine even in cases of grave illness, stating that this is a matter of dispute among jurists. But he soon invokes the renowned contemporary jurist Baha al-Din al-'Amili to argue that it is lawful when life itself is at stake, and in the book's subsequent chapters uses that license to talk freely about wine, its benefits, and the proper way of consuming it in the company of others.[78]

---

[76] Ashuftah-i Natanzi, *Naqavat al-asar*, 73.

[77] Junabadi, *Rawzat al-Safaviyah*, 604. A Similar poem appears in Ashuftah-i Natanzi, *Naqavat al-asar*, 75.

[78] Elgood, *Safavid Medical Practice*, 40; Falsafi, *Zindigani-yi Shah 'Abbas*, 631–32.

Wine was not the only alcoholic beverage consumed at the court. The aquavit included in envoy Ivanovich Chicherin's gift to Shah `Abbas I suggests that Russian ardent liquor was much esteemed in Safavid court circles.[79] The Iranian emissary `Andi Beg in 1595 brought some one thousand liters of vodka back from Russia to Iran.[80] Six years later, court merchant Muhammad Aqa purchased circa three hundred liters of aquavit for the shah in Moscow.[81] European missionaries arriving in Iran via Russia in early 1605 presented Shah `Abbas with gifts that included a small barrel of aquavit.[82]

Even as they portray a court in which wine flowed freely, the sources are nearly unanimous in their insistence that under Shah `Abbas I the consumption of alcohol rarely got out of hand and did not interfere with sound statecraft.[83] One Augustinian Father in 1607 recounts how with his own eyes he had seen the monarch enjoy himself during festivals, joking with the young and the old, surrounded by women, engaged in drinking wine, strolling through squares and streets and visiting homes, all day long. Yet the same observer noted how, half drunk, the shah would continue to give orders and manage his realm, listening and issuing orders.[84] The private parties to which `Abbas often invited visiting envoys were merry gatherings that never seem to have degenerated into drunken orgies. We have the testimony of several of his foreign guests, emissaries from Christian countries, but also ambassadors from neighboring Muslim states, to confirm this.[85]

Far from setting a precedent, Shah `Abbas's reign appears as a period of relative sobriety, for under his grandson and successor, Shah Safi, unbridled drinking resumed at the court. Safi was the first Safavid ruler to have grown up in the confines of the harem, a place ill-equipped to prepare a future ruler for the rigors and responsibilities of real life. After a brief moment of sobriety following the shah's enthronement, his physicians advised him to take up wine, with the argument that it would dispel the "cold" that his opium use had introduced into his system.[86] This

[79]Della Valle, *Viaggi*, 1:836.

[80]Fekhner, *Torgovlia russkogo gosudarstvo*, 58.

[81]Bushev, *Istoriia posol'stv, 1586–1612 gg.*, 347.

[82]Florencio del Niño Jesús, *Biblioteca Carmelitano-Teresiana*, vol. 2, *A Persia (1604–1609)*, 117.

[83]Falsafi, *Zindigani- yi Shah `Abbas*, 630–31.

[84]Alonso, "Due lettere," 161, P. P. Diego di Santa Ana, Isfahan to Pope Clement VIII, 7 Dec. 1607.

[85]Bushev, *Istoriia posol'stv, 1586–1612 gg.*, 259–60; idem, *Istoriia posol'stv, 1612–1621 gg.*, 219–20; idem, "Posol'stvo V. G. Korobina," 138–39, 141; Silva y Figueroa, *Comentarios*, 2:93; Della Valle, *Viaggi*, 1:642; and Munajjim Yazdi, *Tarikh-i `Abbasi*, 441.

[86]Anon., *Chronicle of the Carmelites*, 1:350; Krusinski, *History of the Late Revolutions*, 1:47.

points to the use of alcohol as medication, something that the Mughal emperor Jahangir (r. 1605–27) refers to when in his autobiography he recalls that he was first given arak as an infant as a remedy against a cough.[87] VOC agent Jan Smidt, visiting the court only months after Safi's accession in early 1629, describes a royal banquet where the guests had to wait three hours before the shah himself showed up, deep in his cups, accompanied by the son of Imam Quli Khan, the governor of Shiraz, who was equally as inebriated. Smidt also wrote that on several occasions, drunken courtiers had insulted each other and even exchanged blows in the presence of the shah, and that this diminished the respect the new monarch enjoyed among his entourage.[88]

The hard drinking at Shah Safi's court had a negative effect on policy making in other ways as well. As several well-documented stories suggest, momentous decisions might be made during royal bacchanals.[89] The most dramatic, and a particularly grisly, example of this occurred in 1633, when, during a drinking session, the shah ordered Imam Quli Khan, the powerful governor of Shiraz who ruled virtually autonomously over the entire southern half of the country, executed with two of his sons.[90] Less macabre but as telling is an event, told in the Persian as well as the European sources, that took place on a night in July of 1634, when three prominent court officials, among them Ughurlu Khan Shamlu, the *ishikaqasi-bashi* (master of ceremony), were the guests of grand vizier Mirza Abu Talib Beg Urdubadi. They left the latter's residence drunk, and Ughurlu Khan, arriving at the palace gate that he was scheduled to watch that night, got into an argument with a gatekeeper and beat the latter with a stick. The next day the shah heard about the incident and, when engaged in a drinking party himself, reprimanded the grand vizier for having given these royal officials so much to drink, asking him if he thought it was proper to serve wine on the eve of the Muslim holy day. When the grand vizier responded by saying that the door to his house was open to all guests, the shah drew his sword, struck the grand vizier in the face, and ordered his palace guards to behead him on the spot. Ughurlu Khan and Hasan Beg, one of the other

---

[87]Jahangir, *Tūzuk-i Jahāngīrī*, 1:307.

[88]Dunlop, ed., *Bronnen*, 738, 741, 746–47, diary Jan Smidt.

[89]For this phenomenon in general, see Heine, *Weinstudien*, 110. Under the pre-Islamic king Ardashir, the chance that this might have terrible consequences was apparently mitigated by a custom of having two court scribes write down everything the shah said when intoxicated, which was then read back to him the next day. See Christensen, *L'Iran sous les Sassanides*, 403.

[90]NA, VOC 1106, Overschie, Isfahan to Heren XVII, 8 May 1633, unfol; Valah Qazvini Isfahani, *Khuld-i barin*, 148–49.

revelers, fled in panic but did not get very far: They were hauled back and cut down as well.[91]

Shah Safi drank until the end of his life, his boozing clearly contributing to its brevity. The *Khuld-i barin* contains a few lengthy passages from the last years of Safi's rule that suggest the extent of this addiction and the effect it must have had on his governing capacities. In 1639, en route to Gilan and when residing in the Safi Abad garden outside Qazvin, the shah threw a drinking party that lasted several days. At the end of the festivities his health gave way and he had to take to bed for a number of days.[92] A mere thirty-one years old, Safi died, on 11 May 1642, on his way to recapture the eastern frontier city of Qandahar from the Mughals, "overmuch drinking and other ryots [having] hastened his end."[93]

The reign of Safi's successor, Shah `Abbas II (1642–66), began with a general ban on wine, possibly in reaction to the alcohol-drenched reputation of his father.[94] In their narration of events of his first years on the throne, the chronicles contain the obligatory references to the annual New Year's festivities, but wine drinking is absent in their description of the Nawruz *bazm*.[95] In 1649 `Abbas II reneged on his commitment to a life without alcohol and, for most of his reign, is known to have enjoyed nights of quaffing wine with his boon companions in an ambience of merriment and conviviality.[96] Like other high-ranking officials, the shah had his own caves for that purpose. The royal cave is described as a square space with a little pond filled with water in the middle. Tapestries covered the floor and at the four corners of the pond there were four large wine bottles each containing some twenty pints or more. Between these large bottles were ranged a number of smaller ones, each containing four or five pints, with whites and clarets alternating. Around the cave there were niches at several levels, with a bottle in each niche. Natural

[91]Ibid., 201–3; Turkaman, *Zayl-i tarikh*, 144–45; ARA, VOC 1115, Overschie, Isfahan to Heren XVII, 27 Oct. 1634, fols. 99–100; Dunlop, ed., *Bronnen*, 525.

[92]Valah Qazvini Isfahani, *Khuld-i barin*, 291–92, 312; and Qazi Ahmad, *Khulasat al-tavarikh*, 154–55, which notes how the shah's drinking came at the expense of his attention to matters of state. Narrating the events of 1050/1641, Valah Qazvini Isfahani recounts how Safi again got so drunk during a bacchanal organized during a hunting trip that the royal doctors had to intervene to save his life.

[93]IOR records, 17 January 1643, quoted in Anon., ed., *Chronicle of the Carmelites*, 350. See also Tavernier, *Les six voyages*, 1:576. Turkaman, *Zayl-i tarikh*, 256, as well as Valah Qazvini Isfahani, *Khuld-i barin*, 314, confirm that Shah Safi's death was caused by his constant drinking during the spring season. Olearius, *Vermehrte newe Beschreibung*, 664, is the only one to speculate that the shah might have been poisoned.

[94]Valah Qazvini Isfahani, *Khuld-i barin*, 421.

[95]See, for instance, ibid., 406, 412, 424, 430, 434.

[96]Chardin, *Voyages*, 9:418, however, talking about the shah's death in 1666, cites a rumor according to which `Abbas II had been poisoned after ordering the killing of several concubines while in a state of intoxication.

light entered the cave through several windows, with sunlight on the
wine having a brilliant effect.[97]

Shah 'Abbas II typically invited a small number of his favorite
courtiers to his parties and his drinking habits are the best documented
examples of the kind of intimacy and mutual obligation forged by sharing the cup that the ancient Greeks practiced and that had long been an
integral part of traditional Persian court ceremony as well. Among Shah
'Abbas II's (forced) boon companions was Khalifah Sultan, a scion of a
clerical family who for a decade served as grand vizier, who was know
for his piety and learnedness and whom we shall encounter in the next
chapter as the instigator of an antivice campaign.[98] Once the shah drank
so much with Khalifah Sultan and other officials in his entourage that
when they got up to mount their horses, each one of them had to be supported by two servants.[99] Other court officials enjoyed their liquor just as
much. Thus *qullar aqasi* (head of the *ghulam* corps) Siyavush Khan and
his retinue one day were so deep in their cups that they could hardly keep
themselves in the saddle. Of the same official it is said that he did not
consume alcohol in the morning on days when he had see the shah in the
afternoon, so as to appear in a sober state.[100] Safi Quli Beg, the governor
of Yazd, loved wine and threw frequent banquets. His drinking got out
of hand, though, and eventually caused his death.[101] Nasir 'Ali Khan,
who in early 1674 became the new governor Bandar 'Abbas, quickly became better known for his drinking than for his working habits.[102]

Alcohol in this period also figured prominently at official banquets
and audiences, some of which are depicted in the murals that adorn the
walls of the Chihil Sutun palace in Isfahan to this day.[103] From the moment in 1649 that the chronicle announces the shah's decision to take
up the cup, to 1662, the year that it breaks off, the pages of the *Khuld-i
barin* are filled with references to Nawruz festivities and royal hunting
parties where wine flowed freely. For his parties, the shah would often

[97]Tavernier, *Les six voyages*, 1:421–22.

[98]Speelman, *Journaal der reis*, 143–45, 159, 161–63, 182. Nasrabadi, *Tazkirah-i
Nasrabadi*, 24, says of Khalifah Sultan that it was the shah who ordered him to drink
incessantly.

[99]NA, VOC 1178, Sarcerius, Gamron to Batavia, 2 Feb. 1650, fol. 657.

[100]Speelman, *Journaal der reis*, 271, 282. In 1654, the same official requested brandy
from the Dutch. See NA, VOC 1203, Sarcerius, Gamron to Batavia, 21 March 1654,
fol. 787.

[101]Mustawfi Bafqi, *Jami'-i Mufidi*, 196–97.

[102]NA, VOC 1297, Gamron to Heren XVII, 1 April 1675, fol. 1011r.

[103]The Chihil Sutun palace was built in 1647. For its history and features, see Babaie,
"Shah 'Abbas II, the Conquest of Qandahar." For textual evidence that the royal courtesans drank as well, see Tavernier, *Les six voyages*, 1:555.

request the company of European residents of Isfahan who represented Western nations or trading companies.[104] During a farewell audience for Dutch envoy Johan Cuneaus, the shah, surrounded by a select group of courtiers, had a gold cup "fully inlaid with precious stones, mostly uncut rubies" go around.[105] On one occasion in 1665, he invited several French and Dutch guests to join him in spending a day in a festive mood. The party, which started at nine in the morning, was enlivened with dancing girls and featured singing by the guests as well, while music was played on the harp and an organ that had been received as a gift from Russia. All the while the goblet went around, with the shah even allowing his foreign guests to drink from his own gold cup.[106]

In keeping with the words of his chronicler, although `Abbas II's governing capacities do not appear to have suffered too much at first, his persisting drinking did eventually take its toll.[107] VOC agent De Lairesse tells the story of how in the summer of 1666 the shah had invited him for a night of drinking in Mazandaran, his temporary residence, after which the monarch did not appear in public for two weeks.[108] Wine consumption at the court must have been substantial, for that year saw a production of 50,000 *man* (some 145,000 liters) of wine for the royal household.[109] `Abbas died in the fall of the same year, felled by a combination of syphilis and throat cancer, with heavy drinking likely to have hastened his untimely demise at age thirty-four.[110]

The next ruler, Shah Sulayman, showed a greater interest in matters of Shi`i orthodoxy than his father and during his reign religion became an increasingly prominent part of public life—as exemplified by the appointment, in 1687, of Muhammad Baqir Majlisi as *shaykh al-islam* of Isfahan, a move designed to "give greater currency to matters of the holy law."[111] Yet, for the time being, this new mood expressed itself in increasingly vehement denunciations of popular forms of Sufism by dogmatic clerics and a tightening of restrictions on non-Muslim communities rather than in stricter vice laws. The shah himself set the tone with his unholy lifestyle. He spent many an evening drinking with high court officials and under him the royal Nawruz festivities seem to have been

---

[104]Manucci, *Storia di Mogor*, 1:41; Abbé Carré, *Travels*, 3:817.

[105]Speelman, *Journaal der reis*, 271.

[106]Kroell, *Nouvelles d'Ispahan*, 19, letter Daulier Deslandes, Isfahan, 15 Feb. 1665; Daulier Deslandes, *Les beautez*, 30–36; and Tavernier, *Les six voyages*, 1:544.

[107]Vahid Qazvini, `Abbasnamah, 131.

[108]NA, VOC 1255, De Lairesse, Gamron to Batavia, 30 Nov. 1666, fol. 814.

[109]Tavernier, *Les six voyages*, 1:734.

[110]Ibid., 582; and Chardin, *Voyages*, 9:399.

[111]Khatunabadi, *Vaqa'i` al-sannin*, 540.

drenched in alcohol.[112] Much more aloof than his predecessors, Sulayman was not in the habit of inviting foreign guests to his private parties.[113] The occasionally unpleasant consequences of Sulayman's drunken states—in one of them he allegedly ordered the blinding of one of his own brothers—are reminiscent of his grandfather's reign.[114]

Speaking about the court of Shah Sulayman, various eyewitness observers claimed that during the early stage of audiences and banquets the shah was served wine in sealed bottles that were opened in his presence by the *nazir*, the steward of the royal household, who first tasted the contents.[115] The bottles used at court were made of crystal and some were decorated with diamond studs, others with gadroon (inverted fluting or beading) patterns, whereas yet others were painted. Each contained approximately a pint, had a foot of about two fingers wide, a round body, and a long swan neck measuring eight or nine inches. The spout had the shape of the beak of a crane. The bottles were sealed with wax, tied on top with a piece of pink silk, and secured with the seal of the *shirahchi-bashi*, the royal sommelier, on a silk ribbon.[116] It was the *shirahchi-bashi*'s task to provide the royal table with various wines from all over Iran and with Russian aquavit as well as to entertain important guests and official visitors from Christian lands. The same official also supervised those who had a license to make wine and who sold it in the country.[117] This makes it likely that the *shirahchi-bashi* was an Armenian, as was the case for

---

[112]See, for example, the description of the New Year's celebration of 1103/1692 in Mashizi (Bardsiri), *Tazkirah-i Safaviyah-i Kirman*, 606, which notes that all the attendees got drunk. One of the shah's boon companions may have been Mansur Khan, the *qullar-aqasi* in the 1660s, who was said to follow Bacchus more than Muhammad. See Bedik, *Chehil Sutun*, 252.

[113]The Polish envoy Bogdan Gurdziecki, who in 1684 visited Isfahan on behalf of the Russian crown and who once spent an entire night quaffing in the shah's company, is an exception. See Józefowicz, "Z dziejów stosunków Polsko-Perskich," 334; Krusinski, *History of the Late Revolutions*, 1:130–31.

[114]The queen mother, the apocryphal story has it, intervened on behalf of the victim, but this only provoked a greater fury in the shah, who drew his sword and wounded her. Denied medical treatment at her son's orders, she reportedly committed suicide by jumping from the top of the palace. See IOR, G/36/106, Gombron to Surat, 29 April 1672, fol. 96; ibid., Gombroon to Surat, 27 November 1672, fol. 38. Father Krusinski later noted that different opinions existed as to whether Sulayman's mother had killed herself or had been killed by her own son. In reality she survived her son, for on his death in 1694 she made an endowment of a copy of the Koran on his tomb. See Mudarrisi Tabataba'i, *Turbat-i pakan*, 1:170. My thanks to Prof. Modarressi for bringing this reference to my attention.

[115]Sanson, *Voyage*, 60; and *Lettres édifiantes et curieuses*, 4:115, Lettre de révérend Père H. B. à Monsieur le comte de M.

[116]Chardin, *Voyages*, 9:361.

[117]Ibid., 359–60.

most of the reign of Shah Safi.[118] The position was worth a fortune, for he only allowed Muslims to produce and consume alcohol in return for gifts and bribes. According to Chardin the *shirahchi-bashi* had a "thousand ways of extorting from Christians and Jews, even in the remotest provinces, various fines that he imposes, accusing them of selling wine to Muslims, against the legal ban, and making them accountable for the disorder caused by wine." This official had, however, no control over resident Europeans.[119]

The reign of Shah Sulayman also offers the best documentation on the custom of the ruler forcing his subordinates to drink. The shah was notorious for forcing his abstemious grand vizier, Shaykh `Ali Khan, to quaff in his presence. The temporary dismissal of Shaykh `Ali Khan as grand vizier in 1673 seems to have come after his refusal to join the shah in a drinking session.[120] For the forced drinking, a huge goblet made of gold was used, the contents of which are variously given as about a pint and almost a gallon. Its name, *hazar pishah* (a thousand vocations), refers to the belief that those who had emptied it two or three times were capable of speaking randomly about a whole array of arts and professions.[121] No exact descriptions of this wine container exist, although the aforementioned large gold cup inlaid with rubies may be a reference to the *hazar-pishah*. If correct, the vessel was clearly different from the many wine bowls that have come to us from the Safavid period.[122] The issue is complicated by the fact that in the Persian sources the term *hazar pishah* only refers to the traveling kit filled with royal necessities carried by the master of the royal wardrobe (*mihtar-i rikabkhanah*), who always accompanied the monarch.[123] This

---

[118]Valah Qazvini Isfahani, *Khuld-i barin*, 342. Under Shah Safi, the position was first held by Bayindir Beg and later by Amin Beg, who was succeeded by his son Safi Quli Bayg.

[119]Chardin, *Voyages*, 9:359–60.

[120]Mashizi (Bardsiri), *Tazkirah-i Safaviyah*, 387–88. See also Fasa'i, *Farsnamah-i Nasiri*, 489–90; and the references in Matthee, "Administrative Stability and Change," 85.

Forced drinking had been practiced by Shah Safi, who on at least one occasion forced his courtiers to empty a huge wine cup in his presence, as well as by Shah `Abbas II, who often made his European guests drink with him. See Tavernier, *Les six voyages*, 1:544, 558. Not even religious objections would be accepted as an excuse for a guest not to comply. Thus, `Abbas II made the poet Mir `Aqili drink, despite the latter's remonstrations and invocations to the Imam `Ali that he did not consume alcohol. See Falsafi, "Sar-guzahst-i `Saru Taqi," 299–300; Nasrabadi, *Tazkirah-i Nasrabadi*, 394.

[121]Sanson, *Voyage*, 67–68; Manucci, *Storia di Mogor*, 1:40. Chardin, *Voyages*, 3:216, mistakenly translates *pishah* as "chimeras" after the headaches drinking the goblet was supposed to produce.

[122]For illustrations and descriptions of these, see Melikian-Chirvani, *Islamic Metalwork*, 266ff.

[123]Mirza Rafi`a, *Dastur al-muluk*, ed. Afshar, 530 (42); Minorsky, ed. *Tadhkirat al-Muluk*, 138.

The *qazi* (judge) of Hamadan in a drunken state, Lalchand, seventeenth century. Credit: The Freer Gallery of Art, Smithsonian Institution, Washington, D.C.

large drinking vessel recalls the chariot-wheel-sized bowl offered to Shah Isma'il I, and although it is not recorded before the Safavids, there is no reason to assume that it was not in use earlier.

Several reasons underlay this practice. Often it simply provided a form of entertainment for the shah. Thus, whenever Shah `Abbas II felt like joking with someone or wished to mete out light punishment, he would force the person involved to empty the *hazar pishah* in his presence, as he did several times with French goldsmiths in his service for delivering work that did not please him.[124] Shah Sulayman loved to see high officials being carried away like corpses after downing a *hazar pishah*.[125] The same ruler also seems to have taken a perverse pleasure in inflicting humiliation on pious court officials. There was a political rationale, too, reminiscent of what Herodotus had said about pre-Islamic Iranian kings: drinking loosened the lips and enabled the ruler to extract secrets from his courtiers.[126] Following the appointment of Mirza Tahir Vahid Qazvini as Shah Sulayman's new grand vizier in early 1691, the shah presented him with a full *hazar pishah*, and subsequently made him explain what in his view were the most pressing needs of the country.[127] Conversely, court officials found it in their interest to have a bibulous shah, as this enabled them to bamboozle him while wielding power with a free hand.[128] Finally, even issues of honor and exclusion might be involved in the use of the *hazar pishah*. During an assembly in late 1691 Shah Sulayman offered one to a number of courtiers, but not to the *qurchibashi* (head of the royal guard), Saru Khan Sahandlu, who had incurred the ruler's displeasure and who was beheaded following the meeting.[129]

After Shah Sulayman, the abstemiousness of Sultan Husayn (r. 1694–1722) appears natural, a swing of the pendulum reminiscent of Shah `Abbas II's initial sobriety. Exceedingly pious, Shah Sultan Husayn in fact established his credentials as the new ruler in 1694 by solemnly proclaiming wine drinking and an array of other frivolous pastimes banned, in a move that reminds one of the measures instituted by Shah Tahmasb a century and a half earlier. But, in his case, early resolutions proved too hard to live up to. Initially banned, wine soon crept back into court life,

---

[124]Manucci, *Storia di Mogor*, 1:40–41.

[125]Sanson, *Voyage*, 67–68.

[126]Ibid. See also *Lettres édifiantes et curieuses*, 4:118, Lettre du Révérend Père H. B. à Monsieur Comte de M. Della Valle, *Viaggi*, 1:668, speculated that Shah `Abbas I, too, used wine for this purpose. For wine as a means to make subordinates speak without inhibition, see also Heine, *Weinstudien*, 110.

[127]Kroell, ed., *Nouvelles d'Ispahan*, 30; Sanson, "Nouvelles de Perse," Isfahan, 8 April 1691.

[128]Krusinki, *History of the Late Revolutions*, 1:72.

[129]Kroell, *Nouvelles d'Ispahan*, 39; Sanson, "Nouvelles de Perse du 13 août 1691."

and, as will be seen in the next chapter, the shah himself gave in to drinking. His decision in 1699 to appoint Gurgin Khan *beglerbeg* of Qandahar, at a time when Baluchis and Afghans were ravaging the country's southeastern region, was allegedly taken under the influence.[130]

IV: FROM PUBLIC CEREMONY TO PRIVATE PLEASURE

Much of drinking at the early Safavid court combined ceremony with rowdy enjoyment. As Aubin notes, in the case of Shah Isma`il especially, it is hard to distinguish between ritual and recreational drinking.[131] Ceremonial drinking had long been practiced by Eurasian nomads, was an integral part of the Christian liturgy, and also played a role in the Zoroastrian sacrificial festival of Mihragan. An example that recalls the pre-Islamic libation ritual is the shah's behavior following his capture of Baghdad in 1508. The Safavid ruler watched while drinking in a boat on the Tigris as the Qizilbash massacred those among his Aq-Quyunlu adversaries who had stayed in the city.[132] Tenreiro, who in 1524 visited Shah Isma`il's camp as a member of a Portuguese embassy, insisted that the Safavid sovereign followed the ancient custom of Iranian kings according to which the more they could drink without becoming drunk, the more they were esteemed. His description of a ritual bacchanal, held shortly before Isma`il's death, suggests how much drinking was bound up with traditional notions of charismatic kingship:

Most of the days during our stay in the camp, many Moorish Persians arrived in groups, men and women. They would come accompanied by a great noise of instruments and merriment. The Sofi, advised of their arrival, would come out of his tent in his robe, with his sword on his belt, and immediately would drink a cup of wine to honor and welcome them. They would sacrifice a cow in front of him, clamoring that from now on no harm could come to them anymore. Those who had horses, mares, or young girls, would offer these to him. Following this they would leave for their districts, very satisfied and content. I have seen this often at times when I was with the army camp.[133]

---

[130]Brosset, trans. and ed., *Histoire de la Géorgie*, 2:16.

[131]Aubin, "L'avènement des Safavides," 48.

[132]Aubin, "Révolution chiite," 4.

[133]Tenreiro, "Itinerário," 38. The offering of a cow, slaughtered on the spot, is similar to the reception Shah Isma`il is said to have enjoyed when he conquered Baghdad in 1508. The city's inhabitants came out in droves, killed a cow and offered it to him in prayer and supplication. See Khvandamir, *Habib al-siyar*, 4:494.

Ritual drinking was associated with a prevailing belief that wine drinking was not just permissible for a king, who by consuming prodigious amounts of alcohol would show his physical stamina, but actually an integral part of kingship. Fun and merriment, Safavid chronicler Mashizi insists, are necessary for kingship.[134] This notion rested on a common conviction that the shah was exempt from the ban on drinking wine, that it was not a sin for him not to observe the fast during Ramadan but to drink instead. "Kings and princes drink wine," the Mughal Sultan Jahangir told his son Khurram, who until his twenty-fourth birthday had never done so.[135] The French missionary Sanson, who visited Iran in the late seventeenth century, explained the notion that the ruler embodied an autonomous moral realm as follows:

> In his capacity as son of the prophet, the King calls himself the chief of religion, and the Persians hold that he cannot be damned or even judged, regardless of the sins he commits. They are not scandalized when he does not observe Ramadan and drinks wine, for they believe that he is without sin and exempt from all legal observations, by virtue of his being the son of a saint and a descendant of the Prophet.[136]

Following the mostly dry period of Shah Tahmasb's reign and the underreported era of Isma`il II and Muhammad Khudabandah, wine consumption is well documented for the reign of Shah `Abbas I. Yet, Shah `Abbas's reign did not represent a return to the days of Shah Isma`il. Royal drinking persisted, and there still was room for public drinking parties at a court that remained open and informal. But the period no longer witnessed ritualized and orgiastic drinking reflecting Qizilbash beliefs and customs. By definitively curtailing Qizilbash influence, Shah `Abbas finished what Shah Tahmasb had initiated, and the absence of the kind of rowdiness that had marked court revelry in early Safavid times may be seen as a measure of his success in doing so. The attitude toward drinking changed in other ways as well. After the alcoholic excess at Shah `Isma`il's court and the uncompromising rejection of spirits by Shah Tahmasb, Shah `Abbas I's attitude toward alcohol comes across as a self-conscious activity marked by ambivalence masked as obfuscation and manipulation. Wine never lost its dubious standing, and as such was subject to a ritual designed to isolate the illicit act from the actor about to engage in it. At drinking parties, Iranian would first fill a small glass to the brim, taking care that not a drop would fall on their clothing for fear that it would thereby become *najis*, ritually unclean.

[134]Mashizi (Bardsiri), *Tazkirah-i Safaviyah*, 387.
[135]Jahangir, *Tuzūk-i Jahāngīrī*, 1:306.
[136]Sanson, *Voyage*, 17.

They would then murmur a few prayers, words of excuse for flouting the religious law so manifestly, open their mouth, and empty the glass in one gulp, after which they would twist their face in a grimace similar to a sick person who is forced to take his medicine.[137] Shah ʿAbbas I, although never forcing his guests to consume alcohol, liked them to join him in drinking wine, viewing those who did not as hypocrites who by abstaining meant to reproach him for not abiding by the law of Islam.[138] Thus, on various occasions, the shah put pressure on Russian envoys to drink, and whenever they refused, as was the case with F. I. Leontʿev in 1616–17, he would complain of their impoliteness and lack of civility.[139] Writing in the spring of 1619, Della Valle further illustrates how embarrassment might be turned into virtue with a fascinating story of how the shah used alcohol ambiguously to claim the moral high ground vis-à-vis the Russian envoy Chicherin, whose gift to the shah included a large amount of aquavit. Della Valle surmised that ʿAbbas felt uneasy about having accepted such an enormous amount of alcohol because it branded him, if not exactly as a drunk, as prone to drinking. The shah, ready to go up to his winter quarters at Farahabad, thus took his leave from the Russian delegates by returning all the aquavit to them, saying that he had taken as much as he needed and that he returned the rest because he knew how much they liked to drink themselves, and that because such wonderful liquor was nowhere to be found in Iran, he did not want them to suffer. With this sly gesture, Della Valle noted, Shah ʿAbbas managed to pin the stigma of alcoholic excess on the Russians rather than on himself.[140]

Shah Safi does not seem to have shared his grandfather's qualms about alcohol. Drinking at ʿAbbas II's court, by contrast, only began in late 1649, seven years into his reign, at about the time that the ruler reached maturity.[141] The ʿAbbasnamah describes how ʿAbbas had his first taste of wine on the banks of the Helmand River in western Afghanistan, on the way back from an expedition to Qandahar, the frontier fortress that had long been in the hands of the Mughals and whose "closed gates he had just opened with world-opening keys." The context—a successful campaign and an idyllic, verdant setting alongside a life-giving river—suggests the time-honored bazm.[142] Yet, in their description of the event, the chroniclers do not simply exult in a royal

---

[137]Du Mans," ʿEstat' de 1660," in Richard, Raphaël du Mans, 2:103.

[138]Della Valle, Viaggi, 1:642.

[139]Bushev, "Posol'stvo V. G. Korobina," 129.

[140]Della Valle, Viaggi, 1:836–37.

[141]Tavernier, Les six voyages, 1:561, 581. The Dutch are the ones to provide the specific date. See NA, VOC 1178, Sarcerius, Gamron to Batavia, 2 Feb. 1650, fol. 657.

[142]Vahid Qavini, ʿAbbasnamah, 131.

shindig celebrating victory. Valah Qazvini Isfahani, reporting on the episode, offers a twofold excuse for the shah's lapse into conduct unbecoming of a devout Muslim. He implicitly absolves the shah by referring to God's law, in which happiness and pleasure are permitted, especially in the bloom of youth, and turns explicit in his exoneration by blaming high-ranking officials for their excess and persistence in urging the shah to take up the wine cup.[143] Vahid Qazvini follows a somewhat different, more formalistic path. He rather self-consciously seeks to justify the shah's public breach of Islamic precept by resorting to a distinction between cause and effect, arguing that although the act of drinking is objectionable by religious standards, it is evident that the monarch's behavior did not thereby become tainted: "Although he [Shah ʿAbbas II] drinks incessantly from morning till evening, and from sunset to sunup, his face does not shown the signs of drunkenness." The author's interpretation could thus be taken as either a sign of religious propriety or an approving reference to the traditional ideal of an Iranian king whose physical prowess remains undaunted by a large intake of alcohol.[144]

Shah Sulayman imbibed as prodigiously as any of his forebears. But, like Shah ʿAbbas I, he drank with a guilty conscience. As said, he liked to force alcohol on his subordinates and took particular pleasure in demeaning his persnickety grand vizier Shaykh ʿAli Khan in this manner. Shaykh ʿAli Khan's persistent refusal to drink wine regularly provoked the monarch's wrath and mockery, causing him to humiliate the vizier by forcing him to drink, throwing wine in his face, and making him shave his beard. But Sulayman made his chief minister drink precisely because the latter's abstinence served as a stinging reproach to his own drinking. Instances of cruelty alternated with demonstrations of remorse. After a night of gross insult, the shah frequently would offer Shaykh ʿAli Khan a robe of honor as a token of appreciation for his services.[145]

Royal drinking, the examples of Shah ʿAbbas II and Sulayman suggest, did not necessarily diminish in impetuosity or lose its burlesque character. What it rather seems to have lost by the later Safavid period is its unselfconscious character and with that its unquestioned place at the royal court. Wine drinking continued to be central to the courts of Shah Safi I and Shah ʿAbbas II. In fact, one gets the distinct impression that the large amount of space the *Khuld-i barin* devotes to the latter's frequent celebrations after 1649 in part serves to compensate for a lack of political events—mostly wars and rebellions—that tended to preoccupy

---

[143]Valah Qazvini Isfahani, *Khuld-i barin*, 480.

[144]Vahid Qazvini, *ʿAbbasnamah*, 131.

[145]Chardin, *Voyages*, 3:116, 121–27; NA, VOC 1285, De Haeze, Shiraz to Batavia, 13 September 1673, fol. 411v.; Fasaʾi, *Farsnamah-i Nasiri*, 489–90.

the chroniclers. But by the time of Shah Sulayman wine had lost its visibility beyond the confines of the palace, in a reflection of how Safavid kingship was evolving. Although not tribal themselves, the Safavids came to power as heirs to a nomadic tradition that saw campaigning as the ruler's main occupation and in which peacetime provided a brief respite for him to hunt and engage in the pleasures of the harem. In keeping with the Central Asian tradition, the early Safavid shahs were highly mobile as well as highly visible and approachable—in contrast to the Ottoman sultans who had been rather reclusive from the time that Istanbul became their capital.[146] This tradition continued well into the seventeenth century. Shah ʿAbbas I especially was famous for his informal governing style, and even under Shah ʿAbbas II the court was open and accessible, even to non-Shiʿi foreigners. Beginning with Shah Sulayman, the Safavid ruler became more and more immured in his palace, invisible to all but the most intimate of his courtiers. In the twenty-eight years of his rule, Shah Sulayman never left his capital to lead his troops into battle, and in his later years he occasionally stayed out of public view for months.

The sources allow one to trace these developments, although in the case of the Persian ones only up to a point. Early Safavid chronicles are quite open and unapologetic about the alcoholic excess at the court. They routinely exult in the revelry and carousing the shah and his entourage engaged in following a victory in battle or in celebration of the onset of a new spring. By late Safavid times, when formal religion had made inroads into society, chroniclers are more sparing in the details with which they describe festivities and leisure time in such vivid detail, even if they still employ the term *bazm* for the New Year's festivities and continue to mention wine drinking as part of royal celebrations. Western sources corroborate that at such celebrations, as well as during audiences and receptions for visiting diplomats, wine continued to be served. Yet, they also suggest that under Shah Sulayman especially, the nocturnal parties at court became more and more private. Because no court chronicles have come to light for the reign of Shah Sulayman, it is difficult to trace this type of change through the Persian sources. The anonymous ʿAlam-ara-yi Shah Tahmasb, which dates from the time of Shah Sulayman, in its retroactive description of a wedding under Shah Tahmasb might provide a clue to a presumed transition of the discourse on wine from the public to the private sphere.[147] As Sholeh Quinn argues, the exuberance of the descriptions referring to the time of Shah Ismaʿil written at a time when the practices had disappeared or at least could not

---

[146]For this contrast, see Necipoğlu, "Framing the Gaze," 304–7.
[147]Quinn, "Rewriting Niʿmatuʾllāhī History," 220–21.

longer be openly celebrated, perhaps suggest a nostalgia for the "good old days" when shahs were still engaged in the revelry of the traditional *razm u bazm.*

This development culminated with the famously devout Shah Sultan Husayn, the last of the Safavid monarchs, whose reign is also the period in the dynasty's history when wine consumption was at it lowest. The shah clearly drank, as did at least some high-ranking courtiers,[148] and the *shirahchi-bashi* continued to be a member of the royal household staff.[149] Yet, royal drinking seems to have taken place mostly in the privacy of the palace. Alcohol never occupied the pivotal place it had held under most of his predecessors, and to the outside world at least the court appeared dry during most of the period. Thus, when the Russian envoy Artemii Petrovich Volynskii arrived in Tabriz in 1717 and offered vodka as a gift to the local governor, he was upbraided for doing so with the comment that Shah Sultan Husayn did not drink and that his subordinates were not supposed to either.[150]

CONCLUSION

Pietro della Valle was right in claiming that "In Persia, though it is a country of Muslims, all drink wine with alacrity, without scruples or shame," but only as far as the elite is concerned.[151] At the same time that ordinary people quenched their thirst with little more than water, the ruling classes and above all shah and his entourage consumed alcohol in the form of wine and arak, in considerable quantity. Drinking indeed seems to have been a hallmark of the elite as opposed to the common people, something they simply did and were expected to do.

The prodigious consumption of alcohol among the elite in Safavid times harkens back to multiple traditions. One is the pre-Islamic, Iranian tradition that equated kingship with power beyond that set by religion. The other is the tribal legacy of the Central Asian (and wider

---

[148]Of Fath `Ali Khan Daghistani, Shah Sultan Husayn's grand vizier between 1715 and 1720, it is said that he complained about the shah while engaged in heavy drinking with Mikhri Khan, the governor of Tabriz, in early 1720. This expression of dissatisfaction with the monarch became public and was used by his enemies as an excuse to bring him down. See Beneveni, *Poslannik Petra I*, 54, Beneveni, Tehran to St. Petersburg, 25 May 1720.

[149]Mirza Rafi`a, *Dastur al-muluk*, ed. Afshar, 587(90); and Minorsky, ed., *Tadhkirat al-Muluk*, 137–38, where he is called *sahib-i jam`* of the *shirah-khanah*. This official only receives passing mention in the *Tadhkirat al-Muluk*. The same is true for the *shirahchi-bashi* in the *Dastur al-muluk*, presumably in a reflection of the diminished status of wine at the time.

[150]Bushev, *Posol'stvo Artemiia Volynskogo*, 79.

[151]Della Valle, *Viaggi*, 1:441.

Eurasian) steppe, where hard drinking in a highly visible setting was the norm. The third was a propensity in more extremist forms of Sufism to use alcohol as a means to achieve ecstasy. The final one was the Christian environment of Armenia and Georgia, societies with which Safavid Iran interacted in intimate ways. All four traditions mixed ritualized and ceremonial drinking with recreational drinking.

In alcohol consumption in Safavid times we see, first and foremost, a continuation of Iran's pre-Islamic *razm u bazm* tradition of hard fighting and hard drinking as the expected pursuits of warriors. Consuming alcohol in large quantities had a worldly as well as a spiritual dimension. The king was not just allowed to drink; he was supposed to drink, both as a sign of his status and stature as a "big man," and as a demonstration that, as the descendant of the sinless Imam, he was beyond the strictures of Islam, occupied his own autonomous moral space and thus personified the body politic. Royal drinking lent the shah a suprareligious stature, connecting him at once to the unseen and to the natural order.[152]

A metaphor for power, wine also served to delineate hierarchical gradations, to mark the (shifting) boundaries of inclusion and exclusion. Royal drinking was a ritual of shared pleasure that forged bonds and cemented loyalty in a society "where even kinship bonds were notoriously fragile and unreliable."[153] Whoever was invited to join the shah in his drinking parties enjoyed royal favor in a way that harkens back to the classical image of the Islamic ruler surrounded by his boon companions. That Western visitors might not just be included in these assemblies but were even allowed to share the shah's own cup reflects the secular makeup of a court willing to transgress the generic Islamic ban on drinking as well as the more specifically Iranian-Shi`i anxiety about ritual purity.

Wine in Safavid society presents us with the fundamental paradox of a substance that, although formally forbidden, played an important role in society, its rituals, and its conventions. That it was among the gifts that accompanied an important Safavid mission to the Mughal court in 1620 suggests how much wine was part of a shared cultural idiom in the eastern half of the Muslim world.[154] Yet, as much as alcohol permeated society, wine drinking retained its dubious religious status and thus remained socially and morally unintegrated. Wine was a social lubricant, but it could never be officially accepted as such, let alone become the

---

[152]This symbolism is found in many societies, among them sub-Saharan African ones in modern times. See Akyeampong, *Drink, Power, and Cultural Change.*

[153]Dale, *Garden of the Eight Paradises,* 182.

[154]Junabadi, *Rawzat al-Safaviyah,* 876.

"metaphorical lifeblood" of civilization, the function it had around the Mediterranean.[155] Its ultimate fate was simultaneously furtive embrace, a means to achieve quick oblivion, and public disavowal.

Little of this was visible in early Safavid times, when wine was celebrated in an exuberant way and consumed in ecstatic fashion by a cult-like group—the Qizilbash. Over time, as the Safavid state moved toward greater conformity to scriptural Shi`ism, the approach to alcohol began to change and one sees a growing preoccupation with the discrepancy between norm and practice. Whereas Shah Isma`il and his entourage were open and unapologetic about their excessive drinking, his successors increasingly showed an awareness of the inherent ambivalence surrounding alcohol in a Muslim milieu. As Qizilbash beliefs and habits were suppressed and as heterodox Sufi practices invited clerical rebuke, the frequency of drinking did not necessarily diminish but the act itself lost so0me of its ritual connotations and turned into a self-conscious activity in which pleasure competed with guilt. This process began with Shah Tahmasb's famous repentance, which represents a crucial phase in the loss of the shah's divine pretensions that the Safavid defeat at Chaldiran had set into motion. Later shahs continued to drink, but the ambiance had changed. Shorn of its orgiastic dimension, drinking continued to enliven official events at the court and might remain a source of raucous fun during evening parties, but guilt was never far from the surface. First visible under Shah `Abbas I, this development culminated during the reign of the pious Sultan Husayn. Following a highly publicized yet short-lived ban, wine was still consumed at the court but, having lost its public visibility, it was now relegated to the privacy of the palace.

We should be careful not to attach fixed labels to this meandering, often dialectical trajectory. Extrapolating from the limited and scattered examples the sources yield about each individual ruler to detect a long-term trend is fraught with risk. A great deal of variation existed from ruler to ruler and, depending on personal predilections and circumstances, even within the reigns of individual shahs. Yet, it is clear that over two centuries Safavid ideology underwent a profound transformation, with the image of the shah evolving from incarnation of the unbounded divine to that of trustee of the imam, watchdog of Islamic orthopraxis. The next chapter will trace that trajectory from a different angle by taking a closer look at the bans to which wine was periodically subjected, in an effort to identify the forces behind their seemingly random occurrence.

---

[155]Sherratt, "Alcohol and Its Alternatives," 20.

CHAPTER 3

Wine in Safavid Iran II: Ambivalence and Prohibition

فساد روی زمین از شراب می زاید   کدام دیو که در شیشه نیست صهبارا

مدار خویش بزرگی که بر شراب نهاد   بنای دولت خودرا به روی آب نهاد

> Depravity on earth grows out of wine. Which demon is not found in a bottle of wine?
> A man of name who bases his life on wine, builds his fortune on water.
> Mulla Muhammad Baqir Sabzavari, *Rawzat al-anwar-i `Abbasi*

> Persians respect the law of the Prince more than that of Muhammad.
>
> Jean-Baptiste Tavernier, *Les six voyages*

INTRODUCTION

It was seen in the previous chapter how, the prodigious drinking throughout the Safavid period notwithstanding, alcohol's inherent status in Islam as an objectionable substance did make itself felt in a growing awareness of a discrepancy between norm and practice. It is not surprising therefore that the two centuries of the dynasty's life span are punctuated by numerous bans on its consumption. Nor is it surprising that the ulama often had a hand in such bans. Although mostly known for its initially quietist approach to matters of sin and its prescriptions for eradicating it, Shi`i Islam over time yielded a theoretical corpus on issues of behavior deemed contrary to the sacred law no less elaborate than that produced by Islam's Sunni variant.[1] In early Safavid times, moreover, Shi`i scholars developed the idea that, in the absence of the Hidden Imam, a qualified jurist might undertake the task of leading the community of the faithful in its efforts to uphold the divinely ordained social order.

This sanctioning of clerical activism put some muscle into the claim of the ulama to have the right of direct intervention in state affairs. Such claims were certainly made. `Ali Naqi Kamarah'i Shirazi, *qazi* of Shiraz,

---

[1] Cook, *Commanding Right*, ch. 11.

in 1634 wrote a treatise in which he exhorted Shah Safi I to consult the religious leaders in matters of statecraft and to allow them control over shari`a-related issues.[2] Muhammad Baqir Majlisi, Shah Sulayman and Shah Sultan Husayn's *shaykh al-islam*, was equally as explicit in his call for clerical supervision. Reluctant to deal with what they considered an illegitimate state, radical clerics went even further by hesitating or even refusing to accept its positions and favors. Yet, the vast majority of the ulama, including the outspoken Majlisi, could not be brought to foreswear their allegiance to, or cooperation with a state to which they were beholden for official functions and financial support.[3]

The complex relationship between secular and clerical power this suggests will serve as an entry into this chapter's exploration of the incidence of bans on alcohol in the Safavid period. It will be seen that, periodic outbursts in response to specific circumstances notwithstanding, the ulama put but little energy in their push for a society free of vice. This was in part a matter of political impotence. The religious authorities lacked the power to enforce measures designed to eradicate wayward behavior without the cooperation of the secular administration—the shah, who was the ultimate arbiter of the judicial system, and his representatives, who implemented his commands.

The manner in which injunctions against the consumption of alcohol were proclaimed and enforced in the Safavid period reflects a functional division of jurisdiction and labor between the ulama and the state. Although the former saw themselves as the guardians of morality, they did not control the levers of power, and thus could do little more than exhort the ruler to uphold the religious order. Dependent on the same ruler—who appointed them and could dismiss them—and the ambient administrative order, they generally were quite content to provide ideological cover for a social and political system that fell far short of what they envisioned.

The adjudication of issues involving moral conduct bears this out. There is some question with regard to the officials in charge of public morality in the Safavid polity. In early Islam the *muhtasib*, or market inspector had been the official responsible for maintaining the ordering of social life, and whose task it was to "enjoin good and forbid evil." In Safavid times the office of *muhtasib* remains obscure and little defined. The early period records the position of chief *muhtasib* of the realm, the *muhtasib al-mamalik*.[4] Individual cities may have had their own *muhtasib*.[5] Yet, the paucity of references to his existence and activities raises questions about

---

[2]Ja`fariyan, "Guzarish-i andishah'ha-yi siyasi," 20ff.
[3]Calder, "Legitimacy and Accommodation," 95; Arjomand, *Shadow of God*, 184, 206.
[4]Qazi Ahmad, *Khulasat al-tavarikh*, 1:455, 456.
[5]Turkaman, *Tarikh-i `alam-ara-yi `Abbasi*, 630.

his significance. It is clear that, although the post of *muhtasib* did exist in the Safavid period, the scope of his activities was so circumscribed that his function cannot be considered an important one.[6] The *muhtasib* at this point was the market inspector, the official in charge of regulating prices and checking on weights and measures.[7] The late Safavid manual, *Dastur al-Muluk*, suggests the evolution of the position. It lists the *muhtasib* but insists that, although the function used to be an important one, his primary responsibility concerned market prices and most of his duties had devolved on the *shaykh al-islam*, the judges, and the *sadrs*.[8]

Formally, the task of upholding the moral order in Safavid times indeed counted among the responsibilities of the *shaykh al-islam* and, to a lesser extent, of the *sadr*, the chief of religious officers who oversaw the religious endowments. Judging by the prominence of Shaykh `Ali al-Karaki, the supreme jurist of the Shah Tahmasb era, and of Mu`izz al-Din Isfahani, the shah's *sadr*, this was as true for the early period as it was for the seventeenth century. Olearius refers to the *sadr* as the official who in 1637 enacted antiwine measures. The *farman* (royal decree) issued by Shah Sulayman in 1079/1668–69, appointing Mirza Hidayat as the *shaykh al-islam* of Mashhad, lists his tasks as "commanding right and forbidding wrong."[9] Muhammad Baqir Majlisi built his reputation on his activism in combating improper behavior, and eradicating vice was among the official tasks assigned to him by Shah Sultan Husayn.

Yet, although the *shaykh al-islam* and the *sadr* were charged with maintaining the moral order, and although the fiction was upheld that they had executive power in this matter as well, reality was often different, depending as it did on the power base of a local *shaykh al-islam* and the degree of his popularity. On a theoretical level, the injunction to command the good and forbid evil seems to have elicited little enthusiasm among some of the major the jurists of the day. A good example is Baha al-Din al-`Amili (d. 1621), one of the preeminent religious scholars

[6]Ja`fariyan, *Safaviyah dar `arsah-i din*, 1:365, citing Shah Tahmasb, *Tazkirah*, 30, and Sabzavari, *Rawzat al-anwar-i `Abbasi*, 485. Ja`fariyan points to the occurrence of the term in Shah Tahmasb's autobiography and the fact that Muhammad Baqir Sabzavari (1608–79), in his *Rawzat al-anwar* lists the appointment of a *muhtasib* as one of the duties of the shah. Yet Sabzavari's exhortation represents an ideal rather than that it reflects reality and thus does not prove that the *muhtasib* was an existing function in this period.

[7]Floor, "The Office of Muhtasib"; Minorsky, ed., *Tadhkirat-al-Muluk*, 48–49, 67, 83, 90, 149.

[8]Mirza Rafi`a, *Dastur al-Muluk*, ed. Afshar, 556(68) This situation is corroborated in the Dutch sources, which list the position of "supervisor of victuals." See NA, VOC 1886, Oets, Isfahan to Jacobsz., Gamron, 9 Sept. 1715, fol. 211.

[9]See Busse, *Untersuchungen*, 200–1; and Ja`fariyan, *Din va siyasat*, 104.

of his time who under Shah `Abbas I served as *shaykh al-islam* of Isfa-han. In his *Jami`-i `Abbasi*, a legal compendium written at the behest of the shah and a work that was to remain the official legal manual for the remainder of the century, al-`Amili devotes little space to the ethical obligation to command good and forbid evil. Arguing that most jurists called it individually incumbent (`*ayni*)—as opposed to the responsibility of the community, *kifa'i*—he restricts it to "nonviolent persuasion in cases where no damage to Muslims is likely to ensue."[10] This reasoning reflects a pragmatic attitude that could accept and live with sin as long as it stayed indoors.

On a practical level, religious officials might exhort the shah and they did often serve as his consultants on issues involving complex religious matters. Yet, it was the ruler who ultimately decided whether and when decrees outlawing improper behavior were to be issued, and it was the *divanbegi*, the chief justice, who was responsible for their implementa-tion.[11] As elsewhere in the Islamic world, the practical enforcement of such decrees, as well as the overall control of the public space, rested with secular public authorities, such as the city's *darughah*, the prefect of police, and the *ahdas*, the city police who patrolled the urban streets at night.[12] Another secular official, the *mash`aldar-bashi*, supervised the taxation and management of prostitutes and entertainers. Those who vi-olated the rules were brought before secular courts and tried according to common law, `*urf*, which in Safavid times prevailed over religious law except in civil cases involving matters such as divorce and inheritance.[13] In provincial towns, too, justice was administered by the tribunals of local governors.[14]

I. SHAH TAHMASB'S SINCERE REPENTANCE

The timing, the circumstances, and the effect of bans on alcohol in Safavid times all suggest continuity with previous times. Ghazan Khan, the first Il-Khanid ruler to convert to Islam, took measures to combat both the rampant prostitution and alcohol consumption in his realm. He forbade drunkenness in public places and issued a edict to that effect. Drunks in the bazaar were arrested and tied naked to a tree.[15] In 1320,

---

[10]al-`Amili, *Jami`-i `Abbasi*, 146; Arjomand, *Shadow of God*, 175.

[11]Chardin, *Voyages*, 6:68–69; and Floor, "Secular Judicial System," 25, 31.

[12]Minorsky, ed., *Tadhkirat al-Muluk*, 82; Chardin, *Voyages*, 6:78–79. For the situation elsewhere in the Muslim world, see Zubaida, *Law and Power*, 56–57.

[13]Chardin, *Voyages*, 6:71, 75.

[14]Chardin, *Voyages*, 5:234–35.

[15]Gronke, *Derwische im Vorhof der Macht*, 77.

during the reign of Abu Sa'id (1317–35), terrible hailstorms prompted the ulama to urge a ban on improper behavior, so that wine reserves were destroyed in various towns.[16] Mubariz al-Din (r. 1354–59), the first ruler of the Muzaffarid dynasty, enacted severe laws against drinking soon after seizing control of Shiraz, in a measure that the great Persian poet Hafiz refers to in one of his *ghazals*.[17] Herat under Husayn Mirza Bayqara (r. 1470–1506) seems to have been quite a jolly place, although at least on one occasion it saw the promulgation of a similar ban on wine consumption.[18]

The Safavid preoccupation with wine, in turn, began long before their emergence as a political dynasty. The founder of the order, Shaykh Safi al-Din, battled against the moral degeneracy resulting from Mongol rule, including sodomy, prostitution, and mixed dancing. Viewing the consumption of alcohol a cardinal sin, he is said to have taken severe measures, including execution, against those who contravened the religious law.[19]

Safi al-Din's campaign had little long-term effect, and the turbulent days following his death once again necessitated measures to cleanse Ardabil of untoward practices. This led to an edict, issued in 1361–62 at the instigation of the town's inhabitants, that sought to end prostitution and the consumption of alcohol.[20] The next century and a half saw a relaxation of these strictures. No antivice decrees are known from the period of Safi al-Din's successors, Junayd and Haydar; nor is there anything to suggest that Shah Isma'il I ever followed the example of his ancestor. Few competent ulama were available to provide guidance during this turbulent formative period; and most clerical energy went into emphasizing and bolstering the fledgling dynasty's anti-Sunni credentials.[21] The first clear instance of a ban on wine occurred under Shah Tahmasb I. As a young boy, Tahmasb apparently engaged in the same revelry as his father. One noncontemporaneous Persian source claims that this episode lasted from the time when he was sixteen until he was twenty years of age.[22] Because Tahmasb was born in 919/1514, this would mean that he drank from 935/1528–29 until 939/1532–33. Yet the Portuguese Tenreiro during a visit to Shah Isma'il's camp in early 1524 saw how the

[16]Melville, "'The Year of the Elephant,'" 205.

[17]Browne, *A Literary History*, 3:163–64, 277.

[18]Khami, *Mansha' al-insha*, 164–65.

[19]Gronke, *Derwische im Vorhof der Macht*, 258; Sohrweide, "Der Sieg der Safawiden," 100.

[20]Gronke, *Derwische im Vorhof der Macht*, 57.

[21]Glassen, "Schah Isma'il und die Theologen," 261–63.

[22]Qazvini, *Fava'id al-Safaviyah*, 27.

king's son consumed alcohol like everyone else, and thus suggests that his drinking began much earlier.[23]

Shah Tahmasb turned his back on alcohol soon after coming to power in 1524. In Zu'l-hijjah 932/September 1526, he issued a *farman*, inscribed above the entrance to the main mosque of Ardabil, that outlawed establishments serving wine and various drugs, in addition to brothels, gambling dens and various games deemed to be at variance with the shari`a.[24] But the shah only really renounced alcohol almost a decade later. The exact dating of Shah Tahmasb's so-called Sincere Repentance is a matter of some confusion. Some sources give 940/1533–34 or 941/1534–35 as the year in which Tahmasb gave up and proscribed various forms of raucous entertainment and frivolous enjoyment.[25] Yet, most list 939/1532–33 and place the actual repentance in the context of a pilgrimage that Shah Tahmasb made to the holy city of Mashhad, on his return from campaigning in Khurasan and en route to confront the Ottomans who at that point were threatening Iran-held Iraq.[26] During this pilgrimage, a divine inspiration allegedly prompted the shah to purge the town of "all blameworthy activities that cause good governance to founder." The wine houses, gambling dens and brothels were boarded up, the tax income generated by these activities were stricken from the books, and the measure was next extended to cover the entire country. Opium appears to have the exception. Some chroniclers claim, without specifying a date, that the opium found in the royal palace, worth almost 500 *tumans*, was dissolved into water and destroyed.[27] Khurshah b. Qubad al-Husayni, by contrast, excepts opium from the substances that he claimed had completely disappeared from society following the edict, thus suggesting that opium was not banned beyond the palace or that the authorities had been less vigilant or, more likely, less successful, in policing its use.[28]

The varying dates may not be mutually exclusive. The repentance itself tends to be narrated as a fixed moment in time, but the subsequent morality campaign was evidently a matter of process and development.

[23]Tenreiro, "Itinerário," 36. Although Tenreiro gives the age of the boy as sixteen, he clearly meant Tahmasb.

[24]See Tajbakhsh, *Tarikh-i Safaviyah*, 143–45.

[25]Khurshah, *Tarikh-i ilchi-yi Nizam Shah*, 117–18; and Sabzavari, *Rawzat al-anwar-i `Abbasi*, 167, mention 940. Budaq Qavini, *Javahir al-akhbar*, 166–67, gives 941.

[26]See Rumlu, *Ahsan al-tavarikh*, 323; "Farman-i Shah Tahmasb," in Nava'i, ed., *Shah Tahmasb-i Safavi. Majmu`ah-i asnad*, 513–14; Ghaffari Qazvini, *Tarikh-i jahan-ara*, 265; and Turkaman, *Tarikh-i `alam-ara-yi `Abbasi*, 123.

[27]Valah Qazvini Isfahani, *Khuld-i barin*, 395. For the notion that water was thought to purify unclean items, see Chardin, *Voyages*, 6:325, 338ff.

[28]Khurshah, *Tarikh-i ilchi-yi Nizam Shah*, 118.

An initial ban was proclaimed in or around 1525, suggesting that the issue played out over a number of years. There is good reason to believe that Shah Tahmasb had his definitive change of heart in 1532–33 but that the edict that followed was promulgated around the country two years later. The rescript attached to a shop adjacent to the Masjid-i Mir ʿAmad of Kashan, proscribing wine, *bang* (cannabis), prostitution and pigeon-flying, was issued in 941/1534–35, and the ban was publicized in Herat in the same year as well.[29] Clerical pressure likely influenced the timing of the ban's various installments. It is surely no coincidence that in circa 1526 ʿAli al-Karaki issued a first *fatwa* directed against the Qizilbash, in which the recitation of *Abu Muslim-namah*s, early Islamic epic tales that were particularly popular among the Qizilbash, was outlawed.[30] Nor can we ignore the fact that Shah Tahmasb's repentance took place in the same year that he conferred on al-Karaki the title of *na'ib al-imam*, deputy of the Imam, while giving him a mandate over religious matters and moral issues. Having received this mandate, al-Karaki proceeded to issue a series of commands that included the appointment of prayer leaders in every village to instruct people in the tenets of Shiʿi Islam as well as the expulsion of Sunni ulama from Safavid territory.[31]

The reference to the Qizilbash suggests a link between Tahmasb's repentance and his long-standing conflict with these tribal forces. Safavid chroniclers tell the story of how, during the shah's stay in Khurasan, Ahmad Beg and Pashtan Qara, retainers of Husayn Khan Shamlu, tried to kill Shah Tahmasb by putting poison in his wine and how the plot failed when the shah became suspicious, causing them to flee to Transoxania. One author even goes so far as to attribute the ruler's subsequent repentance to this event.[32] Although Shah Tahmasb's own autobiographical rendering of the episode does not refer to the attempt on his life, it does implicate the Qizilbash in his conversion. He puts the blame for his father's defeat at Chaldiran in 1514 on the drunken state of the Safavid soldiers and castigates Durmish Khan, their Qizilbash commander, for deceiving Ismaʿil by foolishly leading the troops into battle. "Thank God and the Imams," the shah writes, "my army and my realm have given up on wine, vice and all that is illicit, and in my entire domain all wine taverns, liquor houses, and brothels have been eliminated." He then recounts how he outlawed unislamic practices following a dream in which

[29]Nava'i, ed., *Shah Tahmasb-i Safavi. Majmuʿah-i asnad*, 513–14.

[30]Babayan, "Safavid Synthesis," 144.

[31]Khatunabadi, *Vaqa'iʿ al-sannin*, 461. See also Newman, "Myth of the Clerical Migration," 100–1.

[32]Qazi Ahmad, *Khulasat al-tavarikh*, 1:224–25; Budaq Qazvini, *Javahir al-akhbar*, 165.

Mir Sayyid Muhammad (Jabal `Amili), the prayer leader of the royal camp, appeared to him urging him to forswear prohibited practices so as to become victorious in battle—against the Ottomans, whose invasion was reported when the shah was in Khurasan. The next morning, the shah relates, he got together with his vizier, Hamdibeg, and a number of political officials, *umara*, and asked to have this dream explained. Different opinions were voiced. Some functionaries saw the dream as a sign that the shah should abstain from some proscribed things, but cautioned him not to move against wine, which they called a necessity for kingship (*zaruri-yi saltanat*). The shah thereupon decided to follow whatever message the following night's dream might convey to him. This time he saw himself at the foot of the tomb of Imam Riza, the eighth Imam of Shi`ism who is buried in Mashhad, holding the hand of Mir Hadi, the *muhtasib* (of Mashhad?), in a clear signal that a total repentance was in order.[33]

On a strategic level, Tahmasb's repentance and the measures it generated was thus part of his efforts to wrest control from the unruly and rebellious Qizilbash, whose immoderate, ritualistic drinking and sodomy-filled sexual practices represented a primordial world of pagan excess and immorality. It is probably no accident that 1532–33 is also the time when the shah rid himself of Husayn Khan Shamlu, his *vakil* (regent) who was rumored to harbor intentions to overthrow Tahmasb and to put the ruler's brother Sam Mirza on the throne. Husayn Khan's death, it has been argued, marked the official end of the interregnum of the Qizilbash and the assertion of the shah as an autonomous actor.[34] But the ideological import of the gesture is no less important. Given the integral role wine played in the doctrine of the traditional warrior—signaled by the caveat of the royal advisors—the shah's decision to include wine in his repentance was a deliberate move, symbolizing Islam's triumph over syncretistic kingship. Unlike his father, Shah Tahmasb was revered less for his physical prowess and stamina than for being the lineal descendant of `Ali. Abjuring wine was a fitting gesture for a transformative moment, a first step toward a worldview that had no place for the life style of a godlike shah surrounded by wild tribesmen engaged in orgiastic ritual.[35]

[33]Shah Tahmasb, *Tazkirah-i Shah Tahmasb*, 29–30. See also Shirazi, *Takmilat al-akhbar*, 76–77, which gives a different, rather more plausible version of the story, in which the prayer leader of the royal camp, Sayyid Muhammad Jabal `Amili, has the initial dream, with the Prophet Muhammad ordering the shah to desist from unislamic practices. It is not clear, though likely, that the term *buz-khanah* is the same as *burah-khanah* referred to in the *farman* of 1526.

[34]Mitchell, "The Sword and the Pen," 191.

[35]For the difference in the ways Shah Isma`il and Shah Tahmasb were revered by their followers, see Wood, "*Shahnama-i Isma`il*," 119–21.

Tahmasb's repentance spilled across the border to become part of the ongoing war of words between the Shi`i Safavids and their Sunni neighbors, the Ottomans and the Uzbeks. We see this in the ridicule heaped on the Uzbek ruler `Ubaydallah, Tahmasb's adversary, who refused to engage in open warfare with Iran. A caricature of him, most likely by Aqa Mirak, shows him sitting on a chair looking besotted, holding a wine gourd and a musical instrument, clearly a jibe at his Islamic credentials.[36] Given the abandon with which the Qizilbash imbibed, it is no wonder that wine drinking was an issue in the polemic between the Ottomans and Safavids as well, with the former viewing the consumption of alcohol by the latter as proof of their libertinism and godlessness. This clearly reflected reality but it was also of a piece with a long-standing belief in the Sunni world that associated drinking with Shi`is and Shi`is with extremism and heresy, *zandaqa*.[37] Sultan Selim, referring to Shah Isma`il following Chaldiran, thought his rival "always drunk to the point of losing his mind and totally neglectful of the affairs of state."[38] Sixteenth-century Ottoman polemicists insisted that the enjoyment of all kinds of drugs was permitted and customary among the Qizilbash.[39] This may have prompted Shah Tahmasb to raise the presumed association in the vitriolic letter he sent to the Ottoman Sultan Süleyman in 1554. In it, he noted that the Qizilbash had made observing the prophetic shari`a their slogan, obeyed its strictures and refrained from all that was religiously improper, such as drinking wine, fornication, and sodomy.[40] The Ottomans were probably not convinced, judging by the contrast one of their historians made between the wine-filled banquets held at the Safavid court and the sober official ceremonies of Istanbul's Topkapı Palace.[41]

Once put into effect, the ban is said to have caused thousand of sinners to join the shah in repenting and in turning to prayer, pilgrimage, and almsgiving. Some gave up their un-Islamic lifestyle out of conviction and sincerity, whereas others are said to have abstained for fear of the "scourge of the *muhtasib* and the whip of the *darughah*."[42] Punishment was indeed draconian, for those caught engaged in illicit behavior risked losing life and property. The Persian sources claim that many offenders

---

[36]Soudavar, "Early Safavids," 98–102.

[37]See Heine, *Weinstudien*, 56.

[38]Aubin, "L'avènement des Safavides," 63.

[39]Mordtmann, "Sunnistisch-schiitische Polemik," 116–19; Eberhard, *Osmanische Polemik*, 95–96.

[40]Nava'i, ed., *Shah Tahmasb-i Safavi. Majmu`ah-i asnad*, 225.

[41]Necipoğlu, "Framing the Gaze," 311.

[42]Sabzavari, *Rawzat al-anwar-i `Abbasi*, 168–69.

Caricature of `Ubaydallah Khan, attributed to Aqa Mirak. Credit: Arthur M. Sackler Gallery, Smithsonian Institution, Washington, D.C.

were killed and mention a few prominent ones by name. The Turkmen Inuka Ughli was hanged with a wine bottle around his neck. Qasim Abuk Ughli Mawsillu, Shukr Ughli, and Khajah Shah Quli, all three high officials, were condemned to death as well for alcoholism.[43] Khajah Muhammad Salih, the governor of Astarabad in the late 1530s, spent much of his time drinking and fornicating with prostitutes. Arrested and brought before the shah, he was put in a barrel and thrown to his death from the top of a minaret.[44]

It is not surprising, then, that, unlike many later prohibitions, Shah Tahmasb's puritanical edict was taken seriously. The *sadr* of the day, Mu'izz al-Din Muhammad Isfahani (served 1532–39), is credited with having been especially active in rooting out the sources of sin by destroying taverns, brothels, and gambling houses.[45] Several authors further insist that, since the date of the proclamation, none of the outlawed practices and substances—with the exception of opium—had been seen or heard of, that wine taverns had gone out of business and that no one even dared mention the drugs that had been banned.[46] Such idealized statements at most represent a half-truth. Taverns may have ceased operation temporarily, and the shah himself never seems to have touched a glass until his death.[47] But the ban on alcohol was clearly ignored and resisted by some, as is suggested by the story, told by the Venetian envoy Michele Membré, that Tajlu Khanum, the shah's mother, intended to poison her son and put Bahram Mirza, another son of hers, on the throne.[48] Membré, who visited Shah Tahmasb's court in 1540, noted in an observation corroborated by the Persian sources that Bahram Mirza drank a "great deal of aqua-vitae and spirits of spices, and it is known that he died of excessive alcohol consumption."[49] Bahram Mirza is only one of a number of examples. The sources, for instance, offer us Musa Sultan, the governor of Azerbaijan in the 1530s, as an official given to "mirth and play, conversation and wine."[50] The shah also chose to ignore infractions by painters such as the famous Bihzad, who "could not live for a moment without ruby-red wine or the ruby-red lips of a wine bearer," and who, despite the ban, "continued

[43]Cheref-ou'ddîne (Sharaf al-Din), *Chèref-nâmeh*, II/1, 561–62; Qazi Ahmad, *Khulasat al-tavarikh*, 1:225; Budaq Qazvini, *Javahir al-akhbar*, 167; Ghaffari Qazvini, *Tarikh-i jahan-ara*, 265.

[44]Qazi Ahmad, *Khulasat al-tavarikh*, 1:282–84.

[45]Rumlu, *Ahsan al-tavarikh*, 406; Qazi Ahmad, *Khulasat al-tavarikh*, 1:313–14.

[46]Khurshah, *Tarikh-i ilchi-yi Nizam Shah*, 118; and Yahya Qazvini, quoted in Parsadust, *Shah Tahmasb*, 611; Sabzavari, *Rawzat al-anwar-i 'Abbasi*, 170.

[47]Turkaman, *Tarikh-i 'alam-ara-yi 'Abbasi*, 123.

[48]Membré, *Mission to the Lord Sophy*, 31; and introduction, XVI–XVII.

[49]Ibid., 25; and Qazi Ahmad, *Khulasat al-tavarikh*, 1:340–41.

[50]Budaq Qazvini, *Javahir al-akhbar*, 170.

drinking," even as the shah knew about it.[51] What must have been lax enforcement of rules guiding proper behavior in 1554–55 prompted the shah to dismiss Hasan Sultan Rumlu as governor of Mashhad and to appoint his own nephew, Ibrahim Mirza, instead.[52]

A year later, apparently concerned about continuing irregularities, the shah was moved to reaffirm his puritanical stance by issuing another installment of his Edict of Sincere Repentance. Aside from formally outlawing the secular arts (with the exception of painting and calligraphy), it enjoined the Qizilbash to repent for past sins and abstain from forbidden worldly pleasures, and it ordered the closing of taverns, brothels, and gambling dens.[53] It is said that 118 persons in the shah's own entourage heeded this call.[54] The new regulations induced quite a few artists to move to the neighboring Mughal Empire or to the more hospitable provincial court of Sultan Ibrahim Mirza in Khurasan.[55] Although it remains unclear if the timing of this rescript was in any way prompted by the conclusion of the Peace of Amasya a year earlier, the Ottoman chronicler `Ali may have been right in surmising that the dissolute lifestyle of the shah's son, Isma`il Mirza, contributed to its proclamation.[56] His son cannot have been the only scofflaw, though, for on 12 Sha`ban 972/15 March 1565 the shah had yet another dream enjoining him to end various "novelties," *mubtada`at*. The next morning he summoned all state officials to have the dream explained, after which he donated all income derived from taxes, in the amount of 30,000 *tumans*, to the cause of the Imams. And again, orders, inscribed on stone and distributed around the country, went out to cease all improper behavior and to close the taverns and the gambling parlors.[57]

II. Shah `Abbas I

No examples of bans on un-Islamic practices are on record for the reign of Isma`il Mirza, Shah Tahmasb's successor, who, having been released from the prison to which his father had confined him for twenty years, ruled for less than two years as Shah Isma`il II (1576–77). Instead, once

[51]Soudavar, "Between the Safavids and the Mughals," 51, based on Budaq Qazvini, *Javahir al-akhbar*.
[52]Qazi Ahmad, *Khulasat al-tavarikh*, 1:380–81.
[53]Ibid. 1:386.
[54]Röhrborn, *Provinzen und Zentralgewalt*, 71.
[55]Soudavar, "Between the Safavids and the Mughals," 51.
[56]Hinz, "Schah Esma`il II," 37.
[57]Qazi Ahmad, *Khulasat al-tavarikh*, 1:449–50.

in power, he persisted in the dissolute lifestyle for which he was known. The next shah, the pious and purblind Shah Muhammad Khudabandah, began his reign, in classic fashion, by establishing his religious credentials. Shortly after coming to power, he issued a *farman* that outlawed wine and other activities at variance with shari`a rules.[58] Nothing is known about the effectiveness of this command, but since the shah himself soon became known for his involvement in "lust and play," it is unlikely that it made drinking disappear.

The reign of Shah `Abbas I was marked by an alternation of periods when the consumption of alcoholic beverages was officially permitted and periodic bans that was to be typical for the remainder of the Safavid period. In 1593, the shah had Darvish Khusraw, the leader of the heterodox Nuqtavi sect, executed after jugs of wine had been found in the latter's cloister.[59] Religious sensibilities seem to have played at most a subordinate role in the shah's decisions to allow or outlaw drinking. Some instances appear motivated by little more than personal whim and suggest the autonomous power of the shah to issue decrees of moral import. In 1600, for instance, Shah `Abbas forced the royal astrologer, Jalal al-Din Muhammad Munajjim Yazdi, to break his personal repentance by sending him a drinking cup. Once, during a time when alcohol was banned, `Abbas exempted a tavern owned by one particularly handsome young man, giving orders to have a stamp put on the hands of those who frequented his watering hole so as to keep them from being harassed by the authorities. When the shah was in a particularly good mood, he would also allow people to engage in public wine drinking for a period of three days. On such occasions, the streets of Isfahan would be filled with revelers. After the term expired, punishment would await anyone caught drinking.[60]

No formal bans are recorded during the first fifteen years of Shah `Abbas's reign, the period when he was busy consolidating his power. In 1603, when the shah was about to move decisively against his main domestic enemies, the Qizilbash, wine was banned on pain of death.[61] It is impossible not to see a connection between the campaign and the proscription, especially as the army seems to have been the source of the problem. This ban may still have been in effect in 1606, when Nicolao de Orta Rebelo passed through Shiraz and reported that the local governor, Allah Virdi Khan, had prohibited the consumption of wine (as well

[58]In Nava'i, ed., *Shah `Abbas. Majmu`ah-i asnad*, 1:117–19.
[59]Turkaman, *Tarikh-i `alam-ara-yi `Abbasi*, 476. For the context of this execution, see Babayan, *Mystics, Monarchs, and Messiahs*, 3–7.
[60]Falsafi, *Zindigani-yi Shah `Abbas*, 645.
[61]Tectander, *Abenteuerliche Reise*, 65.

as prostitution) by Muslims, on pain of confiscation of goods and execution. The reason, he noted alluding to anxieties about public disorder, was a concern that soldiers were wont to spend all their money on alcohol and women. Rebelo added that the ban did little to prevent the sale of wine in the city.[62]

The ban of 1603 had either become moot or been repealed by 1608. An incident that took place in December of that year, coinciding with Ramadan, again suggests the power of the sovereign to allow or forbid drinking in his realm and, more particularly, Shah ʿAbbas's success in subordinating the country's ulama to his authority. During a meeting that included some Portuguese missionaries as well as clerics, including the highest religious official of the realm, Shah ʿAbbas ordered that wine be brought for the Christian guests. He then invited everyone to drink a small amount. According to Antonio de Gouvea, the narrator of the story, the shah whispered to him: "When you leave here and meet the Pope, tell him how, during Ramadan, I ordered wine in the presence of all my judges and their chief, and made them all drink it. Tell him that, though I am not a Christian, I am worthy of his esteem."[63]

More than a decade later a new ban was instituted. Della Valle reports that on 28 August 1620 the news spread in Isfahan that, when residing in Farahabad, the shah had prohibited the consumption of wine for all Muslims. It could not even be sold to them, on penalty of death for both the consumer and the vendor—the consumer by having molten lead poured down his throat, and the vendor by being disemboweled. According to Della Valle the motive of the proscription remained unclear, though he said that it was most likely because of an (unspecified) illness from which the shah had been suffering for some months.[64] Khuzani Isfahani refers to the same proclamation as a form of repentance, *tawbah*, on the part of the shah, and thus gives it a religious connotation.[65] Although neither source explicitly mentions clerical exhortation, Baha al-Din al-ʿAmili may have been involved, just as he had a hand in the persecution of Iran's Armenian population a year later.[66] Writing on 23 February 1621, Della Valle insisted that the ban was strictly adhered to, not just in Isfahan but throughout the realm, and that already one individual had lost his life

---

[62]Rebelo, *Un voyageur portugais en Perse*, 125. Referring to the Shiʿi institution of *mutʿa*, Rebelo added that soldiers were still allowed to engage in temporary marriages of up to one year.

[63]Gouvea, *Relation des grandes guerres*, 499–500.

[64]Della Valle, *Viaggi*, 2:143–44.

[65]Khuzani Isfahani, "Afzal al-tavarikh," fol. 414.

[66]For the persecution of Armenians in the summer of 1621 and the alleged role Baha al-Din al-ʿAmili played as its instigator, see Anon., ed., *Chronicle of the Carmelites*, 255–56.

ignoring it.[67] This may have involved the same person mentioned by Jacques de Coutre, a Flemish diamond trader who in the same year witnessed the gruesome execution of someone who had violated the ban.[68]

Christians were exempted; they could still manufacture wine, provided they did not sell it to Muslims. There were other exceptions as well, and as no other, this episode shows how competing interests complicated the issue of alcohol consumption. First of all, the shah himself used the illness as a justification to continue to drink—in secret and in moderate quantities, so as not to give cause for scandal—an unspecified number of cups, as prescribed by his doctors, for a defect in his complexion. Some high-ranking officials, using the excuse that they suffered from a similar illness, were also allowed to drink—surreptitiously and indoors. The province of Fars, the center of Iran's viticulture and viniculture and a semiautonomous region whose inhabitants never saw and hardly recognized the shah as their sovereign, refused to heed the ban as well. In the capital, it was the courtesans who, feeling the effect of the prohibition most keenly, did their utmost to have it repealed. They offered large sums of money to various officials in charge of punishing criminal behavior, in addition to Dallalah Chizi (Qizi), the shah's court jester, arguing that without the drinking that accompanied their conversations, they would lose their jobs and starve. Della Valle, claiming that Muslims were envious of the Christians for being allowed to drink wine, noted that the number of Muslims visiting his house had increased considerably since the interdiction—as a result of which he often had to allow them to spend the night as well, so they would lose all outward signs of having imbibed.[69]

Della Valle predicted that the ban might remain in effect, as it solved many social problems and prevented public scandals, quite aside from saving money on military expenditure. Yet, eight months after it went into effect, wine was made legal again. The official motive did not refer to appeals by a prostitution lobby or pressure from the elite but was compelling all the same. Deprived of wine, Safavid soldiers apparently took to opium. The damage this did to their corporal strength and battle-readiness prompted the shah on 24 April 1621 to replace the wine prohibition with a ban on opium: as long as they did not get drunk, people could now drink wine.[70]

[67]Della Valle, *Viaggi*, 2:143–44. Khuzani Isfahani, "Afzal al-tavarikh," fol. 414, that anyone violating the decree was to lose his head.

[68]Verberkmoes and Stols, eds., *Aziatische omzwervingen*, 227. De Coutre claimed that ban included tobacco as well.

[69]Ibid., 144–45. For prostitution in Safavid Iran, see Matthee, "Courtesans, Prostitutes and Dancing Girls." The *mash`aldar-bashi*, the chief torchbearer, was the official in charge of the royal lightning but also collected the taxes from all professions of ill repute.

[70]Della Valle, *Viaggi*, 2:209.

III. Measures under Shah Safi and Shah ʿAbbas II, 1629–66

Shah Safi's enthronement was enveloped in religious symbolism: he was the first Safavid monarch to be anointed by the *shaykh al-islam* of the capital.[71] This did little to make the new ruler heed Islam's proscription of alcohol, however, and if it did it was for little more than a few months after coming to power in early 1629.[72] Persuaded by his physicians, who sought to wean him off the opium to which he had become addicted during adolescence, he soon took to the bottle.[73] Yet, less than two years into his reign, a series of military challenges, ranging from rebellions and Uzbeg incursions into Khurasan, Kurdish unrest, Arab Bedouin raids, and war at Qandahar, seems to have triggered a passing bout of temperance. The contemporary *Khulasat al-siyar* makes the shah's sudden abstinence follow the news, in the fall of 1630, that the Ottoman army was advancing toward Baghdad and had set up camp near the Tigris in anticipation of the arrival of artillery. The ensuing ban thus assumed the character of a penance. The shah, Isfahani insists, had come to the conclusion that this calamity was not to be averted by counsel or war, but that only humility and supplication would make it go away, and thus ordered that the ban on wine proclaimed earlier be enforced. The result was that "the clamor of drunkards was transformed into the religious invocation (*takbir*) of the devout and the prayers of the pious replaced the shouting of wine drinkers," and that "the ruler whose face had always been illuminated by the wine goblet now took on the facial expression of a pious man and henceforth earnestly begged God to forgive him his sins." As part of this new demeanor, the shah engaged in all kinds of pious deeds and, once the Ottoman danger had subsided, performed the pilgrimage to the holy city of Karbala.[74]

The rhetorical flourish with which Isfahani presents the measure notwithstanding, the fact that no other chronicle even refers to it reinforces the impression that it was purely symbolic as well as ephemeral. We know in effect that the ban did not last very long. As early as the summer of 1631, notified that the Ottomans were once again moving toward Baghdad, the shah decided that this time the danger was not quite as serious, and reacted by reaching for the goblet during festivities.[75] This lapse does not seem to have applied to all, though, at least not officially, for Olearius, visiting Iran in 1637, reports that, although the shah and

---

[71]Isfahani, *Khulasat al-siyar*, 37–38. The *shaykh al-Islam* in question is likely to have been Mir Muhammad Baqir Damad.

[72]Dunlop, ed., *Bronnen*, 738, 741, diary Jan Smidt.

[73]Anon., ed., *Chronicle of the Carmelites*, 350.

[74]Isfahani, *Khulasat al-siyar*, 99–100, 108.

[75]Ibid., 116–17.

his court were given to drinking, the *sadr* had gave orders for the wine containers of Isfahan's Armenians to be smashed.[76] This may be in reference to another short-lived ban, proclaimed as an act of contrition after an incident whereby the shah, having returned drunk from the house of the *kalantar* (mayor) of New Julfa, had stabbed his own mother. As Tavernier, the author of this possibly apocryphal story, notes, the ban was short-lived, and within a year everyone made and consumed wine again.[77] At any rate, the shah himself drank until his last days, paying little heed to clerical disgruntlement, until his addiction overtook him in May of 1642.[78]

On his accession in 1642, Shah `Abbas II engaged in an archetypal gesture by banning the consumption of alcohol, ordering even the wine barrels broken that had been set aside for the crown in Shiraz.[79] Matters turned even more serious with the appointment as grand vizier of Khalifah Sultan (Sultan al-`Ulama), a scion of a clerical family known for his erudition and piousness who had been chief minister under Shah `Abbas I and who in October 1645 was called to serve in the same capacity by `Abbas II. Although he himself was known for his mystical tendencies, Khalifah Sultan's appointment reflects the ascendance of those who abhorred the influence of popular Sufism in society. The appointment, at the behest of Khalifah Sultan, of `Ali Naqi Kamarah'i (d. 1650) as *shaykh al-islam* of Isfahan in the same year, is emblematic of this trend as well. On the face of it, these clerics stood for a stricter, more literal interpretation of the holy law as well. Thus in his *Himam al-thawaqib*, written during the reign of Shah Safi, `Ali Kamarah'i had urged the ruler to heed the advice of the ulama and to see to it that people followed the precepts of the shari`a.[80] In late 1645, two months after Khalifah Sultan had been reinstated as grand vizier and following `Ali Kamarah'i's appointment, a royal *farman* announced a ban on alcohol and the closing of the wine taverns of the capital, so that soon "instead of water liquid ruby ran through the gutters of the streets and bazaars wherever wine taverns were found."[81] The contemporary chronicles describe this measure as part of an overall purification campaign that also involved the outlawing of prostitution and an order for brothels to shut their doors, as well as measures designed to safeguard Shi`i society against

---

[76]Olearius, *Vermehrte newe Beschreibung*, 577.

[77]Tavernier, *Les six voyages*, 1:575–76.

[78]For the clerical disgruntlement with Shah Safi, see Arjomand, *Shadow of God*, 147–48.

[79]Mulla Kamal, *Tarikh*, 98; Mahdavi, *Zindiginamah-i `Allamah Majlisi*, 1:144.

[80]See Ja`fariyan, "Andishah'ha-yi yik `alim-i Shi`i"; and idem, "Guzarish-i andishah'ha-yi siyasi," 20–24.

[81]Valah Qazvini Isfahani, *Khuld-i barin*, 421.

pollution, such as a ban on Armenian fur merchants selling their wares to Muslims.[82]

Anti-Sufi rhetoric played a role in this and other morality campaigns. Yet, matters are a good deal more complicated than enthusiasm for the enforcement of the obligation to combat evil on the part of the ulama and their growing outspokenness against Sufis and non-Muslims who tended to drink. Several modern authors have shown how the anti-Sufi tendencies in seventeenth-century Iran followed no linear course and that it would be a mistake to see the controversy between religious scholars and Sufis in the Safavid period as two irreconcilable forces locked in their own visions of purity and probity. Some of those who vilified Sufi practices dabbled themselves in mysticism. The relationship between the two was marked by mutual influence, a fluidity of perspectives and a dialectic of opposition and cooptation.[83] Tensions between the two have to do as much with power as with doctrinal difference. The ulama were not so much against Sufism as against folk Sufism, with its associations of *qalandar* subversiveness and political unrest and the threats this posed to the status quo, especially in times of scarcity and penury.[84] The Sufis, in turn, ridiculed the hypocrisy of the ulama and criticized their coziness with worldly power.

The state was wary of manifestations of popular religious sentiments as well. But it also had to contend with critical ulama. Overall, it seems to have followed a policy of divide and rule, balancing the interests and demands of outspoken, shari`a-minded clerics and popular religious movements, all in an effort to maintain enough bargaining power to stay on top of the fray. Shah `Abbas II, for instance, paid his respects to Sufis, engaging in discussions with them and building lodges for them, but he did not let himself be coopted by either them or the ulama. The motives behind the various bans decreed by Shah `Abbas II are not always easy to discern and seem to have varied between clerical pressure in response to adversity ranging from impending war or military defeat and economic malaise to the shah's medical condition, which in the case of Shah `Abbas II involved syphilis and cancer of the throat.[85]

What remained constant is the autonomy of a ruler who might occasionally be swayed by the arguments of high-ranking ulama but who did not tolerate the state's subordination to their agenda. As noted in the

---

[82]Ibid., 421–22; Mulla Kamal, *Tarikh*, 98, 102; Vahid Qazvini, `Abbasnamah, 71–72; and Keyvani, *Artisans and Guild Life*, 129, quoting Muhammad Tahir Vahid, "Divan-i Rizvan," Library of University of Tehran, Ms. 4344.

[83]Ja`fariyan, Safaviyah dar `arsah-i din," 522; Abisaab, *Converting Persia*, 115, 144.

[84]Zarrinkub, *Justiju dar tasavvuf*, 259–60.

[85]Chardin, *Voyages*, 9:417–18; 10:88.

previous chapter, by late 1649 Shah `Abbas II turned his back on sobri-
ety and enjoyed his first alcoholic *bazm* with his courtiers when returning from a successful campaign at Qandahar.[86] Yet, in that same year, he
dismissed the *qurchibashi*, Murtaza Quli Khan, on account of drunkenness and other (unspecified) failings.[87] In 1653, faced with the possibility
of losing Qandahar to the Mughals, the shah was again encouraged by
the country's highest-ranking cleric to give up drinking. The reference is
most likely to Muhaqqiq Sabzavari, at that point the *shaykh al-islam* of
Isfahan, whose *Rawzat al-anwar al-anwar-i `Abbasi* contains a warning
that frivolous behavior and the neglect of affairs of state were leading to
the decline of the realm. He singled out the alcoholism of rulers as responsible for this state of affairs, argued that monarchs who gave up
drinking were stronger and happier and more likely to live longer—hence
the longevity of Shah Tahmasb I's reign—and by allusion enjoined Shah
`Abbas II to follow his ancestor's example.[88] Shah `Abbas II complied by
renouncing alcohol himself and in the summer of 1653 issued a total ban
on its manufacture and consumption.[89] The result was that "all the wine
was seized on and spilt, and all vessels to make it in broken, no mans accepted."[90] The measure extended to Safavid-controlled Armenia and thus
seems to have been proclaimed throughout the realm.[91]

The ulama may have attributed Iran's military weakness to the shah's
dissolute life style, but the poor performance of the ill-fed and ill-
equipped Safavid soldiers stationed on the eastern front owed at least as
much to the desperate situation of state finances.[92] The antivice campaigns of 1645 and 1653 played themselves out against the backdrop of
considerable economic problems. These had been gestating for some time
and were the outgrowth of the Safavid economy's structural flaws—
exemplified in the country's dependence on foreign bullion—that were
exacerbated by measures such as the conversion from state to crown
lands that Shah `Abbas I had initiated or intensified. When the precious
metal flow from the Ottoman Empire, the lifeblood of the Safavid economy, dried up as a result of the outbreak of a round in the Ottoman-
Venetian wars, the result was a dramatic bullion shortage.[93] The quality

[86]Vahid Qazvini, `*Abbasnamah*, 131; Valah Qazvini Isfahani, *Khuld-i barin*, 480;
NA, VOC 1178, Sarcerius, Gamron to Batavia, 2 Feb. 1650, fols. 657–58.

[87]Mulla Kamal, *Tarikh*, 113.

[88]Sabzavari, *Rawzat al-anwar-i `Abbasi*, 74, 167–71.

[89]NA, VOC 1201, Sarcerius, ship Robijn to Batavia, 16 Aug. 1653, fol. 832.

[90]Foster, ed., *English Factories in India, 1651–1654*, 189, Spiller and Park, Shiraz
to Surat, 11 July 1653.

[91]Zak`aria of Agulis, *Journals*, 51.

[92]See the observations on this issue by Speelman, *Journaal der reis*, 211–12, 249,
286, which are discussed in greater detail in Matthee, "Politics and Trade," 101.

[93]NA, VOC 1162, Gamron to Batavia, 16 April 1647, fols. 317–20.

of Iran's currency underwent a sharp deterioration and provincial mints throughout the Safavid realm were forced to close in large numbers. Whereas under Shah `Abbas I some forty mints been active in Iran, the number dropped to twenty-six under Shah Safi, and to nineteen by the time Shah `Abbas II came to the throne in 1642. During the last decade of his reign, only ten of those were still in operation.[94]

This context helps explain the targeting of Iran's religious minorities in this period, both in terms of the anxieties and the need for scapegoats lean times tend to produce, and in terms of the actual money the authorities likely hoped to extract from them as a price for relenting bans on their activities. We know that in the campaign of late 1645 money played a role, if not as the motivating force, certainly in its denouement. Less than a week after the institution of the ban, the Dutch reported how the headman of the Armenian community of New Julfa had been incarcerated and falsely accused of having promised to raise 1,000 *tumans* for the shah for the right to work side by side with Muslims.[95] At the behest of the ulama, a campaign to convert the country's Jewish population was organized on at least two occasions between 1645 and 1657. In 1655 the Armenians of Isfahan were forced to evacuate the center of the capital.[96] Armenian sources suggest that the shah's decision to have the Armenians moved to New Julfa was in part motivated by a desire to prevent them from supplying wine to Muslims.[97] A *farman* prohibiting the sale of alcohol to Muslims indeed survives in archives of the Julfa Cathedral.[98] Trespassing the ban carried a fine but could result in far more severe punishment: the cropping of one's nose, the abscission of one's ears, or even disembowelment.[99] Shortly after the ban was issued, the English reported the execution of some of the shah's own servants for having violated it. Manucci also witnessed the parading of two men bound on camels, with their bowels protruding. Their offense was having caused a disturbance after overindulging in wine.[100] The proscription did not affect the privileges of the Dutch and the English in Shiraz, and initially wine in Shiraz was left untouched. Yet in the late summer of 1653 the governor of the city decided to make it applicable to these foreigners as well, smashing the urns in their compounds. Both complained with Mirza Tahir, the

---

[94]For this, see Matthee, "Mint Consolidation," 505–39.

[95]NA, VOC 1152, Extract dachregister Bastijncq, 8 December 1645, fol. 249.

[96]For more information on this, see Moreen, "Persecution of Iranian Jews"; Matthee, "Career of Mohammad Beg."

[97]Brosset, trans. and ed., *Des historiens arméniens*, 57; and Darhuhaniyan, *Tarikh-i Julfa-yi Isfahan*, 60–61.

[98]Herzig, "Armenian Merchants of New Julfa," 70.

[99]Brosset, trans. and ed., *Collection d'historiens arméniens*, 1:482–83.

[100]Manucci, *Storia do Mogor*, 1:30.

shahbandar (tollmaster) in Bandar `Abbas and the brother in law of the governor of Shiraz, but to no avail.[101]

On the proclamation of the ban in the early summer of 1653 the English resident of Shiraz speculated that, as the grapes in the local vineyards were ripe, the command was unlikely to outlast the month of Ramadan—coinciding with August.[102] He was not far off the mark. Whether or not the ban died that quickly in Shiraz remains unknown, but it probably did not last beyond the end of the year. In Armenia, it became moot after six or seven months.[103] We also know that royal drinking resumed in the last years of Shah `Abbas II's reign and continued at least until a few months prior to the monarch's death in late 1666.[104] VOC agent de Lairesse, who may have been the last foreigner to see the shah, in November of that year reported how, following a period of heavy drinking in Mazandaran, the shah had just issued a decree outlawing the sale and consumption of wine throughout his realm.[105]

Rather than to a further dramatic downturn in the economy or military defeat, the timing of this final ban may have been related to a challenge some prominent clerics posed to the shah's very legitimacy at this point. The Persian sources offer some evidence for this in their allusions to clerical discontent with royal behavior they deemed improper, and we know that high-ranking ulama advocated the active participation of religious leaders in governmental affairs with the argument that their vigilance against sin would save the country from decline and ruin.[106] Chardin provides the details. According to him, many ulama disagreed with the notion that the shah was the legitimate representative of the Imam, arguing that the one to represent the Imam should not only be of his ethnic background but also without blemish and endowed with wisdom in the highest degree. How come, they would ask, that these undisciplined rulers of ours, who drink wine and are slaves of their passions, are God's agents and communicate with the heavens to receive the light necessary for the guidance of the believers? How can people who are barely literate solve problems of conscience and doubt relating to

[101]Foster, ed., *English Factories in India, 1651–1654*, 189, Spiller and Park, Shiraz to Surat, 11 July 1653; NA, VOC 1201, Sarcerius, ship Robijn to Batavia, 16 August 1653, fol. 832.

[102]Foster, ed., *English Factories in India, 1651–1654*, 189, Spiller and Park, Shiraz to Surat, 11 July 1653.

[103]Zak`aria of Agulis, *Journals*, 52.

[104]See, for example, NA, VOC 1242, Van Wijck, Gamron to Heren XVII, 31 December 1662, fol. 1211v.

[105]NA, VOC 1255, De Lairesse, Gamron to Batavia, 30 November 1666, fol. 814.

[106]Newman, "Fayd al-Kashani," 43. On Kamarah'i, see Ja`fariyan, "Andishah'ha-yi yik `alim-i Shi`i"; and idem, "Guzarish-i andishah'ha-yi siyasi," 20–24.

matters of faith? Our kings are unjust and their rule represents a tyranny to which God has subjected us by way of punishment after removing the legitimate successor of the Prophet from this world. The supreme throne of the universe belongs to a *mujtahid*, a cleric in possession of saintly qualities and surpassing wisdom. Because the *mujtahid* would be a man of peace, kingship is still necessary to carry the sword of justice, but the monarch should be no more than his deputy.[107]

In 1666, Chardin continues, the authorities had just rid themselves of a cleric by the name of Mulla Qasim who openly preached these doctrines. A former schoolmaster, this mullah had retreated into a hermitage in a suburb of Isfahan, where his sermons attracted a large audience, including the *divanbegi*, who became one of his most devoted followers.[108] He openly spoke out against the government, practically within earshot of the shah and his ministers, saying that the ruler and his court were a disgrace for breaking the law, that God would want to destroy this cursed branch, and that the son of *shaykh al-islam* Mirza `Ali Riza should be elected ruler.[109] The court allowed this to go on for more than six months, but then decided that something had to be done about it. Mullah Qasim was apprehended and sent to Shiraz to be imprisoned.[110] He was never seen or heard of again, and so it was presumed that he had been thrown off a cliff on the way. Mirza `Ali Riza was told to keep his son under house arrest. Pleading innocence, both the father and the son ended up receiving a robe of honor from Shah `Abbas II. Afterward, no one talked about the affair anymore, so that it seemed as if nothing had happened. Chardin concludes by saying that had encountered various men of religion and of letters who held similar beliefs, though he adds that the prevailing idea according to which the shah was above the law and in possession of supernatural virtues remained intact.[111]

IV. SHAH SULAYMAN AND SHAH SULTAN HUSAYN

In keeping with Chardin's observation about the unbroken power of the shah, wine drinking once again became a feature of court life following

---

[107]Chardin, *Voyages*, 5:215–16.

[108]The *divanbegi* in 1666 was `Abbas Quli Khan. See Shamlu, "Qisas al-khaqani," fol. 148.

[109]Chardin, *Voyages*, 9:481, gives the name of the *shaykh al-islam* as Mirza `Ali Riza. He was a brother of grand vizier Mirza Mahdi, and his son, whose mother was a daughter of Shah `Abbas I, was a cousin of the shah.

[110]According to Shamlu, "Qisas al-khaqani," fols. 147v–148, he was sent to the fortress of Alamut.

[111]Chardin, *Voyages*, 5:217–19, and 6:58–84.

the coronation of Shah Safi II in late 1666. We only have negative evidence for this in the form of the Frenchman's claim that the shah gave up alcohol in 1667, prior to his second accession that same year, when he took the name Sulayman. This decision, it seems, was caused by his bad health and in particular an inflammation of the throat, clearly a congenital ailment, which his physicians attributed to too much drinking and which was among the ominous signs adduced by the clerics that had prompted the shah's very recoronation.[112]

Several revealing incidents from the dry period that followed are on record. In 1673, the story goes, grand vizier Shaykh `Ali Khan, who was known for his moral probity, including an abhorrence of alcoholic beverages, informed the shah that inebriated young men were causing disturbances near the royal palace. The shah ordered that anyone found drunk would have his belly cut open, except for those who had permission to drink wine (from sealed bottles). This right was then immediately extended to all who were habitués at the king's drinking sessions.[113] In the same period, Sulayman repeatedly humiliated Shaykh `Ali Khan by forcing him to drink in his presence, only to utter apologies and bestow a robe of honor on his vizier after sobering up.[114]

Like his father, Shah Sulayman went through more than one episode of momentary abstinence. It is often difficult to discern motives beyond his notoriously erratic behavior. The Venetian traveler Ambrosio Bembo in 1674 reported that the shah himself drank but that his subjects were not allowed to touch wine.[115] This changed a year later, for in the spring of 1675 wine was again allowed at the court and, following the great quantities that were consumed, became expensive.[116] The reason for the new tolerance remains unknown. It is just as unclear why in 1678 the ruler, who by that time often remained hidden from public view for long periods of time, decided to abstain from drinking on the days around `Ashura (the holy day on which Shi`is commemorate the massacre of the Imam Husayn on the battlefield of Karbala in 680), so that he could administer justice in a proper fashion.[117] It is perhaps at this point that the shah came close to ordering the execution of Muhammad Tahir b. Muhammad Husayn Shirazi Qumi, the *shaykh al-islam* of Qum who

---

[112]Chardin, *Voyages*, 10:88. When the shah's health did not improve, the court physicians and astrologers decided that he had been crowned under a bad omen and recommended that he be recrowned, which was done later that same year.

[113]Chardin, *Voyages* 3:116.

[114]Matthee, "Administrative Stability and Change,"

[115]Bembo, "Viaggio e giornale," fol. 236.

[116]IOR, G/37/107, Rolt, Gamron to Surat, 17 April 1675, fol. 88.

[117]NA, VOC 1323, Casembroot, Istaham to Bent, Gamron, 2 March 1678, fol. 688.

had criticized the ruler for his alcoholism.[118] The policy was still (or again) in effect in 1684. Kaempfer reports on an official dinner for the Swedish ambassador that year, where wine—together with female singers and dancers—was conspicuously absent. As told by the same informant, such rectitude followed admonitions by royal physicians concerned about the shah's health rather than religious scruples. The shah's doctors had forbidden him from drinking, and in all of Iran wine had thus been officially banned.[119] Once again, the abstinence did not last, and by 1691 Shah Sulayman had taken to the bottle again.

The last Safavid ruler, Shah Sultan Husayn, established such a reputation for piety that he received the nickname Mullah Sultan Husayn. Yet under him, too, wine drinking fluctuated over time in swings that were dictated more by circumstance than principle. The shah's initial abstemiousness was famously inspired by the traditionalist cleric Muhammad Baqir Majlisi. *Shaykh al-islam* of Isfahan since 1687, Muhammad Baqir evidently had made little headway imposing his agenda on the court as long as Sulayman was alive. The coming to power of the impressionable Sultan Husayn, who governed under Majlisi's spell until the latter's death in 1699, gave him a new chance. Majlisi's influence was felt as soon as the shah was enthroned on Saturday, 7 August 1694. Breaking with the tradition of having Sufis gird the monarch's sword during the coronation ceremony, Sultan Husayn requested that Majlisi perform this task. When the shah asked him how he wished to be compensated, the cleric requested, among other things, that the shah outlaw wine and set himself the example. That very day Sultan Husayn banned the consumption of wine on pain of death. He gave orders to break all bottles that might be found, beginning with the six thousand that his father had stocked in the royal wine cellar.[120] Orders went out to close taverns, opium dens, gambling parlors, and brothels. Injunctions were also issued for people to refrain from engaging in popular games that were deemed frivolous, such as kite-flying and wolf-baiting, and for women to behave modestly, not to mingle with nonrelated men, and not to appear in public. A *farman* to that effect, dated Shawwal 1106/May–June 1695, was engraved in stone and, in keeping with established practice, attached to the entrance portal of mosques.[121]

In addition to suggesting the persuasiveness of Muhammad Baqir Majlisi, the episode reveals the poignant dilemma between lucrative vice

---

[118]Only the intervention of other officials saved the cleric's life. Ja'fariyan, *Safaviyah dar 'arsah-i din,* 567.

[119]Kaempfer, *Am Hofe des persischen Grosskönigs,* 281–82.

[120]Kroell, ed., *Nouvelles d'Ispahan,* 68; Gemelli Careri, *Giro del mondo,* 2:154.

[121]See Nasiri, *Dastur-i shahriyaran,* 29–52; Nakhchavani, "Masjid-i Jami'-i Tabriz," 36–38; and Di Borgomale, *Mazandaran and Astarabad,* 7.

and gratuitous virtue. Shah Sultan Husayn is said to been approached by representatives of the treasury who cautioned him that the taxes on prostitution and other forms of entertainment were vital at this time of great expense and meager revenue. The income they generated was so huge, in fact, that if it had to be expressed in terms of gold and divided over the days of the year, a ban would mean a loss to the royal treasury amounting to a daily sum of ten *man-i shah* (ca. 50 kg.) in gold. The shah angrily dismissed this counsel by proclaiming that ill-gotten revenue could never be used for the furtherance of pious ends.[122]

So strict was the enforcement of this ban, once source contends, that when wine was needed for someone in Isfahan who was ill, none could be found, until it was finally obtained from the Armenians of New Julfa.[123] The edict reverberated in the provinces as well. The *farman* announcing the ban was sent to the governors and orders were given to have it read in all mosques.[124] Several stories suggest that, at least in Armenia, the officials meant the ban on alcohol to go beyond the Muslim population. Villotte, claiming that not just the consumption but the storage of wine had been outlawed, recounts that state officials would visit even the homes of Christians for inspection and would smash any jars containing wine they would find. He notes, however, how the agents of the shah, during a visit to the Jesuit convent in Yerevan had found the wine cave but had chosen to seal its door in such a way that it could be opened and closed without breaking the seal.[125] This story should be read together with the account in the Armenian sources according to which Shah Sultan Husayn sent Murtaza Quli Khan to Armenia in an official function. Once in Yerevan, he began to work on his ambition, to become the local governor, directing requests and gifts to the court for that purpose. When his ambition was left unfulfilled, he began to put pressure on the region, claiming that the shah had resolved that the Armenians should not be exempted from the ban on alcohol. He thus sent officials with the task of sealing up all wine barrels in the area. When not just wine jars but also vessels containing milk and soup were subsequently sealed, unrest spread throughout the region. Local leaders petitioned Isfahan to be released from the ban and sent money to strengthen their case. The court acceded to the request, swayed, it seems,

[122]Abu Talib Mir Findiriski, "Tuhfat al-ʿalam," Library of University of Tehran, Ms. 2465, fol. 197, quoted in Ishraqi, "Shah Sultan Husayn dar Tuhfat al-ʿalam," 90–91; Nasiri, *Dastur-i shahriyaran*, 40.

[123]Nasiri, *Dastur-i shahriyaran* 39.

[124]Ibid., 38.

[125]Villotte, *Voyages*, 313–14. Villotte was not an eyewitness, for he only came to Iran in 1696.

more by the payment than by the argument that, as Christians, Armenians should be exempted from the decree.[126]

Shortly after Shah Sultan Husayn's enthronement, a *farman* confirmed Majlisi as *shaykh al-islam* of the capital and spelled out his responsibilities. Including commanding right and forbidding wrong among them, the decree stipulated that all secular authorities, including viziers, governors, and the *divanbegi*, should obey his commands and that no one had the right to interfere with his activities.[127] This did not affect the palace, however. For all his piety, Sultan Husayn, too, relaxed his ban on wine soon after his accession, and not just for his subjects in Armenia. On 10 November 1694, while Gemelli Careri was in Kung, a messenger arrived in that port confirming that the new king drank as hard as his father had done. Assuming that the messenger had taken three weeks to cover the distance from Isfahan to the Persian Gulf coast, the royal prohibition must have ended no later than mid October, some two months after it had gone into effect.[128] The Dutch in December of the same year confirmed that the shah had been seduced by Bacchus.[129]

The circumstances of this repeal, as told by missionary sources, are revealing. According to them, the edict was much resented by the influential court eunuchs, who preferred a bibulous ruler oblivious to their activities to a sober and vigilant one. In an attempt to have it repealed, they turned to the shah's great-aunt, Maryam Bigum, a Georgian Christian who lived to almost one hundred and who until her death in 1721 wielded enormous power at the royal court. Addicted to alcohol herself, Maryam Bigum "feigned herself sick and had conveyed to the young monarch the impression that, if he valued her life, he should permit her to drink a little wine, that being, according to her physicians, the sole remedy that would relive her." The shah agreed and sent a servant to New Julfa to fetch some wine. The Armenians, suspecting a trap, claimed not have a drop left, however, so that the resident Polish envoy—who as a representative of a Christian country was allowed to have alcohol in his possession—was approached. Maryam Bigum drank some and insisted that the shah follow suit, using the time-honored argument that he was above the law. Having followed his grandmother's suggestion, Sultan Husayn drank a cupful and "took such fancy to it that he abandoned himself completely to indulgence in it, so that . . . it was rare to find him sober."[130]

[126]Le diacre Zakariya, in Brosset, ed. and trans., *Collection d'histoires arméniennes*, 2:144–45.

[127]Mahdavi, *Zindiginamah-i `Allamah Majlisi*, 1:260–64.

[128]Gemelli Careri, *Giro del mondo*, 2:274–75.

[129]NA, VOC 1549, Verdonck, Gamron to Heren XVII, 9 December 1694, fol. 617r.

[130]Anon., ed., *Chronicle of the Carmelites*, 470–71.

CONCLUSION

With the possible exception of the ephemeral Isma`il II, all Safavid shahs following Isma`il I issued bans on drinking. Such bans were never formally repealed but tended to fall into desuetude. The causes for issuing them varied, ranging from the accession of a new shah or a particularly zealous grand vizier, the perceived need to propitiate the divine at the onset of campaign, or to atone after military defeat, the urge to find scapegoats for adverse economic conditions or to squeeze money from a minority, or the shah's illness and the advice of his physicians that he should give up drinking.

The role in such episodes played by religious leaders was usually instrumental and sometimes crucial. As the state moved away from its tribal, semipagan past, their influence grew, and they showed themselves increasingly unhappy with the dissolute lifestyle of the shah and his entourage. Their position was greatly strengthened with al-Karaki and his colleagues, who changed the religiopolitical discourse with their innovative claim that, in the absence of the Imam, a qualified jurist might undertake the task of shielding the community from sin and dissipation.

Their initiative set a precedent, although it hardly established a moral imperative. It is true that every time an activist cleric gained influence at the court, the customary pattern of permissiveness might be momentarily interrupted by a regime of rebuke, prohibition, and punishment. Yet, prohibitions never lasted long—they had to be reissued periodically and the royal wine cellar was never destroyed but merely locked shut for their duration[131]—so that drinking remained the coin of the realm, causing one to conclude that the ulama were either less than wholly dedicated toward its eradication or unable to make good on their moral exhortations.

In reality they were both. Bans on alcohol were ostensibly designed to stamp out religiously proscribed behavior, but such measures betray not so much a determination to extirpate vice altogether—anyhow an impossible task—as a preoccupation with the preservation of public order—a shared concern of both secular and religious authorities. The best way to preserve public order was to make untoward activities "disappear" by relegating them to the inviolable private domain. Islam provided sanction for this. The Koran ensures the privacy of the home and condemns prying and spying. Traditional Islamic law, in turn, charged the *muhtasib* with the preservation of the good in the public domain yet forbade him from intruding on the private sphere. Ghazan Khan's edict contained an explicit clause prohibiting the authorities from entering people's homes to check for untoward behavior. In Safavid Iran, too,

---

[131]Kaempfer, *Am Hofe des persischen Grosskönigs*, 152.

private drinking was rarely tackled, in part, to be sure, because it was much harder to tackle, but more fundamentally because it did not disrupt the social order and the appearance of conformity that Islamic societies have tended to insist on so emphatically.[132]

It is important to realize in this context that the ulama were not utopians. Their professional status forced them to profess an attachment to the religious prescribed ideal of sober Muslims. But, aside from the fact that some drank themselves, they also had an interest in finding a *modus vivendi* between theory and practice, so that they generally did not clamor too loudly for the enforcement of the bans they called for in their writings.

Most important, the high-ranking ulama lived in a symbiotic relationship with the state: they needed it for status and livelihood as much as it needed them for ideological vindication and validation. The ulama might bring the authorities on their side whenever the shah and society stood in need of God's good graces and intercession—at the accession of a new ruler, before a military campaign of uncertain outcome, in times of economic malaise—but real power, including the power to ignore or rescind a ban on wine, rested with the secular ruler. Chardin, the Frenchman who left such a penetrating description of Safavid society, was probably closest to the truth when he said that the degree of tolerance for drinking depended on the mood of the sovereign (and the avarice of the governors).[133] It was the shah who appointed (and could, though rarely did, dismiss) the *sadr* and the *shaykh al-islam*.[134] Sultan Husayn's mandate for Majlisi explicitly subordinated the agents of worldly power—though, significantly, not the ruler himself—to the deputy of the Imam, and as such represented official ideology. But it was little more than fiction. The notion that secular authority served religious authority could not conceal an opposite reality: clerics had a consultative and exhortatory function; executive power was the province of the shah and his deputies. Ultimately, the ulama bowed before a state that offered them legitimacy and income. Calls to clerical heroism in opposing the state could periodically be heard but they remained rare; most were happy to accept positions and favors from the state. Despite their occasional expressions of dissatisfaction with the behavior of the shah and the populace, the ulama were content with a functional division of labor, whereby they catered to the spiritual health of the community and the state managed its political affairs.

---

[132]For a discussion of the notion of the private sphere and the implications for vice control in Islamic societies, see Cook, *Commanding Right*, 80, 591–95.

[133]Chardin, *Voyages*, 4:70–72.

[134]For the rarity of the *shaykh al-islam* being dismissed by the shah, see Stewart, "The First Shaykh al-Islām," 402.

CHAPTER 4

Opium in Safavid Iran: The Assimilated Drug

از آن افیون که ساقی در می افکند

حریفان را نه سر ماند و نه دستار

From the opium that the cupbearer threw into the wine,
our banquet companions were left with neither head nor turban

Hafiz

INTRODUCTION

Although its record does not go back as far as that of wine, opium boasts a respectable history. Originating somewhere in the eastern Mediterranean basin, most likely in Asia Minor, opium was cultivated in lower Mesopotamia in circa 3400 B.C.E. The first real sample of opium has been found in a Pharaonic grave in Egypt dating from approximately 1500 B.C.E. By the end of the second millennium B.C.E., knowledge of opium was widespread throughout Europe, the Middle East, and North Africa.[1] Known for its medicinal value, opium is mentioned in Homer's *Odyssey* as the drug that "quiets all pains and quarrels."[2] Its healing properties became part of the Greek pharmacological canon through the works of Hippocrates (466–377 B.C.E.), and also figure in those of the Roman physician Galen (130–200 C.E.).

Moving eastward, opium is believed to have come to Iran with the campaigns of Alexander the Great. The first mention of opium in an Iranian context occurs in a Sasanian text.[3] The Greek connection is exemplified in the fact that in Persian (and Arabic), opium is called *afyun*, a word derived from the Greek *opion*, and alternatively is known as *taryak*, which is also derived from Greek, *theriake*, meaning antidote to

[1]Booth, *Opium*, 16.
[2]Scarsborough, "The Opium Poppy," 4.
[3]Neligan, *The Opium Question*, 1–3.

a poisonous snakebite. A aphorism by the thirteenth-century poet Saʿdi illustrates this meaning:

تا تریاق از عراق آید   مار گزیده مرده باشد

Until opium arrives from Iraq, he who's bitten by a snake will die

Opium has long been an indispensable pharmaceutical agent in west Asia, serving not just as an antidote to venom but as a panacea against all kinds of diseases. Until the Safavid period it continued to be used in Iran mainly as a medicine. But recreational use was not unknown either. The well-known Persian historian Abu'l Fazl Bayhaqi (995–1077) claims that the famous physician-cum philosopher Ibn Sina (Avicenna) (980?–1037) engaged in much debauchery and was addicted to opiates as well. Ibn Sina indeed is said to have died of an overdose of opium mixed in with wine.[4] Yet, although theriacs are included in Ibn Sina's most famous medical textbook, the *Qanun* (Canon), opium does not seem to have been widely known at the time, judging by the fact that there is no entry for either *afyun* or *taryak* in the *Zakhirah-i Khvarazmshahi*, a Persian-language medical compendium written by Sayyid Ismaʿil Jurjani for the Kharazmshahi ruler, Qutb al-Din Muhammad (r. 1097–1127) that borrowed heavily from Ibn Sina's *Qanun*. This lends weight to the hypothesis, advanced by Petrushevsky, that the use of the opium poppy was not widely known in Iran until the end of the eleventh or twelfth century. Iran in this reading only became better acquainted with opium under the Mongols, who may have been particularly interested in opium because of their leaders' fears of being poisoned by their rivals and enemies. The Mongols were instrumental in spreading the use of opium to China. The Il-Khanid ruler Abu Saʿid in 1332 sent a large amount of *taryak* to China by way of tribute.[5] But even under the Mongols, Iran produced only small amounts of opium, judging by the rarity of references to it in the tax records.[6]

I. Opium in the Safavid Period

In the Safavid period, the earliest time for which we have extensive references other than literary ones, the consumption of opium was widespread. So was its indigenous cultivation. Olearius in the 1630s refers to

---

[4]This is controversial. See Gutas, "Avicenna, Biography," 67–68.

[5]Allsen, *Culture and Conquest*, 155.

[6]Petrushevsky, "Iran under the Il-Khans," 502. By contrast, opium does frequently occur in the literary sources as of the eleventh century. See Shahnavaz, "Afyūn," 594.

cultivation around Isfahan.[7] A few decades later De Thevenot noted that in the vicinity of Shiraz a great amount of opium was manufactured and that large tracts of land around the city were planted with white poppies.[8] By the late eighteenth century, opium from Kazirun, also in Fars province, was considered to be superior to any produced in Asia.[9] Kazirun was a center of poppy cultivation already in the Safavid period; *taryak-i kaziruni* is mentioned in a *farman* issued by Shah Tahmasb I as one of the items to be supplied to the royal palace.[10] It is not clear if Iran at that time was self-sufficient in producing opium for the needs of its own population. It appears that some Iranian opium was taken to India, exported via Hurmuz, the principal entrepôt of the Persian Gulf and the western Indian Ocean. But Hurmuz in the sixteenth century also served as a conduit for imports, with opium originating in the Red Sea basin, in Egypt and Yemen, being shipped from Cairo and Aden.[11]

As was true in Antiquity, in early modern Europe, and especially in India, opium's reputation in Safavid Iran mostly derived from its medicinal status and use. Accordingly, throughout Safavid (and Qajar) times it was taken as a painkiller as well as a remedy for a host of ailments and illnesses.[12] These included diarrhea, toothache, stuffed ears, bronchitis, rheumatic pains, chronic eye infections, colick, bladder, catharr, and coughing.[13] There was some disagreement over its place in the Galenic scheme. According to the eighteenth-century pharmacological compendium *Makhzan al-adviyah*, the physicians of ancient Greece all held it to be cold and dry, with its coldness being considered extreme. Their Indian colleagues, however, considered opium to be hot and dry. Iranian physicians and pharmacologists mostly followed their Greek colleagues and deemed it cold.[14]

Most people who took opium typically did so in the form of a regular daily dose, ingesting it in the form of a pill.[15] Called *hashim begi*, after the person who presumably invented them, these pills were the size of a pea. People would, however, typically start with a needlepoint of opium and gradually increase their intake until it had reached the size of a pea

---

[7]Olearius, *Vermehrte newe Beschreibung*, 597.

[8]De Thevenot, *Voyage*, 3:443.

[9]IOR G/19/25, Manesty and Jones, "Trade in the Persian Gulf, 1790", fol. 261.

[10]Anon., *`Alam-ara-yi Shah Tahmasb*, 409.

[11]Magelhães-Godinho, *L'Economie de l'empire portugais*, 598–99. For the opium trade in the Muslim world at that time, also see Bouchon, "Notes on the Opium Trade."

[12]Munajjim Yazdi, *Tarikh-i `Abbasi*, 95.

[13]Polak, *Persien*, 249. The Russian diplomat Korf, who visited Iran in 1834–35, relates how opium was used as a remedy for coughing. See Korf, *Vospominaniia o Persii*, 242–43.

[14]`Aqili Khurasani, *Makhzan al-adviyah*, 155.

[15]Olearius, *Vermehrte newe Beschreibung*, 597.

or even half a walnut. Having arrived at this point, users did not dare discontinue their intake for fear of dying or of becoming addicted to wine instead. Yet, contrary to received wisdom in the modern West, committed opium users did not need a steadily increasing daily dosage to achieve the same result. Most users would reach a plateau, then continue to ingest the specific dose that suited them, and often did this into old age. The Safavid physician ʿImad al-Din Shirazi quotes one Mulla Adham, a poet, who said he had used opium for seventy years, taking a certain amount in the early morning each day, and that he had never been ill, weak or lost weight.[16]

Yet, some did become addicted. ʿImad al-Din Shirazi notes that the effect of opium was rather insignificant unless one took it every day. He also made a distinction between the "people of discernment and understanding," who might take opium but only rarely became addicted, and ordinary people, who often imitated the former but did not know how to handle opium and would get hooked on it.[17] Addicts were called *taryaki*. European observers, echoing Shirazi, insist that this term was meant as an insult, similar to the term "drunkard" in Europe. Tavernier claimed that among addicts one saw young ones with pale faces, dejected and beaten down, as if they had lost their speech. As long as they were under the influence of the drug, users engaged in all kinds of ridiculous acts and uttered extravagant speech, but as soon as the effect had worn off they would feel as cold and stupid as before so that they were forced to take another dose. This was the reason that real addicts did not live very long and that, at age forty, they would be suffering from pain caused by the drug's poisonous effect.[18] Chardin agreed that addicts rarely reached old age and that those who lived beyond fifty would be incapacitated by the nerve pain and aching bones caused by this slow poison.[19] The devastating effects of this drug, Chardin claimed, had prompted the government to try to prevent and curb its consumption on several occasions.[20]

In the early eighteenth century, Jonas Hanway observed that Iranians consumed less opium than the inhabitants of the Ottoman Empire and only occasionally took it "by way of amusement," implying that the drug's medicinal use continued to prevail over its recreational consumption.[21] In chapter 8, we will see that he was wrong about the first proposition.

[16]Shirazi, "Afyuniyah," fol. 20.

[17]Ibid., fol. 22.

[18]Chardin, *Voyages*, 4:78; Tavernier, *Les six voyages*, 1:715.

[19]Ange de St. Joseph, *Souvenirs de la Perse*, 104–5; Chardin, *Voyages*, 3:73–74, 77.

[20]Chardin, *Voyages*, 3:77.

[21]Hanway, *Historical Account*, 1:229.

Although the line between medicinal and recreational use is not necessarily obvious, the second part of his statement cannot be taken at face value either, for there is no question that opium served as a euphoric as well in Iran. People took it to alleviate the tedium of daily life, to stiffen their courage in battle, and to control and prolong their sexual performance.[22] These latter functions made the alternative term for the opium pill: *habbah-i nishad* (pill of enjoyment), a particularly appropriate one.

II. Opium at the Royal Court

As is true in the case of wine, the sources suggest that opium consumption was particularly widespread in court circles and among the governing elite. The shah himself took the lead in this. The *mihtar*, the shah's chamberlain, who was always a eunuch, at all times could be found at the side of the ruler, both during meetings and during outings, armed with a silk-embroidered purse or a little gold casket in which the monarch's personal items were kept. These included handkerchiefs, nail clippers and files, a watch, perfumes, and various opiates.[23]

The Persian sources have little or nothing to say about royal opium use but offer quite a few stories about courtiers and high officials that involve opium. Iskandar Beg Munshi tells a story about an opium addict by the name of Aqa `Aziz Isfahani, who served as *avarajah-nivis* (accountant) of Khurasan under Shah `Abbas I. Implicated in a financial scandal, he was arrested and thrown in prison. The shah punished him by depriving him of opium. Soon Aqa `Aziz Isfahani, "as a result of not having consumed his regular dose of opium, was shaking all over, and his body was twisted by spasms of pain . . ." but he kept refusing the opium offered him by another courtier who felt sorry for him, until the shah relented and allowed him to use opium again.[24] His opium addiction contributed to the death of Ibrahim Beg, the governor of Lar, during one of Shah `Abbas's campaigns in Khurasan.[25] Muhammad Riza Beg, Shah Sultan Husayn's ambassador to France in 1714, used opium when in France.[26]

---

[22]Opium is a sedative and as such cannot be called an aphrodisiac. Used in moderation, it is said not so much to excite the sexual drive as to serve as an "aid to sexual stamina." For opium and sexual performance in China, see Dikötter et al., *Narcotic Culture*, 88–92. Although Iranians commonly (and rightfully) believed that it reduces sexual potency, opium, mixed in with other ingredients, clearly had a role in spiking sexual pleasure among the Safavid elite.

[23]NA, VOC 1379, Report Casembroot, 25 November 1682, fol. 2736v; Chardin, *Voyages*, 5:349–50, 378–79; De Thevenot, *Suite de voyage,* 3:349.

[24]Turkaman, *Tarikh-i `alam-ara-yi `Abbasi,* 953.

[25]Khuzani Isfahani, "Afzal al-tavarikh," fol. 145r.

[26]Herbette, *Une ambassade persane,* 59.

Bahram Mirza, Shah Tahmasb's brother, was addicted to opium as well as *barsh* or *bersh*. The latter was a compound drug of unclear etymology and composition that is also mentioned as a hallucinogenic used in Egypt.[27] *Barsh* could be administered as an antidote to opium, as happened with Bahram Mirza, whose doctors prescribed *barsh* containing ingredients such as bezoar stone (*fad zahr* or *bad-zahr*), zedary (*jadvar*), pepper (*filfil*), saffron (*za'fran*), gum euphorbium (*farfiyun*), and dracunculus (*'aqaqirha*). In order to get him slowly used to it, he was given a mixture in which one portion of opium was added to eight *misqal* of the antidote, for six days. After six days 'Imad al-Din Shirazi was asked about the cure. Given the fact that in his own medical compendium he compared the use of *barsh* as a way of killing an opium addiction to running from the rain by sitting under a gutter, it is not surprising that he rejected the mixture, prescribing instead one that contained sandal wood (*sandal*), indigo (*nilufar*), pumpkin seeds (*tukhm-i kadu*), bamboo sugar (*tabashir*), and such.[28]

The line from Hafiz at the beginning of this chapter suggests how opium and wine were traditionally intertwined. This symbiotic relationship continued into Safavid times, but seems to have operated mostly at the elite level—where, as we saw, drinking was most common. The seventeenth-century physician Ibn Kashif al-Din prescribed opium, taken in the form of a lentil-sized pill and washed down with coffee, as a favored antidote to hangovers.[29] Conversely, Della Valle, observing that many in Iran were addicted to opium and that it was difficult for them to kick the habit, insisted that to do so required ingesting a large amount of wine—which also served as an antidote in case of opium overdose—or other intoxicating substances. He added, however, that people were typically loath to give up opium for wine.[30] Nor did the remedy always cure the patient. Shah Safi had been given large amounts of opium as a youngster, in the years before he assumed power.[31] As noted in the previous chapter, the royal physicians, seeing the ruler's addiction to opium, prescribed the use of wine to him, but the result was that the shah became addicted to alcohol.[32] Chardin makes a different and equally revealing comment on the seesaw relationship between wine and opium by saying that those who abstained from wine for religious reasons tended to take opium.[33]

---

[27]For *barsh*, see Rosenthal, *The Herb*, 31–33.

[28]Qazi Ahmad, *Khulasat al-tavarikh*, 1:340–41. See also Shirazi "Afyuniyah," fols. 25, 29. A *misqal* was a weight equaling 4.25 grams.

[29]See Āl-e Dawud, "Coffee," 894.

[30]Della Valle, *Viaggi*, 2:284–85; Chardin, *Voyages*, 4:77.

[31]Tavernier, *Les six voyages*, 1:571.

[32]Anon., ed., *Chronicle of the Carmelites*, 1:350; Krusinski, *History of the Late Revolutions*, 1:47.

[33]Chardin, *Voyages*, 4:73.

Despite the reality of a drug that suppresses rather than heightens sexual arousal, opium in Asia has long had the reputation of being an aid in sexual activity. This is true for China and India as much as it is for Iran.[34] Foreigners linked the use of opiates to lewdness, referring to the fact that, although opium dulls rather than excites the senses, it is a sedative that does lengthen the sexual act—provided it is taken in light doses—quite aside from stimulating the erotic fantasy.[35] Various sources claim that Shah Sulayman used it in great quantities for this purpose. The shah apparently ordered doctors to come up with libido enhancing agents, and opium, either in the form of pills or in the form of a drink, sweetened with sugar or mixed in with amber, was among the ones that served the purpose.[36] Another substance added to opium for this purpose was *nux vomica, P. kuchulah,* known as poison nut in English, an extremely bitter strychnine-containing seed that had a reputation for enhancing the libido.[37]

This function as a sexual aid offers one important clue to the cultural acceptability of opium in the Iranian context. Gelpke, noting that the sexual act itself is performed in a state of intoxication, insists that any analysis of the use of intoxicants that ignores the multifaceted, interactive nature of sex and drugs in the Islamic cultural realm is bound to end up as an accumulation of material without the key to open up the real meaning of those facts.[38] It is easy to make too much of this and it would certainly be an exaggeration to posit a stark contrast between practices in the Christian and the Muslim world in this regard.[39] But it is nevertheless true that the Iranian-Islamic tradition does not deny man's physical tendencies and instincts and has always embraced the erotic as part of the natural world far more than Christian tradition as it evolved in the early centuries. From the lack of inhibition that marks the portrayal of the Prophet's amorous life in the classical sources, to the vivid description of paradise in the Koran, to the factual openness with which religious commentators have always talked about the physical aspects of love, Islam not just accepts sexuality as an integral part of natural life but celebrates the sexual act as an entry into the world of the sacred. In

[34]For China, see Spence, "Opium Smoking in Ch'ing China," 144; and Dikötter et al., *Narcotic Culture,* 88–92. For Iran, see Shirazi, "Afyuniyah," fol. 39–40.

[35]Pires, *Suma Oriental,* 2:513. See also Sangar, Intoxicants in Mughal India, 203–4.

[36]NA, VOC 1379, Casembroot Report, on the state and conditions of the Persians, 14 June 1682, fol. 2733; Chardin, *Voyages,* 5:349–50, 378–9; Kaempfer, *Am Hofe des persischen Grosskönigs,* 37.

[37]Shirazi, "Afyuniyah," fols. 24–25; Polak, *Persien,* 2:264.

[38]Gelpke, *Vom Rausch im Orient,"* 33.

[39]As Smith, *Consumption and Respectability,* 72, argues, in early modern Europe, too, the attractiveness of exotic consumables lay in part in their supposed aphrodisiac qualities.

Islamic thought, one's corporeality is not to be negated and sublimated but accepted and hailed as God's gift, and there is a redemptive quality to surrendering to the desires of the flesh, provided its is done in licit ways. Anything that fosters and heightens these desires is validated as well, and pharmacology has always been an essential part of the art of maximizing one's erotic fulfillment.[40]

As was true in Roman times—Hannibal ended his life by way of opium—and later in China, India as well as in nineteenth-century Britain, opium in Safavid times was a favorite way of committing suicide, and sometimes murder. The best known, though controversial instance of opium being used as a murder weapon concerns the death of Shah Isma'il II on 24 November 1577. As the story goes, the shah, after a night of wandering about town with his boon companion, Hasan Beg Halvachi-ughlu, ingested an overdose of *filuniya*, an opium-based electuary, that may or may not have been tampered with by his enemies and died as a result.[41]

Much more common than murder by opium was suicide by way of taking an overdose, in Iran as much as in Mughal India, where Man Bai, Sultan Jahangir's first wife, in 1605 killed herself in this manner out of grief over her son's rebellion against his father.[42] Those who intended to commit suicide by opium would first take a large piece of *taryak*, chase it with vinegar so as to make it impossible for those around them to administer a vomit-inducing substance, and die in a state of laughter.[43] 'Imad al-Din Shirazi notes that opium became particularly lethal when combined with sesame oil, *rawghan-i kunjid*.[44] Numerous cases of suicide by opium are on record for the Safavid period. Mir 'Abdallah, an official under Shah Tahmasb, killed himself with opium in 932/1526.[45] The Dutch report a dramatic case in the early seventeenth century involving Shah 'Abbas I's son Safi Quli Mirza, who was blinded by his own father in Farahabad. When he returned to Isfahan, Safi Quli Mirza killed his own four-year-old son by strangulation, exclaiming that his son's fate would not be any better than his own, after which he took his own life by ingesting opium.[46] High officials frequently seem to have taken their own lives anticipating the wrath of the shah and possible

---

[40]Bouhdiba, *La sexualité en Islam*, 184.

[41]Turkaman, *Tarikh-i 'alam-ara-yi 'Abbasi*, 218–19.

[42]Jahangir, *Tūzuk-i Jahāngīrī*, 1:55–56; and Findly, *Nur Jahan*, 115. For opium and suicide in India, also see Bouchon, "Opium Trade in Southern Asia," 97.

[43]Du Mans, "'Estat' de 1660," in Richard, *Raphaël du Mans*, 2:105; Chardin, *Voyages*, 4:78; Tavernier, *Les six voyages*, 1:716.

[44]Shirazi, "Afyuniyah," fol. 45.

[45]Horn, ed. and trans., *Denckwürdigkeiten Schâh Tahmâsp's*, 23.

[46]Dunlop, ed., *Bronnen*, 224, Visnich, Gamron to Batavia, 13 Feb. 1628.

execution following a botched up diplomatic mission or defeat in battle. In 1637 Biktash Beg, the commander in chief of the Safavid army defending Baghdad, committed suicide by eating opium after hopes of keeping the city from falling to the Ottomans grew dim.[47] Naqd `Ali Beg, the Safavid ambassador to England, in 1628 is said to have died of a surfeit of opium, out of fear that, having overstepped his mandate abroad, he might be in for a dire fate on returning to Iran.[48] When in late 1645 Agha Parvanah, the treasurer of Mirza "Saru" Taqi, the grand vizier who served both Shah Safi and Shah `Abbas II, was given a bastinado and subjected to other forms of torture to force him to disclose his master's wealth, he, too, committed suicide by way of opium.[49] Women who did not get along with their husbands often took an overdose of opium and died from it.[50] Suicide by opium continued to be the preferred method of taking one's life in Iran well into the twentieth century, in particular in the large towns, and women especially were said to still die in this way in significant numbers.[51]

III. Use Among Common People

Although the sources, in their focus on the elite, suggest that the popularity of opium was particularly pronounced among the ruling classes, it is clear that the appeal touched all segments of society. Indeed, rather more than in the case of alcohol, opium, which was perfectly legal and had no negative religious connotations attached to it, was not limited to the shah and his courtiers. Opium use seems to have been especially widespread among Sufis and literati.[52] Persian literary sources from the Safavid period contain a number of references to poets using and being addicted to opium. Sam Mirza talks about Salami Isfahani, a receiver of fines at the ambulant army market (*urdu bazaar*), who ingested so much opium that he was about to give up the ghost.[53] The same author, talking about Mawlana Kamal al-Din Husayn Qissah-khan (story teller), claims that his opium habit had produced a striking alteration in his face and his gait, to the point at which he had become so emaciated that one felt he had undergone a metamorphosis.[54]

[47]Turkaman, *Zayl-i tarikh-i `Abbasi*, 218–19.
[48]Ferrier, "An English View of Persian Trade," 202.
[49]NA, VOC 1152, Extract Dachregister Bastijncq, 25 November 1645, fol. 248.
[50]Olearius, *Vermehrte newe Beschreibung*, 597.
[51]Neligan, *The Opium Question*, 23.
[52]Ange de Saint-Joseph, *Souvenirs de la Perse*, 152–53.
[53]Sam Mirza Safavi, *Tuhfah-i Sam Mirza*, 262. The Persian contains a pun, *qabiz*, receiver (of fines) and *qabiz al-arwah*, the receiver of souls, that is, the angel of death.
[54]Ibid., 138–39.

But use went far beyond Sufi circles and their quest for transportation to an ethereal realm. There is a consensus among seventeenth-century foreign observers that a great many Iranians took opiates and that opium was the drug of choice for the masses.[55] Du Mans estimated that out of a thousand people a mere twenty would not be involved in the consumption of opiates.[56] There are several reasons for this. Most important, opium was cheap, hence its name *hashish al-fuqara*, hashish of the poor.[57] Like hashish, it also suppresses the appetite. The combination made it an excellent substitute for food. Financial means clearly determined what type of opium one consumed but, unlike the situation in China, the choice does not seem to have been bound up with an elaborate calibration of social status. Although opium was within reach of common people, some were too poor to afford the regular extract. They used the husks of the poppy, *pust-i khashkhash*, and a decoction thereof, instead, and were known as *pustys*.[58] According to 'Imad al-Din Shirazi, the husk could be used in two ways, either in ground form, *kuftah*, or by mixing it with water and drinking the extract. The latter method, he claimed, was common in Transoxania and India. It also served as a way for people to wean themselves off their opium addiction.[59]

Its low price made opium affordable to many, but its pharmacological effects account for its popularity. Opium relaxes and fortifies. As in the Mughal state, where soldiers were in the habit of taking opium, Safavid soldiers, too, consumed it, especially before going into battle.[60] Herbert noted that, "the footmen use it too as a preserver of strength."[61] As importantly, opium distracts. It was a great antidote to the drudgery of daily life. In Mughal India, opium was mostly taken by manual laborers to cope with the tedium of hard labor.[62] Fryer, writing in the 1670s, made the same claim for Iranians by insisting that, "to divest their care and labours, they are great devourers of opium."[63]

Yet, at the popular level, opium remained most commonly used as medicine taken for a variety of ailments and in general was used as an analgesic. 'Imad al-Din Shirazi dwells at length on its wholesome properties and calls its many medicinal benefits the main reason why "people

---

[55]Thevenot, *Suite de voyage*, 3:330–31.
[56]Du Mans, "'Estat' de 1660," in Richard, *Raphaël du Mans*, 2:106.
[57]Brunel, *Le monachisme errant*, 381; Gelpke, *Vom Rausch in Orient*, 79, 80.
[58]Teixeira, *Travels*, 200.
[59]Shirazi, "Afyuniyah," fols. 24–25.
[60]Hedin, *Verwehrte Spuren*, 278, quoting the observations of Nils Mattsson, a Swedish traveler who visited Iran in the 1640s and 1650s.
[61]Herbert, *Travels in Persia*, 261.
[62]Sangar, "Intoxicants in Mughal India," 203.
[63]Fryer, *New Account*, 3:99–100.

in east and west have been using it for thousands of years."[64] Thomas Herbert, who was in Iran in 1627–29, had this to say about this aspect of opium consumption:

> Opium (the juice of poppy) is of great use there also. Good, if taken moderately; bad, nay mortal, if beyond measure; by practice they make that familiar which would kill us, so that their medicine is our poison. They chew it much, for it helps catarrhs, cowardice, and the epilepsy, strengthens (as they say) Venus; and, which is admirable, some extraordinary foot-posts they have who by continued chewing this, with some other confection, are enabled to run day and night without intermission, seeming to be in a constant dream or giddiness.[65]

V. Variants

a. Kuknar

Barsh was by no means the only opium blend. Of the various forms in which opium could be ingested, *kuknar* was the most addictive. *Kuknar*, which is the Persian word for the actual poppy but here refers to "a liquor made by soaking in water the bruised capsules of the poppy after the seeds have been taken out," was a dark brown and bitter bouillon and had been known since Antiquity. Iranian physicians such as Razi and Ibn Sina (Avicenna) knew of it and wrote on it. There is, however, no evidence that this laudanum was used as a recreational drug before the Safavid period.[66] Fryer, writing in the later seventeenth century, noted that Iranians would quaff *kuknar*, "when they have a mind to be merry."[67] Thus, although regular opium, eaten, was an everyday antidote to the tedium and drudgery of life, *kuknar*, drunk like a boullion, was consumed as a pastime drug. Du Mans describes how *kuknar* users needed ever larger daily amounts to get the same effect and that those who were addicted would die within three of four hours of suffering if they did not get their fix on time.[68] A nineteenth-century visitor to Iran and Central Asia confirmed this, albeit not in similarly dramatic terms: "Temporary exhilaration," he wrote, "is soon succeeded by stupefaction, and that by nervous prostration. The *kukhnar* drinker is soon forced to take large quantities several times a day, and to use the greatest caution

---

[64]Shirazi, "Afyuniyah," fol. 13.
[65]Herbert, *Travels in Persia*, 261.
[66]Ravandi, *Tarikh-i ijtima'i-yi Iran*, 7:228.
[67]Fryer, *New Account*, 3:99–100.
[68]Du Mans, "'Estat' de 1660," in Richard, *Raphaël du Mans*, 2:105.

in his diet; above all he must abstain from very hot and from very sour drinks."[69] The *Tazkirah-i Nasrabadi* has several references to poets who were addicted to *kuknar*. Of Mulla Makhfi Rashti, Nasrabadi says that he was addicted to *kuknar* and that his wit was perfect at times when he was high on opium and alcohol. Mirza Abu'l Baqa, one of the many poets from the Safavid period who migrated to India, was rumored to be addicted to *taryak* and *kuknar*. Nasrabadi confesses to being a *kuknar* addict himself who could not give up his daily dose even after repenting from other drugs.[70]

Kuknar was served in the so-called *kuknar-khanah*s, seedy dens where addicts would gather to drink their *kuknar*. *Afyun* or *taryak*, solid opium, was not to be had in the *kuknar-khanah*, but was sold at separate shops and also seems to have been among the offerings of the regular coffeehouses that as of the first decade of the seventeenth century flanked the newly built royal square, *maydan-i naqsh-i jahan*, of Isfahan.[71] *Kuknar-khanah*s could be found all over town, but they seem to have been concentrated around the old square, which was also the site of a large number of regular coffeehouses and the scene of large crowds of people drinking, engaged in discussions, taking a breath of fresh air, or simply there for devotional reasons, as the tomb of Harun Vilayat was nearby.[72] Du Mans called the *kuknar-khanah*s establishments where all kinds of rumors and news could be gathered, but he also suggests that they were places avoided by honest and more private people.[73] Chardin describes the atmosphere in these drug dens as follows:

> It is very entertaining to be part of those who take in those cabarets, and to observe them before, during and after they take a dose. When they enter the cabaret, they are gloomy, defeated and languid. A short while after taking two or three cups of this beverage, they become peevish and like enraged; anything annoys them, they rebut everything and they are querulous; in the end, however, they make peace, and each gives himself to his overriding passion, the amorous showers his lover with sweetness; another one, half-sleeping, laughs up his sleeve, yet another one does rodomont, and another tells absurd stories; in sum, it is as if one were in a lunatic asylum. A type of drowsiness and stupor follows this uneven and disorderly gaiety; but the Persians, far

---

[69]Schuyler, *Notes of a Journey*, 1:127. According to the *Burhan al-qati`*, *kuknar* refers to the extract of the opium poppy, `*asarah va fishurdah*. See Tabrizi (Burhan), *Burhan-i qati`*, 3:1734.

[70]Nasrabadi, *Tazkirah-i Nasrabadi*, 167, 395, 668–69.

[71]Junabadi, *Rawzat al-Safaviyah*, 771.

[72]Chardin, *Voyages*, 7:449–50.

[73]Du Mans, "`Estat' de 1660," in Richard, *Raphaël du Mans*, 2:105.

from seeing it for what it is, call this ecstasy and maintain that there is something supernatural and divine to this state.[74]

b. Bang and Hashish

Another hallucinatory drug used with abandon in the cabarets, where each afternoon many people congregated to find oblivion from their boredom or misery, was *bang*.[75] *Bang* has a long history in the Islamic world and in Iran in particular. It is likely that the word is etymologically related to the Avestan *banha/bangha*. Pre-Islamic Iranian texts refer to it as a drug that was either used medicinally to lessen injury or that, as an ingredient in an "illuminating" drink, was integral to ecstatic practices.[76] *Bang* refers to the dried leaves and small stalks of Indian hemp (*cannabis Indica*), and is thus identical to hashish.[77] Observers of Safavid Iran describe *bang* as hempseed, or refer to it as a mixture of poppyseed, hempseed, and *nux vomica*. *Bang* came in different forms. The Indian type consisted of pure cannabis. This is likely the substance referred to by Fryer when he said that Iranians never smoked a pipe without the "Leafs of the intoxicating Bang, and Flowers of the same, mixed in with their Tobacco."[78] Tavernier calls it a beverage, like *kuknar*, bitter and mean to drink, and nastier than anything else. Its effect was so potent, the same informant tells us, that it would send the user into a strange rage, which is why its use was illegal.[79]

If it is not obvious what *bang* refers to in each case when it is mentioned, it is not altogether clear where and when *bang* originated either. Arab commentators suggest that the drug came from the east, most likely India, and spread westward, and Hadith literature even implies that hashish came originally from Iran. Several Arabic sources also locate the introduction of hashish in twelfth-century Iranian Sufi circles from Khurasan, and more specifically Qutb al-Din Haydar of Zavah (modern Turbat-i Haydariyah), the founder of the Haydari Qalandars (d. 1221–22), whose center was Nishapur and who is credited with having discovered the intoxicating effect of the cannabis leaf.[80] The fifteenth-century Egyptian historian al-Maqrizi is among those who called hashish "the wine of Haydar," and he specifically attributed the growing spread and popularity of hashish in Khurasan and later across all of Iran to the influence of the Haydari

---

[74]Chardin, *Voyages*, 4:78–79 (my trans.).

[75]Chardin, *Voyages* 4:82.

[76]Pur-i Davud, *Hurmazdnamah*, 93–96; Gnoli, "Bang," 689.

[77]Yule and Burnell, *Hobson-Jobson*, 59.

[78]Fryer, *New Account*, 100.

[79]Tavernier, *Les six voyages*, 1:716.

[80]Karamustafa, *God's Unruly Friends*, 46.

Qalandars. Others, among them the renowned theologian Ibn Taymiyah (d. 1328), saw the influence of Central Asia and, more specifically the Mongols.[81] Although the association of the evil of hashish with the evil represented by the Mongols makes such claims suspect, a Central Asian origin of hashish is indeed plausible in light of the fact that it does seem to have spread westward with the Mongol conquest of the eastern half of the Islamic world. As late as the nineteenth century, opium was said to be rare in Turkistan, and people would typically smoke *bang* as a narcotic.[82] And it is also widely reported that hashish was a favorite drug among Sufis and especially Qalandars, the antinomian Sufis we encountered in chapter 2. Opium consumption may have further spread in the subsequent Mongol period, following the expansion of dervish orders and their practices, which in many cases included the permissibility of using hashish.[83]

Also customary in Central Asia, especially in Uzbeg territory, and likely introduced to Iran from Central Asia, was a stronger mixture of hempseed, hemp, and *nux vomica*. Du Mans insisted that, of late, the Uzbeks had taught the Iranians to use this. Tavernier and Chardin tell the same story but it is not clear if they came to this independently or heard it from Du Mans.[84] Hemp mixed in with honey was customary as well. Olearius said that Iranians used hemp, both the seeds and the leaves, as a means to arouse sexual appetite, although he expresses puzzlement about this given the fact that Safavid herbal manuals declared that *bang* had the opposite effect. He describes how the leaves would be gathered before the seeds appear on the stems, were laid to dry in a shady place and pulverized, after which they were mixed with honey and turned into balls the size of pigeon eggs. People would eat two or three of those and resume their activities. The seeds also were roasted and sprinkled with salt. Olearius mentions that Imam Quli Sultan, the Safavid envoy Shah Safi sent to Holstein in response to the mission accompanied by Olearius, and a man of approximately seventy, used cannabis in this manner on his journey through Russia after he had taken a young wife in Astrakhan. In Iran itself, he added, those who used *bang* for the purpose of this type of sexual arousal did not enjoy a good reputation.[85]

Ma'jun was the name of yet another confection of opiates and additives, including poppyseeds, flowers of the thorn-apple, *nux vomica*, and sugar. Its name, which derives from Arabic, means "kneaded," referring

[81]Brunel, *Le monachisme errant*, 281; Rosenthal, *The Herb*, 45–46, 49–50, 54; Lane, *Early Mongol Rule*, 247–49.

[82]Schuyler, *Notes of a Journey*, 1:127.

[83]Gronke, "La religion populaire," 213–14.

[84]Tavernier, *Les six voyages*, 1:716; Chardin, *Voyages*, 4:79–80.

[85]Olearius, *Vermehrte newe Beschreibung*, 594.

to the fact that *ma'jun* was a "compound of medicines kneaded with syrup into a soft mass."[86] Like *bang*, it may have come from India or Central Asia. The early Indian Mughals in the person of Sultan Babur and his entourage consumed it frequently.[87] Du Mans remarks on the delirious effect *ma'jun* had on its users, who would wander the streets talking to themselves, laughing at the angels, joyful as long as the drug did its work. Once its effect wore off, the user would descend into a sullen and testy mood, leading to a saying in Persian about someone argumentative and testy: *magar taryak-i tu narasidah ast?* Hasn't your opium had its effect [lit. "reached"] yet?[88] *Ma'jun* was used at the Safavid court as well. A well-known anecdote recounts how one night Shah Sulayman, drunk, told Shaykh `Ali Khan that his refusal to take alcohol exposed the blameworthiness of his own drinking and ordered him to liven up by emptying a glass with him or by taking some *ma'jun*. The grand vizier chose *ma'jun* and, not being used to it, soon manifested strange behavior, at which point the shah called out his other courtiers to laugh at the hapless servant, and ordered his beard shaven. The next day, Shaykh `Ali Khan tendered his resignation as chief minister.[89]

Another electuary of uncertain provenance was called *filuniya*. The word itself points to a Greek origin, *filonia*, referring to an antidote allegedly invented by Philon of Tarsis, but its etymology is as unclear as the precise composition of the drug.[90] Mir Sadr al-Din Muhammad of Shiraz in the late sixteenth century wrote a letter to Khan Ahmad Khan, the ruler of Gilan, in which he requested the sending of strong filuniya (*filuniyah-i pur jawhar*, lit. *filuniya* full of jewels).[91] This may suggest that the *filuniya* of the Caspian region was known for its potency, but unfortunately we lack further documentation to corroborate this. We do know that *filuniya* was not confined to Iran. The Mughal emperor Jahangir (r. 1605–27) in his memoirs recounts how he took to *filuniya* in order to wean himself off alcohol, to which he had become addicted, and how he lessened his drinking as he increased his intake of the drug.[92]

---

[86]Yule and Burnell, *Hobson-Jobson*, 539.

[87]Dale, *Garden of the Eight Paradises*, 143, 181, 282, 300, 301, 315, 316, 322.

[88]Du Mans, "`Estat' de 1660," in Richard, *Raphaël du Mans*, 2:106. Prof. Modarressi tells me that the expression survived in Iran until a few decades ago but, rather, referred to an edgy addict in need of a dose.

[89]Fasa'i, *Farsnamah-i Nasiri*, 479.

[90]Jahangir, *Tūzuk-i Jahāngīrī*, 1:308, fn.

[91]Afshar, "Tazah'ha va parah'ha-yi iranshinasi," 77.

[92]Jahangir, *Tūzuk-i Jahāngīrī*, 1:308.

VI. Prohibition

Opium naturally was among the substances whose enjoyment was not allowed during the month of Ramadan. This evidently was not easy for addicts. And addiction was common, even though many used opium in moderation. Della Valle expressed amazement at the large quantities those addicted to it would consume on a daily basis.[93] Fryer, himself a physician, also drew attention to the addictive properties of opium, explaining how people would step up the dose they took from a grain to half an ounce, "without any harm, besides a frolicksome sort of drunkenness; by means whereof, without any sustenance, they are qualified to undergo great travels and hardships." But having once begun, Fryer continues, "they must continue it, or else they dye; whereby it becomes so necessary, that if they mis-time themselves, as in their Ramzan [*sic*], or on a Journey, they often expire for want of it: Yet those that live at this rate are always as lean as Skeletons, and seldom themselves . . ."[94]

'Imad al-Din Shirazi's treatise on opium includes a lengthy description of ways for people to overcome their opium addiction. Because it took a long time to become addicted, he insisted, it stands to reason that it also should take time to wean oneself off opium. There were several ways of doing so. One could either postpone taking opium by an hour each time until one had not taken it for a period of four days without feeling nervous. Because acute sickness tends to last four days, this was a sign of being cured of the addiction. A second way of ending the addiction was by lowering the amount of opium. One could do this by taking the same amount while making sure the opium was moist, thus containing a great deal of harmless weight. Or one could lower the weight. If the result would be that one didn't feel well, however, it would be advisable not to lower it any further, until one got used to the new amount, after which lowering it further would be in order. The addicted individual in question did not even have to be aware of this gradual process, Shirazi adds. He gives the example of a wife who lowered the amount of her husband by putting wax in his opium without his knowledge, gradually increasing the amount until all he would eat was wax. Another way of achieving the same result was to replace opium gradually by the husk of the poppy.[95]

In his remedial prescription, Shirazi differentiated between those who took only one pill a day, those who were used to taking two, and real addicts, who ingested at least three. The first, he insisted, should not have a problem, for they could simply take their pill in the early morning,

[93]Della Valle, *Viaggi*, 2:284.
[94]Fryer, *New Account*, 3:100.
[95]Shirazi, "Afyuniyah," fols. 22–24.

before the onset of fasting. For those who were used to taking two daily pills, he recommended that during Rajab and Sha`ban, the two months preceding Ramadan, they gradually change the time of day to early morning and night, so that during the month of fasting they would take their dose naturally before daybreak and after sunset. Those who took opium three times day had to make sure to lower the frequency to twice a day in the period before Ramadan, so that they would not have a problem when fasting came around.

If the attempt to regulate one's intake failed because of forgetfulness or inability, Shirazi recommended that the user resort to a suppository, that is, insert a cartridge, *fatilah*, filled with opium into his rectum, securing it by attaching a string to it so that it could always be taken out. One should be careful with this method, he argued, for failure to take the cartridge out on time could damage the rectal muscle, causing it to lose control over the emission of feces.[96]

Little information is available on government measures against opium and its variants. Given the embeddedness of opium and other hallucinatory drugs in social life—Tavernier noted that it was hard to find a man in Iran who was not addicted to any of these substances[97]—and the absence of religious proscription—none of these hallucinogenics appears in the Koran or the Hadith—it may be assumed that this relates to a paucity of incidents rather than a persistent omission in the sources. Opium, around since time immemorial and not explicitly excoriated in the Koran, was so thoroughly indigenized that it barely provoked religious and sociopolitical resistance. *Bang* was different. It is not mentioned in the Koran either, but it does figure in Islamic manuals of jurisprudence (*fiqh*) as the standard prohibited intoxicant. As noted, its users enjoyed a bad reputation. Tavernier claimed that, unlike the other drugs, *bang* was illegal in the Safavid period, but he does not elaborate, and neither do other sources from the period.

Opium and its derivatives nevertheless did not entirely escape the periodic measures aimed at forbidden substances and blameworthy practices. *Bang* was certainly among the drugs proscribed as part of Shah Tahmasb's repentance of 1532–33. In his autobiography the shah specifically mentions *zumurd-i sudah*, pulverized emerald, a reference to the green color of hashish, as one of the illicit euphorics.[98] Among the establishments that were ordered to close their doors were the *bang-khanah*, the *ma`jun-khanah*, and the *buzah-khanah*.[99] Various sources suggest

---

[96]Ibid., fol. 36.

[97]Tavernier, *Les six voyages*, 1:716.

[98]Shah Tahmasb, *Tazkirah-i Shah Tahmasb*, 30.

[99]Nava'i, ed., *Shah Tahmasb-i Safavi. Majmu`ah-i asnad*, 513.

that opium itself was included in the shah's interdiction as well, with one chronicler ascribing his decision to dissolve the stash that was found in the palace in water to the ruler's extreme fastidiousness.[100] Yet, it seems unlikely that opium was among the stimulants and taking it among the practices that were subsequently prosecuted.

Shah ʿAbbas I, known for his dislike of other substances, is also on record for having taken antiopium measures. In 1005/1596 he issued a *farman* in which courtiers who were addicted were given the choice of quitting, going to Uzbeg territory, or returning their past wages, for "I do not retain addicts and headless types." The result, according to Munajjim Yazdi, was that most courtiers gave up using opium, even though quitting was not without pain. The author, who was Shah ʿAbbas's court astrologer, includes himself in this, telling his readers that he had been addicted for nineteen years.[101] But the need for money clearly was in competition with any royal compunction about the use of opium. Khuzani Isfahani in his account of the same year introduces Qunbur Beg, one of the shah's *silahdars*, weapon-bearers, who was addicted to opium so that the shah always called him *taryaki*. He is said to have requested the ruler to have the opium users of the realm become his subjects. The shah conceded and granted him Iran's opium production as his prebend, *tiyul*. Each year his officials would go out to the various parts of the country to collect the appropriate tax.[102]

None of this apparently had any effect, and many continued to use opium with great abandon. Chardin sums this up when he says that, over time, the government had made several attempts to restrict the use of opium but that it was so widespread and ingrained that it proved to be ineradicable. The main reason why opium use could not be stamped out, Chardin noted, was that out of ten people hardly one could be found who did not indulge in ingesting it. Wine, he insisted, as if alluding to the futility of Shah ʿAbbas's endeavor to substitute it for opium, was the only antidote but, not being as pleasurable, it was not a good replacement. Opium addicts who tried to overcome their habit with wine tended to come back to opium, arguing that without it they would not longer have any fun in life and would rather depart from it.[103]

Another episode that confirms Chardin's contention occurred during the reign of Shah ʿAbbas I, who after many soldiers had switched to opium following an initial ban on wine in 1621, outlawed opium and

---

[100]Khurshah, *Tarikh-i ilchi-yi Nizam Shah*, 118; Valah Qazvini Isfahani, *Khuld-i barin*, 395.

[101]Munajjim Yazdi, *Tarikh-i ʿAbbasi*, 157.

[102]Khuzani Isfahani, "Afzal al-tavarikh," fol. 101v.

[103]Chardin, *Voyages*, 4:77.

again allowed wine drinking short of inebriation. Any container with *kuknar* found was smashed, and the death penalty awaited all who were found drinking it.[104] This measure betrays the shah's typical pragmatism rather than religious concerns, and it is clear that little effort was exerted to enforce it beyond perhaps the military. Opium, or at least the sale of hashish, *chars-furushi*, finally, was included in the ban on un-Islamic activities issued by Shah Sultan Husayn upon his accession in 1694.[105] But this measures seems to have been as desultory as all previous (and subsequent) attempts to curtail its use.

CONCLUSION

Unlike alcohol, which was mostly confined to the court and the elite, opium in Safavid times was truly a drug of the masses. It is no doubt for this reason that it received little attention from domestic and foreign observers alike. Opium was too common and unremarkable to be the object of much curiosity, no religious stigma was attached to it, and only excessive use and obvious addiction merited comment.

Taken in pure, solid form, blended with a variety of other substances, or consumed in liquid form, opiates were used in great quantity in court circles, as a form of medicine, as an aphrodisiac, and as a euphoric. It was extraordinarily popular among mystics, and especially wandering dervishes are said to have used it without exception and in great quantity. The majority of common people used it as well, mostly, it seems, for its soothing effect, for its capacity of produce pleasurable dreams, to make dull lives of hard labor a little more bearable and, of course, as a panacea against all and sundry aches and pains in an era when self-medication was typically the only form of medication. Yet, most users took it in moderation and in such a way that it did not interfere with the flow of life. Hence, the comparison foreign observers made with the use of wine in southern Europe.

Despite the insistence of some that Iranians knew how to deal with opium it is clear that that addiction to opiates, especially in the form of heady cocktails such *kuknar* and *ma`jun*, was not uncommon. Opium was clearly socially accepted and altogether unremarkable inasmuch as it was integrated into the texture of life. No social or religious stigma was attached to it, although to be a *taryaki*, someone unable to control his intake, was perceived negatively. *Bang*, by contrast, does not appear to have been viewed as positively. The ulama condemned it and the

---

[104]Della Valle, *Viaggi*, 2:209.
[105]Nakhchavani, "Masjid-i jami`-yi Tabriz," 37.

little information we have indicates that its use, regardless of dosage, was illicit.

The sources suggest that opiates only rarely were the target of governmental anti-vice campaigns. Although opium was included in the substances targeted in the context of Shah Tahmasb's Sincere Repentance, enforcement seems to have been lax to nonexistent outside the confines of the palace. Too popular to eradicate and, in the case of opium not burdened by religious stigma, both opiates and cannabis continued to flourish among large segments of the Iranian population.

CHAPTER 5

Tobacco in Safavid Iran:
Pleasure and Proscription

تنباکو چیست آفت برگ امید   گلخن به از آن گلو که این دود کشید

از تنباکو نفع توان داشت گمان   از دود اگر خانه توان کرد سفید

What is tobacco? A calamity arising from a leaf of hope
A fireplace is better than the throat that draws its smoke
One could imagine benefits coming from tobacco
If only you could whitewash the house with smoke

Muhammad Tahir Nasrabadi,
Tazkirah-i Nasrabadi

INTRODUCTION

Of all the psychoactive substances that spread around the world following the so-called age of discovery and exploration, none was dispersed with such lighting speed, embraced with such alacrity and integrated into social life with such ease as tobacco. Tea and coffee, cocoa, and distilled liquor took centuries to circumnavigate the globe; some of these stimulants never crossed certain cultural divides, all went through a gestation period of at least a century before they became part of the social fabric of the countries where they were introduced, and it often took quite a bit longer for them to gain genuine popularity beyond the upper classes or, in some cases, the common people, who had first developed a taste for them. Tobacco, by contrast, invariably and usually within decades after being introduced, made converts out of all those who were exposed to it, regardless of social rank, occupation and, quite often, gender. In the words of one historian, "Tobacco has been, especially when smoked, the most universal new pleasure mankind has acquired."[1]

With the other stimulants, tobacco played a role in the shaping of the early modern world; it brought about a shift in patterns of consumption, it was accompanied by the emergence of new forms of sociability,

---

[1]Kiernan, *Tobacco*, 227.

and the public place most directly associated with it, the coffeehouse, became a venue for early capitalist business activity and the literary and political discourse of a rising middle class. Alternatively hailed for its salutary working and vilified for its diabolical properties, tobacco drew the attention of doctors who recommended its use for various ailments and of clerics who associated it with vanity and moral rot. Governments, wary of the bullion the new drug was thought to drain from the treasury, as well as apprehensive of the political discourse that tended to thrive in the establishments where men gathered to enjoy their pipes and coffee, were suspicious of tobacco and frequently prohibited its use—until they discovered it as a taxable commodity.

Such forms of impact and response are near universal in early modern times, though our most detailed knowledge and understanding of them comes from European societies. This chapter seeks to extend this knowledge to Iran under the Safavids, a society that embraced some of the new stimulants, but especially tobacco, with such eagerness and enthusiasm that smoking appears to have been taken up by all layers of society well before it became a habit elsewhere in the eastern hemisphere. Two basic questions with regard to tobacco will be explored. The first involves the origins and spread of tobacco and smoking in Safavid Iran and, more particularly, the exceptionally rapid adoption and acceptance of smoking by the Iranian populace. The second concerns the process of commodity indigenization, that is, the specific ways in which tobacco was integrated in social life in Safavid society, as well as the forms of resistance and rejection it encountered in the process.

I. THE INTRODUCTION OF TOBACCO

Over time, different ideas have been advanced with regard to the timing and the source of Iran's acquaintance with tobacco. In the eighteenth century there were those who believed that the Iranians knew of and used tobacco before Europeans sighted the New World. The context of this belief was a broader conviction that the origins of tobacco did not lie exclusively in the Americas and that the plant was indigenous to various regions in Africa and Asia.[2] Such beliefs likely go back to stories and rumors that circulated in Iran itself in the seventeenth century and that were picked up and given currency by foreign visitors, most notably the

---

[2]For examples, see Tiedemann, *Geschichte des Tabaks*, 208ff; Wiener, *Africa and the Discovery of America*, vol. I; and Becker, "Zur Ethnologie der Tabakspfeife"; and, more recently, Balabanova, "Tabak in Europa vor Kolumbus." For a refutation of the non-American origin of tobacco, see Stahl, "Zur Frage des Ursprungs des Tabaksrauchens."

widely read Chardin.[3] Since the nineteenth century, however, the prevailing opinion has been that Iran, like the rest of the Old World, received its first tobacco following the European exploration of the American continent. Yet, disagreement remained as to the source of transmission and diffusion. Some have insisted that the Iranians learned about tobacco from the Ottomans during the Safavid-Ottoman war of 1609, when Shah ʿAbbas, hearing that his soldiers spent much of their pay on tobacco, outlawed its use, threatening violators of the ban on smoking with the cropping of their nose and lips. Their claim goes back to the story told to that effect by the German traveler Olearius, who visited Iran during the reign of ʿAbbas's successor, Shah Safi.[4]

There is no reason to doubt that Iranian soldiers hailing from the north and fighting in Azerbaijan and eastern Anatolia spent their money on tobacco during the wars against the Ottomans. In the Ottoman Empire tobacco was known by that time. Tobacco may have been introduced into Syria as early as 978/1570, although 1000/1591 is also mentioned as a date.[5] The Ottoman historian Naima claims that Europeans had first brought it to Istanbul in 1009/1600–01.[6] Olearius, however, does not say that tobacco was *introduced* in that manner. He does not express an opinion on the issue. The problem is that there are virtually no eyewitness accounts of the actual use of tobacco during the reign of Shah ʿAbbas I. Thomas Herbert, who visited Iran in 1627–29 and who often but erroneously is claimed as the earliest reference to the actual smoking of tobacco in Safavid Iran, is one of the few exceptions.[7] Another is the Spanish envoy Don Garcia y Silva de Figueroa who, a decade before Herbert, witnessed how Shah ʿAbbas I, though he had banned tobacco in his realm, allowed the visiting Mughal ambassador Khan ʿAlam to smoke during an audience.[8] Tobacco was allegedly the subject of a learned debate between the two.[9]

The Safavid-Ottoman wars of the early seventeenth century may have been one conduit for the dissemination of tobacco in Iran, but it is clear that tobacco smoking was introduced earlier. How much earlier is difficult to establish, because the evidence is scanty and contradictory. Tobacco was readily available in 1612, the year when Uzbeg ruler Vali Muhammad Khan came to Iran. Still in Khurasan, far from the urban

---

[3]Chardin, *Voyages*, 3:303.

[4]Olearius, *Vermehrte newe Beschreibung*, 645. See also Corti, *History of Smoking*, 144.

[5]These dates occur in al-Karmi, *Tahqiq al-burhan*, 16. Thanks to Prof. Modarressi for bringing this work to my attention.

[6]Birnbaum, "Vice Triumphant." See also Tiedemann, *Geschichte des Tabaks*, 213ff.

[7]Herbert, *Travels in Persia*, 261.

[8]Silva y Figueroa, *Comentarios*, 2:403.

[9]Islam, *Indo-Persian Relations*, 75.

areas where smoking is likely to have begun, the members of the Uzbeg delegation asked for tobacco, and before long "tobacco was repeatedly smoked."[10] According to Kamal al-Din, an Iranian physician, Iran was introduced to tobacco in 1605, a date that accords well with that of its presumed introduction elsewhere in South Asia and Southeast Asia. Some Persian sources claim a slightly earlier date. A medical treatise by another physician, Husam al-Din Mutattabib, dating from the turn of the seventeenth century, says that tobacco was introduced at the time of its writing.[11] Elsewhere, a precise date of 1001/1601 is given for the introduction of tobacco into Iran.[12]

A radically different, altogether precocious date of tobacco's introduction is suggested by a set of two Persian poems that refer to the water pipe, *qalyan*, and that allegedly date from the early sixteenth century. The oldest of these is a *ruba`i* from the hand of an anonymous poet from Shiraz who died in 942/1535–36:

قلیان ز لب تو بهره ور میگردد   نی در دهن تو نیشکار میگردد

بر گرد رخ تو دود تنباکو نیست   ابریست که بر گرد کمر میگردد

From your lips the water pipe draws enjoyment
In your mouth the reed turns sweet as sugar cane
It is not tobacco smoke around your face
It is a cloud that swirls around the moon[13]

A second quatrain is by a poet by the name of Basiti:

کمتر باشد غم تنهائی   مایوس شدم به عالم تنهائی

صحبت به کسی گو اگر نیست چه باک   قلیان کافیست همدم تنهائی

For me the pain of solitude is not so great
I used to become sorrowful in a world of being by myself
Converse with someone, but if no one is around, who cares
The intimacy of the water pipe is sufficient against my loneliness

---

[10]Munajjim Yazdi, *Tarikh-i `Abbasi*, 439.

[11]*Fihrist-i nuskhah'ha-yi khatti-yi kitabkhanah-i Malik*, 8:386–87. I owe this reference to Prof. Modarressi.

[12]Agha Buzurg, *al-Dhari`ah*, 4:436.

[13]See Simsar, "Nazari bih paydayish-i qalyan," 15; and idem, "L'apparition du narghileh," 84.

In the early sixteenth century, the people of the Iberian Peninsula were the only inhabitants of the Old World who knew of tobacco, the first samples having been brought back from the New World with the return voyage of Columbus in 1493. Given a *terminus ad quem* of 1535 for the first poem and the arrival of the Portuguese in the Persian Gulf in 1505, there is the theoretical possibility that tobacco first reached Iran in the early sixteenth century.

Yet, the introduction of tobacco more than a half century before a generally accepted date of penetration anywhere in Asia cannot be taken at face value and recently has led Willem Floor to call the authenticity of Shirazi's poem into question. Floor argues that "either a later poet might have written or adapted the poem," or that "something other than tobacco was used in it, which seems more likely." He then speculates that the poetic references are to indigenous tobacco, refers to the rumors recounted by Chardin about the existence of such a substance prior to the introduction of the nicotian weed but, unable to establish evidence for it, fails to reach a definitive conclusion about a likely date of its entry into Iran or the identity of the ones who first brought it to Iran.[14]

The early date of the first *ruba`i* indeed raises several questions. First of all, it remains puzzling how three quarters of a century could have lapsed before tobacco smoking was noticed and described by foreign observers, for whom the habit, if not completely new, must have been noteworthy given the unusual manner in which tobacco tended to be consumed in Iran. Even allowing for the remote possibility that an intermittent supply and logistical obstacles kept the habit of smoking confined to the country's southern regions for the better part of the sixteenth century, nothing explains why neither early English visitors such as Arthur Edwards (1566), Richard Willes (1568), John Newbery (1588), or John Cartwright (1606), nor Portuguese travelers such as Luis Pereira de Lacerda (1604–05), Gaspar de S. Bernardino (1605), or Nicola de Orta Rebelo (1606), make any mention of tobacco in Iran.[15]

Second, nothing in the sources suggests that the knowledge and sporadic use of tobacco spread beyond the Mediterranean world during the first half-century following Columbus's voyage. Theoretical knowledge advanced through works such as the popular *Agriculture et maison rustique*, a book on horticulture by Jean Liebault, and the *Cruydeboeck*, written by the Flemish Rembertus Dodonaeus in 1554 and held to be

---

[14]Floor, "Art of Smoking," 48–50.

[15]The accounts of the early English travelers can be found in Hakluyt, ed., *Principal Navigations*, vols. 2 and 3. For the Portuguese travelers, see Gulbenkian, ed., *L'ambassade de Luis Pereira de Lacerda*; Bernardino, *Itinerário da Índia*; and Rebelo, *Un voyageur portugais en Perse*.

the oldest reference to the cultivation of tobacco in Europe.[16] Jean Nicot, whose name is immortalized in the addictive substance in tobacco, contributed to the early knowledge by describing tobacco while he served as the French ambassador to the Portuguese crown in 1560. The first to use tobacco in Europe were the soldiers and sailors who set out on military expeditions and commercial ventures from the ports of Lisbon, Genoa and Naples. Trade took tobacco further north. The English, who would later become the chief distributors around the world, took up smoking in the late sixteenth century. The first clay pipes, modeled after Indian examples, began to be manufactured in London in about 1580. Sailors and travelers brought the tobacco habit from Portugal and England to Holland, and further on to Norway, where tobacco appeared in the import duty records in 1589.[17] Elsewhere in Europe commercial channels were instrumental as well. English merchants thus introduced tobacco to Russia in the 1560s. War and commerce similarly furthered the spread beyond Europe's coastal regions. The Thirty Years' War disseminated tobacco into Central Europe, where English troops in the service of Frederick of Bohemia in 1620 were seen smoking as they marched through Saxony. Before long, Germany was cultivating its own tobacco and served as a springboard for the spread to Austria and Hungary.[18]

In Africa and Asia tobacco penetrated by way of Portuguese and Dutch sailors and merchants but, aside from the early use of tobacco in the Philippines, few references predate the seventeenth century.[19] Smoking was reported in Sierra Leone as early as 1607, whereas southern Africa was only exposed to tobacco with the Dutch founding of the Cape Colony in 1652.[20] In most of Asia, tobacco penetrated in two ways, either through direct contact with the seafaring Europeans or, in the case of landlocked regions, via coastal areas. Japan, for instance, learned of smoking directly from the Portuguese. Tobacco probably spread to Korea and Manchuria with the Japanese occupation of the Korean peninsula at the same time that it was introduced in southern China by the Portuguese from Macao.[21] Central Asia, by contrast, seems to have acquired the tobacco habit via Iran. The story of the Uzbeg envoy requesting tobacco from the Iranians in 1612 suggests that smoking was not yet common in Central Asia at that time.

---

[16]Brongers, *Pijpen en tabak*, 14; Rival, *Tabac, Miroir du temps*, 13.

[17]Price, "Tobacco Adventure to Russia," 8.

[18]Tiedemann, *Geschichte des Tabaks*, 165–6.

[19]See Höllmann, *Tabak in Südostasien*. The Philippines received its first tobacco in the 1570s, directly from South America across the Pacific.

[20]Ibid., 191.

[21]See Satow, "Introduction of Tobacco into Japan."

Whether or not we put the early poem on hold for being an isolated and uncorroborated case, it seems clear that, like most of Asia, Iran received its first tobacco from Portuguese merchants and sailors. The eighteenth-century Persian pharmacological dictionary *Makhzan al-adviyah*, states this as a fact, and so do most seventeenth-century sources.[22] Unfortunately, none of them are forthcoming about their own sources and informants. The friar Ange de St. Joseph, who may have been the first to assert that the Portuguese were responsible for the introduction of tobacco in Iran, failed to mention his source. The same is true of Engelbert Kaempfer, another seventeenth-century observer who credited the Portuguese for introducing tobacco to Iran. Chardin is hardly more specific in simply claiming several Iranians as his informants.[23] The Iranian scholar Pur-i Davud estimates that the Portuguese brought tobacco to Iran a short while after doing so in India, and that the Iranians first became acquainted with the herb in the last decade of the sixteenth century.[24] Neither he nor the nineteenth-century author he invokes, however, mentions an original source for this contention.[25]

As the Portuguese entered the Persian Gulf from the west coast of India, where they had settled shortly before, it seems reasonable to assume that Iran became familiar with tobacco at the same time that India did. The likelihood that Safavid Iran learned about tobacco from or rather via India is enhanced by the fact that the country imported much of its tobacco from the Subcontinent during the early seventeenth century, when tobacco had yet to turn into a cash crop in Iran. All early references in the Dutch maritime sources to tobacco in Safavid territory are to imports from India, by western companies and indigenous merchants alike.[26] Yet, there is not a single allusion to the knowledge and use of it in India (or the Ottoman Empire) from the period before the 1580s, and the *Alfaz al-adviyah* maintains that it was first recorded in India in the early reign of Sultan Jahangir (1605–27).[27] One source claims that tobacco was brought to India in 914/1508–09, though that it did not become popular until the reign of Sultan Akbar (1556–1605),[28] which reminds one of the early poetic reference to the water pipe, both in the

[22]'Aqili Khurasani, *Makhzan al-adviyah*, 275.

[23]Ange de St. Joseph, *Souvenirs de la Perse*, 102–5; Kaempfer, *Amoenitatum exicotarum*, 640; and Chardin, *Voyages*, 3:303.

[24]Pur-i Davud, *Hurmazdnamah*, 198. See also the references in Comes, *Histoire, Géographie, statistique du tabac*, 218–19.

[25]The source Pur-i Davud quotes is Bleibtreu, *Persien*, 71, 96, fn. 1. Bleibtreu claims that the Portuguese introduced tobacco in 1599.

[26]Dunlop, ed., *Bronnen*, 35, 176.

[27]Gokhale, "Tobacco in Seventeenth-Century India," 485; Seligmann, ed., *Ueber drey höchst seltene Persische Handschriften*, 41.

[28]Dahlavi, *Shar-i Mina Bazar*, 105.

startlingly early date it proposes and the lack of historiographical context. Until more evidence comes to light, possibly from Portuguese archival sources, the matter must remain unresolved.

II. The Water Pipe

We might explore the question of origins and initial introduction a little further by examining the water pipe. From the inception of smoking in Iran, the most popular smoking device in Iran has been the water pipe, *qalyan* in Persian, *huqqah* (lit. orb, jar, receptacle) in India, and *nargilah* or *shishah* in Arab lands. All Western visitors to Safavid Iran mention the *qalyan* as a curiosity that did not exist anywhere in the West. Some claim that it was used in India as well.

The water pipe may actually be much older than the sixteenth century. A type of water pipe seems to have been used to smoke cannabis in Ethiopia in the thirteenth and fourteenth centuries.[29] But details are missing and we remain in the dark about possible transmission beyond East Africa. Meanwhile, most Iranians and many scholars, Iranian and non-Iranian alike, believe that the *qalyan* is an Iranian invention that spread from Iran to other parts of the Middle East.[30] The evolution of the water pipe seems to confirm this. A drawing of a Persian *qalyan* is included in the earliest European compendium on tobacco, the *Tabacologia*, written by Johann Neander and published in the Netherlands in 1622.[31] Water pipes also appear in several early-seventeenth-century Persian drawings and paintings by Riza 'Abbasi and his pupil, Muhammad Qasim Tabrizi, respectively.[32] Contrary to what one might expect, however, the images are not of primitive and crude contraptions improvised from coconut shells, presumably the first material from which water pipes were constructed, but of highly elaborate and intricate devices. The high-quality craftsmanship suggests a relatively long process of technical advancement and aesthetic refinement and appears to corroborate, if not the early poetic reference, at least a relatively long period of gestation. Over time, the water pipe certainly acquired an Iranian connotation. In eighteenth-century Egypt, the most fashionable pipes were called *Karim Khan*, after the Iranian ruler of the day.[33]

[29]See Van der Merwe, "Cannabis Smoking," 78.

[30]See, for example, Razpush, "Galyān," 263; and Tanner, "Rauchzeichen," 23; Floor, "Art of Smoking," 61.

[31]Neander, *Tabacologia*, 247, 249.

[32]See Martin, *Miniature Paintings*, plate 159; and Rogers, ed. and trans., *Topkapı Saray Museum*, plate 124.

[33]Niebuhr, *Travels through Arabia*, 1:127. They were known under that name in late-eighteenth-century Iran as well. See Ives, *Voyage from England to India*, 224.

Early image of a water pipe, taken from J. Neander. *Tabacologia medico-cheururgico pharmaceutica* (Leiden, 1622).

The most compelling argument for Iranian primacy is the story that the first person said to have passed the smoke of tobacco through a bowl of water was an Iranian poet-cum physician by the name of Abu'l-Fath Gilani (1547–89).[34] Yet that fact, if true, does not make the *qalyan* an Iranian invention. Gilani had moved to India in 1575 and it was at the court of Sultan Akbar, where he had been welcomed and attained high rank that he allegedly smoked his first water pipe.[35] The story rather points to Indo-Islamic origins. (In India, water pipes became common in the northern "Muslim" regions, but not in the south.) The first reference to the water pipe in the Subcontinent dates from 1615, long before foreigners noted this type of smoking in Iran.[36] On etymological and physiological grounds, it also is more likely that the water pipe was first developed in India, or at least that it came to Iran from or via India. The term *qalyan*, at any rate, does not point to an Iranian origin, for it is a derivative of *ghalyan*, a word that, in turn, derives from the Arabic verb *ghala*, meaning to "boil" or to "bubble." The early water pipe was a simple device consisting of a hollowed-out coconut, into which a straight (bamboo) reed was inserted through which the tobacco smoke was filtered.[37] This type long continued to be used by poor people in (southern) Iran and India alike.[38] The very word *nargilah*, meaning coconut in Sanskrit, refers to those origins.[39] As the coconut is not indigenous to Iran but does grow in southern India, it stands to reason that the water pipe originated in the subcontinent. It is quite possibly via trade channels originating in western India that more elaborate water pipes, consisting of a glass bowl, reached Yemen, where early-seventeenth-century water pipes similar to models found in western India have been recorded.[40] Merchants, whether Indian, Arab, or Iranian, also spread the water pipe throughout the coastal areas of East Africa.[41] As with the documentation on smoking per se, the evidence about the origins and early development of the water pipe remains scanty and elusive. Yet,

[34]Elgood, *Safavid Medical Practice*, 41.

[35]Karamati, "Abu'l Fath Gilani," 107.

[36]In Laufer, *Tobacco and Its Use in Asia*, 12.

[37]Early images of water pipes all show this straight reed. See, for example, the drawing in Neander, *Tabacologia*, 247; Chardin, *Voyages*, atlas, plate XIX; and Bedik, *Chehil sutun*, 288. This strengthens the assertion by a Persian source that the coiled tube, *marpich*, was invented under Shah Sultan Husayn (r. 1694–1722). See Mustawfi, *Zubdat al-tavarikh*, 138.

[38]Ives, *Voyage from England to India*, 224. Another creative way poor people used to construct a water pipe was by using the tibia of a sheep, observed by O'Donovan in Central Asia in 1881. See O'Donovan, *Merv Oasis*, 2:440.

[39]Pur-i Davud, *Hurmazdnamah*, 208.

[40]See Armin Schopen, "Tabak in Jemen," 447.

[41]Laufer et al., *Tobacco and Its Use in Africa*, 10, 17.

even a rejection of the notion that tobacco was adopted prematurely and skepticism about the Iranian origins of the water pipe do not alter the fact that Safavid Iran was one of the first societies outside of the New World and the Iberian Peninsula where tobacco was diffused and became a commonplace article of consumption.

II. POPULARITY, CULTIVATION, AND TRADE

Regardless of the exact timing of the introduction and diffusion of tobacco in Iran, it is clear that by the mid-seventeenth century smoking was extraordinarily popular among Iranians. The German traveler Heinrich von Poser, visiting Qandahar in 1621, spoke of the "excessive drinking of tobacco" in that city.[42] Sixteen years later, Olearius noted that Iranians of all classes found so much pleasure in tobacco that they smoked it everywhere, even inside mosques. He added that it was imported from Baghdad and, by insisting that Iranians did not know how to prepare it, implied that, at the time, tobacco was not yet widely cultivated in Iran itself. The Iranians, Olearius claimed, loved European tobacco, which they called *inglis tambaku*, referring to the English as importers.[43] More than a generation later, Chardin insisted that *tanbaku inglisi* stood for the Brazilian tobacco that the English had brought to Iran circa fifty years earlier. Chardin added that the Iranians did not like the strong flavor of this tobacco and also thought it was too expensive.[44] The origin of this tobacco must have been Virginia, which as of the 1620s had become the main supplier of tobacco to England. The English indeed imported tobacco into Iran in 1628–29, but the quantity seems to have been small and a lack of follow-up in the sources creates the impression that the initiative met with little success.[45] In the early part of the seventeenth century, great quantities of a cheaper grade of lesser quality also seem to have been carried overland from the Subcontinent, for Herbert in the 1630s witnessed how forty camels loaded with tobacco and coming from India entered Qazvin.[46] Indian tobacco reached Iran via the maritime trade as well.[47]

It did not take long for tobacco to become an indigenous crop. By the mid-1600s, tobacco foreign imports had largely come to an end. Rather

[42]Poser, *Tage Buch*, unpag.

[43]Olearius, *Vermehrte newe Beschreibung*, 597.

[44]Chardin, *Voyages*, 3:302.

[45]Sainsbury, ed., *Calendar of State Papers*, 628–29, Burt et al., Gombroon to Surat, 20 Feb.–May 1629.

[46]Herbert, *Some Years Travel*, 198.

[47]Dunlop, ed., *Bronnen*, 35, 176.

than importing it from India and Mesopotamia, Iran as of the mid-seventeenth century exported its homegrown tobacco to the Subcontinent, the Ottoman Empire, and Russia.[48] Iranian water pipes, too, found their way to India. It is said that four thousand were shipped to Surat each year by 1700.[49] Tobacco by that time had turned into a cash crop that was cultivated all over Iran. *Tanbaku*, the fine tobacco used for water pipes, was grown in the south-central and eastern parts of the country, whereas *tutun*, the coarser tobacco used for regular pipes, grew in the western regions. By late Safavid times, tobacco had turned into one of the major trade items in the city of Qum.[50] Kazirun in the same period had become a center of *tanbaku* cultivation, producing more than ten varieties. Tobacco from Kazirun sold for three mahmudis per *man-i Kaziruni*.[51] The environs of Isfahan and Kashan continued to produce fine tobacco, but since late Safavid times Iran's best grades have been grown in Fars. In Ma'in, a village north of Persepolis, the "choicest tobacco of Persia" was found.[52] Its inhabitants called Ma'in a "tobacco village," and by the late seventeenth century many of its former orchards had yielded to the "stinking herb."[53] Armenia, finally, grew tobacco as well in late Safavid times.[54]

So popular had the weed become by the mid-seventeenth century that Iranian soldiers brought their water pipes to the army and carried them with them during campaigns, and that the device accompanied travelers during trips.[55] The majority of Iranians, Tavernier noted, would rather forego bread than their tobacco, adding that, as soon as a worker had received his daily salary, he would first go buy tobacco and use the remainder of the money for bread and fruit. The first thing Iranians would do at the breaking of the fast during the month of Ramadan was light their pipes.[56] Fryer concurred when he said that "the Poor, have they but a Penny in the World, one half will go for Bread and dried Grapes, or Butter-milk, and the other for Snow and Tobacco."[57] Khatunabadi's

[48]Chardin, *Voyages*, 3:302; 4:165–66; Gopal, *Indians in Russia*, 97, 130.

[49]Barendse, "Trade and State in the Arabian Seas," 220.

[50]Petis de la Croix, *Extrait du journal*, 135.

[51]See Salati, *I viaggi in Oriente*, 31.

[52]Fryer, *New Account*, 2:228.

[53]Kaempfer, *Reisetagebücher*, 95.

[54]Pitton de Tournefort, *Relation d'un voyage*, 2:139.

[55]Poullet, *Nouvelles relations*, 2:328–29. One observer of early-nineteenth-century Iran noted that all who smoke in the army were followed by cinderbearers, "who were of themselves sufficient to compose a small army." See Kotzebue, *Narrative of a Journey*, 142–43.

[56]Tavernier, *Les six voyages*, 1:598–99.

[57]Fryer, *New Account*, 2:248. See also De Bruyn, *Reizen over Moskovie*, 137, who insisted that tobacco was the "main delicacy and pastime of the Iranians."

Iranians smoking at a coffeehouse, Safavid period. J.- B. Tavernier, *Les six voyages de Jean Baptiste Tavernier . . . fait en Turquie, en Perse et aux Indes,* 2 vols. (Paris, 1676).

chronicle offers another telling example of the popular craving for tobacco. He reports how in 1127/1715, a time of economic hardship and political turmoil in Iran, huge price increases for basic necessities led to a popular revolt in Isfahan, with people slandering Mir Muhammad Baqir Khatunabadi, the leading cleric of his age, who reportedly had said to the shah that if the people were able to buy tobacco for eight `abbasis they could certainly afford to buy bread for eight *bistis*.[58]

Given this passion, it should not come as a surprise that the *qalyan* house, possibly synonymous with the coffeehouse, was a standard feature of Iranian cities by the later seventeenth century. Kaempfer, passing through Rasht, the capital of the northern province of Gilan, in 1683, noted that, "every third or definitely every fourth house here is a *qalyan* house, in which orators as well as beggars can be heard." De Bruyn, too, remarked on the tricksters who performed in great numbers in the

[58]Khatunabadi, *Vaqa'i` al-sannin,* 567–68. For more on this episode, see Matthee, "Blinded by Power," 187. The `*abbasi* was a Safavid coin that was first produced under Shah 'Abbas I and named for him. The *bisti* was a small copper coin.

country's tobacco and coffeehouses.[59] In Rasht as well as in other cities, including Isfahan and Kashan, the *qalyan* houses were located in the heart of town, often flanking the main square.[60] One of the reasons why water basins were found in the middle of coffeehouses was to allow people to fill their water pipes.[61] In addition to the coffee- and tobacco houses there were many tobacco stalls, *dukkan-i tanbaku-furushi*, lining the streets and avenues of Isfahan and ubiquitous street vendors selling tobacco to passers by.[62] In sum, all the evidence about the urban environment confirms that Iran was decades ahead of Europe in fully integrating smoking into the fabric of society and in turning tobacco into an article of mass consumption. In Europe tobacco has been called "the first of the range of non-European exotica to establish itself permanently as a European commodity."[63] It was, however, only in the later part of the seventeenth century that it became a widely consumed commodity in countries such as Holland and England, whereas others, such as Austria and France, took until the middle of the eighteenth century to reach that level.

We might pursue the question of the rapid integration of tobacco smoking in Iran a little further by considering it in connection with other stimulants. It is tempting to see a causal link between the quick acceptance of tobacco and the near simultaneous introduction of coffee in Iran. Smokers metabolize caffeine much faster than nonsmokers and thus require a greater coffee intake to feel the same effect from it.[64] To consider one as the vector of the other in an effort to explain the speed of the process is merely to beg the question, however. To be sure, both became important accessories to life in Iran, each other's pendant, so to say, in that tobacco calms while coffee stimulates.[65] According to a Persian saying, "coffee without tobacco is like soup without salt."[66] Yet, there is no intrinsic reason why this should have been the case. The quick and total acceptance of tobacco by Iranians can possibly be explained as a form of convergence and fusion of a different order, involving other, preexisting mind-altering drugs. Some of these had been widely used in Iran long

[59]Fryer, *New Account*, 147.

[60]Kaempfer, *Reisetagebücher*, 65, 77, 78.

[61]Petis de la Croix, *Extrait du journal*, 114.

[62]Du Mans, "'Estat' de 1660," in Richard, ed., *Raphaël du Mans*, 2:104. The term *dukkan-i tanbaku-furushi* appears in a *vaqfnamah* issued by Shah Sultan Husayn in 1118/1706–07, which turned a great many shops and worshops, including tobacco shops, in Isfahan, into waqf property. See Umidyani, "Nigarishi ba yik vaqfnamah-i tarikhi," 23.

[63]Goodman, *Tobacco in History*, 59.

[64]Courtwright, *Forces of Habit*, 20.

[65]Schivelbusch, "Die trockene Trunkenheit des Tabaks."

[66]In Ouseley, *Travels in Various Countries*, 341.

before the introduction of tobacco. Among those, opium comes to mind. Opium, however, is a good example of fusion following rather than preceding the dissemination of tobacco smoking, as until the early nineteenth century it was only ingested in Iran. (See chapter 8.)[67] The same is not true for *bang*, or cannabis, a hallucinogenic that had long been known to Iranians and whose widespread use may have facilitated the adoption of tobacco. It is true that early references to hashish suggest that in medieval times it, too, was consumed in solid form rather than smoked.[68] Yet, this does not alter the fact that tobacco and cannabis are highly complementary, and in Iran, as virtually everywhere else, had long been used together (and continued to be consumed in combination in the Qajar period).[69] In suggesting a connection between tobacco and hashish, one does not have to follow those who have surmised that the water pipe may have been used to smoke hashish long before the introduction of tobacco, thus rejecting the possibility of a spontaneous invention in the world of Islam.[70] It is quite possible to entertain the idea that the water pipe, whether it originated in Iran or India, was an original invention *and* to argue that the rapid acceptance of tobacco and the concomitant development and refinement of the water pipe followed a process of fusion between existing and newly introduced habits of hallucinogenic drug-taking. For this to be the case it is irrelevant whether or not hashish was ever smoked by way of a water pipe. That the two, tobacco and hashish, were consumed jointly in the seventeenth century merely strengthens this hypothesis.[71] Thus, the Englishman John Fryer in the 1670s noted that the Iranians "never smoked a pipe without the leaves of the intoxicating bang and flowers of the same mixed with their tobacco."[72]

[67]In China, by contrast, opium was smoked already in the seventeenth century. Jonathan Spence calls the habit of opium smoking in China "an offshoot and development in tobacco smoking" but fails to explore how opium was used before the introduction of tobacco in China at the turn of the seventeenth century. See Spence, "Opium Smoking in Ch'ing China," 146–47.

[68]Rosenthal, *The Herb*, 64–65.

[69]Courtwright, *Forces of Habit*, 105. For their combined use in the Qajar period, see Polak, *Persien*, 2:244.

[70]Laufer, *Tobacco and Its Use in Asia*, 27; Goodman, *Tobacco in History*, 88; and Keall, "One Man's Mede is another Man's Persian," 275–85.

[71]For the hypothesis that the water pipe and hashish smoking were originally linked, see Hartwich, *Die menschliche Genussmittel*, 231, quoted in Tanner, "Rauchzeichen," 24.

[72]Fryer, *New Account*, 3:99–100. According to Du Mans and Tavernier, the Uzbegs had (recently) taught the Iranians to mix tobacco with cannabis. See Du Mans, "'Estat' de 1660," in Richard, ed., *Raphaël du Mans*, 2:104; and Tavernier, *Les six voyages*, 1:716–17.

III. CLASS AND GENDER

In many parts of the West different social classes gravitated toward different forms of smoking. The pipe, which in modern times was to become the emblem of class and style, was originally the preferred device of the common people, beginning with the sailors and soldiers who acquired the smoking habit from the indigenous peoples of South America. The upper and upper-middle strata of society in countries such as Italy, France, and Germany in the late seventeenth century took to snuff, surrounding its taking with an aura of ritualized distinctiveness designed to accentuate the status of consumers and to separate them from the common people. Some parts of the Islamic world, such as North Africa, and certain groups, such as the nomadic peoples of the Maghrib, adopted snuff. In Iran, snuff was reportedly used by some high-ranking officials in the eighteenth century, but it never found wide acceptance beyond Sistan in the southeast.[73] Class distinctions in Iran seem to have expressed themselves in part in the choice between different forms of smoking, in part in the degree of refinement and decoration of the accessories used, the elaborateness of the surrounding ritual, and the social codes inscribed in a pastime that was sociable rather than individual in nature. The old, the rich and the poor, noblemen and commoners, all indulged in smoking with the same gusto.[74] Yet, the well-to-do tended to smoke water pipes, whereas members of the poorer classes, leading lives and doing work that involved greater mobility, more often seem to have smoked the more portable regular pipes. In so far as the poor smoked qalyans, they used simple devices that were made with a base of coconut, or alternatively a gourd (qabaq).[75] The wealthy, by contrast, had their water pipes made of painted glass or crystal and ornamented with chiseled silver or gold or even encrusted with diamonds, surviving examples of which attest to the fact that, whether the qalyan originated in India or in Iran, it attained its acme of design and sophistication in the latter country.[76]

---

[73]NA, VOC 2417, Leypsigh, Isfahan to Koenad, Gamron, 26 December 1736, fol. 4193; Floor, "Art of Smoking," 82–83.

[74]Du Mans, "'Estat' de 1660," in Richard, Raphaël du Mans, 2:106; Neander, Tabacologia, 247.

[75]Olearius, Vermehrte newe Beschreibung, 597; and Bembo, "Viaggio e Giornale," fol. 244. Edward Ives makes a reference to qalyans made of a coconut shell and a bamboo reed being used on the island of Kharq in 1758. See Ives, Voyage from England to India, 224. The eighteenth-century pharmacological compendium Makhzan al-adviyah contains a reference to the use of the coconut shell as the bowl of a water pipe. See 'Aqili Khurasani, Makhzan al-adviyah, 857.

[76]Neander, Tabacologia, 247. The so-called karna'i bowls seem to have been the best. See Rustam al-Hukama, Rustam al-tavarikh, 100–1; and Keyvani, Artisans and Guilds Life, 83. for royal water pipes made with gold, see Silva de Figueroa, Comentarios, 2:403; Valentyn, Oud- en nieuw Oost-Indiën, 5:277; and Bushev, Posol'stvo Artemiia Volynskogo, 119.

Water pipe carrier on horseback, late Safavid period. Cornelis de Bruyn, *Reizen over Moskovie, door Persie en Indie* (Amsterdam, 1714). Courtesy of Koninklijke Bibliotheek, The Hague.

People of high rank also took to employing someone called a *qalyan-dar*, or a water pipe holder, who would follow them either on horseback or on foot while carrying the various implements needed for smoking.[77] De Bruyn refers to this servant in describing his arrival in Shamakhi in Shirvan. The city authorities, he noted, came riding out to welcome his party, accompanied by "servants who rode around, each of them carrying a *qalyan* or Persian tobacco bottle in his right hand, to serve his master. These bottles are made of glass, and are nicely decorated at the top with gold or silver." Other servants had a copper kettle hanging at the side of their horses, in which a fire was kept steadily alight, so as to be able to offer the *qalyan* to their masters at his desire.[78]

De Bruyn's printed travelogue contains a striking illustration of a servant on horseback with such as kettle dangling from his horse's side. This phenomenon, incidentally, gave rise to a further differentiation along religious and social lines, for in Safavid times Armenians are said to have been prohibited from having their tobacco gear thus carried behind them.[79]

[77]Chardin, *Voyages*, 4:25. Muhammad Riza Beg, Safavid ambassador to France in 1714–15, during his entire visit was accompanied by a *qalyan-dar*, who went with him "wherever he went." The envoys was said to be inseparable from his water pipe, smoking it in the carriage on his way to an audience with Louis XIV, while bathing, and even while attending the Paris opera. See Herbette, *Une ambassade persane*, 35, 51, 154, 156, 192, 207.

[78]De Bruyn, *Reizen over Moskovie*, 102–3.

[79]Fryer, *New Account*, 2:259. This rule must have been instituted under Shah Sulayman, for, according to Tavernier, Iranian Armenians were privileged over other non-Muslims in being allowed to ride richly caparisoned horses. See Tavernier, *Les six voyages*, 1:468.

The shah's own *qalyan-dar* kept the royal *qalyan* at his side at all times.[80]

The same sort of class distinction can be observed with regard to the regular tobacco pipe. In addition to "wet" smoking, Iranians adopted "dry" smoking, done through long-stemmed pipes with a small bowl, which were quite similar to the ones used in England and Holland, where they were first seen in the early seventeenth century. Originally made of clay, these pipes were known in Turkish and Persian as *chupuq* or *chapuq*, a cognate of the Persian word for wood, *chub* and rendered in English as *chibouk*. The tobacco used for the *chapuq* was called *tutun*, a word that may derive from the Portuguese-Brazilian word *petun*, and differed from *tanbaku*, which was used for the water pipe, in being of lesser quality.[81] Hamadan and Bihbahan were two areas in western Iran were so-called *tutun-i kurdi* (Kurdish tobacco) was grown.[82] The distinction between the *qalyan* and the *chupuq* was in part class-based, in part regional. The *chupuq* became especially popular in the northern and northwestern, Turkish-speaking parts of Iran. Class distinctions played a role as well, however. The wealthy over time took to using richly decorated pipes of engraved silver, whereas the poor smoked simple wooden pipes. The poor in Safavid times also were in the habit of assembling and fixing broken pipes.[83]

Unlike the situation in most early modern Western societies, no overt gender division seems to have existed in Safavid (and Qajar) Iran with regard to tobacco smoking. Both men and women smoked.[84] Two paintings by Muhammad Qasim Tabrizi from the mid-seventeenth century vividly illustrate female smoking.[85] Textual evidence corroborates the phenomenon. As one observer noted: "All people, men and women, smoke, indiscriminately and avidly, day and night."[86] It was rather location that separated the sexes. Whereas men enjoyed their pipes in the many coffeehouses that sprang up in the Safavid urban centers in the seventeenth century, (respectable) women rarely ventured outside and appear to have indulged in the habit in the confines of the private sphere.

---

[80]Du Mans, "'Estat' de 1660," in Richard, ed., *Raphaël du Mans*, 2:78, 267.

[81]Pur-i Davud, *Hurmazdnamah*, 205. On the possible Portuguese-Brazilian origin of the word *tutun*, see Comes, *Histoire, géographie, statistique du tabac*, 228.

[82]Ange de St. Joseph, *Souvenirs de la Perse*, 103–5; and Polak, "Beitrag zu den agrarischen Verhältnissen," 143.

[83]Tavernier, *Les six voyages*, 1:675.

[84]Kaempfer, *Reisetagebücher*, 79; and Du Mans, "'Estat' de 1660," in Richard, ed., *Raphaël du Mans*, 2:104.

[85]In *Treasures of Islam*, 119; and Rogers, *Topkapı Saray Museum*, 124, 182. Thanks to Massumeh Farhad for bringing these two paintings to my attention.

[86]Bedik, *Chehil sutun*, 286.

IV. Resistance: Criticism, Proscription, and Resignation

As in many places around the world, tobacco in the early stage of its introduction in the Middle East aroused medical interest, provoked moral rebuke among clerics, and caused economic anxiety on the part of bureaucrats. Like their counterparts in the West, Muslim physicians discussed the effect of smoking on physical health. In keeping with traditional humoral pathology, some Muslim doctors and pharmacologists considered tobacco to be dry and cold, though most followed European practice by placing tobacco among the dry and hot substances. Controversy surrounded the alleged effects of smoking on the body. Although it was held to be salutary for people with a humid disposition, some believed that it weakened the brain.[87] Similar to European beliefs, tobacco smoke was thought to repel pestilence.[88] Overall, however, tobacco in the Islamic world never gained the medicinal reputation it enjoyed in early modern Europe.

Clerical authorities in the Middle East, by contrast, showed themselves highly preoccupied with the potentially detrimental effects of the novelty on piety and propriety. Christian preachers railed against tobacco as a satanic invention, referring to its origins in heathen territory. Muslim scholars, unable to find references to tobacco in the Koran, resorted to analogical reasoning to determine whether smoking was permitted or should be condemned and banned as contrary to religion. As tobacco did not resemble any of the forbidden substances mentioned in the Koran, the prophetic Sunna, and the Hadith, proscribing it, other than on the basis of *bid`a*, innovation, was not a simple matter. Nor was it yet easy to "prove" that tobacco in itself was bad, or harmful to one's health. One way of arguing for proscription, therefore, was to equate tobacco with the foul things that Sura VII:157 declares forbidden, to associate it with the "avoidance of things evil" contained in Sura III:104, or to argue that the Prophet who, according to a Hadith, appreciated sweet odors, would certainly have loathed tobacco's disgusting smell. An attempt was even made to associate smoking with the smoke and fire that is held to precede the Last Judgment. Proponents of smoking invoked Sura II:28 (al-Baqara), which refers to the benefits of everything that God has created on this earth.[89] Some religious scholars argued that smoking was a wasteful habit, whereas others criticized it as

---

[87]Seligmann, ed., *Ueber drey höchst seltene Persische Handschriften*, 41.

[88]`Aqili Khurasani, *Makhzan al-adviyah*, 275.

[89]Klein-Franke, "No Smoking in Paradise."

a sin for being associated with infidel foreigners, who after all had been the ones to introduce tobacco to the Islamic world.[90]

In the Shi`i world, tobacco inspired similar debates. A number of Iranian theologians from the Safavid period are on record as having written treatises that discuss the religious status of tobacco smoking, weighing the potential health benefits ascribed to it by some doctors against possible religious objections. Arguments for and against tobacco were often made in the context of the controversy between the representatives of a literal-minded version of religion, who tended to reject tobacco, and members of Sufi orders, who smoked in great numbers and whose beliefs and practices increasingly became the object of clerical vilification in the seventeenth century. Those who spoke out against the habit for the most part seem to have belonged to the Akhbari school of thought, a theological current that rejected the validity of recourse to rationalist legal argumentation and, instead, relied on the sayings of the Prophet and the Shi`i Imams.[91] `Ali Naqi Kamarah'i (d. 1650), the activist `alim who argued that the government had a strict obligation to uphold public morality and who under Shah Safi served as qazi, judge, of Shiraz and later as shaykh al-islam of Isfahan, was one of those who considered tobacco a satanic weed. In a treatise on the impermissibility of smoking tobacco he adduced a number of religious and social reasons why tobacco was to be rejected. Tobacco, he noted, counted among the foul-smelling substances, khaba'ith mentioned in the Koran, tobacco smoking was devilish because mostly practiced by the unemployed, the ignorant, and the depraved, the implements, which were often made of gold and silver, involved enormous and wasteful expense, and the first to smoke and to spread the habit had been Western (farangi) unbelievers.[92]

Another staunch opponent of the water pipe was `Abd al-Hayy Razavi Kashani, a cleric who lived in the waning days of the Safavid state and who was fiercely critical of the moral laxness of the Safavid rulers and the society they governed. His Hadiqat al-Shi`ah includes a chapter on the qalyan. Although seemingly resigned to the staying power of tobacco, which he calls bound to "remain with us until the Day of Judgment," the author criticizes tobacco smoking, albeit not on religious grounds. Instead, he complains about the bad smell caused by the ubiquitous water pipe, which was even carried into the mosques by

---

[90]See Berger, "Ein Hertz wie ein trockner Schwamm."

[91]Ja`fariyan, `Ilal-i bar uftadan-i Safaviyan, 351–54; a list of Shi`i anti-smoking tracts appears in Aqa Buzurg Tihrani, al-Dhari`ah, 11:173–75.

[92]See Ja`fariyan, `Ilal-i bar uftadan-i Safaviyan, 351–64; idem, ed., "Risalah fi bayan hukm shurb al-tutun wa'l qahwah," 88–90, which gives the text of Kamarah'i's objections to tobacco as rendered by Hurr al-`Amili; and idem, Safaviyah dar arsah-i din, 1143–44. For the political career and ideas of Kamarah'i, see Ja`fariyan, "Andisha'ha-yi yik `alim-i Shi`i."

tobacco addicts. Kashani mentions wastefulness as another objectionable aspect of the water pipe. People spent large sums of money on devices studded with precious stones, all of which, he argues, merely detracts from the pursuit of religion.[93]

As well as from clerical leaders, tobacco encountered resistance from social commentators pursuing the traditional literary genre of *adab* literature, which paired entertainment with rules of etiquette and propriety. The author of one such treatise holds tobacco responsible for several diseases. Before tobacco became widespread, he notes, the disease of leprosy was rare. Sucking the air needed to smoke, he continues, also puts a strain on the roots of teeth and weakens them, and when the smoke reaches the chest it leads to coughing, as a result of which shortness of breath and suffocation occur and the body and mind are damaged and the human life span is shortened. He goes on to invoke a clearly apocryphal saying of Hippocrates to the effect that humans would live longer if there were no tobacco, as well as the thirteenth-century Muslim philosopher Ibn al-`Arabi, to whom the quote "At the end of time tobacco will appear and it will entice man, but it is one of Satan's temptations" is spuriously attributed. After a passage in which the author dwells on the danger of tobacco's bad fumes poisoning the liver and causing cholera, he ends his treatise by criticizing tobacco for not having anything to do with essentials such as food and drink, and smoking for being a frivolous pastime that causes people to fritter away their household money.[94]

From the colonial authorities in Mexico to the Zealots of Piety in Russia, from Catholic popes to Chinese emperors and Japanese shoguns, governments around the world in the seventeenth century issued decrees that outlawed smoking. Preachers and moralist, associating tobacco with vanity, idleness and dissolution, inveighed against the habit, but moral objections rarely played a decisive role in proscriptive measures. Some authorities were apprehensive that importing tobacco would exacerbate the outflow of bullion, the ultimate dread for mercantilists. It was, however, mostly the fear of fire that prompted early modern governments in Europe to curb public smoking. Such, for example, was the case in Russia and in many German states, where the ban on smoking was lifted no sooner than the 1848 revolution.[95] The contemporaneous Islamic world was no exception to this pattern. Following clerical disapproval, Muslim rulers tended to present and articulate prohibitive measures as a "return to the true faith," but it would be erroneous to take this rhetoric at face

---

[93] Ja`faryan, *Safaviyah dar arsah-i din*, 1091–92.
[94] Qazvini, "Dar Mazarrat-i dukhaniyat," 372–74.
[95] Matthee, "Exotic Substances."

value, for their real motives typically lay elsewhere or at least went beyond mere considerations of piety. The Mughal Emperor Jahangir banned smoking in 1617, convinced that its consumption created "disturbance in most temperaments."[96] Similar motives, spelled out in greater detail, are recorded in the Ottoman Empire, where tobacco was first proscribed in the reign of Sultan Ahmad (1603–17), who issued numerous bans on tobacco and the places where it was smoked. Of his successors, Sultan Murad IV (r. 1623–40) was most vehement in waging war on smoking. His aversion to tobacco derived as much from its religious status as innovation, bid`a, as from a concern with order and discipline, thought to be undermined by those who frequented tobacco shops, and his fear of political opposition by the Janissaries, who owned many of these establishments.[97] In 1627 a ban was issued on tobacco cultivation in Ottoman territory. Six years later the sultan, possibly persuaded by Istanbul's fiery Friday mosque preacher Kadizadeh Mehmet Efendi, used a huge fire that destroyed thousands of houses in Istanbul as a pretext to outlaw smoking and to close all coffee shops. Among those who were found smoking many were executed.[98]

In Safavid Iran, governmental attempts at curbing tobacco consumption are quite rare and limited to the reigns of Shah `Abbas I and Shah Safi I. His personal dislike for tobacco and concerns about the waste it represented seem to have motivated the former in his antismoking measures. Shah `Abbas outlawed the use of tobacco at an unspecified date in the early 1600s, apparently because his soldiers spent too much of their pay on smoking, and punished offenders by having their noses and lips cropped or even by having them burned.[99] He also is known to have ridiculed his smoking courtiers by offering them ground horse manure, claiming it was a special tobacco from Hamadan.[100]

Yet, as an anecdote related by the Frenchman Gabriel de Chinon illustrates, the shah lived up to his reputation for pragmatism in dealing with the tricky issues this measure raised. An Armenian cleric was found to have violated the shah's ban on smoking tobacco and was condemned by a judge in Isfahan to the usual burning at the stake. Khajah Nazar, the Armenian kalantar, mayor, of New Julfa, thereupon pleaded with the shah to offer clemency to the priest. The shah responded by saying that he could not contravene a law that he himself had promulgated and enforced so severely. He added, however, that he would make it easy

[96]Sangar, "Intoxicants in Mughal India," 210.
[97]Saraçgil, "Generi voluttuari e ragion di stato."
[98]Rycaut, History of the Turkish Empire, 1:52, 59, 71, 79; and Zilfi, "The Kadizadelis."
[99]al-Jaza'iri, al-Anwar al-nu`maniyah, 4:56.
[100]Chardin, Voyages, 3:306–7.

for the Armenian community to save the offender and ordered that the execution should take place in Julfa, where the Armenians would be able to rescue him from the hands of the executioner. This is indeed what happened. On the day of the execution, the fire was lighted and the priest was led to the pyre. Before the execution could take place, however, a group of women armed with sticks poured out of their houses and rescued the priest, having been ordered to do so beforehand by Khajah Nazar. Complaints to Shah ʿAbbas were futile, De Chinon concludes, as the ruler's response was that the Armenians were a difficult people to govern and that they were so keen on their priests that they all would rather be torn to pieces than have the shame of seeing one of them die ignominiously.[101]

Outlawing tobacco proved little successful in general, for it merely drove smokers underground—literally so, according to al-Jazaʾiri, who claims that people would dig holes in the ground to indulge in their passion, making sure to burn rags close by so that the smell would not be obvious.[102] The shah apparently found so many violators and so much contraband that in the end he was forced to give in to the passion of his people by allowing tobacco to be planted in public.[103] Yet, his resignation to the proliferation of the foul weed did not prevent him from proclaiming another ban in 1621.[104] This is likely to have been the one Thomas Herbert refers to for 1628.[105] If so, the measure remained in effect until the shah's death, only to be rescinded by his successor, Shah Safi, a few days after acceding to the throne in early 1629, as part of a series of measures designed to establish his legitimacy and to propitiate his subjects, many of whom, according to the contemporary Persian sources, had grievously suffered from the previous ban.[106] At least one eyewitness observed how the Shah Safi himself smoked shortly thereafter.[107] The same ruler is known to have banned tobacco several more times, for reasons that remain unknown, but each time the effect was minimal and the measure temporary.[108] Tobacco thus continued its unstoppable march in Iran, as it did everywhere else.

If it is not quite known what prompted Shah Safi to ban tobacco, one possible impulse behind his allowing or even encouraging smoking is

---

[101]de Chinon, *Relations nouvelles*, 262–63.

[102]al-Jazaʾiri, *al-Anwar al-nuʿmaniyah*, 4:56.

[103]Ange de St. Joseph, *Souvenirs de la Perse*, 1025.

[104]Verberckmoes and Stols, eds., *Aziatische omzwervingen*, 227.

[105]Herbert, *Travels in Persia*, 203.

[106]For the repeal of the ban, see Valah Qazvini-Isfahani, *Khuld-i barin*, 12; Isfahani, *Khulasat al-siyar*, 39; Qazvini, *Favaʾid al-Safaviyah*, 48.

[107]See Dunlop, ed., *Bronnen*, 738, Dairy Jan Smidt, 24 May 1629.

[108]Tavernier, *Les six voyages*, 1:599.

not far to seek. Many a European government in this same period banned tobacco and other stimulants only as long as the awareness had not set in that the stuff, aside from being an olfactory nuisance, was also a great source of revenue. In England, James I hated tobacco and even wrote a treatise lambasting it as a foul-smelling weed that corrupted morals and damaged the brain. Yet, rather than prohibiting smoking, he pragmatically ended up taxing it in 1608.[109] Iran was no different. Prohibitions, Tavernier noted, would never last long, for banning the sale and use of tobacco would cost the shah a great deal of money. Isfahan alone, he explained, yielded 40,000 *tumans* in annual revenue from taxing tobacco, whereas Tabriz brought in 20,000 and Shiraz 10,000 *tumans*.[110] Shah `Abbas I only relented in his abhorrence of tobacco to impose a tax on it, ostensibly to deal a blow to the tobacco trade and its consumption. The effect, however, was the opposite, and tobacco became a major source of government revenue.[111] A *farman* from 1709 declares the money annually levied on tobacco sales and road tolls (*rahdari*) in the northern town of Ganja to be 164 *tumans*, 1,640 *dinars*.[112] Sanson claimed a smaller but still respectable total state income from tobacco of 2,500,000 *livres*, or more than 55,000 *tumans* for the entire country (the magnitude of which can be gauged in relation to reported total royal annual revenue of 600,000 to 700,000 *tumans*).[113] Du Mans and Fryer, confirming the involvement of the state in tobacco consumption, claimed that "there is an heavy tax laid upon tobacco."[114]

Among the ulama, too, there were many who fell victim to the seductive properties of the herb or who in time came to realize that fighting tobacco was an exercise in futility. In the Ottoman Empire, *shaykh al-islam* Baha' al-Din Efendi in the 1650s declared smoking lawful, and, though tobacco was forbidden a few more times by the Ottoman authorities, both the state and the clergy ultimately resigned themselves to its spread.[115] The Iranian ulama, too, eventually gave in. Prominent clerics from the late Safavid period such as Muhammad b. al-Hasan al-Hurr al-`Amili (d. 1693), Mirza `Abd Allah Afandi Isfahani (d. 1718), and

---

[109]James I, *A Counterblast to Tobacco.*

[110]Tavernier, *Les six voyages*, 1:599.

[111]al-Jaza'iri, *al-Anwar al-nu`maniyah*, 4:56.

[112]In Musävi, *Orta äsr Azärbajän tarichinä dari fars dilindä jazilmyš sänädlar*, doc. 17.

[113]Sanson, *Voyage*, 99.

[114]See Du Mans, "`Estat' de 1660," in Richard, ed., *Raphaël du Mans*, 2:106; Fryer, *New Account*, 3:7.

[115]The muftis of Istanbul, Damascus and Cairo officially bowed to the widespread use of tobacco by permitting it in the late 1710s. See Rafeq, "Socioeconomic and Political Implications," 131.

Sayyid Ni`mat Allah al-Jaza'iri (d. 1700) stated that they were not convinced by the arguments of tobacco's foes. Afandi pragmatically argued that, even if the objections of antitobacco clerics were sound, they pertained to a time when addiction was not yet an issue. Now that it was, he said, giving up tobacco would cause harm and might even result in death.[116] Hurr al-`Amili neither smoked nor drank coffee. But, as he informed a curious Shah Sulayman during a disputation on coffee and tobacco, this only was because these substances did not accord with his disposition. He went on to state that he was not prepared to declare either religiously impermissible, because neither coffee nor tea was mentioned in the Koran or the writing of the Shi`i Imams.[117]

Clerics who themselves had succumbed to the habit probably had the strongest incentive to connive at smoking. Muhammad Taqi Majlisi, a prominent cleric, and his even more illustrious son, Muhammad Baqir Majlisi, are good examples of this. A fervent smoker, the former wrote a public pronouncement on tobacco that is rife with ambiguity and essentially accords with Hurr al-`Amili's opinion. Asked if he approved of tobacco, he said: If it has merit, *naf`*, it isn't bad, but if it has harm, *zarar*, it is bad. And if it has neither merit nor harm, there is the fear of wastefulness. It is better not to smoke, but if people smoke, I will not declare it *haram*, for it has to be harmful in the eye of the smoker. It is not appropriate for the ulama to declare it haram, for one does not speak out on things that are unknowable.[118] It is said that, in real life, he considered smoking permissible even during period of voluntary fasting (*sawm mustahabb* or *sawm al-tatawwu`*) and that he only refrained from tobacco at times of obligatory fasting (*sawm wajib*) so as to avoid controversy.[119] Muhammad Baqiri Majlis (d. 1699), *shaykh al-islam* of Isfahan and the preeminent cleric of his time, was an even greater tobacco aficionado. At times he asked for a water pipe during his lectures, and his addiction was such that he even smoked when preaching from the pulpit.[120] Needless to say, he put his generally hardline position on innovation aside to agree with his father that smoking was religiously permissible. An anecdote recounts how a contemporary cleric by the name of Khalil b. Ghazi Qazvini wrote a treatise in which he declared tobacco *haram*, and sent a copy to Majlisi wrapped in a piece of cloth. Majlisi is said to have read the treatise and to have returned it without the cloth,

[116]Ja`fariyan, ed., "Risalah fi bayan hukm shurb al-tutun wa'l qahwah," 84.
[117]Ibid., 91–92.
[118]Majlisi, "Kitab al-mas'ulat," 698–99.
[119]al-Jaza'iri, al-Anwar al-nu`maniyah, 4:55.
[120]Mahdavi, Zindiginamah-i `Allamah Majlisi, 1:188.

explaining in an accompanying note that of the treatise as presented to him only the cloth had been useful to him—to put tobacco in.[121]

Tobacco remained religiously sensitive beyond the days of Muhammad Baqir Majlisi. Of Muhammad Baqir Khatunabadi, the first *mullabashi* (court chaplain) in the early-eighteenth-century Safavid state, it is said that the grand vizier did not dare smoke tobacco except with his permission.[122] Yet, by this time, clerical resistance to tobacco was little more than a rearguard battle. As al-Jaza'iri `observed at the end of the Safavid era, "People have come to accept this weed so resoundingly that curbing it is no longer possible." His contemporary `Abd al-Hayy Razavi Kashani (d. 1739–40), exclaimed in similar vein: "The *qalyan* is so well known in east and west that its removal is no longer possible. In former times a ruler proscribed it everywhere and ordered the execution of addicts, and people were indeed killed on its account, but all to no avail."[123]

CONCLUSION

Iran may have been one of the first countries in the Eastern Hemisphere to become acquainted with tobacco. Indeed, if we are to believe the veracity and the dating of the poem written by the anonymous poet from Shiraz that refers to the water pipe, smoking may have been introduced decades before anyone outside the Iberian Peninsula became acquainted with tobacco.

All the evidence beyond the anonymous poem, most of it admittedly negative and circumstantial, points to a later date of tobacco's entry into Iran, however. Even the claim that Abu'l Fath Gilani was the first to draw water through the bowl of a water pipe in the late sixteenth century remains an isolated one. No narrative sources, indigenous or foreign, mention smoking before the 1590s, a date that seems in line with the first references to tobacco in other part of maritime Asia.

Even if the early date of its introduction is incorrect, it is clear that the people of Iran learned of tobacco earlier than most Europeans and that smoking had become a passionate pastime for ordinary people at a time

---

[121]Pampus, "Die theologische Enzyklopädie Biḥār al-Anwār," 45. Mahdavi, *Zindigi-namah-i `Allamah Majlisi*, 1:188, recounts a slightly different version, whereby Majlisi returned the cloth as well with the tobacco in it, with the words that he had read the treatise and could not think of a better reward for his colleague's labor than his return gift.

[122]Ja`fariyan, *Tarjumah-yi anajil-i arba`ah*, 50. See also Khatunabadi, *Vaqa'i` al-sannin*, 567–68.

[123]al-Jaza'iri, *al-Anwar al-nu`maniyah*, 4:56; and Kashani, "Hadiqat al-Shi`ah," in Ja`fariyan, *Din va siyasat dar dawrah-i Safavi*, 350.

when in the West the habit was still mostly limited to sailors and soldiers. Iranians took to smoking with such passion and abandon that the habit elicited comments of astonishment from various foreign observers marveling that people would forego their daily bread before giving up on tobacco. Everyone smoked, male and female, rich and poor. Smoking was differentiated by class according to the implements and their accoutrements rather than to the manner of smoking. The rich smoked *qalyans* made of glass or even precious metal, richly decorated and encrusted with gems, and employed their own water pipe bearers, while the poor sucked smoke through a reed stuck in a gourd or a coconut.

The intriguing water pipe was the most popular implement, and it is unfortunate that it remains impossible to penetrate its earliest history or even to confirm that it was indeed an Iranian invention, as common knowledge has it. Although it seems likely that the water pipe originates in India, it clearly made its way to Iran very quickly and reached its full development in the Safavid cultural milieu. It also seems likely that the *qalyan* and its capacity to serve as a conduit for different substances at least contributed to the speedy acceptance of smoking in the country.

As in the West, tobacco initially ran up against objections. Some, such as luxury and wastefulness, cross cultural divides. Others were peculiar to Islam with its suspicion of innovations not encountered in the Koran or known at the time of the Prophet and his companions. Muslim jurists decried tobacco, calling attention to its foul smell and associating it with substances that the Prophet had forbidden or deemed abhorrent. The government chipped in with its own arguments. Beyond a personal aversion in the case of Shah `Abbas I, and objections against perceived frivolousness and wastefulness, the motives often remain rather unclear. In the end, though, censure and proscription were unable to halt the advance of the herb that brought all, layman and cleric alike, under its spell around the globe. All fell for the foul weed, the state on account of the taxes it generated, everyone else, including hard-line clerics who were wont to reject innovation as un-Islamic, on account of its addictive properties.

CHAPTER 6

Coffee in Safavid Iran: Commerce and Consumption

ای سیاه رو که نام اوست قهوه   قاتل نوم قاطع شهوه

Oh black-faced one whose name is coffee, killer of sleep, destroyer of lust

Persian proverb[1]

INTRODUCTION

The introduction and popularization on a global scale of psychoactive substances such as tobacco, coffee, tea, and chocolate are inextricably bound up with the trade revolution that got under way after the European discovery of the Cape route to India at the turn of the sixteenth century.[2] Hitherto unknown to entire continents, these substances soon began to spread from South America or Asia and within 150 years after Columbus's American journey and Da Gama's rounding of the Cape of Good Hope had become staples of a vast trading network that brought them within reach of ever growing numbers of people around the globe.

Coffee, the only one of these stimulants not to originate in either South America or East Asia, was first cultivated in the lands that straddle the Red Sea, Ethiopia in northeast Africa and Yemen in southwest Arabia. With the exception of tea, coffee was also the only substance to spread beyond its original region of cultivation slightly prior to and independently from the tremendous European commercial expansion of the sixteenth and seventeenth centuries. It was, after all, to the Ottoman Empire that coffee was first introduced from Yemen after the Turks conquered Egypt and the Hijaz in the early sixteenth century. Coffee was known in Cairo by 1510, and the first coffeehouse in Damascus opened in 1530. In 1554 the inhabitants of the Ottoman capital, Istanbul, were able to savor the new drink. From Ottoman lands coffee spread to southeastern Europe, where it was sold in Venice in 1638, years before

[1] Quoted in Olearius, *Vermehrte newe Beschreibung*, 599.
[2] See Matthee, "Exotic Substances."

the English and Dutch East India companies began to ship the beans to Western Europe.

Ironically, whereas the introduction and dissemination of coffee in (northern) Europe is fairly well documented, until quite recently its history was much less well known in its west Asian lands of origin and early spread. The last two decades have brought change, so that the Ottoman Empire is now relatively well covered.[3] For Iran the situation remains more rudimentary. Nasrullah Falsafi and, more recently, Aladin Goushegir have looked into the history of coffee in early modern Iran, but the limited source material available to them has prevented their work from going much beyond a rather static focus on consumption.[4] This chapter seeks to expand our knowledge of coffee in Safavid Iran, by exploring aspects of its consumption—the identity of consumers, the function of coffeehouses in social and religious life and, most importantly, the reaction of the country's religious and political establishment to coffee and coffeehouses—but also through an examination of the maritime network that supplied it to the Persian Gulf ports, focusing on origins and channels of introduction, on merchants and on patterns of dissemination.

I. COMMERCE

It is unclear how much time it took for Iran to become familiar with coffee after it first spread from its origins in Ethiopia in the fifteenth century. The term under which it became known in Arabic and Persian, *qahwah* and *qahvah*, respectively, had been known in the Middle East since at least the eighth century C.E., but for more than half a millennium it referred to red wine. When the hot drink coffee made its appearance in Yemen it was initially called *bunn*.[5] Goushegir concludes on the basis of early-seventeenth-century commentators, who presumably borrowed from earlier authors, that coffee may have been known among some Iranian physicians and literati in the early sixteenth century.[6] Such an early date for a theoretical knowledge among Iranian men of letters is not implausible in light of the cosmopolitan intellectual milieu of the time. Yet, Badr al-Din al-Qusuni, whose treatise dates from 974/1566–67, insists

---

[3]See Hattox, *Coffee and Coffeehouses*; Brouwer, *Cauwa ende comptanten/Cowa and Cash*; and the contributions in Tuchscherer, ed., *Le commerce du café*.

[4]Falsafi, "Tarikh-i qahvah va qahvah-khanah"; and idem, *Zindigani-yi Shah ʿAbbas*, 2:353–6, 703–9; See also Goushegir, "Le café en Iran"; and idem, "Forme et évolution."

[5]Goushegir, "Forme et évolution," 174.

[6]Goushegir, "Le café en Iran," 77.

that he was unable to find any written references to coffee and that his knowledge was based on his own experience.[7]

Medical treatises are the first to mention coffee in Iran, reflecting the fact that, as in Europe, coffee in Safavid society was initially seen and used as a medicinal agent rather than as a tasty beverage. Early on there was also an association between the mildly intoxicating drink and popular mysticism. According to a well-known story, the Sufi Shaykh al-Shadhili was instrumental in the initial spread of coffee from Ethiopia to Yemen. As long as coffee remained restricted to Ethiopia and southern Arabia, that is, until the middle of the sixteenth century, the main consumers were members of Sufi orders. This may have been true in Iran as well, just as Sufis likely were instrumental in coffee's entry into the country. Salik al-Din Muhammad Hamavi Yazdi, the author of a late-sixteenth-century Persian treatise on stimulants, said that in Arab lands "everyone" and in Iran "most people are now used to drinking it." Claiming that in the Ottoman Empire and Iraq it was considered a necessity by the pious (*zuhhad va 'ubbad*) and the sinful (*ahl-i fisq va fisad*) alike, he also insisted that after becoming popular in Arab lands, especially Mecca, it now had spread to Iran as well.[8] The association between coffee and Sufism continued in Safavid Iran with the establishment of the coffeehouse and the role Sufis and itinerant dervishes played in it, both as customers and as popular storytellers.

In Europe, there was a considerable lag between the first mention and the popularization of coffee. European travelers and botanists discussed coffee in their travelogues and treatises long before it was consumed anywhere in the West. Some seventy-five years were to lapse between their first references to the drink and the establishment of the first coffeehouses in Italy, England and Holland, and it took another half century before coffee became truly popular in the West.[9] Something analogous may have been true in Iran, where a broader acquaintance with the drink as an article of consumption cannot be dated with any certainty before the turn of the seventeenth century. No Persian chronicle refers to coffee until the 1590s. Similarly, none of the foreign travelers and merchants who visited the country in the sixteenth century makes any mention of coffee as

---

[7]al-Qusuni, "Fi bayan ahwal al-qahwah," fol. 58.

[8]Hamavi Yazdi, "De veneris celeberrimis," fol. 54.

[9]The earliest example of a European traveler in the Middle East mentioning coffee is Leonhard Rauwolf, who learned of coffee in Aleppo in the 1570s, and referred to it in his *Aigentliche Beschreibung*, 102–3. Possibly the earliest scientific reference in Europe is from the hand of the Italian physician Prosper Alpinus in his *De plantis Aegypti liber* (Venice, 1592). Europe's first coffeehouse, in Venice, opened its doors in 1645. England followed in 1650; Holland in 1663–64. For an analysis of this time lag in the case of England, see Smith, "Early Diffusion of Coffee Drinking in England."

either a trade commodity or a consumer item.[10] A category of visitors who surely would have commented on the exotic beverage had it been served on official occasions are the foreign envoys and ambassadors who frequented Shah `Abbas I's court in great numbers.[11] The only one to do so until the 1620s was the Austrian envoy Georg Tectander, who visited Iran in 1602–04. In a likely reference to coffee, he reported that the Persians drank "boiled water with all kinds of spices" as an alternative to wine, which was prohibited.[12] But even in the Persian Gulf region, where coffee may have been first introduced, it was not common at that time, judging by the claim of the Portuguese friar Gaspar de S. Bernardino that the locals drank water mixed with raisins and sugar, clearly a reference to *sharbat*.[13]

Nor is this remarkable. It was only in the 1570s, with the establishment of Ottoman control over Yemen, the attendant rise of al-Mukha, and the stabilization of Ottoman-Portuguese trade relations in the Indian Ocean, that the trade in coffee took off in the Red Sea and beyond.[14] Coffee spread quickly throughout the region after that. Baghdad was the site of at least one coffeehouse in 1601,[15] and by the late sixteenth century coffee was common in small towns in Anatolia.[16] In 1609 India is said to have received coffee from Arabia. Iran is unlikely to have been bypassed on the way.[17] A small volume probably reached the country by way of the annual hajj caravan that returned to Iran via Basra. Caravans may have brought coffee to Masqat, and ships likely took the beans to the Iranian side of the Gulf, heavily Arab-influenced through language and trade links. Coffee may have also been imported via the desert route through Baghdad or via Tabriz by way of the east

[10]For the Portuguese and Italian travelers, see Barbosa, *Book of Duarte Barbosa*, 1:100ff; Pires, *Suma Oriental*, 1:28–31; Baiao, ed., *Itinerarios da India a Portugal*; Membré, *Mission to the Lord Sophy*; Tucci, "Relazione di Giovan Battista Vecchietti"; and Teixeira, *Travels*. The English accounts may be found in Morgan and Coote, eds., *Early Voyages*, 1:41–152; 2:384–414; and in Hakluyt, *Principal Navigations*, vol. 3.

[11]The various Russian embassies to Safavid Iran are discussed in Bushev, *Istoriia posol'stv, 1586–1612 gg.*; and *Istoriia posol'stv, 1613–1621 gg.* Other European missions include those of the Englishman Anthony Sherley, whose adventures are described in Sherley, *Sir Anthony Sherley*; and in Don Juan of Persia, *Don Juan of Persia*; of the Portuguese envoys to Iran in 1604–5, narrated in Gulbenkian, ed., *L'ambassade en Perse de Luis Pereira de Lacerda*; of the Portuguese Augustinian missionary-cum diplomat Antonio de Gouvea, *Relation des grandes guerres*; further documented in Alonso, "El P. Antonio de Gouvea O.S.A."; and idem, "La embajada persa de Denguiz-Beg."

[12]Tectander, *Eine abenteuerliche Reise*, 65–66.

[13] "água cozida com passas a açucar." See Bernardino, *Itinerário*, 140.

[14]See Tuchscherer, "Commerce et production du café en Mer Rouge."

[15]Teixeira, *Travels*, 61.

[16]Faroqhi, "Coffee and Spices," 92.

[17]Jourdain, *Journal of John Jourdain*, 86.

Anatolian trade route. And if trade was not the vehicle, the catalyst for the spread of coffee into Iran may well have been warfare, the other form of contact between the Ottoman and Safavid states. In particular, the near-continual state of hostilities in the late sixteenth century, which temporarily brought Iraq under Safavid control, may have been a conduit.

The introduction of coffee in Iran thus clearly predates the arrival of organized Western maritime trade in the form of the EIC and VOC at the northern shores of the Persian Gulf in the early seventeenth century. We know that in the early 1600s, at the time when the Europeans were just beginning to participate in the trade, coffee was already a known commodity in Iran's urban areas. The first reference to a coffeehouse in Iran dates from 1006/1597.[18] The construction of the coffeehouses that flanked the *maydan-i naqsh-i jahan* in Isfahan must have taken place in or shortly after 1603–04, when the square itself was finished and the buildings around it were completed.[19] An early witness to the existence of coffeehouses in the center of the capital is Don Garcia de Silva y Figueroa, who visited Isfahan as Spanish ambassador in 1619.[20] Pietro della Valle, who was in Iran between 1617 and 1622, also referred to the capital's familiarity with "cahue."[21] Incontrovertible evidence that coffee was imported into Iran at that time is moreover provided by the observation of an EIC official in 1618 about coffee being "worth heere 24 (25 and 26) shahees per maen which is brought from Mocca to the Indies and from thence transported into these partes (used to bee drunke heere as tobacco in England for idlenesse, it is to be had at Mecca)."[22]

Although nothing is known about the antecedents of local suppliers, the first EIC suggestion that coffee might be shipped to Iran was made in 1619, long before the directors in London requested it for the home market. In that year the EIC agent in Surat informed his colleague at al-Mukha, the source of the beans, that "the factors in Persia advisinge for commodities there vendable, do mencion cowha to be there worth 24 shahee the 13 parte of royall of eight."[23] As it happened, however, the coffee in question, presumably shipped by so-called Surat merchants, was more profitable in Surat, its first port of destination, and thus was never transshipped to Iran's main gateway, Bandar `Abbas.[24] It is quite unclear

[18]Khuzani Isfahani, "Afzal al-tavarikh." fol. 100b.

[19]Junabadi, *Rawzat al-Safaviyah*, 760; and Munajjim Yazdi, *Tarikh-i `Abbasi*, 236.

[20]Silva y Figueroa, *Comentarios*, 2:380.

[21]Della Valle, *Viaggi*, 2:25. See also Zolli, "Il caffè di Pietro della Valle," 64–65.

[22]Ferrier, "An English View of Persian Trade," 208. The *shahi* was a small Safavid coin.

[23]Foster, ed., *English Factories in India, 1618–1621*, 83, Kerridge, Surat to factors at al-Mukha, 15 March 1619.

[24]Ibid., 143–4, Kerridge, Surat to Barker, Persia, 29 October and 6 November 1619.

The *Maydan-i naqsh-i jahan*, Royal Square, in Isfahan, late Safavid period. Cornelis de Bruyn, *Reizen over Moskovie, door Persie en Indie* (Amsterdam, 1714).

how much coffee the English managed to import, if any at all, during these early years, either directly from al-Mukha or, more likely, via Surat, for the next entry in the records pertaining to coffee is again a negative one. William Bell, reporting from the interior, noted in early 1622 that "Cowha [. . .] in seeds is an excelent commodity in these parts, and is worth at present in Spahan 50 shahees the maunde shah. Regret that none was sent from Surat, owing to the late arrival of the Mokha iurk."[25]

The Dutch, the main competitors of the English in the Persian Gulf, were not standing by idly in the meantime. Indeed, of the European maritime companies it was the VOC which first opened up the seaborne coffee trade from the source in Yemen, although the Dutch were not the first to explore commercial opportunities in Arabia Felix.[26] VOC agent Pieter van den Broecke had learned about the "little black beans" as early as 1616, and the Dutch soon established a factory in order to initiate the trade in coffee to other parts of Asia.[27] Coffee, however, did not figure as a commodity in the first decade of the Western exploration of the Yemeni market. It was not until 1628 that the VOC first bought coffee destined for the Iranian market. In that year, Job Christiaansz. Gryph is said to have purchased 40 *bahar* or cica 15,000 pounds in al-Mukha in the hope that it would yield a 70 percent profit in Iran.[28]

After this initial foray into the coffee trade in the early 1620s, political unrest in Yemen and hostilities between Arabs and Turks in the Red Sea prevented the Company from supplying the Iranian market until the 1638–39 season, when the Dutch agent in Iran requested a shipment of 2,000 *man*, or circa 60,000 pounds.[29] Responding to the great demand for coffee in Iran as well as to expanding commercial opportunities at al-Mukha, the VOC equipped a ship from Batavia laden with sugar, spices and chinaware. Of its return cargo, 4,880 Dutch pounds of coffee were brought ashore in Bandar ʿAbbas. Bought for five *stuivers* per pound in

---

[25]Foster, ed., *English Factories in India, 1622–1623*, 23, Bell et al. at "Kuhestek" to Surat, 24 January 1622.

[26]The English first explored commercial opportunities at al-Mukha in 1609–10 and 1611, but were unsuccessful in setting up a factory. See Macro, *Yemen and the Western World Since 1571*, 4–5.

[27]For the early history of the Dutch presence in Yemen as well as the VOC coffee trade conducted from al-Mukha, see Brouwer, *Cauwa ende comptanten/Cowa and Cash*, and the chapter on coffee in Glamann, *Dutch Atlantic Trade*.

[28]Brouwer, *Cauwa ende comptanten/ Cowa and Cash*, 49. A *bahar* was 194.5 kg.

[29]See Dunlop, ed., *Bronnen*, 617. The *man* used for coffee seems to have been the so-called Surat *man* of thirty pounds. For this unrest, see IOR E/3/11, Relation of William Knightbridge concerning the passages of the Mocho trade in the Red Sea from June 1625 until August 1629, fols. 36–37.

al-Mukha, the beans were sold in Iran for 122, that is, at a 150 percent gross profit. The company directors in Batavia, the Asian headquarters of the VOC, expressed their satisfaction at this result. As long as profits on coffee in Iran continued to be this high, they noted, it would not be advisable to transport any to Holland beyond a small sample.[30]

Al-Mukha thus seemed to be turning into a successful westward addition to the widening intra-Asian network from which the Dutch Company trade derived much of its viability. The ideal for each Asian factory was a balance between the goods it exported and those it received as return cargo. Yemen in this scheme was to yield coffee and bullion, and in return would absorb Indian cloth and spices. In ideal circumstances, this reciprocity might guarantee great profitability but, as the Europeans were soon to discover, the feasibility of conducting trade with Yemen was determined by a number of variables, of which profits on coffee was only one.

If coffee deliveries by the companies to Iran proved irregular, this was in part because of price fluctuations, caused by the variable quality and quantity of the harvest in Yemen as well as by the state of the market in Iran and elsewhere in southwest Asia.[31] What exacerbated these uncertainties of the market, however, was the companies' fundamental weakness, their insufficient control over production, transportation, and distribution networks. This weakness began in Yemen, where the foreign companies failed to penetrate both the production process and the transport system between the coast and the highlands where the coffee was cultivated. The process of procurement and transportation to the coast preceding the sale at the market of Bayt al-Faqih, where the local merchants tended to purchase their coffee, involved a system of advance payment and middlemen that put outsiders such as the Europeans, who traded on the coast, at a distinct disadvantage. Put simply, local, Arab, merchants were in a better position to buy cheaply because they were able to make direct purchases from the cultivators.[32]

The vagaries of maritime transportation further contributed to the precariousness of conducting trade with Yemen. The circumscribed nature of the shipping season—ships had to reach the Red Sea before the monsoon winds turned against them in late May—mandated careful

[30]Coolhaas, ed., *Generale Missiven, 1639–1655*, 18 December 1639, 39; 30 November 1640, 114–15. The pound used by the Dutch was the so-called Amsterdam pound, equaling 494.090 grams. Coffee was indeed barely known in Holland, or anywhere in northern Europe for that matter. It was only in 1641 that the VOC directors in Amsterdam requested a first sample. See NA, VOC 316, Copiebrieven, 5 September 1641, fol. 340.

[31]Chaudhuri, *Trading World of Asia*, 366–67.

[32]Brouwer, *Cauwa ende Comptanten/Cowa and Cash*, 63.

timing at the risk of nondelivery.[33] Piracy, moreover, was a problem that continually jeopardized the security of the route between the Red Sea and the Persian Gulf.

On the receiving end of the line connecting Yemen with the Persian Gulf, control eluded the Europeans as well. From the limited information preserved in the English and Dutch maritime sources on trade procedures, it is evident that, having been brought ashore in Bandar ʿAbbas, coffee was purchased by the same wholesale merchants who bought most wares from the Western companies and private merchants. These merchants then transported and distributed the beans to various parts of the country by caravan. Little is known about the logistics. A rare glimpse of the inland trade comes from a Persian source from the 1670s, which states that coffee was offered for sale by merchants from Lar in the Maqsud ʿAssar caravanserai at Isfahan.[34] We also know that coffee was carried far into the interior, as far as Khurasan.[35] In 1689 a caravan carrying coffee, among other merchandise, between Bandar ʿAbbas and Herat was robbed in the vicinity of Kirman.[36] The maritime companies had no role in any part of this distribution system.

Competition, from private Western and local merchants alike, proved to be the main obstacle to commercial success for the Europeans. A year after the initial venture, an encouraged VOC sent another ship to Yemen, this time sailing from Surat with a cargo that consisted, aside from spices, of cotton cloth, and returning with, among other things, coffee for Iran. The spices presented no problem and yielded a handsome profit, but of the cloth only half was sold. Indian cloth proved to be just as hard to vend in the next few years, and disappointing gross profits of just 15 percent resulting from subsequent journeys to al-Mukha obviously dimmed the enthusiasm of the Dutch. This was to become a pattern, until in 1654 the VOC directors decided that coffee neither repaid the effort involved in the precise timing of its purchase and delivery, nor compensated for the Company's miserable overall trade performance in Yemen, and issued an order to halt the direct trade to al-Mukha.[37]

In Iran itself, meanwhile, rapidly growing competition made the initial coffee euphoria short-lived as well. Coffee cups, an ancillary commodity the VOC had begun to import, continued to be in great demand

---

[33]Ovington, *Voyage to Suratt*, 450.

[34]"Dar danestan-e karavansaraha-ye Esfahan"; facsimile and German trans. in Gaube and Wirth, *Der Bazar von Isfahan*, 274.

[35]IOR, E/3/52/6285, Lee, Mashhad to Owen, Gombroon, 9 October 1696, unfol.

[36]Mashizi (Bardsiri), *Tazkirah-i Safaviyah-i Kirman*, 566–67.

[37]NA, VOC 317, Copiebrieven, 8 October 1654, fol. 402r–v.

and commanded good prices.[38] Coffee itself, however, quickly fell in price from the 37½ *larins* per Surat *man* of 30 pounds it had commanded in Bandar ʿAbbas in 1638 to 29 a year later, a decline that was because of competition by the English and Portuguese, the latter selling coffee in Kung for 25 *larins*.[39] Subsequent years, which witnessed an overall trade slump in Iran, brought no improvement. In January 1641 the VOC director in Bandar ʿAbbas, Geleynssen de Jongh, lamenting that prices had dropped to 23 *larins* and that the latest supply lay unsold, suggested that no more coffee should be sent from al-Mukha.[40] Nor was this the nadir. In April of the same year the price in Bandar ʿAbbas fell to a new low of 20 *larins*,[41] whereas the town's index for commodity prices for May registered an even lower price of 16.[42] In al-Mukha, meanwhile, competition from English and Gujarati merchants drove up retail prices.[43] As a result, in this entire period EIC sources only record one coffee delivery, transshipped via Surat, in April of 1641.[44]

Private traders fared better than the companies. In the following year private English merchants and Gujarati traders imported the considerable amount of 150,200 pounds from al-Mukha.[45] By contrast, the VOC during the shipping season of 1642 carried 100 bales or 29,100 pounds to Iran, where they were sold at 19 *larins* per Surat *man*.[46]

Although the VOC sources are scanty in their information on the company's coffee dealings in the period from 1642 to 1655, they yield enough data to gain an impression of the quantities of Dutch imports into Iran. As Table 1 shows, the VOC in this period delivered a total annual average of approximately one hundred thousand pounds in Bandar ʿAbbas. Other

[38]The VOC in 1636 calculated that an annual total of two hundred thousand coffee cups might be profitably imported into Iran. See Dunlop, ed., *Bronnen*, 565. In 1644–45, the VOC indeed sold 268,998 cups in Iran, and for years shipped an average of 50,000 to Bandar ʿAbbas. See NA, VOC 1152, Sarcerius, Gamron to Batavia, 11 March 1651, fol. 84.

[39]NA, VOC 1133, Westerwolt, Gamron to Pieterssen, Surat, 4 December 1639, fol. 409v. The *larin* was the most widely used currency in the Persian Gulf region for most of the sixteenth and the early part of the seventeenth century. The *larin* was valued at 10 Dutch *stuivers* or Hfl. 0.50.

[40]NA, Coll. Geleynssen de Jongh 97a, Gel. De Jongh, Gamron to Croocq, Gujarat, 11 January 1641, unfol.

[41]NA, VOC 1135, Gel. De Jongh, Gamron to Batavia, 5 April 1641, fol. 800.

[42]NA, VOC 1135, Price list Gamron, May 1641, fol. 733.

[43]Van Santen, *Verenigde Oost-Indische Compagnie*, 60; Brouwer, *Cauwa ende Comptanten/Cowa and Cash*, 90.

[44]NA, VOC 1135, List of shipping movements at Gamron, 29 December 1640–28, April 1641, fol. 770.

[45]NA, VOC 1144, Gel. de Jongh, Gamron to Batavia, 25 February 1643, fol. 541; idem in NA, Coll. Geleynssen de Jongh 158, unfol.

[46]NA, Coll. Geleynssen de Jongh 157a, Gel. de Jongh, Gamron to Croocq, Surat, 9 February 1643, unfol.

TABLE 1
VOC coffee deliveries in Bandar `Abbas, 1642–53, in Dutch pounds

1642–43	39,100	1648–49	120,600
1643–44	96,201	1649–50	120,000
1644–46	none	1650–51	156,000
1646–47	55,485	1651–52	78,337½
1647–48	125,333	1652–53	126,880

Sources: NA, VOC 1150, 1152, 1165, 1168, 1170, 1180, 1185, 1188, 1195, 1201; Coll. Geleynssen de Jongh 157a.

than the 1644–46 period, when no coffee was bought because of exceedingly high prices in al-Mukha, quantities remained fairly constant and prices and profits were generally deemed acceptable. Table 2 shows how prices in Bandar `Abbas's competitive market fluctuated between 25 and 15 *larins* per pound in the period from 1640 to 1656. (The high price of 1655 possibly reflects the withdrawal of the VOC from the al-Mukha coffee market and the resultant drop in supply to Iran.) Profits, by contrast, steadily eroded from the year 1645, which saw gains of 71 percent, to 41 and 50½ percent in 1647, and further down to almost 28 percent in 1651, before they rose again to almost 70 percent in 1653.[47]

TABLE 2
Coffee prices in Bandar `Abbas 1638–56, per pound, in *larins*

1638	37½	1648	15
1639	25–29	1649	18
1640	16–20	1650	16
1641	22–24	1651	18½
1642–43	18–19	1652	17¾
1644	20	1653	24
1645	23	1655	34–38
1646–47	23	1656	24

Sources: NA, VOC 1135, 1137, 1141, 1150, 1152, 1165, 1168, 1180, 1185, 1188, 1195, 1201, 1215; Coll. Geleynssen de Jongh 157a, 162, 171, 296, 296a.

[47] See NA, VOC 1152, Constant, Gamron to Batavia, 11 March 1645, fol. 85; VOC 1165, Verburgh, Gamron to Batavia, 19 March 1647, fol. 170v; VOC 1168, Verburgh, Gamron to Batavia, 19 December 1647, fol. 774v; VOC 1185, Sarcerius, Gamron to Batavia, 25 March 1651, fol. 578v; VOC 1180, Boudaen, Basra to Batavia, 18 Aug 1651, fol. 824; VOC 1201, Sarcerius, Gamron to Batavia, 5 April 1653, fol. 779v.

Disappointing sales in al-Mukha and the hazards of navigation following the outbreak of the First Anglo-Dutch War (1652–54) made the
VOC directors decide to suspend direct shipping from Surat and the
Persian Gulf to al-Mukha. Very little coffee appears to have been imported by the Dutch for a number of years after this decision was taken,
for coffee does not figure in any of the subsequent lists of goods sold by
the VOC in Bandar 'Abbas Indeed, aside from a 22,102-pound consignment in early 1661, none are recorded.[48] The English appear to have
concentrated their activity in the period around 1650 on the Basra coffee market, which for a few years yielded them considerable profits.[49]
The Dutch, always keen on keeping track of their main competitors,
only recorded a combined English private and company delivery of 700
bahar or more than 250,000 pounds to Bandar 'Abbas for 1656.[50] All in
all, from 1655 until the early 1680s, when the private trade again
opened up in al-Mukha, the English and the Dutch only occasionally ex-
pedited a ship to Yemen with the intent of exploring the market. None
of these ad-hoc missions proved particularly successful, however.[51]

Following the resumption of normal trade links with Yemen in the late
1680s dramatic changes occurred in the coffee trade with Iran. For one,
the safety of shipping lanes became permanently endangered, in the Red
Sea as well as in the Persian Gulf basin.[52] Most significant, however, was
that the development of a new and more promising market for coffee
lessened the attractiveness of supplies to the Persian Gulf area. As prices
dropped in Bandar 'Abbas, a demand for coffee was emerging in northwestern Europe. Before long, this resulted in a shift in the destination of
most of the coffee shipped by the maritime companies. Amsterdam received its first coffee supply of 22,102 pounds in 1661,[53] whereas in
England, where the first coffeehouses had opened their doors in the 1650s,
the drink had already become "quite popular" by that time.[54] Because of

[48]Van der Chijs, ed., *Dagh-Register Batavia, 1661*, 3.

[49]NA, VOC 1180, Daghregister Basra, 12 August, 1651, fol. 877; Boudaen, Basra to
Batavia, 18 August 1651, fol. 824; Boudaen, Basra to Heren XVII, 5 October 5 1651,
fol. 824; VOC 1188, Boudaen, Basra to Heren XVII, 21 August 1652, fol. 493v.

[50]In NA, VOC 1210, Willemsz., Gamron to Van Wijck, Isfahan, 27 August 1656,
fol. 416v; idem in VOC 1217, fol. 372v; VOC 1224, Willemsz., Gamron to Heren XVII,
21 November 1656, fol. 320v.

[51]See NA, VOC 317, Copiebrieven, 12 April 1656, fol. 431; 13 October 1656,
fol. 465; VOC 882, 21 September 1658, fol. 489.

[52]Ovington, *Voyage to Suratt*, 464, mentions how the war between the English and the
Mughals in 1687 as well as the activities of European pirates in subsequent years ruined a
number of Arab, Turkish, and Indian merchants. For the Persian Gulf, see also Das Gupta,
Indian Merchants, 71–72.

[53]Van der Chijs, ed., *Dagh-Register Batavia, 1661*, 13 January 1661, 3.

[54]Coolhaas, ed., *Generale Missiven, 1655–74*, 16 January 1660, 310.

this early domestic demand the English rose to the occasion well before the Dutch. They imported 44,912 pounds in 1664, a quantity that was to go up to almost 300,000 pounds in 1690.[55] VOC orders, by contrast, only reached a quantity of 50–60,000 pounds as of 1686, and it was only in the 1690s, when consumption took off and the English threatened to corner the al-Mukha market, that the VOC directors insisted on receiving vastly increased supplies.[56] This trend continued into the eighteenth century; orders went up from 200,000 pounds in 1700–01 to one million in 1712.[57]

VOC interest in the domestic Iranian coffee market had long waned by that time. Yet, the vast quantities requested from Holland and the continued insecurity of supplies from al-Mukha made that the Persian Gulf continued to play a role in the Dutch involvement in the coffee trade. Surat and Bandar ʿAbbas, and even Malabar were mobilized to supplement the huge orders, to the point where local VOC agents were ordered to spend the available funds on coffee rather than on other, less lucrative wares.[58] In the later seventeenth century, the VOC also received some of its coffee supply, including that destined for the home market, from Masqat, which in the early 1680s developed into a prominent coffee market.[59]

The importance of this Persian Gulf transshipment connection can be gauged from the fact that in the last decade of the seventeenth century, before the regular shipping link with al-Mukha was reestablished, a request for coffee destined for the Dutch home market was invariably included in the order to Iran. The volume of these demands was continually high. For the period 1689–91, the Amsterdam directors requested 75,000 to 80,000 pounds each year. This slackened to annual figures fluctuating between 20,000 and 50,000 pounds in the period from 1694 to 1701. No amount even approaching these figures was ever supplied in these years, however, for little coffee could be procured in the insecure climate that began to prevail in the Persian Gulf.[60] As Portuguese-Omani rivalry intensified in the late seventeenth century, piracy increasingly plagued the shipping lanes around Masqat. Matters became particularly serious in 1695, when merchants from al-Mukha were apprehensive to

[55]Chaudhuri, "Kahwa, Trade with Europe," 454.

[56]See NA, VOC 323, Copiebrieven, 24 August 1694; 7 September 1696, unfol.

[57]NA, VOC 1635, Instructie voor ondercoopman Dirk Clercq, 28 March 1701, fol. 759v; VOC 325, Copiebrieven, 1 August 1712, unfol.

[58]NA, VOC 323, Copiebrieven, 31 July 1697, 27 June 1699; VOC 325, Copiebrieven, 1 August 1712, unfol.

[59]See, for example, NA, VOC 1476, Van Leene, Gamron to Heren XVII, 29 Nov 1690, fols. 496v–97r.

[60]NA, VOC 110-112, Resoluties Heren XVII, 1687–1699, unfol.

venture into the Gulf after the Omani Arabs raided and partly destroyed the Iranian port city of Kung, where the Portuguese had a stronghold.[61] This naturally contributed to high coffee prices at Masqat and made the VOC in Iran reluctant to buy any quantities for either the Iranian or the home market.[62] Basra, riven by massive unrest and civil war at the turn of the eighteenth century, was no alternative either.

Political turmoil and commercial insecurity continued into the early eighteenth century. The control they gained over the important islands in the Gulf, from Qishm to Hurmuz and Bahrain, enabled the Omani Arabs to dominate trade in the entire Gulf, or at least obstruct that of others. As a result of growing insecurity—at times Omani ships even attacked targets in the Red Sea—the need for vessels to travel in convoy protected by Dutch armed ships, became common as of the late seventeenth century.[63] All this is reflected in continually high prices for coffee in Iran.[64]

The VOC by this time had shifted its coffee routes. Most of the coffee the Company purchased in Yemen after 1700 appears to have been destined for the home market and was transshipped via Surat, Ceylon, and Batavia.[65] But Yemen itself was to be engulfed by turmoil as well. Political strife and the ruler's extortion of the merchant community in the 1720s proved extremely harmful to commerce and motivated the Europeans to try and find alternative coffee markets. In 1723 the price of coffee in al-Mukha, added to the ever-increasing marginal expenses, had become so high and profits so low that the VOC thought of giving up its factory in Yemen.[66] This did not happen, but as of the 1720s the main reason for a continued Dutch presence in al-Mukha became maintaining high coffee prices through manipulation in order to safeguard the production in new areas of cultivation. Java, and to a lesser extent Ceylon, became the principal coffee-producing regions for the Dutch. In 1721 coffee purchases in al-Mukha still exceeded those made in Java nine to one; in 1726 the proportion had become the exact reverse.[67]

[61]NA, VOC 926, Batavia's Uitgaand Briefboek, 21 October 1695, fol. 1683.

[62]NA, VOC 1598, Bergaigne, Gamron to Batavia, 31 August 1697, fol. 10.

[63]See, for example, Coolhaas, ed., *Generale Missiven 1698–1713*, 29 Nov. 1710, 705; 30 November 1711, 792; NA, VOC 1635, Instructie voor coopman Dirk Clercq, 28 March 1701, fol. 746; VOC 1660, Rapport reis naar Mokka van Dirck Clercq, 1701, fol. 807. For a description of the convoy system between India and Yemen, see Das Gupta, *Indian Merchants*, ch. 2.

[64]MAE, Paris Corr. pol., Perse 5, Projet de commerce pour les français en Perse et dans le sein persique et aux Indes (1718), fols. 200–5.

[65]Coolhaas, ed., *Generale Missiven, 1713–1725*, 26 November 1714, 119; 18 February 1715, 156.

[66]Ibid., 735. For a confirmation of the high coffee prices in the early eighteenth century, see the price chart of coffee sold in Cairo, in Raymond, *Artisans et commerçants au Caire*, 1:70.

[67]Knaap, "Coffee for Cash," 36.

How did the indigenous trading network fare in this entire period? Although the European foray into the coffee trade undoubtedly affected the business of the Arab and Gujarati merchants who plied their vessels around the Arabian Peninsula, there is clear evidence that the latter continued to ship coffee to the Persian Gulf region. Indeed, there is little doubt that the local merchants never ceased to surpass the European companies in the quantities they supplied. Already in the 1648–49 season the EIC noted that the trade between Surat and Jiddah and al-Mukha had "decreased, from the great number of Arabian ships which had been employed by it."[68] In the same season the four hundred packs of coffee delivered from Masqat were said to have caused a glut in the Isfahan market.[69] A similar reference is found in the 1655 reports that attributed the decline in coffee prices to the great supply by "Moorish" ships to Basra, Masqat, and Bandar 'Abbas.[70] In 1675 a VOC missive noted that the company could easily have sold its coffee for a good price in Bandar 'Abbas were it not for the cheap supply of six hundred to eight hundred pounds from Kung by Banyan (Indian) merchants, which forced the Dutch to lower their price as well.[71]

We saw how much of the indigenous coffee trade that served Iran used Masqat, which emerged as an entrepôt of Arab and Gujarati traders after the Omani Arabs took the city from the Portuguese in 1650.[72] Its low customs rate of 2½ percent—as opposed to at least 10 percent in Bandar 'Abbas—attracted a great quantity of merchandise, much of which was subsequently taken to the numerous ports beside Bandar 'Abbas that fell outside the purview of the Safavid toll masters as well as that of the European company agents. In 1664 it was said that 125 to 150 ships had docked at Masqat in one year, a number that far surpassed the traffic at either Bandar 'Abbas or Kung.[73]

After 1654, when the VOC ceased to buy coffee directly in al-Mukha, the role of Arab and Gujarati traders can only have increased. An EIC letter, written in 1674 from Surat, noted that coffee of late had become more expensive because of "the great quantities being carried to Egypt, Basra, and Persia."[74] The coffee that was sold in Iran in the 1690s was

[68]Bruce, *Annals of the Honourable East-India Company*, 1:428–29.

[69]NA, VOC 1178, Sarcerius, Gamron to Batavia, 16 October 1649, fol. 629; idem in Sarcerius, Gamron to Surat, 16 October 1649, fol. 634r–634v.

[70]NA, VOC 1215, Sarcerius, Gamron to Surat, 6 October 1655, fol. 800; VOC 1210, Sarcerius, Gamron to Heren XVII, 23 October 1655, fol. 852.

[71]NA, VOC 1297, Bent, Gamron to Heren XVII, 1 April 1675, fol. 1010v.

[72]NA, VOC 1261, Generale Missiven, 5 October 1667, fol. 88v.

[73]NA, VOC 1242, Van Wyck, Gamron to Heren XVII, 20 June 1664, fol. 1091.

[74]IOR, G/36/87, 2nd ser., Swally to London, 12 January 1674, fol. 85.

apparently all shipped in Arab vessels.[75] In 1705 and 1706 VOC reports from Basra speak of "trankies" (local boats) taking sugar and coffee from al-Mukha via Masqat and Kung.[76] In 1714, finally, Iranian merchants operating in al-Mukha were transporting considerable amounts of coffee home every year.[77]

Nor did the overland supply, delivered via the traditional caravan trade, cease to exist as a result of either the European company activity or the indigenous maritime supply. Coffee from Yemen in the early eighteenth century apparently continued to pass Tabriz in transit to Erzurum.[78] Some of this may have gone north, for a French report from the same period mentions that Armenian merchants transported coffee from Iran to Moscow.[79] Much earlier, the Dutch had pointed at Tabriz as the city where more coffee was traded than anywhere else in Iran.[80] Some coffee destined for Iran continued to come from Arabia via the caravan trade. In the course of the eighteenth century, however, the abovementioned shift in the main areas of coffee cultivation began to affect the supply line to Iran as well: Java began to surpass al-Mukha as the major supplier of coffee consumed in Iran.[81]

II. Consumption

As in contemporary Europe and the Ottoman Empire, coffee in Safavid Iran was known as a beverage with medicinal properties. De Silva y Figueroa, noting that the Persians considered coffee a medicine as much as an agreeable drink, specifically drew attention to their belief that coffee was salutary for the stomach.[82] Don Garcia's claim is corroborated in various seventeenth-century medical and botanical dictionaries that discuss coffee on the basis of the humoral pathology of Galenic medicine. Echoing a contemporary (though not unanimous) European conviction, these treat coffee as a cold (*barid*) and dry (*yabis*) substance that causes

---

[75]Coolhaas, ed., *Generale Missiven, 1686–1697*, 8 February 1696, 772.

[76]NA, VOC 1732, Macare, Basra to Casteleyn, Gamron, 9 November 1705, fol. 414; and idem in ibid., 20 December, fol. 575; and VOC 1747, Macare, Basra to Casteleyn, Gamron, 14 July 1706, fol. 317.

[77]NA, VOC 1856, Everts, al-Mukha to Batavia, 21 August 1714, fol. 38.

[78]Zarinebaf-Shahr, "Tabriz under Ottoman Rule," 190–91.

[79]MAE, Paris Corr. pol, Perse 5, fol. 188.

[80]NA, VOC 1133, Westerwolt, Gamron to Pieterssen, Surat, 4 December 1639, fol. 409v.

[81]Polak, *Persien*, 2:267.

[82]Silva y Figueroa, *Comentarios*, 2:380.

insomnia and weakens sexual desire.[83] The pharmacologist Hamavi Yazdi seems to have expressed a majority view among his colleagues in writing that the dryness of coffee prevailed over its coldness.[84] In his early-seventeenth-century treatise, he hails coffee as beneficial against fatigue and exhaustion (a`ya va kuftigi), as well as tenseness of the muscles. The author also cites its reputation as a cure for hemorrhoids, but doubts the veracity of this.[85] The *Alfaz al-adviyah* asserts that coffee *causes* hemorrhoids, in addition to colic, consumption, and nightmares, but also lists some remedial benefits such as its curative effect on gastric weakness and, in general, on ailments carried by people with phlegmatic and humid temperaments.[86] The author of the *Tuhfah-i Hakim Mu'min* confirmed the salutary working on the stomach and in addition called coffee an agent effective against phlegmatic cough, catarrh, in soothing boiling blood, and in the removal of fatigue, measles, blood rashes, and vapors.[87] Olearius referred to a belief among Iranians that coffee killed the libido.[88]

As well as being regarded as a drink with medicinal qualities, coffee in late Safavid Iran was considered what it has universally become: a tasty beverage consumed in a social setting. Drunk hot and without sugar from little china cups, it was often served with sweets and pistachio nuts, both of which enhanced its flavor, as Tunakabuni asserted.[89] Coffee, Kaempfer noted, was predominantly a winter drink; in the summer Iranians preferred sherbets.[90]

---

[83]Tunakabuni, *Tuhfah-yi Hakim Mu'min*, 697; al-Qusuni, "Fi bayan ahwal al-qahwah," fol. 58; Seligmann, ed., "Ueber drey höchst seltene persische Handschriften," 40–41; and Qazvini, "Dar mazarrat-i dukhaniyat," 373. See also Goushegir, "Le café en Iran," 82; and Matthee, "Exotic Substances." European pharmacological opinion agreed on the dryness of coffee but could not agree on whether it was hot or cold. See Weinberg and Bealer, *The World of Coffee*, 99–100.

[84]Hamavi Yazdi, "De venenis celeberrimis," fol. 54.

[85]Ibid.

[86]Seligmann, "Ueber drey höchst seltene persische Handschriften," 40–41.

[87]Tunakabuni, *Tuhfah-i Hakim Mu'min*, 697.

[88]Olearius, *Vermehrte newe Beschreibung*, 414.

[89]Tunakabuni, *Tuhfah-i Hakim Mu'min*, 697. The habit of drinking coffee without sugar can be deduced from the various references to the bitterness of the drink. Don Garcia, for example, called coffee "muy amarga." See Silva y Figueroa, *Comentarios*, 2:380. Thomas Herbert described coffee as "a drink imitating that in the Stigian lake, black, thick, and bitter." See Herbert, *Some Years Travel*, 241. Later negative evidence also suggests that coffee was not sweetened. Olivier at the turn of the nineteenth century noted that villagers laughed at the habit of Europeans of putting sugar and milk in their coffee, as well as of drinking it when eating bread. See Olivier, *Voyage dans l'Empire Othoman*, 5:119. Polak, *Persien*, 2:267, claimed that Iranians often added a little cinnamon to their coffee. Valentyn, *Oud-en nieuw Oost-Indiën*, 5:195, observed that in the Ottoman Empire cardamom was sometimes added to coffee. Della Valle, *Viaggi*, 1:75, confirms this and also asserts that the Turks did add sugar to their coffee. Tectander, *Eine abenteuerliche Rise*, 65–66, refers to the addition of spices to coffee.

[90]Kaempfer, *Am Hofe des persischen Grosskönigs*, 151.

Coffee consumption in Safavid Iran involved a wide range of the social spectrum, beginning with the royal court. Indeed, coffee was a fixture in the shah's very household, for a member of the royal retinue was invariably the coffee master, the so-called *qahvahchi-bashi*. The royal palace in Isfahan included a "coffee kitchen," in which the coffee consumed by the royal household was stored, roasted, and prepared under the supervision of this official.[91]

Various accounts from the period of `Abbas I's reign to that of Shah Sultan Husayn refer to coffee as a common drink in Safavid court circles. The visits Shah `Abbas frequently paid to the coffeehouses of Isfahan are reflected in the accounts of numerous foreign visitors.[92] VOC ambassador Van Leene, who in 1691 conducted lengthy negotiations in Isfahan, noted the inclusion of coffee in the royal "sugar banquet" offered to the shah's guests.[93] In the late Safavid chronicle *Dastur-i shahriyaran*, moreover, we read how on the occasion of the visit to Mashhad of the Mughal Prince Akbar in 1696 an official banquet was organized during which coffee, rosewater, and sweets were served prior to the appearance of 150 dishes of food and an equal number of plates of sweetmeats.[94]

By the mid-seventeenth century, coffee was a standard beverage in governing circles outside the royal court as well. Speelman in 1652 called coffee a "very common drink" in the country, and in his dairy referred to a reception given by a high official where coffee was offered.[95] Du Mans claimed that, after tobacco, coffee was the second item offered to guests in Iran.[96] John Fryer, who was in Iran in 1677, is one more

[91]Ibid., 152; Sanson, *Voyage*, 64; Mirza Rafi`a, *Dastur al-muluk*, ed. Afshar, 90; and Minorsky ed., *Tadhkirat al-Muluk*, 68, 100. The latter source also lists a functionary called the *sahib jam`*, who was in charge of all coffee pots, roasters, cups, and trays.

[92]Among them is Ivan Ivanovich Chicherin, who stayed in Iran in 1618–19 as the representative of the Russian tsar Mikhail Romanov and had taken over the command of the embassy after the death of its original leader Mikhail Petrovich Bartiatinski. Chicherin was one of the official guests taken on `Abbas's nightly tour of Isfahan on 14 June 1619. His reference to coffee is brief—he simply mentioned the selling of "black water" alongside the *maydan-i naqsh-i jahan*—yet appears unmistakable. Given the several other eyewitnesses who mention coffee in their accounts of the same occasion, there seems little ground for Bushev's suggestion that Chicherin's remark may refer to oil (*naft*) for illumination. See Bushev, *Istoriia posol'stv, 1613–1621 gg.*, 218. Another example is Fedot Kotov, a Russian state merchant who in 1623 was sent to Iran with the task of collecting information on the itinerary from Moscow to Isfahan and on circumstances in Iran. According to him, Shah `Abbas visited the coffeehouses along the *maydan* almost daily. See Kotov, *Khozhenie kuptsa Kotova*, 43, 81. In none of these sources it is said that Shah `Abbas himself drank coffee. Both Della Valle and Chicherin's account give the impression that the shah only drank wine during his visit to the coffeehouse.

[93]NA, VOC 1501, Diary Van Leene, 28 March 1691, fol. 515.

[94]Nasiri, *Dastur-i shahriyaran*, 117.

[95]Speelman, *Journaal der reis*, 141, 158.

[96]Du Mans, "`Estat'de 1660," in Richard, *Raphaël du Mans*, 2:75–76.

witness to government officials' routinely serving coffee to their guests. He recounted how he was entertained with "coho," tea, and rose water by the governor as well as the *shahbandar* of Bandar `Abbas.[97] The Scotsman John Bell, finally, in 1717 was the guest at a dinner party at the home of a high city official in Isfahan where "coffee and sherbett were carried about by turns."[98]

Coffee was not just confined to state banquets and official receptions but was also enjoyed in the public sphere. The drink was served during nocturnal festivities as well as in bathhouses frequented by the wealthy, where it awaited the customers as they emerged from the bath to put on their clothes. No visit to a bathhouse in Safavid (and Qajar) Iran, it seems, was complete without an offering of refreshments afterward. Fryer described the aftermath of a visit to a bathhouse as follows: "When they retire to put on their Cloaths . . . there awaits them a collation of fruit, sweetmeats, and variety of perfumes, as rosewater, rackbeet, and the like, with all befitting Attendants, besides the usual servitors to administer either coho, tea, tobacco, or brandy, if faint."[99]

But the most common locale for the enjoyment of the beverage was the coffeehouse. Don Garcia's account of Shah `Abbas's court offers a vivid description of the coffeehouse to which the monarch took him with a number of other envoys.[100] Some twenty years later, Olearius also testified to the existence of coffeehouses in the Safavid capital when he wrote: "The cahwa chane are those places where they take tobacco, and drink of a certain black water, which they call cahwa."[101] All refer to the coffeehouses along the north side of the *maydan-i naqsh-i jahan*, near the entrance to the Qaysariyah bazaar.[102]

Chardin gave the most colorful and detailed description of these establishments:

> These houses, which are big spacious and elevated halls, of various shapes, are generally the most beautiful places in the cities, since these are the locales where the people meet and seek entertainment. Several of them, especially those in the big cities, have a water basin in the middle. Around the rooms are platforms, which are about three feet high and approximately three to four feet wide, more or less according to the size

[97]Fryer, *New Account*, 2:162.
[98]Bell, *Travels from St. Petersburg*, 1:115.
[99]Fryer, *New Account*, 3:33–34.
[100]Silva y Figueroa, *Comentarios*, 2:380–81.
[101]Olearius, *Vermehrte newe Beschreibung*, 558; English trans. from the English edn. of 1662, 298.
[102]Tavernier, *Les six voyages*, 1:448–49; Gemelli Careri, *Giro del mondo*, 2:153.

of the location, and are made out of masonry or scaffolding, on which one sits in the Oriental manner. They open in the early morning and it is then, as well as in the evening, that they are most crowded.[103]

The basin in the middle seems to have been a regular feature of the coffeehouse, with its water used to refill water pipes.[104] The upper parts of the coffeehouses along the royal square in Isfahan were painted in gold colors and had wooden latticework on both sides, through which the "Qizilbash watch the game without paying for it," as Kotov put it in an apparent reference to the absence of the Qizilbash among the coffeehouse clientele. Glass holders filled with oil and a wick, to be lit at night, were held by wires hanging from the roof.[105] Fryer described the nocturnal appearance of coffeehouses in similar terms: "At night here are abundance of lamps lighted, and let down in glasses from the concave Part of the Roof, by Wires or Ropes, hanging in a Circle."[106]

Over time, the number of coffeehouses in Isfahan grew from the original few along the *maydan*. In the later part of the century they numbered at least seven, according to information provided by Muhammad Badi`, a central Asian man of letters who spent a few years in Iran in the 1680s.[107] By that time, several coffeehouses also seem to have been located near the Jubarahah gate, alongside the Chahar Bagh, Isfahan's main thoroughfare, as well as inside the Qaysariyah bazaar.[108] Chardin further referred to a place in Isfahan by the name of Tahtagah as being "among the most famous spots in the city." Here, he noted, an infinite number of coffee and opium cabarets always drew an enormous crowd of people drinking, engaged in discussions, taking a breath of fresh air, or simply there for devotional reasons, as the tomb of Harun Vilayat was nearby.[109] Kaempfer informs us that coffeehouses were often part of *madrasa* complexes.[110] In the early eighteenth century, coffeehouses also graced the gardens outside of Isfahan where the shah frequently spent time.[111]

---

[103]Chardin, *Voyages*, 4:67–68 (my trans.).

[104]Tavernier, *Les six voyages*, 1:449; Kotov, *Khozhenie kuptsa Kotova*, 43, 80–81.

[105]Ibid. The tradition to paint the interior of coffeehouses has continued until recent times. See Sayf, *Naqqashi-yi qahvah-khanah*.

[106]Fryer, *New Account*, 3:35.

[107]McChesney, "Anthology of Poets," 61.

[108]Ibid; Valentyn, *Oud en Nieuw Oost Indiën*, 5:256; Nasrabadi, *Tazkirah-i Nasrabadi*, 326.

[109]Chardin, *Voyages*, 7:449–50; and 215.

[110]Kaempfer, *Am Hofe des persischen Grosskönigs*, 149.

[111]NA, VOC 1856, Oets, Isfahan to Jacobsz., Gamron, 10 March 1714, fol. 685.

Coffee consumption probably knew its most spectacular growth in Isfahan and the people of Isfahan may have consumed more coffee than those of other Safavid cities, but the existence of coffeehouses was by no means restricted to the capital. Coffee in the seventeenth century quite possibly spread beyond the ranks of the wealthy and the perimeters of the capital city as a result of greater availability and lower prices following a growing supply via the sea-borne trade. Reference has already been made to the lively coffee trade of Tabriz. Chardin mentioned the existence of "cabarets à café" in the same city, as did the Italian traveler Gemelli Careri a generation after him.[112] In the late 1620s Farahabad, Shah `Abbas's resort town in Mazandaran, had at least one coffeehouse.[113] Coffeehouses existed in Qazvin, Nakhchavan, and Shiraz, too.[114] We have a record of the establishment of a coffeehouse in the city of Yazd in 1678.[115] The renowned Ottoman traveler Evliya Celebi, describing the northern town of Shamakhi, noted their existence in that place.[116] Muhammad Badi` refers to two coffeehouses in Mashhad and to one such place in Nishapur.[117] All in all, coffee was clearly widespread in Iran's urban centers, though not nearly as much as in the neighboring Ottoman Empire, where in the mid-sixteenth century Istanbul alone is said to have boasted about fifty coffeehouses, a number that went up to a fantastic six hundred by the seventeenth century.[118]

The extent of coffee consumption outside Iran's urban centers is difficult to gauge. We know that in the later 1600s coffee was consumed in villages, or at least in those that lined the caravan routes, as well as in the caravanserais that served as halting places for travelers. Kaempfer referred to the existence of coffeehouses in the villages of Shabaran, Imamzadah, and Asupas, all located in the south, along the Isfahan to Bandar `Abbas route.[119] Travelers were served coffee in the caravanserai at Mayar, 40 kilometers south of Isfahan.[120] Yet, there is good reason to believe that coffee was by no means a household item everywhere. A Dutch report from 1640 referred to coffee as being preferred over tea in Iran but, as tea was a rare drink at the time, this says little about the actual dissemination of coffee.[121] The claim in various sources that, compared to the Ottoman

---

[112]Chardin, *Voyages*, 2:297, 322; Gemelli Careri, *Giro del Mondo*, 2:42.

[113]Ross, ed., *Journal of Robert Stodart*, 52.

[114]Chardin, *Voyages*, 2:390; 297; 8:418.

[115]Mustawfi Bafqi, *Jami`-i Mufidi*, 3:226–27, 228.

[116]Efendi, *Narrative of Travels in Asia*, 2:160.

[117]McChesney, "Anthology of Poets," 61.

[118] Kırlı, "Struggle over Space," 34–35.

[119]Kaempfer, *Reisetagebücher*, 41, 66, 92, 115.

[120]Valentyn, *Oud- en nieuw Oost-Indiën*, 5:256.

[121]Coolhaas, ed., *Generale Missiven, 1639–1655*, 30 November 1640, 115.

Empire, Iran consumed moderate amounts of the beverage, suggests that coffee had not penetrated all regions and all social classes. François Bernier in the late seventeenth century insisted that "they drink very little of it in India and Persia," claiming that not much passed through the seaports and that very little reached the interior. The situation, he affirmed, was very different in the Ottoman Empire, where coffee was everywhere widely known and cheaply available, with all Turks enjoying it every morning and evening, either at their homes or in public places.[122] Jonas Hanway, writing in the early eighteenth century, echoed this opinion by claiming that Iranians drank coffee in small quantities.[123]

Irrespective of the dissemination and the quantities involved, the references to the ambience in which coffee was consumed in seventeenth century-Iran are unequivocal in their suggestiveness. They convey a picture of public leisure and conviviality in a society that evidently could afford the importation of the new luxury commodity that coffee was. From all the information provided by foreign observers coffee emerges as a drink that was enjoyed by the upper and middle strata of late Safavid urban society. As in Ottoman territory, in Safavid Iran coffeehouses appear to have been an entirely new phenomenon. They were the first public places other than mosques and bathhouses, hammams, where respectable urbanites could socialize in a leisurely manner and under the enjoyment of stimulants such as coffee and tobacco.[124] The coffeehouse thus struck a happy balance between the mosque, which was a public space but lacked worldly entertainment, and the taverns and gambling houses, which were avoided by upstanding members of the community for serving alcohol and providing disreputable entertainment for the lower classes.[125] Hamavi Yazdi notes that coffee was called the "wine of the Arabs (khamr al-`Arab).[126] In Iran, coffee clearly did not supplant wine, but the drink and the ambience in which it was consumed did offer a largely legitimate alternative to the public consumption of alcohol. As in Catholic countries, where church and tavern often rubbed shoulders, allowing male believers to enjoy a drink after the service or even to slip out for the duration of the sermon, coffeehouses in Iran and elsewhere in the Middle East were frequently located near

---

[122]Letter from Bernier to Dufour, in Dufour, *Traitez Nouveaux*, 178–85.

[123]Hanway, *Historical Account*, 1:226.

[124]This is one of the main arguments of Hattox, *Coffee and Coffeehouses*, in his discussion about the Ottoman Empire. How inseparable the combination of coffee and tobacco, over time became in Iran is reflected in the saying, "coffee without tobacco is like food without salt, quoted in Ouseley, *Travels in Various Countries*, 1:341.

[125]See Hattox, *Coffee and Coffeehouses*, 122–25, for the Ottoman Empire.

[126]Hamavi Yazdi, "De venenis celeberrimis," fol. 54.

mosques, enabling the faithful to socialize over coffee and a water pipe before or after prayer.[127]

Leisure went hand in hand with liveliness, for more than one foreign visitor described the spirited atmosphere in the Safavid coffeehouses. The social function of coffeehouses, places where people gathered to exchange news and gossip, is brought out in a description by Chardin:

> People engage in conversation, for it is there that news is communicated and where those interested in politics criticize the government in all freedom and without being fearful, since the government does not heed what the people say. Innocent games [. . .] resembling checkers, hopscotch, and chess, are played. In addition, mullahs, dervishes, and poets take turns telling stories in verse or in prose. The narrations by the mullahs and the dervishes are moral lessons, like our sermons, but it is not considered scandalous not to pay attention to them. No one is forced to give up his game or his conversation because of it. A mullah will stand up, in the middle, or at one end of the *qahvah-khanah*, and begin to preach in a loud voice, or a dervish enters all of a sudden, and chastises the assembled on the vanity of the world and its material goods. It often happens that two or three people talk at the same time, one on one side, the other on the opposite, and sometimes one will be a preacher and the other a storyteller.[128]

John Fryer's words that "hither repair all those that are covetous of News, as well as Barterers of Goods, where not only Fame and common Rumor is promulged, but Poetry too, for some of that Tribe are always present to rehearse their Poems," confirm Chardin's description and draw attention to the much-noted function of coffeehouses as public places where folktales were narrated and poetry was recited.[129] Earlier, Olearius had commented on the presence of "poets and historians" who, seated on high chairs, tell their "histories and fables."[130] The content of these stories varied, ranging from the *Shahnamah* to the exploits of the early Safavid shahs, Isma`il and Tahmasb, to epic romances of historical figures in the Islamic tradition, folk heroes such as Hamzah, an uncle of the Prophet, and Abu Muslim, a leader of the eighth-century `Abbasid revolt. It was for this reason that benches in coffeehouses were often arranged in the shape of an amphitheater, allowing spectators to watch performances.

---

[127]For this phenomenon in the late Ottoman Empire, see Georgeon, "Les cafés à Istanbul," 41.

[128]Chardin, *Voyages*, 4:68 (my trans.).

[129]Fryer, *New Account*, 3:34.

[130]Olearius, *Vermehrte newe Beschreibung*, 558.

Members of the religious classes were among those who performed in coffeehouses. Gemelli Careri, entering one of Isfahan's coffeehouses in 1694, observed the spectacle of a mullah entertaining the assembled. The mullah, he recounted,

> sitting down without an upper vest and turbant, very gravely began a speech in commendation of Scia Abas the Great and of Scia Sofi, extolling their Actions and Conquests. He grew so hot in his Panegyrick that he cry'd out like a Madman, and roar'd like a Bull, foaming at the Mouth, expecially when he mention'd an particular exploit, the Hearers applauding him by clapping their Hands, and Pipes. This confusion lasted two Hours, after which the Mullah went about gathering an Alms of one or two Casbis a Head, and carry'd off two Abassis.[131]

These eyewitness accounts, combined with Kaempfer's remark about the propinquity of the coffeehouse and the madrasa, and the information Persian sources yield about the performance of wandering dervishes as popular storytellers, show an unmistakable link between the coffeehouse and the religious sphere. This link was not necessarily positive or unproblematic, however. It would be a mistake to conclude from the political and religious associations suggested in eyewitness accounts that the coffeehouse was simply a substitute for or even an extension of, the mosque, a happy symbiosis between piety and pleasure, or no more than an outlet for polite discourse and edifying entertainment. Such an interpretation obscures the tensions that existed between politics and religion in Safavid Iran. These tensions were expressed in various moral and intellectual debates that made the coffeehouse, or rather the activities associated with it, controversial, and that gave rise to measures designed to alter its nature and function.

Objections to the coffeehouse as it had emerged in the early seventeenth century come under various rubrics. One involved politics and the concerns of a centralizing state. Already Shah `Abbas I, worried that coffeehouses might undermine discipline and foster political disorder, interfered in their daily schedule by arranging for a mullah to enter the premises early in the morning. The cleric would then proceed to edify the assembled for a few hours with religious homilies and poetry, after which he would stand up and urge his audience to leave the place, admonishing them that it was time to go to work.[132] Tavernier is our only source for this, and since he does not specify a date, it is unclear when exactly this measure was introduced. Although it is tempting to see in it

---

[131]Gemelli Careri, *Giro del Mondo*, 2:153–54; trans. *A Voyage Round the World*, n. p., n.d., 1:147–48.

[132]Tavernier, *Les six voyages*, 1:449.

a link with the shah's crackdown on wine, enacted in 1619, the two do not seem to have coincided since the sources that mention the ban on wine do not refer to coffeehouses.

The other, better documented, issue involves clerical objections to the type of entertainment offered in the coffeehouses and has to do with a large-scale assault against Sufi beliefs and practices on the part of the ulama, reflecting a fundamental shift in Safavid Iran away from a tolerance for expressions of popular religiosity to a growing emphasis on a strict interpretation of the faith. We saw how the anti-Sufi movement had its origins in the reign of Shah Tahmasb; its first protagonist was Shaykh `Ali al-Karaki (d. 1534), the supreme jurist of the period and the same cleric who is likely to have been instrumental in that ruler's Sincere Repentance. He was the most prominent representative of a group of literal-minded ulama, many of them drawn from the ranks of Arab immigrants, who associated Sufi beliefs and practices with the deviant, heterodox ways of the Qizilbash, accusing their adherents of espousing heretical beliefs, of disregarding the external obligations of the faith, and of exercising a deceptive influence on the populace. Over time, this group generated a voluminous anti-Sufi polemic that excoriated practices such as swinging, dancing, swooning, and hand clapping, as well as deviant forms of sexuality, lumping all together under the rubric of *ghuluww*, extremism, and *zandaqah*, heresy.[133] With this came a suspicion of the practice of storytelling, which the literalist ulama considered unislamic as it dealt with the mythical and the imaginary and distracted the faithful from the straight path. These objections led al-Karaki to issue a *fatwa* that declared the entire genre of storytelling un-Islamic.[134] Opprobrium in particular concerned certain narratives, above all that of Abu Muslim, the standard bearer of the `Alid cause in the `Abbasid revolt. Kathryn Babayan has shown how Shah Isma`il I used the oral tradition of the *Abu Muslim-namah*s as a propaganda tool, focusing on the similarities between Abu Muslim's public appearance, *khuruj*, and his own in order to rouse people for the Safavid cause. But ultimately the shah betrayed the revolutionary ideology that had brought him to power, and to do so he had to discard the Abu Muslim analogy and outlaw its public recitation. The tales of Abu Muslim, popular among the Qizilbash, in particular had to be excised from collective memory, for they reminded the Safavids of their own heretical past in representing a competing version of history and a genealogy from which they wished to escape. The subsequent controversy turned on the question of whether Abu Muslim had been a true and loyal Shi`i, as faithful to the house of

---

[133]Newman, "Clerical Perceptions"; and idem, "Sufism and Anti-Sufism."
[134]Ja`fariyan, *Safaviyah dar `arsah-i din*, 860–62.

the Prophet as popular imagination made him out to be, or the real founder of the usurping dynasty of the ʿAbbasids, who had raised their banners in the name of ʿAli only to betray him afterward. Al-Karaki, one of those convinced of Abu Muslim's lack of credentials as a good Imami Shiʿi, issued a *fatwa* condemning Abu Muslim and his followers.[135] Presumably influenced by al-Karaki, Shah Tahmasb had Abu Muslim's grave destroyed on conquering Khurasan and threatened to cut out the tongue of anyone who recited the story.[136]

The outpouring of writings against popular Sufism of the "bazaari" kind (as opposed to high-minded and philosophical mysticism) reached a high point a century later, during the reign of Shah Safi and Shah ʿAbbas II. Most active were religious scholars such as Mir Lawhi and his student Muhammad Hamavi, who wrote against all who continued to defend Abu Muslim, among them the Sufi-minded and popular Muhammad Taqi Majlisi the elder (d. 1660 or 1663).[137] The surge in anti-Sufi rhetoric exemplified by these tracts no doubt played a role in the anticoffeehouse measures taken under Shah ʿAbbas II, even though the anti-Sufi movement was by no means unconditionally supported by the shah. Shah ʿAbbas II at times accommodated the ulama in their anti-Sufi sentiments, but also paid his respects to Sufi representatives, engaged them in discussions, and built a lodge for them.[138]

What seems to have aroused the ire of the clerics beyond the narration of subversive stories is something else commonly associated with Sufism of the Qalandar type: an atmosphere of merriment that served as a screen for depravity and more specifically public pederasty. Don Garcia, taken on his nightly tour by Shah ʿAbbas I, commented on the numerous youths, predominantly Circassians, Georgians, and Armenians, who performed "immodest" dances in these establishments.[139] Della Valle, taking part in the same tour, confirmed the Spanish ambassador's words with his account of pretty "coffee youngsters" who served the customers and entertained them with Persian, Uzbeg, and Tatar dances. Dressed in

---

[135]Babayan, *Mystics, Monarchs, and Messiahs,*" 121ff.

[136]See Hamavi, *Anis al-muʾminin,* 141. Jaʿfariyan, "Sih risalah dar barah-i Abu Muslim," 254. Hamavi was a disciple of al-Karaki who expressed satisfaction that Shah Tahmasb had outlawed the reading and recitation of the *Abu Muslim-namahs,* which, he argued, had recently been falsified. Jaʿfariyan, 257, argues that there is good reason to believe that Abu Muslim was not a Shiʿi and even anti-Shiʿi.

[137]See Babayan, *Mystics, Monarchs and Messiahs,* 148–49, and 409, in which she argues that the context of this second wave of tracts was a personal controversy between Mir Lawhi and Majlisi the Elder.

[138]Jaʿfariyan, *Safaviyah dar ʿarsah-i din,* 523–24.

[139]Silva y Figueroa, *Comentarios,* 2:380. See also the reference to Georgian, Circassian, and Russian boy dancers and prostitutes in ibid., 50–51.

effeminate clothes, these youths also engaged in other "games," which, the author averred, were meant to incite the customers' libidinous desires.[140] The boys would dance around the central water basin, holding bells or playing the tambourine, the flute (*zurna*) and bagpipes, their heads covered with gilded turbans and their waists girded with gilded belts.[141] Chardin, speaking retrospectively, claimed that coffeehouses used to be places where one was served and entertained by pretty Georgian boys, aged from ten to sixteen and dressed in a lascivious manner, with hair strung in female fashion. They were made to dance and perform, uttering a thousand immodest things in order to excite the spectators, who would take these boys wherever it pleased them, vying among themselves to have the most beautiful and engaging. These places, the Frenchman claimed, were veritable houses of sodomy that filled wise and virtuous people with horror.[142]

This situation, Chardin affirmed, had come to an end under Khalifah Sultan, Shah `Abbas II's vizier, whom we encountered in chapter 3 as the instigator of an antivice campaign. Aside from wine taverns and brothels, which had to close their doors at his behest, he also targeted coffeehouses, cleansing them of the practices described by Chardin.[143]

The chapter on wine showed that the overall purification campaign of which the clerical drive for moral rectitude was part occurred against the backdrop of precarious financial circumstances, but also suggested that, although important, these do not suffice as an explanation. The timing suggests that Safavid authorities may have acted in emulation of a similar campaign waged in the Ottoman Empire a decade earlier. In Istanbul, coffee had more than once ran into serious government opposition. Sultan Selim II (r. 1566–74) outlawed the use of coffee shortly after its introduction and spread. In 1633–34 Sultan Murad IV, encouraged by a puritanical movement known as Kadizadeli, ordered the outright closure of coffeehouses and wine taverns. As elsewhere, such measures tended to be directed less against the beverage (except in the case of wine) than against the venues where it was consumed, reflecting clerical concerns that many officials spent more time drinking coffee than praying, the association of coffeehouses with other questionable habits such as tobacco smoking, and, most important, a fear that coffeehouses were "hatcheries for crime and sedition."[144]

---

[140]Della Valle, *Viaggi*, 1:25.

[141]Kotov, *Khozhenie kuptsa Kotova*, 43, 81.

[142]Chardin, *Voyages*, 4:69.

[143]Vahid Qazvini, `*Abbasnamah*, 70–72; Chardin, *Voyages*, 4:69.

[144]Zilfi, *The Politics of Piety*, 138–39. See also Valentyn, *Oud- en nieuw Oost-Indiën*, 5:194; Kissling, "Zur Geschichte der Rausch- und Genussgifte," 347; Faroqhi, "Coffee and Spices"; and Kırlı, "Struggle over Space," 34–36.

It also was seen how the move immediately reflects the ascendance of the "literalist" faction of *ulama* at the Safavid court, most notably Khalifah Sultan and his contemporary, `Ali Naqi Kamarah'i. An advocate for an activist clerical role in society, the latter considered coffee itself un-Islamic because it was one of the words used for wine.[145] Kamarah'i was one of the ulama who were dismayed at the little heed Shah Safi paid to the tenets of the faith and who saw the accession of a new ruler, weak and, still a minor, also impressionable, as an excellent opportunity to launch a campaign against heterodox tendencies that stood in the way of the institutionalization of orthodox Shi`ism as the ideology of the state.[146]

Chardin, writing some twenty years after the events, claimed that the measures had put a halt to these dubious practices.[147] Other sources, too, hint at a transformation of the coffeehouse in the reign of Shah `Abbas II by suggesting that by that time its clientele consisted for the most part of the learned and the literate, people in search of contemplation and intellectual discussion. Nasrabadi's comments on the change in his personal life epitomize this transformation. In his youth, he tells us, he led a life of pleasure and dissolution. Later, having converted to a life of rectitude and study, he sought the company of upright believers and chose the coffeehouse as his residence. Writing in the 1660s, he calls coffeehouses places where men of letters and learning congregated and lists a number of poets who frequented such establishments, or even owned them. Of the Shirazi poet Mulla Ghurur, Nasrabadi says that he settled in Isfahan at the end of his long life—he was to die at the age of eighty— where he took up residence at a coffeehouse. People of spirituality would come to the coffeehouse to listen to his discourse.[148] The *qahvah-khanah* had acquired the same function in the provinces, for Evliya Celebi, describing Shamakhi, called its coffeehouses gathering places for "wits and learned men."[149]

Anticoffee measures were not confined to the Muslim world. In early modern Europe, too, coffee variously met with opposition from beer brewers, clergymen, and bureaucrats. In Restoration England, for instance, coffeehouses were the object of suspicion on the part of state officials, who saw in them "nurseries of idleness and pragmaticalness," establishments that spawned all kinds of antiroyalist conspiracies. In late 1675, a government controlled by high clergymen ordered the closure of these public places. The implementation of the decree was only averted following a storm of public protest. See Ellis, *Penny Universities*, 94–97; and Pincus, "`Coffee Politicians Does Create'."

[145] Ja`fariyan, ed., "Risalah fi bayan hukm shurb al-tutun wa'l qahwah," 90. See also idem, "Andishah'ha-yi yik `alim-i Shi`i"; and "Guzarish-i andishah'ha-yi siyasi," 20ff.

[146] Babayan, "Waning of the Qizilbash," 255ff.

[147] Chardin, *Voyages*, 4:69.

[148] Nasrabadi, *Tazkirah-i Nasrabadi*, 255, 290, 295, 313–14, 376–77.

[149] Efendi, *Narrative of Travels*, 2:160.

We should, finally, be careful not to see total and irrevocable social transformation in this and other such measures. The 1645 campaign followed a common pattern in that it fizzled as quickly as it had emerged. No clear reasons for this are found in the sources, but in the case of the forcible conversion of the Jews bribery by wealthy members of their community clearly played a role. There were also costs involved for the treasury. Each Jew, after all, was offered two *tuman*s as an incentive to convert to Islam, and converts were exempted from the poll tax imposed on non-Muslims. A curbing of entertainment in coffeehouses similarly must have led to a fall in tax revenue.[150] In sum, Khalifah Sultan's initiative did not end the long-term incidence of public drinking and prostitution, and it is not likely to have stamped out all "immoral" behavior associated with coffeehouses either. The next government attack on unislamic practices, mounted in the wake of Shah Sultan Husayn's accession in 1694, showed itself mostly concerned with alcohol consumption. It did explicitly target coffeehouses by imposing a suggestive restriction on them: minors unaccompanied by adults were no longer allowed to enter.[151]

CONCLUSION

In its conquest of the world, coffee first spread to the countries nearest to its principal area of cultivation in Ethiopia and Yemen. The first region to be exposed to the new drink was the Ottoman Empire, but neighboring Iran, connected through commerce and warfare, cannot have remained far behind. Although coffee was known quite early among Iranian physicians and herbalists, its actual spread and popularization did not occur until the late sixteenth century.

Although the Dutch and English East India Companies did not introduce coffee, they were quick to include it into their activities as a potentially lucrative addition to the wares that lubricated their intra-Asian networks. A promising start notwithstanding, they found coffee to be an elusive commodity. Burdened with high overhead costs, deficient in their knowledge of local circumstances, and unable to penetrate the production process, the Europeans had little to match the low cost and the

[150]Coffeehouses as well as brothels and disreputable professions such as prostitution, dancing and music-making all fell under the supervision of the *mash`aldar-bashi*, an official who also collected the taxes these institutions yielded. See Nasiri, *Dastur-i shahriyaran*, 40.

[151]Ibid., 35–51; Gemelli Careri, *Giro del Mondo*, 2:154; Kroell, ed., *Nouvelles d'Ispahan*, 68; and Di Borgomale, *Mazandaran and Astarabad*, 7–10. For the restrictions, see the *Tuhfat al-`alam*, as cited by Ishraqi, "Shah Sultan Husayn," 99.

expertise of local, Arab and Gujarati, merchants who had long plied their trade along existing routes. However, soon after falling profits caused the maritime companies to terminate direct shipping links between Yemen and Surat in the 1650s, new opportunities beckoned. With the emergence of an infinitely more profitable coffee market in northwestern Europe, the Persian Gulf gradually lost its appeal as a region of uncertain demand, low prices, and increasing instability. The ones to profit from this retreat were the indigenous merchants, who had never given up their major share in the coffee traffic.

Although it remains unclear how popular coffee was in Safavid Iran, the centrality of its position in the (urban) public sphere can also be deduced from the location of coffeehouses in the very heart of the capital city, the heart of entertainment and social interaction. Nor was consumption limited to Isfahan; coffee reached far and wide across the country and the existence of coffeehouses is attested for a number of provincial towns, caravanserais and villages along commercial routes. Yet, for all its popularity in the public domain, there is little to suggest that coffee was consumed in the private sphere, and it remains unclear to what extent it had penetrated rural areas beyond the main trade routes.

Safavid sources confirm Ralph Hattox's conclusions about the significance of coffee in the Ottoman Empire. In Iran, too, its introduction signaled a qualitative difference in patterns of entertainment and leisure. As a public place in which the upper segments of society had the opportunity to enjoy a stimulant in an atmosphere of leisure and conviviality, the coffeehouse was a novelty. Hitherto, no outlet for this had existed than the tavern and the mosque, both of which had their limitations for either respectable Muslims or those who sought more than spiritual enjoyment.

As elsewhere in the Middle East, a certain association between coffeehouses and religious circles existed in Safavid Iran. The location of coffeehouses in the vicinity of religious colleges and the intellectual character of their clientele suggest such a link in a society in which literacy and learning were virtually synonymous with religious education. As the scene of the narration of epic folktales by wandering dervishes, coffeehouses also served as a forum for a Sufi-dominated counterculture subversive of the changing self-identification of the Safavids. Early Safavid coffeehouses, finally, appear to us as places of homoerotic interaction between servers and clientele in the form of suggestive dancing and music making by young boys who would be available for sex with customers. Shah `Abbas I, preoccupied with urban unrest, had the coffeehouses patrolled. Following the lax reign of Shah Safi, these establishments again came under scrutiny under Shah `Abbas II. As religious authorities espousing Shi`i orthodoxy gained in prominence, Sufis became the objects of clerical vilification. The coffeehouse, frequented by mystics and the scene of untoward behavior often associated with them, became a target as well.

The ban that followed is said to have made lewd dancing, music making, and pederasty disappear from coffeehouses, and to have turned the establishments into gathering places for those wont to engage in board games and intellectual discourse and those interested in public spectacle in the form of (officially sanctioned) religious harangues or readings of poetry and folk tales. Pressure from above sanitized the coffeehouse but did not make it disappear.

PART II

Qajar Period

CHAPTER 7

Wine in Qajar Iran: From Flouting the Religious Law to Flaunting Unbelief

> I met several parties riding out with their servants, for the purpose of eating onions and getting intoxicated with rum in the beautiful gardens, a custom followed much by noble and wealthy Persians
>
> Lieutenant-Colonel Stuart, *Journal of a Residence in Northern Persia and the Adjacent Provinces of Turkey*, 1854.

I. Introduction: Between Safavids and Qajars

The Afghan interlude (1722–36) represents a fascinating twist on the preceding Safavid period with regard to the consumption of alcoholic drinks. Said to be averse to alcohol, the Afghans drank water rather than wine.[1] Nadir Shah (r. 1736–47), too, for all his similarities to the great Central Asian world conquerors of yesteryear, stood out for being rather abstemious, certainly compared to most Safavid rulers. The literature of the period casts his reign as a departure from Safavid patterns, emphasizing revival and reinvigoration after moral decadence and military dissolution. In a proto-nationalist bout of dramatization that links sobriety to military vigilance and military vigilance to the survival of the realm, the contemporary chroniclers castigate the Safavids for having squandered the nation with their profligacy and decadence, and justify their demise as punishment for their misdeeds. They portray Shah Sultan Husayn as a pious weakling whose preoccupation with religious matters came at the expense of proper state management and military discipline, but they reserve their most scathing words for his son, the feeble Shah Tahmasb II, whose brief reign (1729–32) was cut short by Nadir Shah. Tahmasb II, Marvi, the author of the `Alam-ara-yi Nadiri*, contends, had from early childhood been inattentive to the affairs of state while drinking wine and engaging in lust and play, *lahv va la`ib*.[2] Muhammad Muhsin Mustawfi depicts Tahmasb in similar fashion, detailing how after his disastrous defeat against the Ottomans in 1730, he went to

[1]Krusinski, *History of the Late Revolutions of Persia*, 1:147.
[2]Marvi, `Alam-ara-yi Nadiri*, 1:63.

Isfahan to lose himself in frivolous play and drinking. Following this, Nadir Shah used Tahmasb's scandalous demeanor as an excuse to have him deposed and replaced by his three-month-old son, `Abbas. While the infant was put on the throne as `Abbas III, real power fell to Nadir Shah.[3] In all these narratives Tahmasb is portrayed as the decadent, insouciant ruler who squandered his reputation and neglected his duties, whereas Nadir Shah emerges as the virile warrior, the savior of the realm who deservedly took power and used it to reestablish order.

This image was not just a matter of propaganda. In January 1734 the governor of Isfahan banned wine and arak and invited the city's Muslim residents to fast and pray for Nadir's victory (against the Ottomans). Two days later, the Indian residents of Isfahan were told that they could no longer drink wine or arak either.[4] Nadir Shah himself did not quite live up to the image, however, for reports from March of the same year suggest that, while residing in Shiraz, he had succumbed to heavy drinking during daylong sessions with his officials. He had extended the right to drink and engage in prostitution and sodomy to his soldiers as well, commandeering a consignment of wine sent by the English to Bandar `Abbas for distribution among his troops.[5] It is not clear, though likely, that Nadir gave up this lifestyle once he set out for his next campaign a few months later.

There is little information on the incidence of actual wine drinking, as there is little on social life in general, in the period between the fall of the Safavids and the rise of the Qajars. It is not unreasonable to suggest that the lack of security in this chaotic period made public life suffer to the point where few taverns survived, as is true of another public space, the coffeehouse (to be discussed in chapter 9). Yet, this does not mean that the period represents a phase in a linear process. Following the Afghan interregnum and the reign of Nadir Shah and his mostly ephemeral successors, Iran's regent (*vakil*), Karim Khan Zand (r. 1763–79) resumed the royal tradition of heavy drinking. He apparently took to alcohol only after being in power for ten years. But once he had started drinking he retained, in John Perry's words, his "huge alcoholic and sexual appetites . . . until one year before his death, when he was in his seventies."[6] Suggesting the continued influence of Christian elements in Iran, the Carmelite fathers reported about him that, "through his intercourse with Armenians

[3]Mustawfi, *Zubdat al-tavarikh*, 155, 157, 158–59; Mar`ashi, *Majma` al-tavarikh*, 82; Rustam al-Hukama, *Rustam al-tavarikh*, 199–200. See also Lockhart, *Nadir Shah*, 2.
[4]NA, VOC 2323, Spahans daghregister, 9 January 1734, fol. 939; 11 January 1734, fol. 948.
[5]Ibid., 27 March 1734, fols. 985–86.
[6]Kalantar-i Fars, *Ruznamah*, 73; Perry, *Karim Khan Zand*, 290.

and Georgians [he] has abandoned himself to drinking wine to excess."[7] Some of the atrocities he committed seem to have taken place during drunken spells.[8] His capital Shiraz also continued to be the site of numerous taverns and brothels catering to soldiers as much as to townspeople and "guests" of the court.[9]

Karim Khan's death in 1779 ushered in a period of turmoil, with contenders for the throne who were all notorious boozers. Karim Khan's eldest son, Abu'l Fath Khan, who briefly succeeded him, was known for little else than drinking. On the first night after entering Shiraz to take up rule, he "drank wine in gross quantities." Spending his time in idleness, he paid absolutely no attention to the affairs of the realm, and despite admonitions to sober up he continued to neglect his duties while drinking so much that, in the words of one chronicler, "not even one hour was his blood without the heat of wine." This comportment prompted his uncle Sadiq Khan, governor of Basra, to move to Shiraz to depose and blind him.[10] Zaki Khan, a cousin and a half-brother of the *vakil*, was another contestant. Notorious for his cruelty, which culminated in his massacre of the population of the town of Yazdikhast, he may have wanted to atone for his misdeeds by ordering the closing of wine taverns and the smashing of wine jars.[11] A final pretender to the vacant throne was `Ali Murad Khan, a son of Zaki Khan's sister and a stepson of Sadiq Khan. Following Karim Khan's death, he took control of Isfahan and Tehran. `Ali Murad Khan, too, became a drunkard "because of the bad conditions of the state and the depravities which were spreading."[12]

II. The Qajar Period: The Shah Sobers Up

Although the eighteenth century represents a variegated landscape with regard to the consumption of alcohol, the Qajar period resumed the tendency toward less prodigious drinking that had begun with the Afghans and that Nadir Shah had rhetorically affirmed. Agha Muhammad Khan, the founder of the Qajars, drank, or at least he did when his power did

---

[7]Anon, ed., *Chronicle of the Carmelites*, 665.

[8]Ibid, 666.

[9]Perry, *Karim Khan Zand*, 286–87.

[10]Kalantar-i Fars, *Ruznamah*, 73; and Rustam al-Hukama, *Rustam al-tavarikh*, 15–16. The text from the *Ruznamah* appears in translation in Fasa'i, *History of Persia*, 10–11. See also Perry, *Karim Khan Zand*, 199, and the sources given therein.

[11]Rustam al-Hukama, *Rustam al-tavarikh*, 426.

[12]Kalantar-i Fars, *Ruznamah*, 82; trans. in Fasa'i, *History of Persia*, 20; Also see Isfahani, *Tarikh-i giti-gusha*, 178–79.

not yet extend beyond his home base in Mazandaran. George Forster, visiting Sari in 1783, noted how the Armenians who lived nearby manufactured a spirit distilled from grapes, "of which Aga Mahomed [drank] freely." The tradition of the ruler being exempted from the normal strictures on alcohol apparently was at work here, for, as Forster insists, Agha Muhammad's drinking habits did not "seem to operate to the prejudice of the people."[13] Yet, as in the case of Shah `Abbas I, drinking never seems to have interfered with his governing abilities. The *Tarikh-i `Azudi* has it that Agha Muhammad Khan led a frugal life and did not care for luxury and fine clothes.[14] Other sources confirm the notion that he was the first of a series of shahs who sobered up. According to John Malcolm, the EIC envoy who visited Iran twice between 1800 and 1810, "It was the usage of some of former kings of Persia to indulge openly in drinking wine; but none of the reigning family have yet outraged the religious feeling of their subjects by so flagrant a violation of the laws of Mahomet."[15] Malcolm's immediate reference is to Fath `Ali Shah (r. 1797–1824), the second Qajar ruler and the one who brought a modicum of stability to Iran. It took some time for Fath `Ali Shah to establish a reputation for piety, to be sure. If we are to believe Aqa Ibrahim, a Shirazi merchant who boasted of having been his former boon companion, Fath `Ali Shah, or Baba Khan, as he was called before becoming shah, drank quite openly as long as he was prince-regent of Fars between 1792–93 and 1797. What made Baba Khan publicly renounce his "wicked ways," Malcolm claims, was fear of his uncle, Agha Muhammad, and the mullahs. His "repentance" has all the elements of the inauguration ritual known from earlier times: the religious leaders of Shiraz made him "march around the city to break all the vessels which contained wine, in order that young and old should be aware of the sincere repentance of the Heir Apparent of the throne of Persia."[16]

But, in keeping with time-honored patterns, a ruler's public disavowal was not the same as abstemiousness in private. Robert Ker Porter echoed Malcolm's claim by insisting that Fath `Ali Shah and his sons observed the ban on drinking.[17] The Russian envoy Kotzbue, also writing at the time of Fath `Ali Shah, sounds similar in averring that the Qajars were very strict in observing this part of the law of Muhammad.[18] Yet, Fraser, although calling him "temperate in his habits, seldom tasting wine or

---

[13]Forster, *Journey from Bengal to England*, 2:222.

[14]`Azud al-Dawlah, *Tarikh-i `Azudi*, 144. See also Malcolm, *History of Persia*, 2:311.

[15]Malcolm, *History of Persia*, 2:549.

[16] [Malcolm], *Sketches of Persia*, 1:115–16.

[17]Porter, *Travels in Georgia, Persia, Armenia*, 347–48.

[18]Kotzbue, *Narrative of a Journey into Persia*.

spiritous liquors," reveals that the shah indulged moderately in English beer, the use of which had been recommended to him by his physicians.[19] The Englishman in 1833 attended a royal banquet where an "excellent Madeira, very good wine of Isfahan, and a sort of champagne" were served.[20] And the Russian diplomat Korf, who visited Iran in 1834–35, just after Fath `Ali Shah had died, insisted that the sovereign had been known to drink in private, adding that a large number of bottles of Shiraz wine were found in the vaults of the royal palace following Fath `Ali Shah's death.[21]

Muhammad Shah, Fath `Ali Shah's successor, was not known for extravagant living. He was quite restrained in his harem life and may have been a teetotaler.[22] Fasa'i, commenting on his death in 1848, insisted that, "this king did not soil his hands with things forbidden or his lips with intoxicating liquors."[23] Nor was he content with personal piety. In 1835, one year after coming to power, Muhammad Shah issued a proclamation against the use of alcohol.[24] This decree as well as the shah's overall lifestyle betray the restraining influence of much-maligned grand vizier Hajji Mirza Aqasi, a cunning dervish who had been the shah's tutor and who, following Fath `Ali Shah's enthronement, exercised a bewitching, Rasputin-like spell over him as grand vizier. According to Colonel Stuart, it was this "energetic eunuch, a sober and strict Musulman," who prevented the attendees at a banquet organized by the shah in late 1835, from joining the European guests in raising the glass to the health of the shah.[25] The same Englishman observed how at a banquet given by Muhammad Khan Zanganah, better known as Amir Nizam, the de facto ruler of Azerbaijan at the time, the shah's directives were obeyed to the point where wine was served only to the foreign guests.[26] Over time, however, the fervor seems to have worn off. In 1840, Amir Nizam organized a dinner party in Tabriz for the French envoy Comte de Sercey, at which wine made the rounds among Muslim and Western attendees alike. Later that year, wine was served at a royal dinner party held for the same envoy, and many of the Muslim guests reportedly could hardly keep themselves upright by the time the ambassador raised a toast to the shah's health.[27]

[19]Fraser, *Narrative of a Journey into Khorasān*, 193.

[20]Fraser, *Winter's Journey*, 2:101.

[21]Korf, *Vospominaniia o Persii*, 146.

[22]Amanat, *Pivot of the Universe*, 41.

[23]Fasa'i, *History of Persia*, 280.

[24]Stuart, *Journal of a Residence*, 206.

[25]Ibid., 169.

[26]Ibid., 138, 206.

[27]Flandin and Coste, *Voyage en Perse*, 1:316.

Under later Qajar rulers the tendency toward abstinence or at least moderate drinking continued. Nasir al-Din Shah (r. 1848–96) is known to have enjoyed French wine with dinner, but he did not indulge immoderately, although at one point in his diary I'timad al-Saltanah attributes the dizzy spells the shah sometimes suffered to an unhealthy life that included the (excessive) consumption of Shiraz wine, (frequent) sexual activity, and aimless horseback riding.[28] The women of his harem are said to have drunk wine as well, but this is not corroborated by Persian sources.[29] Nasir al-Din Shah's son and successor Muzaffar al-Din Shah (r. 1896–1907) displayed some of the traditional behavior of Iranian kings by drinking in private while upholding the appearance of abstemious devoutness in public, apparently in the belief that such comportment would help him to have his sins forgiven.[30] The unmistakable penchant for moderation in the alcohol intake of Qajar rulers seen in these examples is remarkable, all the more so because it contrasts so starkly with the situation in the neighboring Ottoman state, where royal drinking seem to have become more conspicuous at that time.[31]

Although it is difficult to find evidence that puts these changes in royal behavior in an explicit ideological context, there is little doubt that issues of legitimacy played an important role in them. Unlike the Safavids, whose authority had been buttressed by a divine aura deriving from the dynasty's alleged descent from the seventh Shi'i Imam, the Qajars came to power without much in the way of religious credentials. They derived their legitimacy mostly from the fact that they had been members of the Qizilbash confederacy and that, as loyal defenders of the Safavid legacy, they had restored the power of Shi'i Islam by reestablishing control over of the territory that had been lost since the fall of the Safavids. It naturally did not help their cause that, subsequently, they lost a considerable portion of that territory to the Russians.

The weak ideological claims of the Qajars were exacerbated by their feeble administrative and military hold on the country—a legacy of a century of regional autonomy that often manifested itself as political chaos. The ones to fill the vacuum and provide continuity had been the ulama. Their growing power vis-à-vis worldly authority and their close

---

[28]I'timad al-Saltanah, *Ruznamah-i khatirat*, 300, 367, 642; Ravandi, *Tarikh-i ijtima'i-yi Iran*, 7:396.

[29]Gasteiger, *Handelverhältnisse Persiens*, 32–33; and Vámbéry, *Meine Wanderungen*, 236. Vámbéry, 236, even claims that Nasir al-Din Shah expelled all French officers in his service when de Gobineau reported that fact, but this, too, remains uncorroborated.

[30]Dawlatabadi, *Hayat-i Yahya*, 1:149. Wilson, by contrast, insisted that Muzaffar al-Din Shah was a "total abstainer from intoxicants." See Wilson, *Persian Life and Customs*, 171.

[31]See Georgeon, "Ottomans and Drinkers," 15–16.

ties to the common people gave them a measure of independence from which they could further challenge the claims of the royal house. They did this by formulating a theory of legitimacy that foregrounded the authority of the clergy as vicegerents of the Hidden Imam while making worldly authority in the form of kingship its handmaiden, charged with the tasks of justice and charity.[32] In practice, the ulama tended to work with the secular state, as they always had done, but this did not prevent the rise of a tenuous relationship, in which the state had to be much more sensitive to the demands of the ulama for fear of antagonizing them than had been the case in the Safavid period. Lacking the aura of the Safavids, the Qajars could naturally not keep up the Safavid status of being above the religious law. One of way of projecting legitimacy in the absence of a natural foundation was to proclaim themselves defenders and practitioners of the true faith, and one way of substantiating that image was to impose sobriety on themselves, or at least to project an image of sobriety to the outside world.[33]

The annalists followed suit. Safavid chroniclers, focusing on the shah and his exploits, had extolled this ability to feast after battle and during New Year celebrations, and many had been quite explicit about the copious amount of wine involved. Their Qajar successors, by contrast, accorded a much less prominent role to the shah and his activities and, in as far as they did, no longer mentioned alcoholic excess. They continued to honor the *razm u bazm* tradition by paying lip service to it in their accounts, praising rulers for their fighting spirit and their capacity to engage in pleasurable activities, but their focus became hunting—also a traditional royal pastime—and sumptuous food rather than alcohol. Under Nasir al-Din Shah the most conspicuous public event involving the court became the annual broth-making festival, held in the autumn.[34] Similarly, the Qajars were much less inclined than the Safavids to invite their foreign guests to private nocturnal parties. English envoy Harford Jones Brydges offers a detailed description of the shah's daily activities but had to confess that he did not know for certain how Fath 'Ali Shah spent his evenings.[35] Continuing a process that had begun in the later Safavid period, the Qajars increasingly were self-consciously withdrawn

---

[32]See Arjomand, *Shadow of God*, 223–29.

[33]In keeping with this image, the performance of female dancers ceased to be part of royal festivities under the Qajars. See Malcolm, *History of Persia*, 2:587; and Dubeux, *La Perse*, 467.

[34]For the annual broth-making, *ashpazi*, event, see Mu'ayyir al-Mamalik, *Yaddashtha*, 74–75; and Qaziha, *Marasim-i darbar*. The first one was held in 1285/1858.

[35]Brydges, *Account of the Transactions*, 423. Brydges had "reason to think" that the shah liked being read to and to listen to music.

and private. They continued to stage public events and communal celebrations, but these now involved the generous offering of soup rather than the excessive consumption of alcohol.

III. State Officials

If the shah projected an image of Islamic probity to the world, many high-ranking court officials were little shy about their drinking habits. This, and especially the heavy drinking that many provincial governors continued to engage in, suggests that the example set by the Qajar rulers lacked the single-mindedness that had brought Shah Tahmasb to his decision, three centuries earlier, to renounce alcohol. The French scholar Bélanger in 1825 attended a reception hosted by `Abbas Mirza, crown prince and governor of Azerbaijan, during which everyone engaged in copious drinking.[36] Even the members of Muhammad Shah's entourage did not necessarily follow the shah's own exemplary behavior. An example is Fath `Ali Khan Rashti, who in 1835 had been governor of Tabriz for almost two decades. This official had become so accustomed to wine that he no longer felt its effects and that no drink could knock him out any longer. He therefore turned to English merchants, who procured a liquor of extraordinary potency for him. Mixing this with rum, he would down two, three or more glasses to attain his goal.[37] Isma`il Khan, a son of Fath `Ali Khan who in the early reign of Muhammad Shah served as governor of Tabriz, was known as a "notorious drunkard."[38] Layard recounts how he was repeatedly invited to the house of a Lur chief, a resident of Isfahan, to participate in drinking parties. These took place in the *andarun*, or women's quarters, where the host would be "safe from intrusion and less liable to cause public scandal." While the guests were served liberally with arak and sweetmeats, dancing girls, who also took part in the drinking, performed for them. These events, Layard concluded, usually ended with the guests getting very drunk, and falling asleep on the carpets, where they remained until sufficiently sober to return to their homes in the morning."[39]

The numerous other local magistrates with a reputation for bibulousness thrown up by the sources include Ardashir Mirza, a half-brother of Muhammad Shah, who in the 1840s served as the governor of Barfurush (modern Babul) in Mazandaran, and the governor of Urumiyah in the

[36]Bélanger, *Voyage aux Indes-orientales*, 2/ii: 376–87.

[37]Ibid., 145–46. For more information about this official—without any references to wine drinking—see Werner, *An Iranian Town in Transition*, 162–65.

[38]Stuart, *Journal of a Residence*, 138, 206.

[39]Layard, *Early Adventures in Persia*, 1:331–32.

reign of Muhammad Shah, a self-proclaimed alcoholic who admitted that he could not go a day without a drink.[40] There is the governor of Bushihr in the early 1860s, a son of the governor of Shiraz, who divided his leisure time between photography—at which he was quite good—and drunkenness. This latter inclination caused such a scandal that his father threatened to write to Nasir al-Din Shah himself to complain about his debauchery.[41] Firuz Mirza Nusrat al-Dawlah (1818–86), a son of `Abbas Mirza who during his career held a variety of gubernatorial posts, was known as a bon vivant. He once fell off his horse in a state of intoxication during the month of Ramadan, causing Nasir al-Din Shah to impose a 10,000-*tuman* fine on him so as to dampen the scandal caused by his behavior.[42] Alcoholism hastened his death.[43]

Surely the most striking case is the ruling Kurdish elite of Kuchan in Khurasan, a region then known for the production of white wine.[44] A series of local chieftains from the ruling family all had a reputation as avid drinkers. Fraser called Riza Quli Khan and his whole court "dead drunk."[45] Most notorious of all was his son Amir Husayn Khan (Shuja` al-Dawlah), who for decades ruled the town. An array of British diplomats and travelers reports on this person's prodigious drinking.[46] The Russian general Grodekoff, who in 1880 visited Khurasan in disguise, gave this description of his court:

> Knowing that he was fond of liquor, we placed several bottles of wine, liqueurs, and *vodka* before him; and in a very short time the Shuja had drunk several glasses of different wines, and then called in his singers and musicians. The men who came with him, his surgeon, and his favourites, Vali Khan and Ramzan Khan, drank themselves stupid, and a regular orgy began. Next day, I went to see the Amir, and presented my documents to him. Bottles were already standing before him, and he explained that he was recovering from his intoxication. During our conversation he repeatedly partook of brandy, opium, *hashish*, and wine, and by noon was quite drunk. In the evening of the same day he invited us to a European supper, and again got intoxicated to the last degree.[47]

[40]Holmes, *Sketches on the Shores of the Caspian*, 173, 192, 194, 205–6; Perkins, *Residence of Eight Years in Persia*, 226.

[41]Ussher, *Journey from London to Persepolis*, 497.

[42]Rivadeneyra, *Viage al interior de Persia*, 2:155.

[43]Bambad, *Sharh-i hal-i rijal-i Iran*, 3:114.

[44]Curzon, *Persia and the Persian Question*, 1:108, thought it "extremely nasty."

[45]Fraser, *Narrative of a Journey into Khorasān*.

[46]Baker, *Clouds in the East*, 276–77.

[47]Quoted in Curzon, *Persia and the Persian Question*, 1:102.

Almost fifteen years later, in 1894, the same official was still at it, drinking large amounts of Russian brandy.[48] The khan's eldest son, Abu'l Hasan Khan, meanwhile, had inherited his penchant for drinking.[49]

The English physician Wills, finally, describes the scene he encountered when he visited Fasa in Fars to attend to the local governor, a man of about thirty-eight, huge and overweight, "a general debauchee, opium eater, wine- and spirit drinker, and bhang smoker," who was suffering from gout. Having been informed about the governor's illness, Wills was offered a tumblerful of "strong spirit." Throughout that same afternoon, the governor drank copiously from a bottle that he produced from under his pillow, and he also took a bolus of opium every two hours. Wills left for dinner and when he returned at about 10 P.M. he found that most everyone in the room was engaged in drinking. Meanwhile, a chorus of dancing boys and singers entertained the patient.[50]

These various eyewitness accounts suggest that, as in so many other respects, the Qajar period knew much continuity with regard to the consumption of alcohol. Many government officials, it seems, drank quite heavily in private. Echoing their predecessors from the seventeenth century, foreign visitors insisted that their real objective was intoxication, and that the strongest wines were thus the most esteemed ones.[51] Both wine and arak were produced in various parts of the country, ranging from Fars to Khurasan and from Luristan to the Persian Gulf littoral. The latter was distilled from the leftovers of the process of wine making, and consisted of a "strong rough spirit" green in color, that was flavored with anise. Made to produce intoxication, much of it was sold in adulterated form, for example by the Armenians of New Julfa.[52] Wherever religious minorities were present, they tended to be involved in producing alcohol for their own needs and, illicitly, those of the Muslim population. In Isfahan and in Sari in Mazandaran, local Armenians made wine, while in Shiraz and Hamadan the manufacture and trade were in the hands of the Armenians as well as the Jews, who in Shiraz numbered around seven thousand and in Hamadan about five thousand at the turn of the twentieth century.[53] The Jewish population of Nahavand in Luristan, numbering twelve in 1875, was allowed to make wine against an annual "contribution" of 28 tumans.[54] But the absence of Armenians or

[48]Yate, Baluchistan and Seistan, 179.

[49]Curzon, Persia and the Persian Question, 1:101.

[50]Wills, In the Land of the Lion and the Sun, 244–46.

[51]Berezin, Puteshestvie po severnoi Persii, 279; Brugsch, Im Land der Sonne, 226–27.

[52]Wills, In the Land of the Lion and the Sun, 360.

[53]Ibid.; Forster, Journey from Bengal to England, 2:222; A&P 1904, vol. C, Trade of Kermanshah and District, 40, 45; Tsadik, "Foreign Intervention," 26.

[54]Rivadeneyra, Viaje al interior de Persia, 2:147.

Jews was not always an impediment to production. Neither groups seems to have been involved in the manufacture of wine in Kuchan. And the (Muslim) inhabitants of Sabzavar, also in Khurasan, made a "very poor kind of wine, in colour somewhat like tea, and of a disagreeable burned flavour . . . " They also manufactured arak, from the plums grown in the neighborhood, and consumed it in great quantities.[55]

Drinking appears to have varied between religious groups and been subject to regional variation, though in both cases the evidence is spotty and even contradictory. Armenians were free to drink and had the reputation of doing so to some excess, but Muslims were not necessarily far behind. Sayyid Hasan Taqizadah in his memoirs reports how sometime toward the end of the nineteenth century an Armenian by the name of Pashayan who was the personal physician of Crown Prince Muzaffar al-Din, established a society to combat drinking among the Armenians of Tabriz. He put great effort into it, and within two years after its foundation, the society counted three hundred members. When Pashayan wanted to establish a similar society for Muslims, on the ground that they drank no less than Armenians—Taqizadah invokes a statistic indicating that more arak was consumed in Tabriz than in Tiflis, the capital of Georgia—he was thwarted in his project by the local ulama, who argued that Muslim drinking was an issue for the pulpit, not the Armenian community.[56]

The Russian S. Lomnitskii makes the following interesting observation concerning the connection between geography and drinking in Qajar Iran:

> One of Tehran's old residents tried to convince me that all Persians drink alike. He is not exactly right. It seems to me that if we divide Persia into three belts, northern, central and southern, and calculate the approximate percentage of those who drink, it will turn out that in northern Persia among the Gilakis, Mazandaranis and residents of the Gaz shore those who drink compose 80 percent of the [area's] population, in the middle zone with Tehran—70 percent, and the southern part of Persia—40 percent.[57]

This did not reflect a consensus. Different observers expressed different opinions on the subject, with some claiming that the Caspian littoral was a region whose inhabitants had, by the mid-nineteenth century, "not yet adopted the wine-drinking habits not uncommon in other parts

[55]O'Donovan, *Merv Oasis*, 1:438.

[56]Taqizadah, *Zindigi-yi tufani*, 43–46.

[57]Lomnitskii, *Persiia i Persy*, 62, 379. It is interesting to note that the heavy drinking areas, according to Lomnitskii, were those in the close proximity to Russia and most influenced by her. Thanks to Elina Andreeva for bringing this source to my attention.

of Persia," and others pointing to Bushihr and the Persian Gulf coast in general as the region where date-brandy was very popular and drunkenness was "a very prevalent vice among all classes," and with one observer calling the people of Fasa "a laughing, careless set, devoid of fanaticism, having indeed very little religion," who "nearly all drank wine to excess."[58] It is probably safe to say that the areas that were most exposed to outside influence knew the highest incidence of drinking. This naturally would have included Iran's northern region, where Russian influence was substantial, the southern littoral with its maritime exposure, and some of the major cities.

IV. The Upper Classes

Members of the governing elite were not the only ones to enjoy alcoholic beverages. The upper classes in general did. Perkins, an American missionary who spent eight years in northwestern Iran during the reign of Muhammad Shah singled out the "higher classes" among those Muslims who drank. Noting that among them "intemperance prevailed to an appalling extent," he insisted that he sometimes saw respectable merchants falling down in the streets or reeling in the arms of their companions.[59] High-ranking people, Von Gasteiger noted, "do not spare any expense in acquiring costly wines."[60] Korf provides more detail:

> The people of the large cities generally do not make a great effort observing the laws of the prophet. As for wine, despite the Quranic prohibition and the efforts of the mullahs who tend to be strict in the observance of the pure faith and morality, this substance is abundantly consumed as contraband among the higher classes and the rich. Obviously, no believer openly dares to defile his lips with a glass of wine, but in the confines of their homes and in rooms far from view, they drink and get drunk in worse fashion than the "unbelievers."[61]

As in Safavid times, many of the well-to-do kept Georgian boys as members of an entertaining entourage, and drinking session typically took place in people's homes, accompanied by music-making and dance performed by these youngsters.[62] These sessions would start three or four hours before the beginning of the evening meal. The boys served

[58]Sheil, *Glimpses of Life and Manners*, 267; Binning, *Journal of Two Years' Travel*, 1:145; Wills, *In the Land of the Lion and the Sun*, 247.

[59]Perkins, *Residence of Eight Years*, 226.

[60]Von Gasteiger, *Handelverhältnisse Persiens*, 32–33.

[61]Korf, *Vospominaniia o Persii*, 146.

[62]Waring, *Tour to Sheeraz*, 53–54.

the guests with drinks and thirst-provoking munchies such as salted pistachios and almonds.

The Hungarian Hermann (Arminius) Vámbéry, visiting Isfahan in 1862, described an evening drinking party at the house of a minor civil servant, with mostly young people, both clerics and laymen, in attendance. After an hour of pleasantries and drinking of brandy, matters turned rowdy, with the men taking off their caps, turbans, and outer garments. Four female dancers showed up and proceeded to dance. What shocked Vámbéry more than anything is that two of the attendees stood up, half-drunk, and proceeded to perform their ablutions and pray in the same room where the party was taking place.[63]

Vámbéry's story is not the only that suggests that mullahs were not above drinking. Griboyedov, the Russian envoy who was to be murdered in Tehran in 1828, noted how, during his wedding to a Georgian girl in Tiflis, the former chief *mujtahid* of Tabriz drank to his heart's desire.[64] Mullah `Ali Asghar, *mullabashi*, royal chaplain of Fath `Ali Shah, was known for his bibulousness and even received the bastinado by royal order for drinking.[65] In 1864 one of Tehran's most popular mullahs was singled out as a scapegoat for a violent storm that had caused many deaths. Because he was given to wine, his enemies, jealous of his popularity, made sure to have him caught in a state of drunkenness. Tehran's supreme religious leader had him condemned to death, but the shah commuted his sentence.[66] Wills tells a funny story of how a mullah helped him make wine in Shiraz, justifying his assistance by saying: "I want to make wine for myself. I can't do it in my own house, I am Mahommedan priest; and if I get the Jews to make it for me, that is worse, for it will be bad, and I am a connoisseur."[67]

V. THE POOR AND THE MARGINAL

Although the consumption of alcohol appears to have been most prevalent among the elite, they were not the only ones to indulge. Tabriz in the early nineteenth century reveals the existence of drinking establishments that appear to have been frequented by people of various class backgrounds. A number of locales run by Armenians and located next to the bazaar served as speak-easies furtively patronized by Iranians of

---

[63]Vámbéry, *Meine Wanderungen*, 175–76.
[64]Kelly, *Diplomacy and Murder*, 173.
[65]Arjomand, "Mujtahid of the Age," 90.
[66]Watson, *History of Persia*, 22.
[67]Wills, *In the Land of the Lion and the Sun*, 229.

all stations and ages. Inside, customers could be found reclining on cushions, cup in hand, with those who had had their fill of wine asking for something stronger under complaints that the wine they had been served did not have enough "kick." Those who were deep in their cups would speak loudly about their domestic travails or criticize the government in the bitterest terms. The government, however, was apparently not particularly concerned about this. All the while the customers were moved to tears by narrators of stories and entertained by young boys performing lascivious dances.[68] Bélanger, the author of this narrative, continues by drawing an apt comparison between these drinking establishments and the coffeehouses that, he (erroneously) claimed, had been closed by Shah ʿAbbas II in the mid-seventeenth century. The activities he describes are indeed strikingly reminiscent of the ones seen in the Safavid coffeehouse. Bélanger ends with the intriguing observation that the Qajar drinking house had really replaced the coffeehouse of the Safavid period. As we will see in chapter 9, he was largely correct.

Claims about abundant alcohol intake and scenes as described by Bélanger should not lead one to believe that alcohol was present wherever people congregated. There is no question that most Iranians, and especially the ones living in the countryside, did not drink, either because of the prescribed punishment of eighty lashes or on grounds of religious principle.[69] Most of Iran's grape harvest was made into raisins destined for export.[70] It is important to emphasize that, giving the nature of their interaction with Iranians, taking the remarks made by foreign visitors at face value easily gives a distorted picture of the situation. We must always be careful not to follow the European traveler accounts to the letter. The observations by Porter and Sheil, who ascribe the ruddy faces of Armenian women living in Bakhtiari territory to drinking, for instance, are gainsaid by Houtum-Schindler, an outsider who was far more knowledgeable about the country than either. Houtum-Schindler, invoking the testimony of a missionary with long-standing experience in the region, noted that brandy was hardly consumed in the area.[71] Most foreigners only socialized with the rich and the powerful and their contacts were heavily urban-based. Some explicitly stated that the spread of wine consumption was uneven. Porter cautioned that, in general, few Iranians drank. There were exceptions, he noted, but imbibing Muslims made sure to drink wine made by Christians "rather than that which is doubly

[68]Bélanger, *Voyage aux Indes-orientales*, 2/ii: 340–41.
[69]Brugsch, *Im Land der Sonne*, 226; Collins, *In the Kingdom of the Shah*, 57.
[70]Stolze and Andreas, "Handelsverhältnisse Persiens," 11; Polak, *Persien*, 2:142.
[71]Houtum Schindler, "Reisen im südlichen Persien," 59.

drenched in sin, by having been the manufacture of a Mussulman."[72] Treacher Collins, who at the turn of the twentieth century spent time in Iran as the eye doctor of the powerful southern governor, Zill al-Sultan, noted that in the four months he had been in Iran he never saw a Muslim drunk. "What drinking there is—and I believe there is a good deal amongst the richer classes—is carried out of sight behind the high walls of the anderun."[73] People in Fars told Preece in 1884 that the date wine to which Marco Polo refers was no longer manufactured in the region.[74] British consular reports from 1893 to 1894 insisted that very few Iranians consumed spirituous liquors, and that the demand for European wines, beer and spirits was very limited.[75]

Among the lower classes, those who drank were often *lutis*. The term covers a variety of groups, some of them dedicated to social justice and manliness reinforced by physical exercise, but here mostly refers to urban hooligans.[76] It is among the latter that wine drinking seems to have been common. Their reputation for thievery, adultery and gambling was intertwined with their propensity to drink, something that Perkins experienced when he was stabbed by a *luti* who reportedly was intoxicated.[77] Examples of drinking among low-level civil servants, *farrashes*, have come to us as well. French envoy Sartiges relates how in December 1845 one of his men, an Iranian national, had been accosted by four *farrashes*, who were totally drunk and who, without any provocation struck the poor fellow in the face with a dagger.[78] Wills tells the amusing story of a servant of his, a cook who had been with him for fourteen years and who had a history of frequent marriages and debts and who for four years had been given to drinking, spending all of his money on alcohol. Dismissal and corporeal punishment failed to deter him and so Wills sent him to the *shaykh al-islam* of Isfahan with a letter asking the shaykh to make him take an oath to abstain. This he did, but instead of a drunk, Wills notes, he now became a fool, having taken to the consumption of opium.[79]

[72]Porter, *Travels in Georgia, Persia, Armenia*, 347–48.

[73]Collins, *In the Kingdom of the Shah*, 57.

[74]Preece, "Journey from Shiraz to Jashk," 423.

[75]*A&P*, 1894, vol. 87, Preece, Report of a Journey made to Yezd, Kerman, and Shiraz, and on the Trade, and of the Consular District of Isfahan, 34; and *A&P*, 1895, vol. 99, Report for the Year 1893–94 on the Trade of Shiraz, 13.

[76]Binning, *A Journal of Two Years' Travel*, 1:273.

[77]Floor, "The Lūtīs," 120, citing Husayn Khan, *Jugrafiya-yi Isfahan*, 86–88. For the stabbing, see Perkins, *Residence of Eight Years in Persia*, 289–90.

[78]AME, Paris Corr. Pol., Perse 21, Sartiges, Tehran to Paris, 31 December 1845, fol. 165.

[79]Wills, *In the Land of the Lion and the Sun*, 379–80.

VI. AMBIVALENCE

Reminiscent of the Safavid period, too, is the ambivalence with which people approached drinking, expressed in attempts to reconcile their indulgence with a desire to be seen as good Muslims. Imbibers might abstain during the month of Ramadan, "taking care to give themselves ample compensation the moment the fast expires."[80] Terminology was a way of deflecting reality. As one observer put it: When a Persian takes on himself the shame of wine . . . "he says he has been eating nightingale's flesh or drinking cold tea."[81] As the guest of the khan of Kuchan, Fraser was offered strong liquor called *ma al-hayat* (lit. life-water), the Arabic equivalent of aquavit, a drink that was highly flavored with oranges and aromatics. His hosts persuaded themselves that it was lawful, "because it was not made from any of the substances expressly prohibited by the Mahometan law."[82] More fundamental was an effort to keep drinking hidden, confined to the private sphere and thus out of public view. As in Safavid times, (reputable) Iranians thus made sure not to drink in public gatherings for fear that this might damage their reputation. The governor of Hamadan in 1875 invited the Spanish consul to Iran, Adolfo Rivadeneyra, to his home for a dinner party but asked his guest beforehand to keep the invitation a secret lest the people find out that the town's first magistrate had hosted a party for an infidel where wine was likely to be served.[83] As Lomnitskii said: "The only difference between a drinking Persian and a drinking European is that a European drinks at every opportunity, day and night and in any season, without being Pharisaical; while Persians drink only at night, mostly on their own or in the company of their most intimate friends." Instead, they would retreat to a separate room in order to imbibe, much in the same way as at a party today in the West a separate room might be set aside for those who want to smoke pot.[84] In this manner, a separation of sorts between public and private spheres within a private ambience would be achieved. As one longtime resident of Iran noted, an Iranian would observe religious rules as long as others watched him, but do what appeared to him as comfortable and pleasant as soon as he was alone. The state, he continued, punished only those drunks who caused a public nuisance and never bothered to intervene with indoor drinking parties, even if in the end all were lying about.[85] As in Safavid times, the person who drank

---

[80]Sheil, *Glimpses of Life and Manners*, 174.

[81]Sparroy, *Persian Children of the Royal Family*, 217.

[82]Fraser, *Narrative of a Journey into Khorasān*, 570.

[83]Rivadeneyra, *Viaje al interior de Persia*, 2:70.

[84]Sheil, *Glimpses of Life and Manners*, 157.

[85]Anon. [Ritter von Riederer], *Aus Persien*, 86.

"drained his glass to the dregs, with his left hand under his chin to catch the drops of wine, lest he should be detected next morning in respectable society."[86]

Clerics naturally had an especially good reason to keep their involvement with alcohol hidden from the public eye. The mullah who made wine for himself by making it for Wills, said: "If I make it here, sahib, I shall make it good, and kill two birds with one stone: you and I will get good wine, and there will be no scandal."[87] Lomnitskii tells a story about mullahs who were invited to a private party at the house of a wealthy Iranian. After performing the evening prayer, the host ordered his servants to bring "something and the hats." When trays were brought in with hats on them, the mullahs took off their turbans and chose a suitable hat. After that they would not worry about drinking alcohol. Declaring, "I am not a mullah any more, but a private person," each of them would start playing games (chess, checkers and cards) and consume that "something." Lomnitskii explains: "This 'something' consisted of a whole battery of bottles; one could find an excellent cognac, vodka, wine, liquors, and all different kinds of beverages." After hearty dining and drinking, and unable to go home, all the guests slept over at the host's house.[88]

VII. THE CASE OF SHIRAZ

Shiraz continued to be the main center of viticulture and wine production after the fall of the Safavids. Its famous wine came from the villages of Bayda, Shul, Adakan, Abrah, Guyum, and Khullar, a place some 50 kilometers from Shiraz whose surroundings counted as the main area of cultivation.[89] During the Zand period, local Armenians continued to make wine in Shiraz. Aside from being consumed locally, Shiraz wine also was carried to Bushihr and thence exported to Basra and India.[90] It was seen how under Karim Khan Zand the town housed a multitude of taverns and brothels. Fifty years later, Shiraz still enjoyed a reputation of looseness compared to other Iranian urban centers.[91]

The Scotsman Charles MacGregor, visiting Shiraz in 1875, noted: "There is one thing in Sheeraz which strikes me as very strange after

---

[86]Colonel Sheil, Note C, in Sheil, *Glimpses of Life and Manners*, 340.

[87]Wills, *In the Land of the Lion and the Sun*, 229.

[88]Lomnitskii, *Persiia i Persy*, 121–22, 380–81.

[89]Tomaschek, "Zur historischen Topographie," 173; Pelly, "Brief Account of the Province of Fars," 176.

[90]Niebuhr, *Reisebeschreibung*, 2:170.

[91]Morier, *Journey through Persia*, 59.

being accustomed to the horror an Indian Mussulman displays at the mention of wine, and that is the very open way in which the Persians drink wine and in which it is made and sold in this town."[92] Vámbéry had a similar take on the city, which he called the place in Iran where people consumed wine with the least embarrassment, and where not just Armenians but Muslims as well were engaged in the manufacturing of wine. Vámbéry claims that everyone in Shiraz, from the poor day laborer to the civil servants, indeed even the ulama, liked to imbibe and took part in drinking parties. In contrast to the situation elsewhere in Iran, the author insisted, women too participated in these festivities.[93]

These observations appear to overstate the case. It is true that the wine of Shiraz, which came in two kinds, red and white, the former "tasting like rough and course sherry, and the latter like a sweet, thin Chablis," was made openly and sold publicly by local Armenians. But it also seems that, even in the city that since Safavid times had held a reputation for Muslim drinking, the followers of Islam were forced to consume wine in secret, so much so that "a man can hardly retire to any place alone, without being suspected of going to taste a forbidden cup."[94] Though Muslims are said to have consumed alcohol as much as Christians, they "refrained from trafficking in it, for fear of too openly defying the bigotry of the few fanatic mullahs, who possess so much influence over the multitude."[95]

No city yields as much information on drinking as Shiraz thanks to the detailed reporting on events in the city by informants for the British over a period of twenty years in the last three decades of the nineteenth century. Their reports, collected in the *Vaqa'i`-i ittifaqiyah*, reveal the magnitude of the social problems caused by drinking, even if much of it took place behind closed doors. The period was one of much turmoil in Shiraz and the surrounding area, with frequent instances of brigandage and theft resulting in a precarious level of security.[96] The incidents recorded typically involve soldiers or *lutis*, portrayed as thugs, or low-level government officials who took part in drinking parties and, once sodden, got into brawls, fought with fists or knives, causing injury and death. Sometimes prostitutes or other, unnamed, females were involved as well. In the period between 1874 and 1893–94 such altercations resulted in eighteen deaths and at least twenty injuries. When arrested, the perpetrators generally landed in prison where they were often given

[92]MacGregor, *Narrative of a Journey*, 1:37.
[93]Vámbéry, *Meine Wanderungen*, 231.
[94]Porter, *Travels in Georgia*, 1:707.
[95]Ussher, *Journey from London to Persepolis*, 512.
[96]Sirjani, ed., *Vaqa'i`-i ittifaqiyah*, 257–58.

lashes or treated to the bastinado. In some cases people's ears were cut off as well. In case the victims died, the killer was beheaded. In a number of instances the attackers sought *bast* (sanctified refuge) in inviolable places, typically the popular shrine of Shah Chiragh.[97] All of this stands in marked contrast to the situation in Tehran in the same period. There, the police reports by Count di Monteforte reveal quite a few instances of public drunkenness for the years 1886–88, but they rarely involved violence, and death through homicide never ensued.[98]

Many of the brawls took place in the Jewish quarter of town. The Jews were among the minorities who had the right to make wine in Shiraz, and the taverns, *shirah-khanah*, also were located in their part of town.[99] The stories told offer us a glimpse of relations between the Jewish and Muslims inhabitants of the town, in addition to occasionally highlighting the role and behavior of the local ulama. In one instance, a couple of *lutis* got drunk in the Jewish quarter. They broke into a Jewish home to get hold of wine. The owners put up resistance and one of them was wounded in the ensuing scuffle. The Jews complained, and the next night two men came back to the house, asked the owner why he had brought charges, and injured him. The Jewish population reacted to this by protesting loudly. An investigation followed, leading to the arrest of a number of the Jews. They received the bastinado and were fined 50 *tumans*. The injured person died from his wounds, the killer disappeared and the Jews ended up keeping a low profile for fear that worse things might happen to them.[100]

Another incident involved local Jews and the ulama in the person of `Ali Akbar Fal Asiri, the well known cleric who played a leading role in the Tobacco Protest that erupted in Shiraz in 1891, and whose frequent agitation against the local Jews exemplifies the hardening attitudes of Iran's ulama in the face of growing Western influence.[101] On 15 Ramadan 1298/11August 1881, Fal Asiri ran into a Jew as the latter was taking a container with arak to the home of a Muslim. Fal Asiri grabbed the

---

[97]Ibid., 5, 33–34, 41, 54, 68, 86, 97, 105, 113, 183, 185, 207, 222, 225, 229, 256, 293, 329, 371–72, 377–78, 467, 504, 532, 552, 567, 612, 695.

[98]Riza'i and Azari, eds., *Guzarish'ha-yi nazmiyah*, 6, 7, 17, 33, 49, 68, 79, 103, 116, 143–4, 155–56, 196, 197, 243, 250, 254, 283, where someone died from drinking too much arak, 284, 301, 311, 316, 347, 371, 379, 394.

[99]Sirjani, ed., *Vaqa'i`-i ittifaqiyah*, 68, 185, 470. Stern notes that the town's Jews were particularly active in running taverns, which he called secret. Insofar as people knew where to find them they cannot have been very secret, however. See Stern, *Dawnings of Light in the East*, 129.

[100]Sirjani, ed., *Vaqa'i`-i ittifaqiyah*, 68, 28 Safar/14 March-2 Rabi` II/16 April 1294/1877.

[101]For the worsening fate of the Jews in late-nineteenth-century Iran, see Tsadik, "Foreign Intervention," esp. 255–330.

container, broke it, and also cut the locks of the Jew. That same night a pamphlet was attached to the door of the cleric's house, asking why he prevented the Jews from selling alcohol, telling him to keep his own mullahs from buying wine from them, and warning that he would be killed if he did this again. The next day Fal Asiri read the text from the pulpit at the Vakil mosque, announcing that the time of the killing of Jews had come. The authorities were notified, and the result was that Fal Asiri was officially reprimanded for having overstepped his jurisdiction. Backing down, the `alim then began to push for the closing of the wine taverns and the prevention of public singing—another activity for which the Jews were known. He also argued that the Jews of Shiraz should cut their locks and not wear conspicuous clothes. The Jews responded to this intimidation by locking their homes for fear of *luti* activities and by hiding their belongings in their basements or in the homes of Muslim friends. Most singers also cut their hair. Following this, Fal Asiri is said to have given up his fiery rhetoric and to have forgiven the Jews.[102]

Yet another incident involving Fal Asiri occurred in October 1894. Jews opened up a *shirah-khanah* on a plot of barren land. Fal Asiri got wind of this and was told that the location used to be the site of a mosque. He thereupon gave orders that any bottle of wine or arak found there should be smashed. The Jews complained, relaying their case to the shah by telegraph. When Tehran responded by ordering the dispatch of soldiers, Fal Asiri threatened armed resistance, defiantly stating that he would never (again) be run out of town and that his death would mean martyrdom for the cause of Islam.[103]

The outcome of the last story remains unclear. The taverns run by Jews were closed in 1903. Drunkenness prompted action, and the Jews of Shiraz were told that they could no longer sell alcohol or even use it themselves. If any bottle was found, the house of the owner was to be destroyed.[104] This did not prevent the Jews from running illegal establishments peddling alcohol, however, for in January 1904 we hear how some unspecified oil functionaries who had recently come to Shiraz had been caught drunk. Asked where they had obtained their alcohol, they pointed to the Jews. Fath Alayalah, the head of the Jewish quarter, was summoned together with the proprietor of the speakeasy and given the bastinado.[105]

[102]Sirjani, ed., *Vaqa'i`-i ittifaqiyah*, 139–40, 5–20 Ramazan 1298/13–28 September 1877. Only fear of the government is said to have kept Fal Asiri from having the Jews of Shiraz massacred. See ibid., 337.

[103]Ibid., 470, 17 Rabi` I 1313/17 October 1894. Fal Asiri's allusion to expulsion refers to his forced removal from Shiraz in 1891 following his agitation against the tobacco concession.

[104]Ibid., 714–15, 3 Jumadi I, 1321/28 July 1903.

[105]Ibid., 718, 4 Zu'l-qa`dah 1321/22 January 1904.

VIII. Antialcohol Measures and Bans

As was the case in Safavid times, public drinking at times prompted the ulama to call for a ban on alcohol, typically following a natural disaster or during adverse economic conditions. Yet the examples from Shiraz suggest the importance of the presence of an activist cleric as a catalyst regardless of the circumstances. A good example is the drought of 1814–15. Mullah Muhammad Zanjani, the *shaykh al-islam* of Tehran, explained the lack of rainfall to his followers as a sign of God's wrath with the drinking of alcohol among the resident Christians, and urged the mob to go raid the Armenian quarter. An Armenian church and several wine houses were thus destroyed. When Fath `Ali Shah heard of this he was irate but the perpetrators sought *bast* in the shrine of Shah `Abd al-`Azim, south of Tehran. Eventually twelve of the culprits were apprehended and brought before the shah, who after lecturing them on the protection enjoyed by the People of the Book, expelled them from the capital. The Armenians, meanwhile, received compensation for the sustained losses and had their church repaired with state funds.[106]

Several cases from the provinces are on record as well. In 1838 the sale of alcohol by minorities caused the outbreak of a riot in Bushihr. A mob moved to the Jewish quarter of the town, targeting the house of the moneychanger, *sarraf*, of the British residence, accusing him of selling alcohol. The assailants ransacked the house, forcing him to take refuge in the resident's lodge.[107] Another instance of a local ordinance involving drinking occurred in Kirmanshah in the winter of 1858. Following the incidence of "public drinking and mischief" on the part of some "lutis and ruffians," the governor, `Imad al-Dawlah, issued a ban on local Jews selling alcohol to Muslims.[108]

Although the ulama were often the ones to incite the populace against the sale and use of alcohol, vice control does not seem to have been part of their actual jurisdiction. Of the religious functionaries who in the Safavid period had been in charge of public morals, the *sadr* and the *shaykh al-islam*, the former had been abolished under Nadir Shah, whereas the latter more and more evolved into a bureaucratic official

---

[106]Natiq, *Iran dar rahyabi-yi farhangi*, 178–79. The contemporary Persian sources do not mention the drought, but present this episode as having resulted from Mullah Muhammad Zanjani's encounter with a drunk and an ensuing altercation. This prompted him to instigate his followers to raid Armenian houses and churches, where they smashed wine bottles and engaged in plundering. See Sipihr, *Nasikh al-tavarikh*, 1:265; I`timad al-Saltanah, *Tarikh-i muntazam-i Nasiri*, 3:1526; as well as Algar, *Religion and State in Iran*, 54.

[107]Kelly, *Britain and the Persian Gulf*, 306,

[108]*Ruznamah-i vaqa'i`- i ittifaqiyah*, no. 360, 6, 7 Jumadi al-ula 1274/24 December 1857. Thanks to Kambiz Eslami for bringing this to my attention.

who dealt with civil matters without having any autonomous standing.[109] The *muhtasib*, meanwhile, performed the same function that he had performed under the Safavids: he was the market inspector, responsible for weights and measures and proper business practice.[110] Jurisdiction over criminal cases rested with the *hakim-i `urf*, the commonlaw judge, and the official in charge of enforcing the ban on drinking, and in general of the morals of people was the *darughah*, the police prefect, whose men, the *farrash*es, patrolled the urban streets.[111] There is little or no difference with the Safavid period in this regard. As was seen in chapter 3, under the Safavids, too, executive power over public order and moral rectitude rested with the *darughah*. The Qajars inherited a dual system, whereby offenses directed against the state or public security generally fell under the jurisdiction of `urf law and shar` law was reserved for personal and commercial litigation.[112] Religious courts might deal with civil cases, including matters pertaining to public order, but since, as Curzon explained, "they pronounce, but they cannot execute judgment," executive power tended to devolve on the offices of government. In a qualifying statement, Curzon added that "the decisions of the *mujtaheds* are seldom disrespected, and are, as a rule, carried into effect, yet the final reference to the civil power is an acknowledgment of its superiority, while it opens the door to the lengthy process of negotiations and bribes that always supervenes when one of the parties engaged is a Persian governor or official."[113]

This observation points to the flexibility of a system that was at all times open to bargaining. The police were "supported by extortions and practice the most vile machinations to trap the rich and those who can afford to considerable sums on the slightest occurrences, which scarcely amount in our conception to immoralities, much less to crimes."[114] Another observer claimed of the *darughah* that "if he detects any of them drinking wine, or in the company of courtesans, he compels them to purchase his connivance at no small expense."[115] According to Wilson, "Wine-sellers, thieves, and lewd men and women were levied upon for hush-money *à la* Tammany." He also claimed that *kalantar*s received 10 percent from the sale of illegal liquor.[116] The *darughah*s had a

---

[109]Binning, *Journal of Two Years' Travel*, 1:338.

[110]Waring, *Tour of Sheeraz*, 68–69; Perry, *Karim Khan Zand*, 234, 283.

[111]Francklin, *Observations Made on a Tour from Bengal*, 30; Waring, *Tour to Sheeraz*, 64–65; Rustam al-Hukama, *Rustam al-tavarikh*, 308, cited in Perry, *Karim Khan Zand*, 282–83. See also Floor, "Change and Development in the Judicial System."

[112]Algar, *Religion and State in Iran*, 12–13.

[113]Curzon, *Persia and the Persian Question*, 1:453.

[114]Stirling, *Journals*, 53.

[115]Waring, *Tour to Sheeraz*, 67.

[116]Wilson, *Persian Life and Customs*, 67.

reputation of being both "harsh and venal."[117] An example that occurred in the city of Yazd in 1880 indeed suggests that shari'a punishment for contravening the ban on drinking could be bought off. Various persons were caught making wine and detained. Two of them especially, both silk workers, were given the bastinado and told that the next day they would both lose their hands. Their fathers thereupon paid the local *farrashbashi* a sum of money in order to avoid this punishment.[118]

As in Safavid times, foreigners were exempted from such bans. Crown Prince 'Abbas Mirza not only allowed the many Russians in his service to drink but even licensed a wine shop in Tabriz for the use of the Russian battalion stationed there.[119]

IX. Drinking as Statement

If in various ways patterns of alcohol consumption remained the same from the Safavid to the Qajar period, some changes did occur. For one, there are signs that the incidence of drinking outside of court circles went up, and the sources create the impression that, as in the Ottoman Empire, arak gained in importance relative to wine.[120] Admittedly negative evidence that the use of alcohol was on the increase by the mid-nineteenth century comes in the form of the agitation against it on the part of the ulama. Complaining to chief minister Mirza Taqi Khan, better known as Amir Kabir, about an alleged increase in public drunkenness, they demanded that the sale of wine and intoxicating liquors be outlawed. Amir Kabir, who was known for his contempt for the ulama, refused, insisting that the sale of alcoholic beverages was to remain permitted and that anyone should be free to drink as much as he wished. He warned, however, that the first person to be found drunk in public would learn the price of violating the law. He kept his world, for when he was informed of an incident involving two men who after drinking too much for their own good, ran around the bazaar as if possessed, he had them arrested and immured with their heads sticking out of the wall. He then ordered one end of a rope to be attached to their heads, and the other end to two horses, which next were made to gallop away, decapitating the poor devils. Following this punishment, Gobineau insists, Tehran saw no more murder and public debauchery.[121]

---

[117]Curzon, *Persia and the Persian Question*, 1:455.

[118]Mahdavi and Afhar, eds., *Yazd dar asnad-i Amin al-Zarb*, 385–86.

[119]Porter, *Travels in Georgia*, 1:348–49.

[120]For the situation in the Ottoman Empire, or at least Istanbul, in the nineteenth century, see Georgeon, "Ottomans and Drinkers."

[121]Gobineau, *Correspondance*, 67–68, letter to Comte de Pokesch-Osten, Tehran, 20 February 1856.

Greater availability of alcohol and its growing visibility as part of a more conspicuous European presence in Iran almost certainly played a role in the (perceived) increase in drinking—and especially in the growing consumption of hard liquor. Lady Sheil speculated that the presence of a Russian squadron near Astarabad was bound to change the non-drinking habits of the inhabitants of Mazandaran.[122] Perkins draws our attention to another aspect of the changing drinking scene in Iran in this period. The consumption of alcohol, he noted, had gone up of late, particularly as European liquors had begun to be imported.[123] There is some evidence that Iran's upper classes followed their Ottoman counterparts in adopting alcohol in imitation of European standards and as a "necessity of civilization."[124] Curzon echoed this when he said that, "the assumption of European tastes carries with it the consumption of European wines, spirits and liqueurs."[125] By the 1830s a considerable volume of alcoholic beverages was imported into Iran. A French report noted that in 1837 two thousand chests of rum were shipped to Iran from England via Trabzon. That year the same Ottoman port saw the transshipment of six thousand bottles of champagne destined for Iran.[126] Shaykh Hasan Karbala'i Isfahani in 1893 wrote a treatise criticizing the tobacco concession that Shah Nasir al-Din Shah had granted to a British national a few years earlier, in which he lamented the increase in the number of foreigners and their influence in Iran. As one of the pernicious signs of Western intrusion he mentioned the appearance of brothels and the proliferation of places where liquor was sold, numbering more than one hundred in Tehran alone.[127] Members of the court, some of whom had accompanied the shah on his various trips to Europe, did not remain immune to these developments. The I'timad al-Saltanah noted how `Ali Asghar Khan Amin al-Sultan had taken to drinking openly and in excess following the his return from Europe in 1889, and how hard drinking and card playing had of late become much more common at court.[128]

Further clues to change, also analogous to the situation in Ottoman lands, come from the aforementioned temperance society founded by Dr. Pashayan, which organized lectures with the aid of the newly introduced magic lantern to present modern arguments having to do with the

[122]Sheil, *Glimpses of Life and Manners*, 267.

[123]Ibid., 226.

[124]Georgeon, "Ottomans and Drinkers," 17.

[125]Curzon, *Persia and the Persian Question*, 2:560.

[126]AME, Nantes, Téhéran A, 21, fol. 104.

[127]Karbala'i, *Tarikh-i dukhaniyah*, 72.

[128]He had accompanied the shah on the latter's third European trip. I'timad al-Saltanah, *Ruznamah-i khatirat*, quoted in Bakhash, *Iran, Monarchy, Bureaucracy and Reform*, 267.

hereditary nature of alcoholism and the bodily harm alcohol causes. They also are found in a treatise on the "decline of order in the world as a result of alcoholic beverages" that in 1874 appeared in serialized form in the newspaper *Iran*. Its author, Mirza Taqi, a physician from Kashan, noted that until fifty years earlier alcohol other than wine had not been readily available in Iran and that in most cities arak was rarely seen at the time. Given the *shar`i* prohibition of alcohol, he loftily insisted, it used to be inconceivable for people to engage in public drinking, the exception being low-ranking types without honor or reputation. With the coming of European knowledge and techniques, however, things had begun to change. People had learned how to manufacture distilled spirits from fruits that had never been used for the purpose, such as apples, pears, figs, melons and watermelons, and different kinds of berries. With the opening of trade with foreign countries alcohol had spread even further, especially among the young with their taste for pleasure. Those taking to alcohol, Mirza Taqi observed, had found excuses to flout the law of the Prophet, some referring to Ibn Sina, others quoting the poems of `Umar Khayyam.[129]

This last remark points to a more indigenous element in changing drinking patterns. Traditional Iranian skepticism about religious verities and disdain for the hypocrisy of religious leaders, famously celebrated by Hafiz and other mystical poets, was nothing new in Iran. "I care nothing for Priests," Malcolm has the Shirazi merchant, Aqa Ibrahim say, "and have never felt the slightest disposition to alter my ways, except when the liquor was bad, but I take care . . . to have it always of the best."[130] But this attitude, coupled with a growing influence of European manners and customs in the course of the nineteenth century, appears to have produced a new consciousness about drinking. Singling out the "higher classes" as the ones given to intemperance, Perkins noted that many of them were "becoming so lax and skeptical in regard to the claims of their religion."[131] Reverence for their religion was diminishing among Muslims, Perkins insisted, "and to a great extent by foreign influence."[132] This was not simply a matter of the well-to-do becoming indifferent to religion. It rather involved an increase in the number of skeptics, agnostics, and antinomians, as well as a growing readiness among people to articulate their skepticism and deist beliefs in the face of the growing intolerance of the ulama.[133] Malcolm in the early

[129]Kashani, "Dar bayan-i ikhtilal-i nizam-i `alam."
[130][Malcolm], *Sketches of Persia*, 1:116.
[131]Perkins, *Residence of Eight Years*, 226.
[132]Ibid., 268.
[133]Amanat, *Resurrection and Renewal*, 80–88.

part of the century and the Russian diplomat Baron de Bode a few decades later drew attention to the progress Sufism had made of late.[134] "The followers of this sect," the latter said, "who formerly dared not avow their sentiments, now openly profess their doctrines, the main object of which is to keep more to the spirit than to the letter of the law, although many have gone beyond the prescribed limits, and have become Freethinkers, or else indifferent, on matters of religion."[135] De Bode attributed the growth of such sentiments in part to the paradoxical loss of clerical prestige among the public and the gain of secular power as seen in decreased royal deference to the religious classes and the state's suppression of the power of the *lutis*, the urban toughs who formed the semicriminal entourage of high-ranking ulama.[136] But as much of this new outspokenness was in reaction to the growing presumptiousness and assertiveness of the ulama in the face of a state with weak religious credentials. The upper classes especially found in radical rationalism a tool to reject revelation and embrace individual judgment in matters of religion, and thus to resist the tyranny, hypocrisy, and intolerance of the ulama.[137]

We have no way of knowing how many Iranians adhered to these doctrines or sympathized with such ideas. Ussher's estimate that one fourth of the populace, including a number of well-educated Iranians, did is as good as any.[138] One observer called them especially prevalent in the country's southern parts,[139] a fact that, if true, would lend credence to Lomnitski's supposition that the incidence of drinking was more widespread in the south than in the north. The number was certainly substantial enough and the voices sufficiently well articulated for European observers to notice and comment on the phenomenon. Layard, describing the drinking parties at the house of a Lur chief to whose house he had been invited, called his host someone who professed to be a "'sufi,' or freethinker." Major Sheil describes being the guest of the son of the (absent) governor of Ardabil in 1833, and how his host would only converse on the topic of wine and brandy. Sheil also noted that those who drank in excess were usually freethinkers who "pretended to laugh at the Prophet's prohibition." He claimed to know one Iranian gentleman, "a shocking drunkard but rather religious, who often bewailed to me his unfortunate

---

[134]Malcolm, *History of Persia*, 2:292.

[135]De Bode, *Travels in Luristan*, 1:47.

[136]Ibid., 47–49.

[137]Sepsis, "Perse, Quelques mots sur l'état religieux," 107; Binning, *Journal of Two Years' Travel*, 1:394–95; and Lewisohn, "Introduction to the History of Modern Persian Sufism," 1:439.

[138]Ussher, *Journey from London to Persepolis*, 6129.

[139]Sepsis, "Perse. Quelques mots sur l'état religieux,"102.

propensity. 'I know it is wrong,' he used to exclaim; 'I know I shall go to Jehennam; every day I make a towbeh (and act of repentance), and every night that rascal, my appetite, gets the better of me.'"[140]

Sheil's wife, Lady Sheil, an astute observer of Qajar life, amplified on the remarkable extent of freethinking and the attendant freedom of speech in Iran:

> With the exception of an open profession of either of the above-named religions [Judaism and Christianity], a Persian Mahommedan may avow any opinions he pleases. Atheism and deism are freely at his choice in his own circle of society. He may revile and ridicule with impunity in the above limits all systems of religion, including Mahommedanism, though of course he would suffer castigation were he indiscreet enough to profess his opinions in public. Atheism is said to be rare, but deism, it is supposed, is widely diffused among the upper classes of society. It is, however, suspected that this latitudinarianism seldom survives youth and health, and that with the approach of years or infirmity a return to old opinions is generally found.[141]

The context that enabled people to express such opinions was the remarkable freedom of speech Iranians enjoyed, a topic already noted by Chardin and on which Sheil had this to say: "Freedom of speech is on an equality with freedom of religion. It is the Persian substitute for liberty of the press, and the safety-valve of popular indignation, Every one may say what he likes. If needy, disappointed, or oppressed, the sufferer may seek consolation in reviling the Shah and his minister, and all their measures to the contentment of his heart."[142]

A particularly colorful example of someone who flouted religious sensibilities and even taunted the clergy with his libertine lifestyle is Malik Qasim Mirza, a son of Fath `Ali Shah. He was fluent in French and able to express himself in English and even some Russian, and wore European clothes and drank wine. Appointed governor of Burujird in Luristan in the reign of Muhammad Shah, "where they have seen very little of Europeans," he was soon accosted by the ulama, who upbraided him for his scandalously infidel behavior. At first civil and evasive in his answers, he later gave them the obligatory answer of libertines, namely, that if he went to a hot place, they were under no obligation to join him,

---

[140]Colonel Sheil, Note C, in Sheil, *Glimpses of Life and Manners*, 327–28.

[141]Sheil, *Glimpses of Life and Manners*, 196.

[142]Ibid., 200. Sheil insisted, though, that latterly the more frequent interaction with the Russian mission had led to the "introduction of some Russian ideas on the subject of the liberty of speech," and that this had had led to its curtailment, at least in the capital, "though in the provinces it subsists in full force."

and that he was free to do as he pleased. Finally, he invited them to see "his" priest. When they agreed, he ordered his servants to open the doors of his residence, and out rushed the greyhounds, spaniels, pointers, large dogs used for fighting wolves and wild boars, and curs of almost every description. Horrified, the mullahs tucked up their robes and began hopping about to avoid being contaminated by touching the dogs and went away spitting right and left and cursing the prince in the most classic Arabic; they never troubled him again.[143]

Brugsch connects the issue of freethinking and the consumption of wine with the inner and outer, the tendency to treat the privacy of the indoors as a haven, a sanctuary for true enjoyment and delight rigorously separated from the public sphere, where social decorum and religious norms must be upheld. It is worth quoting his observations in full:

> Those who anyhow believe in Allah, Muhammad, Ali and the saints, join the teachings and the view of one of the many religious sects, or, by contrast, very quietly follow freethinking and free-spirited views, which often come close to atheism. They read banned books, such as the writing and mystical revelations of the founder of the sect of the much-persecuted Babis . . . or become absorbed in the quatrains of the famous philosopher Omar the tentmaker [Khayyam] . . . or eagerly read the wine and love songs of the immortal Hafez, laughing at the learned exegesis of the orthodox clergy, which distorts the clear and obvious meaning of the text, making it . . . to the faith and the divine. They drink their wine and find in the utter enjoyment of life the real contentment in this earthly vale of tears.[144]

Conclusion

In many respects, the consumption of alcohol in Qajar times followed patterns that had been established in the Safavid period, if not before. Many people drank and drinking with the aim of getting drunk in a minimum of time remained the norm. Even allowing for the skewed sources at our disposal it seems that among those who consumed alcohol the rich, the powerful and the denizens of urban areas were overrepresented. Many examples have come to us of local official in small towns or even tribal areas indulging in wine or arak, especially, it seems, among the Kurds and the Lurs, groups in Iran who were known for

[143]Burgess, *Letters from Persia*, Edward Burgess, Tabriz to George Burgess, 6 April 1844, 60.

[144]Brugsch, *Im Land der Sonne*, 203.

their indifference to orthodoxy and their love of dance and music. Among the poor it was the *lutis* who were seen as particularly prone to drinking. In keeping with tradition, Shiraz, the heart of Iran's viticulture, stood out for a relaxed life style that included a great tolerance for wine drinking. Similarly, the manufacture of wine and spirits, as well as the management of taverns remained the domain of the country's Armenians and Jews.

Drinking, moreover, remained surrounded by ambivalence, for it was still an activity that lacked legal and moral sanctioning and that thus had to take place surreptitiously, in the private sphere. As long as people kept their drinking within the four walls of their homes, the typical response on the part of the state and the ulama was toleration. The continued existence of taverns in quarters inhabited by non-Muslims did not fundamentally affect this understanding, for this concerned a circumscribed public sphere, one that was liminal, quasi-private, and that did not, as such, affect the Muslim public order. In the temporary absence of the coffeehouse, taverns located in the non-Muslim parts of towns and clandestine ones in Muslim quarters, seem to have become an important venue for popular entertainment.

The period witnessed new developments as well. The most important change grew out of the lack of divine aura suffered by the Qajars. In a process that had begun in the late Safavid period, rulers tended to drink less and certainly were less ostentatious in their drinking habits. Thus, Fath `Ali Shah, otherwise known for his lavish spending and extravagant harem, appears to have abstained from drinking. Although several sources belie the notion that Fath `Ali Shah and the members of his entourage were teetotalers, the evidence points to a vastly reduced intake of alcohol on the part of Qajar rulers relative to their Safavid predecessors, and, more importantly, a carefully orchestrated projection of royal sobriety to the outside world. Some shahs still drank, and may cases have come to us of provincial governors who were alcoholics and of local officials who regularly hosted bacchanals, with the town notables and hangers-on, including members of the clergy, in attendance. But the time of the *bazm*, the public and ceremonial drinking session, was over, the food festival having taken its place.

Otherwise, the consumption of alcohol among the upper strata of society does not seem to have diminished. Western imports expanded the variety of alcoholic beverages available, and similar to conditions in the Ottoman Empire, drinking may actually have increased among the elite, even taking into account a far less numerous and conspicuous Western and non-Muslim presence in Iran compared to the Ottoman Empire. Also analogous to developments in Ottoman territory is an incipient medicalization of alcohol, the beginning of a perception of drinking not simply as religiously scandalous but as damaging to the body and the mind.

As in major Ottoman cities, for some upper-class Iranians the consumption of alcohol may have seemed fashionable as a sign of adherence to the values of the modern world. But a more subtle change, in which a long-standing Iranian tradition of religious skepticism shading into deism intersected with growing European influence, involves drinking as public statement. In Qajar times, elite drinking explicitly acquired the connotation of resistance, of protest against the tenets of Islam, and, more directly, against the cant and the intolerance of the ulama, who confronted a state of dubious religious standing and weak disciplinary performance with increasing brazenness even as they remained beholden and in some ways subordinate to it. All evidence suggests that the early to mid-nineteenth century—precisely the time when Sufism suffered great persecution—saw an increase in the number of people professing Sufi notions revolving around the individual pursuit of inner truth. For many of its adherents, drinking became a means to express one's utter contempt for the clergy if not for revealed religion as such, and a way to flaunt one's inner freedom. Although the circumstances had changed, wine thus retained its age-old function of metaphor for the inner soul and the truth it pursues, free and unfettered, expressed as libertinism and freethinking, in contradistinction to the arid formalism of official religion.

CHAPTER 8

Opium and Tobacco in Qajar Iran: From Pleasure to Cash Crop and Emblem of the Nation

> When a person begins to smoke, his faculties appear devoted to the matter at hand, and all his attention is directed to the manipulation of his pipe and lamp
> D. MacLaren, "Opium Eating and Smoking" (1907).

> I have often heard the Persians acknowledge that they can support with greater ease the want of food and drink than the deprivation of the luxury of smoking in the course of the day . . .
> Baron C. A. de Bode, *Travels in Luristan and Arabistan* (1845).

Opium

I. The Transition to the Qajar Period: Continuity

In many ways, the history of opium and its derivatives in the century and a half following the demise of the Safavids stands out for continuation rather than disruption. In 1729 Shah Tahmasb II issued a decree banning the cultivation and consumption of opium. This edict was apparently renewed in 1796, the year when Agha Muhammad Khan inaugurated the Qajar dynasty.[1] But there is little evidence that the consumption of opium was much affected. Karim Khan Zand used opium in great quantity, to the point where his indulgence may have caused an abscess of the throat, so that toward the end of his life he used opiates as a painkiller.[2] Opium was credited with analgesic qualities for toothache and rheumatoid arthritis, as well with healing capacities for a whole array of ailments and diseases ranging from bronchitis to diarrhea and from gonorrhea to eye and bladder infections to colic in babies.[3] As in Safavid times, dervishes without exception used *bang*, the best of which came from Herat.[4] The poor in general consumed *bang* and *kuknar* in great quantity, using these

---

[1]Parvin and Sommer, "Production and Trade of Persian Opium," 249.
[2]Anon., ed., *Chronicle of the Carmelites*, 665; Perry, *Karim Khan Zand*, 102–3.
[3]Polak, *Persien*, 2:246–47.
[4]Ibid.

hallucinogenics to while away their boredom or their misery and, once intoxicated, giving themselves over to daydreaming about their passions and aspirations in life. Dens of folly and stupor, the places that served them occasionally turned into centers of violence, as was observed by the Frenchman Bélanger in Tabriz who recounts a knifing in one of that city's opium establishments.[5]

The astute observations of a number of foreign observers apprise us about other aspects of the use of opium and enable one to see patterns that clearly carried over from the Safavid period but that at that time had not been discerned or analyzed with the same clarity. Olivier, whose observations date from the late eighteenth century, makes some interesting comparative observations about consumer habits, both regionally and in terms of class distinctions. He not only contradicts Hanway's claim that Iranians used opium in smaller quantity than the Turks of the Ottoman Empire, but also clarifies the possible source of Hanway's error by claiming that, although opium consumption was more widespread in Iran than in the Ottoman Empire, among the Iranians far fewer people were seen who took it in excess. Opium in Iran, he noted, was like wine in (southern) Europe: although it was abundantly available, few drunks were seen in public. Educated Iranians and people of high rank, he insisted, extending the comparison, took their opium with as much moderation as people in Europe consumed wine, limiting themselves to a dosage that would not do them any harm. In a further comment on class distinctions, Olivier asserted that the rich never took pure opium but always prepared it with some other substance, so as to make it stronger and alter its stupefying effect. The substances most commonly mixed in with the pills were musk, amber, benzoin (an aromatic resin), nutmeg, cardamom, cinnamon, cloves, and saffron. Users tended to take a dose not generally exceeding a pill of two grains. Some took a bit more but a dose of four grains was rarely ingested. The side effects of consuming excessive doses, weight loss, aching limbs, despondency, and melancholia, were all warning signs that one had taken too much.[6]

How much opium was integrated into daily life and its rituals is further suggested in the following passage:

> In the coffeehouses of which I have spoken, the opium is pure or prepared with various substances. It is offered to those who show up in accordance with their taste and the dose they prefer. From the heads of the poppy boiled in water, to which they add a bit of saffron and various extracts, they also prepare a beverage that is little intoxicating to which the smartest confine themselves, taking just the dose that

[5]Bélanger, *Voyage aux Indes-orientales*, 2:342–43.
[6]Olivier, *Voyage dans l'empire othoman*, 5:277–79.

suits them in order to procure for themselves for a few hours pleasant visions or a joyous delirium.[7]

In a clear reference to *kuknar*, Olivier noted that in the same coffee-houses, a much stronger and much more intoxicating beverage was often sold. Made with the leaves or the ends of the ordinary hemp plant one added a little *nux vomica*. Islamic law, he added, had always prohibited this, and Agha Muhammad Khan Qajar had actually had those distributing or consuming it executed.[8]

Jacob Polak and C. J. Wills, both physicians and as longtime residents of Iran well acquainted with the use of a substances like opium in Iran, corroborate Olivier's observations by affirming that many Iranians from the better classes, and really anyone who could afford it, took a pill in the afternoon for good spirits. Polak noted that the use was especially widespread in the damp Caspian provinces on account of a prevailing belief that the hygroscopic nature of opium neutralized the humidity in the air. Polak, echoing Olivier's observations, cautioned that it would be erroneous to look upon Iranians as opium addicts. Only rarely did one find abuse in the cities, he concluded, and most occurred among the dervishes.[9] As had been the case in Safavid times, dervishes indeed seem to have been one group of people who took opium, as well as cannabis and alcohol, invariably and in great quantity, something that, according to numerous observers, accounted for their often emaciated, haggard appearance and their bewildered looks.[10] Most people, Polak noted, only took up the habit in later life and would stick to the same amount, some five grams per month (twice as much in the Caspian provinces), for decades, so that the effects tended to be minimal. Iranians, he insisted, were convinced that people over fifty should take opium if they wished to stay strong and healthy and live to an old age. By way of illustration, Polak gave several examples of people who had lived to an extreme old age despite their persistent use of opium.[11] And just as with tobacco, the use of opium knew no strict gender division. Old women in particular seem to have been avid opium-eaters in the Qajar period.[12] Wills, who resided in Iran between 1866 and 1881, concurred by saying that "most men of forty among the upper and middle classes" use opium and that "nine out of ten of aged Persians take one to five grams

---

[7]Ibid., 278.

[8]Ibid., 279.

[9]Polak, *Persien*, 252.

[10]Gasteiger (Khan), *Von Teheran nach Beludschistan*, 52; Wills, *In the Land of the Lion and the Sun*, 45.

[11]Polak, *Persien*, 2:248–53.

[12]Ibid., 334.

of the drug daily."[13] Wills estimated that among old people of both sexes almost three out of every four took a small quantity of opium, "from half a grain upwards," every day. The *taryakdan*, or opium pill-box, he noted, was "in as common use in Persia as the snuff-box was in England."[14] He insisted that the moderate use of opium had no appreciable ill effect on people of old age or on those who traveled.[15]

Despite Polak's and Wills's remarks, there can but be little doubt that, beyond dervishes, many people in Qajar Iran were addicted to opium. The prevalence of addiction is illustrated in the difficulty heavy users had in observing Ramadan. James Fraser, writing during the reign of Fath `Ali Shah, drew attention to the extraordinary degree to which opium was part of life and seen as a necessity in his observation about the pragmatism with which opium-eaters managed to evade the rigors of Ramadan:

> For opium-eaters, indeed, there is some degree of indulgence to be purchased; the law, or the moollahs, allow such as cannot without fear of death, or great derangement of the system, abstain from their usual dose for twelve hours, to take what is retired to support them, provided they give a proper consideration for the indulgence, in alms to the poor or the mosque; and I believe there are but few who do not contrive to show cause for it;—but for the poor smokers, I believe, there is no such exemption; the pipe is not considered necessary to life, and may therefore be laid aside for twelve or fourteen hours; but I fear, that few determined opium-eaters or smokers ever trouble themselves to solicit the indulgence, or conquer their craving, but quietly retiring into the recesses of their dwellings, gratify their appetites without reference to priest or moollah.[16]

II. From Eating to Smoking

Polak made an exception to the benign effect of taking opium for smoking it, which he claimed was much more damaging than taking it orally.[17] Whereas the above quote by Fraser indicates that opium was smoked in Iran already in the early nineteenth century, at the time that Polak recorded his observations smoking opium was still much less

---

[13]Wills, *Persia as It Is*, 234, 237–38.

[14]Wills, *In the Land of the Lion and the Sun*, 181.

[15]Ibid.

[16]Fraser, *Travels and Adventures*, 161.

[17]This opinion contrasts with that of Donald MacLaren, the author of a short treatise on opium, published in 1907, in which he stated that ingesting opium in the form of pills is the most injurious manner of using opium, as it causes all the active principles to be introduced into the stomach. See MacLaren, "Opium Eating and Smoking," 508.

widespread than ingesting it, and much less practiced than in the neighboring Ottoman Empire, mostly because, in Polak's words, "public morality" in Iran condemned it, so that it was done only in secret.[18] It was indeed only in the later nineteenth century that Iranians massively took to smoking opium, and by the time Polak wrote an article about the drug, in the early 1880s, smoking had not yet begun to rival eating.[19] Wills, writing in the same period, claimed that "opium smoking is almost unknown and opium when smoked is, as a rule, smoked by a nature doctor's prescription."[20] The police reports of Tehran written by Count di Monteforte in the years 1303, 1304, and 1305 (1886–88), make frequent references to the use of opium and the social problems it caused, and all concern incidences of overdosing or attempted suicide—typically following a domestic dispute—through ingestion.[21] By the 1890s this had changed. A British report from 1894 had this to day about the situation in Khurasan:

> A large portion of the population use it as a drug. They are divided into two classes; the smokers and the eaters. The former may be classed with habitual drunkards who are past redemption. There is no cure, and the opium smoker can be recognised at once by his sallow countenance, sunken cheeks, nervous gait, and, as a rule, filthy appearance. After a time he become unfit for employment, and is spoken of with contempt even by the opium eaters. These latter, as a rule are middle-aged and old people, and simply take one, two or three opium pills morning and evening. When they go beyond that they soon exchange the pills for the pipe.[22]

As the above quote suggests, the transition from swallowing opium in solid form to inhaling it through a pipe, *vafur*, is an important one. This is so in part because it marks a shift from the use of opiates for essentially medicinal reasons to their enjoyment as a recreational drug. The ceremonial laboriousness involved in using a *mangal*, brazier, and tongs to light the *vafur*, and the fact that the pipe tends to be shared by a number of users made smoking opium a communal and sociable affair rather than an activity associated with loneliness, which is what it became in the contemporary West.[23] But the trend toward smoking had

---

[18]Polak, *Persien*, 2:254; idem, "Das persische Opium," 124.

[19]Polak, "Das persische Opium," 124.

[20]Wills, *Persia as It Is*, 237.

[21]Riza'i and Azari, eds., *Guzarish'ha-yi nazmiyah*, 41, 55, 57, 59, 69, 97, 145–46, 152, 155, 172, 191, 241, 247, 266–67, 282, 289, 329, 365, 396, 315.

[22]*A&P*, 1893–94, vol. 95, Thomson, Trade of the Consular District of Meshed, 1892–93, 7.

[23]Gelpke, *Vom Rausch*, 59–60.

more negative consequences as well. The effect of smoking is much more immediate because the lungs instantaneously assimilate the smoke, so that the user is left in a state of extreme lassitude. The same immediacy and the greater difficulty of calibrating the intake increase the chance of becoming addicted. Smoking, finally, is more disruptive of daily routine than eating because of the utensils it involves and the need to be stationary during the process of using them. How did opium smoking make its way to Iran?

Opium smoking was not indigenous anywhere in Asia until the Europeans introduced opium for smoking to China in the seventeenth century. The Spanish were the first to import tobacco and the notion of smoking as such into China from the Philippines, but it was the Dutch who took to smoking their tobacco in Java with a pinch of opium and arsenic, ostensibly in order to fend off malaria. This blend, called *madak*, reached China within a decade, although until the 1680s it remained largely confined to the Dutch trading posts in Taiwan and to the region of Fujian across the Taiwan Strait. When the Chinese state prohibited the use of tobacco, the Chinese began smoking opium.[24]

Opium smoking appears to have spread to Iran from China, although it would take two centuries to do so. Khurasan seems to have been the first region in Iran to be affected by this. It remains unclear whether the pilgrimage traffic to the shrine of the Eighth Imam in Mashhad or Nadir Shah's invasion of India was instrumental in the transmission.[25] Neligan, the physician to the British Legation in Tehran in the 1920s, attributed the conversion to opium smoking in Iran in large part to the place of Mashhad as a point of convergence for Shi`i pilgrims:

> Persians say that the practice was unknown in their country until the nineteenth [century]. Some refer to its introduction to the early years of the century, about 110 years ago; other authorities assert that it did not take place until after 1850. All agree that opium smoking began in Khorassan, the north-eastern province, of which Meshed is the capital. Now the shrine of the Imam Rezah is in that city, and it attracts thousands of Shiah Mohammedan pilgrims every year, of whom many come from the countries east of Persia, the Russian provinces of Central Asia, Afghanistan and India. It is an assumption then, that the opium pipe was first brought into Persia by pilgrims to Meshed. Certain it is that the Khorassanis are to-day more addicted to its use than the people are of any other province. The question as to which country had the doubtful privilege of handing the habit on is now an academic one, but it is

---

[24]Booth, *Opium*, 105; Dikötter et al., *Narcotic Culture*, 32.
[25]Shahnavaz, "Afyūn," 594.

not infrequently discussed by Persians. Some say China, some India, some Afghanistan. It may be noted, however, that opium-smoking took root in Fars later than in other provinces, although Fars had early communications with India; and that though the Chinese method of smoking is very common in Khorassan, the Persians' ordinary method has been developed on lines of their own. . . . All that can be said is that opium smoking reached Persia from further east, probably via Khorassan, and some time in the first half of the nineteenth century.[26]

III. Opium as a Cash Crop

The cultivation of opium in early Qajar times was rather limited; most of it came from Yazd province, the area where opium had long been cultivated, and almost all was for domestic consumption. Hagemeister in 1837–38 estimated that the total production for the entire country did not exceed 500 to 600 *puds*, or 8,200 to 9,825 kilograms. Exports were very limited; in part, it seems, owing to the extreme adulteration of Iranian opium, which made it inferior to that of India.[27] The little that was exported either went to India or was taken overland via Herat to Bukhara, from where it was transported to China.[28]

In the course of the nineteenth century, the cultivation of opium became widespread in Iran, and opium turned into an export cash crop substituting in part for a textile industry in decline. This export drive dates from the 1860s and is said to have been in response to a sharp fall in Indian supplies of opium to China.[29] A complementary explanation, offered by D'Allemagne, focuses more on Iran's domestic conditions. He argued that the sharp increase in Iran's opium production was linked to the Civil War in the United States and the attendant drop in cotton exports from across the Atlantic. The Iranian, like the Egyptians, reacted to this by increasing their cotton production. When the Civil War came to an end, however, and American cotton exports picked up again, the Iranian growers quickly realized that cotton was not such a wise investment after all, and many of them switched to opium.[30]

Already in the 1820s an experiment was made with shipping Iranian opium to China. Shaykh `Abd al-Rasul Khan of Bushihr sent about twenty chests of 160 pounds each to Daman in Arabia, from where they were shipped to Macao. Prospects looked bright, since, the British

[26]Neligan, *Opium Question*, 10–11.

[27]Stirling, *Journals*, 62.

[28]Hagemeister, *Essai sur les ressources*, 34; Abbott, Report on the Commerce of the South of Persia, in Amanat, ed., *Cities & Trade*, 105.

[29]Lucas, "Memorandum on the Opium of Persia," 31.

[30]D'Allemagne, *Du Khorassan au pays des Bakhtiaris*, 62.

argued, Iranian opium was estimated to be as good as any in India and at Bushihr reportedly cost a third of the price commanded by the best Malwa opium in Bombay.[31] Yet, this experiment does not seem to have borne fruit, at least not immediately. In 1848 the British suggested expanding the cultivation of opium in southern Iran with the aim of exporting to it Syria and Istanbul.[32] This suggestion apparently did not go anywhere either. Due to the lack of safety of the road and the expenses involved, it did not take long before this route was all but abandoned. Merchants then began to carry their opium in a semiprepared state to Istanbul. But soon they found that, instead of sending it to the east through Central Asia at great risk and cost, it was easier and cheaper to take it to the Gulf ports, Bushihr, and, to a lesser extent, Bandar `Abbas, and thence ship it to Batavia and from there to China. Using British way stations in India, however, proved to be expensive. An Iranian merchant from Yazd complained in 1871 that he had to pay 600 rupees for a chest touching at the port of Bombay on the way to China, "just for lying in harbour."[33] In order to reduce costs and make good profits, merchants therefore tried to avoid berthing at any British port.[34] In the course of time several routes were tried. At first, Iranian opium was taken to Java and then to Singapore and Hong Kong. At least one Iranian merchant, Hajji Mirza Abu'l Qasim of Shiraz, moved to Hong Kong to establish an opium business in that port, and lived there for ten years before returning to Iran.[35] When the Dutch prohibited the importation into Java, an attempt was made to ship directly to China. Between 1879 and 1882, the importation of Iranian opium into China thus doubled from four thousand to eight thousand chests.[36] This proved to be expensive in freight costs, however, so that Iranian opium ended up first being taken to Aden, whence it was transshipped to China. When the authorities at Aden began to levy transshipment duties, Suez replaced Aden as a port for transshipment. Given the circuitous nature of the Suez run, however, most opium eventually was first taken to Ceylon, where no transshipment dues had to be paid either.[37] A limited quantity of high-quality opium was exported to India and England as well as of 1870.[38] All in all, between 1859 and 1914–15, the annual export of raw

---

[31]PRO, FO60/24, Stannus, Bushihr to Willock, 3 July 1824, fols. 185v–186.

[32]Ibid.

[33]Goldsmid, *Eastern Persia*, 1:175.

[34]PRO, FO60/321, Thompson, Memorandum on the Opium Trade of Persia, 6 March 1869.

[35]Fasa'i, *Farsnamah-i Nasiri*, 1029.

[36]*A&P*, 1884, vol. 79, Dickson, Report on the Trade of Persia, 35.

[37]PRO, FO60/440, Baring, The Persian Opium Trade, 23 September 1881, fols. 388–89; and Stack, *Six Months in Persia*, 1:263.

[38]Neligan, *Opium Question*, 13.

opium from Iran increased from 42,000 pounds to 875,000 pounds and by 1925–26 the export figure had gone up to 1,100,000 pounds.[39] By 1907, one third of Iran's harvest went to London and the rest was sent to India and China, with small quantities heading for the Ottoman Empire via Baghdad.[40]

The optimism of the British resident of Bushihr notwithstanding, one problem that long plagued Iran's export opium was adulteration. Merchants were in the habit of mixing in pure opium with oil, sugar, and starch. This concerned above all opium destined for the Chinese market, which was low in morphine and thus could easily be tampered with, in ways that were not detectable with the testing methods used in China. Opium shipped to India, containing 10 to 11 percent morphine, commanded a price high enough to discourage adulteration. By 1881 quality was said to have improved because the Iranians had suffered heavy losses in exporting opium that, when it was found compromised, had been sent back. Yet, the practice did not disappear altogether. By the early twentieth century, tainted opium still found its way to China (and India), especially in years of poor harvest. Only the opium sent to London was said to be of pure quality at that point.[41] One observer, writing from Yazd in about 1903, noted that, "they are exporting at present to China a quality of so-called opium in which there is absolutely no morphia. The stuff is really an entirely different substance, and very cheap, and it is tied up in bags steeped in a solution of opium."[42] Not surprisingly, the persistently poor quality of Iranian export opium was one of the main reasons why between 1900 and 1905, export revenue fell by over 80 percent.[43]

These developments gave an enormous boost to the cultivation of opium, as peasants found growing opium much more lucrative than planting cereals—grain reportedly yielded circa one third of what opium yielded on the same amount of land. The country's annual output more than trebled between 1859 and 1861, and doubled between 1860 and 1868. An extra incentive for growers was that opium was not taxed, the exception being Kirmanshah, where, as a result, the cultivation was not seen as more profitable than that of cereals because of the expense involved. But even in the Kirmanshah region peasants turned to opium because they found it easier to turn their crops into cash.[44] Large areas were previously none was grown were now devoted to cultivation, with Yazd and Isfahan being the principal and most productive regions.

[39]Ibid., 39.

[40]AME, Brussels, 4265II, 3675, 't Serstevens, Exploration commerciale dans le sud de la Perse, 1907.

[41]Ibid.

[42]Malcolm, *Five Years in a Persian Town*, 155.

[43]Gilbar, "Persian Agriculture," 331.

[44]PRO, FO60/440, Baring, The Persian Opium Trade, 23 Sept. 1881, fols. 401–3.

Poppy cultivation, late Qajar period. Ernst Höltzer, *Persien vor 113 Jahren.* Ed. Mohammad Assemi (Tehran, 2535/1976).

Polak further mentioned `Arabistan, with Shustar and Dizful as production centers, Mahan (in the Kirman region), and Qum and Kashan as areas that yielded inferior opium for local consumption.[45] The British saw this development essentially as beneficial to Iran, since it increased revenue, afforded employment to a large number of laborers, and lessened the need to export specie for the purchase of foreign commodities.[46] Opium, in sum, took on the role silk had once held in Iran: one of the few lucrative export products for a country that had little to offer by way of commodities desired by the outside world.

Many regions took to growing opium poppies, but the cultivation remained unevenly distributed around the country. In the Caspian provinces the yield was negligible and what was produced was of mediocre quality. In Azerbaijan, too, little or no opium was grown. The same is true for the provinces bordering on the Persian Gulf. Cultivation mostly took off in the south-central and eastern parts of the country, around Yazd and Isfahan. The Yazd region stood out for its excellent climate and soil. Isfahan, by contrast, abounded in water and thus held out the promise of a greater extension of cultivation.[47] Production around Isfahan received a great boost when Muhammad Mahdi Isfahani returned from India in 1856–57 to

[45]Polak, *Persien,* 2:248, 255.
[46]PRO, FO60/440, Baring, The Persian Opium Trade, 23 September 1881, fol. 393.
[47]*A&P,* 1876, vol. 84, Report on the Trade of the Persian Gulf and Muscat for the Years 1874–75, 65.

Opium preparation, late Qajar period. J. Dieulafoy, *La Perse, la Chaldée et la Susania* (Paris, 1887).

apply the knowledge he had gathered about poppy cultivation to the region around his hometown.[48] Beginning in the 1870s, production increased in southwestern regions such as Kazirun, Shushtar, Burujird, Kirmanshah and Bihbahan, where the governor, Ihtisham al-Saltanah, encouraged cultivation.[49] Other regions where the authorities stimulated cultivation include Isfahan, whose ruler, Zill al-Sultan, "removed all obstacles in the way of the opium trade." (In order to keep grain from disappearing completely, the governor had ordered that "men shall sow one *jarib* of cereals for every four of poppy.")[50] In Fars, too, many took up the poppy cultivation. Quite a few merchants from the area began to invest in opium and became known as opium merchants, *tujjar-i taryaki*.[51] In response to the exhortations of Mirza Husayn Khan, Iranian consul in Bombay, that more opium be produced for export, Amir Kabir in 1851 initiated experimental cultivation in the vicinity of Tehran.[52]

In keeping with the eastern origins of opium smoking, the bulk of production took place in the eastern half of the country.[53] In Khurasan

[48]al-Isfahani, *Nisf-i jahan*, 124–25.

[49]PRO FO60/321, Memorandum on the Opium Trade, 6 March 1869; FO60/440, Baring, The Persian Opium Trade, 23 September 1881, fols. 374–76; Najm al-Mulk, *Safarnamah-i Khuzistan*, 164, 139.

[50]Stack, *Six Months in Persia*, 1:38, 263; 2:36. A *jarib* equaled 1068 m².

[51]Fasa'i, *Farsnamah-i Nasiri*, 956.

[52]Adamiyat, *Amir Kabir va Iran*, 399; Okazaki, "The Great Persian Famine," 187.

[53]Bricteux, *Au pays du lion*, 195–6.

TABLE 3
Iranian Opium Production, 1871–81

Year	Cases (of 160 lb.)	Value in Rupees
1871–72	870	696,000
1872–73	1,400	1,120,000
1873–74	2,000	1,600,000
1874–75	2,030	1,624,000
1875–76	1,890	1,701,000
1876–77	2,570	2,313,000
1877–78	4,370	4,730,000
1878–79	5,900	5,900,000
1879–80	6,100	6,100,000
1880–81	7,700	8,470,000

Source: PRO FO60/440, W. Baring, *The Persian Opium Trade*, 23 September 1881, fol. 377.

especially, where until 1860 little was grown, opium was ubiquitous twenty years later. The central parts, too, witnessed a tremendous expansion of cultivation. "All around Isfahan," Wills reported in 1881, "where there is good land, and it is not exhausted, nothing can be seen for miles but these fields of poppies, and the scenery is thus rendered very monotonous."[54] The situation was the same around Yazd, where "all the fields around the city . . . were white with poppy."[55] This was not necessarily a linear process. One observer traveling in Sistan in 1872 noted that, because of the drought of the previous years, peasants had given their attention almost wholly to the produce of grain.[56] Yet, overall, the increased amount of land given to the poppy continued, until in 1925, four hundred thousand square miles of the country were devoted to opium cultivation.[57] The result of this development was that, in a span of forty years, Iran turned from a net exporter of cereals to a net importer. Whereas in the late 1850s wheat and barley made up some 10 percent of the country's visible exports, this percentage fell to 2.7 percent in the late 1880s. By the early twentieth century, Iran imported more cereals than it exported.[58]

[54]Wills, *In the Land of the Lion and the Sun*, 173.
[55]Stack, *Six Months in Persia*, 1:262.
[56]Goldsmid, "Journey from Bandar Abbas," 81.
[57]Neligan, *Opium Question*, 13.
[58]Gilbar, "Persian Agriculture," 315.

TABLE 4
Estimates of Opium Exported from Iran, 1862–1906

Year	Annual average quantity (lbs.)	Index 1880–82 = 100	Value in £	Index 1880–82 = 100
1862–65	103,333	12	70,000	11
1867–69	268,200	31	238,400	39
1871–73	192,150	22	113,867	18
1874–76	292,050	33	187,933	30
1877–79	752,850	86	557,667	90
1880–82	874,710	100	618,022	100
1883–85	682,785	78	304,396	49
1886–88	594,990	68	320,425	52
1889–91	835,065	95	435,096	70
1892–94	529,605	60	261,082	42
1895–97	556,965	64	251,443	41
1898–1900	732,314	84	366,014	59
1901–03	724,127	83	293,133	47
1904–06	378,625	43	190,607	31

Source: Ahmad Seyf, "Production and Trade of Opium in Persia, 1850–1906," 246.

IV. Addiction

As in China, where the use of opium exploded in the late nineteenth century, the habit spread rapidly among Iranians in the wake of expanded production.[59] Opinions vary as to the incidence of addiction and the number of Iranians using and being addicted to opium smoking in late Qajar times. Some confirm what Olivier had already observed: that the moderate quantities people tended to take made that few suffered the harmful effect of heavy use. Neligan, writing in the early twentieth century, compared the opium habit in Iran to that of the tobacco habit in Europe, just as Olivier had likened opium in Iran to wine in France.[60] But others, reporting from the eastern half of the country, were less sanguine.

[59]For China, see Dikötter et al., Narcotic Culture, ch. 4.
[60]Neligan, Opium Question, 30.

Opium smokers, late Qajar period. Credit: Rijksmuseum voor Volkenkunde, Leiden, no. 3251.

In keeping with east–west movement of the smoking habit, people living in the eastern half of Iran by century's end were far more likely to smoke than in other parts of the country. In the early 1890s it was estimated that one fifth of the elite of Mashhad and one fourth of their servants smoked opium.[61] Preece in 1894 claimed that nowhere was the incidence of opium smoking greater than in Yazd and Kirman.[62] Yate, reporting in the same period, insisted that in Isfarayin in Khurasan "both men, women, and children . . . were "almost more addicted to opium-smoking than any I had seen."[63] In Kirman, too, opium use was widespread in the early 1900s, with twenty-five thousand people out of a total population of sixty thousand reportedly addicted. Women and child addicts were said to be common in Kirman, and the growing incompetence of workers in the local textile industry caused the trade to pass into the hands of

[61]A&P, 1893–94, vol. 95, Thompson, Trade of the Consular District of Meshed, 1892–93, 7.

[62]A&P, 1894, vol. 87, Preece, Report of a Journey Made to Yezd, Kerman and Shiraz, and on the Trade and of the Consular District of Ispahan, 17–18.

[63]Yate, *Khurasan and Sistan*, 381.

Yazdis, Parsis, and Hindus, none of whom used opium.[64] In Baluchistan opium smoking was "greatly on the increase" as well by century's end. As elsewhere, women especially indulged in the habit.[65]

The extent of the problem is illustrated by the concerns raised by the growing use of opium in the last part of the nineteenth century. In 1881–82, Mirza `Abd al-Wahhab Khan Shirazi (Asif al-Dawlah) launched a campaign against opium after becoming governor of Khurasan. He forbade its use and ordered the shops where opium was sold and the dens where it was smoked closed. It is said that members of the elite in the province who had taken up smoking opium out of fear for the governor's authority no longer dared smoke even in their own homes. Unemployed commoners who were addicted were made to clean the streets in exchange for bread. It remains unclear if despite the social policy aspect, Asif al-Dawlah's measure had any real effect.[66]

Effective measures against the use of opium had to wait until after the Constitutional Revolution of 1905–11. Until a law was approved in 1911 that envisaged a total ban, there was much discussion over the question of whether opium should be banned outright or just restricted. Taking into account the difficulty of enforcing this, it allowed for a phased introduction, with exemptions for certain regions of the country, and with taxes on opium going up progressively with the passing of each year until, seven years after the passing of the law, opium would only be legally sold as a medicinal drug. Only opium destined for export would be exempted from this. In 1913 the Iranian government signed the Hague Convention and adopted a law designed to restrict the production, trade and manufacturing of opiates. In 1919 the Iranian parliament adopted a bill designed to restrict the cultivation and consumption of opium.[67] In 1928 the *majlis* adopted a new law that sought to bring opium under government monopoly, to punish unlicensed use and smuggling, and to reduce consumption by 10 percent annually.[68] But ten years later little had changed. In 1939 more than 40 percent of the people of Mazandaran are said to have taken opium.[69] Opium proved a tenacious adversary, and both the Pahlavi regime and the current Islamic Republic proved unable to eradicate it as the drug of choice of many Iranians.

[64]Neligan, *Opium Question*, 27, 33.

[65]*A&P*, 1896, vol. 88, Sykes, Trade of the Kerman Consular District, 31 December 1895, 12.

[66]Kuhi-Kirmani, *Tarikh-i taryak*, 154.

[67]Latifi-Niya, "Taryak va iqdamat-i anjuman-i mubarizah."

[68]Kuhi-Kirmani, *Tarikh-i taryak*, 23–29.

[69]Ibid., 124–27.

TOBACCO

I. Continuity

The Frenchman Orsolle in the early 1880s offered a colorful description of the tobacco bazaar in Tehran that, aside from the reference to cigarettes, could have been made of the bazaar of Isfahan in late Safavid times:

> Not far from the cloth bazaar stretches the alley of the tobacco merchants, exuding the strong aroma that escapes from the bags of goat leather that contain the tumbaki, a tobacco cultivated in the south, especially in Shiraz, which is so black and so strong that its smoke can only be inhaled after it is softened in water mixed with the rose essence that gurgles in the qalyans. On walls hang strands of tobacco from Isfahan, fine and silky as the skeins of silk, blond like the hairs of a Venetian woman painted by Titian. Packages of tobacco from Rasht sit on shelves next to satchels of tobacco from Latakiyah designated for the manufacture of cigarettes. Copper vases contain tobacco from Revandoz, powdery, yellowish, laced with opium, the kind that camel drivers smoke in the evening while listening to the story of the Thousand and One Nights told by the narrator of the caravan.[70]

As with opium, little indeed changed until the late Qajar period as far as smoking is concerned. The rich smoked their elegant *qalyans*, and the poor puffed on their rough wooden pipes. The bowls of *qalyans* were made from a coconut shell or from glass or crystal made in Isfahan or imported from Russia, plain or ornamented with silver and gold or even studded with precious stones, and the devices cost anywhere between the equivalent of a shilling to £50, with higher prices for the ones owned by the very wealthy.[71] The ones manufactured in Shiraz in the early nineteenth century were "ornamented in the inside with representations of trees, flowers, &c, and sometimes with small medallions."[72] Some fancy water pipes at that time, made of solid gold and bowls of rock crystal, were valued at 100 to 150 *tumans*. Fath `Ali Shah's *qalyan* was entirely studded with pearls, brilliants, rubies and emeralds, to a total worth of over two million francs.[73] The household of Hisam al-Saltanah, the governor of Mashhad in 1872, included *qalyans* with "jars made of Sèvres china, decorated with French pictures," and "bowls

---

[70]Orsolle, *Le Caucase et la Perse*, 232–33.

[71]Ussher, *Journey from London to Persepolis*, 512; Kotzbue, *Narrative of a Journey*, 108; Dupré, *Voyage en Perse*, 2:160; and Rivadeneyra, *Viaje al interior de Persia*, 1:148.

[72]Waring, *Tour to Sheeraz* , 31–32.

[73]Drouville, *Voyage en Perse*, 1:82.

made of solid gold, studded with brilliants and pearls," and equipped with "mouthpieces of gold studded with turquoise."[74]

Of the lower classes nearly every one in northern Iran carried a *chupuq* on his back, in his girdle or in his pocket.[75] In the Persian Gulf area a primitive pipe was used. Between 10 and 17 centimeters long, it consisted of a tube of clay, some $2\frac{1}{2}$ centimeters diameter, bent at a right or acute angle, and constricted in the middle. One side was crammed with *tutun-i kurdi*, a coal was placed on it, and it passed from hand to hand until the contents were burned out.[76] An even more primitive way of obtaining the effect of the water pipe, observed in Central Asia and also reported in Bakhtiyari country, was to dig two communicating holes in the ground, fill one with water and the other with tobacco, put a mouth piece, usually a reed, in the former and inhale the smoke.[77]

As in earlier times, tobacco in the Qajar period ran into some opposition, mostly from the ranks of traditionalists. Even before the Tobacco Revolt of 1890–91, some conservative ulama frowned upon smoking. Cigarette smoking, for instance, met with clerical resistance on grounds that it was a habit adopted by Westernized (*farangi-ma'ab*) types who had given up their faith.[78] A modernizing argument against tobacco was articulated by Crown Prince `Abbas Mirza, governor of Azerbaijan and an energetic reformer. He thought that his countrymen's obsessive smoking was a habit that had gone too far, arguing that "it consumes nearly the whole of the day, and useful occupations are frequently unattended to on its account." To set an example for his troops, he had given up tobacco himself.[79] But all this was little more than a rearguard battle or, in the case of `Abbas Mirza, a precocious argument out of tune with the times, and anyhow futile in the face of the love affair that Iranians had with smoking. Porter, writing in the period of Fath `Ali Shah, described the Iranian passion for the water pipe as follows: "Whether he [the Iranian] is with his women, or in the *divan-kaneh*, in the company of his friends; whether he is going abroad or to court, he is never without his pipe."[80] Drouville in the same period asserted that the *qalyan* was the only passion among Iranians that exceeded that for coffee and that could be considered an absolute need.[81] Baron de Bode referred to the

---

[74]Bellew, *From the Indus to the Tigris*, 363.

[75]Wills, *In the Land of the Lion and the Sun*, 32; and Polak, *Persien*, 2:261.

[76]Wills, *In the Land of the Lion and the Sun*, 33.

[77]See Loftus, *Travels and Researches*, 389; and, for Afghanistan, Ferrier, *Caravan Journeys and Wanderings*, 383.

[78]Riza'i and Azari, eds., *Guzarish'ha-yi nazmiyah*, 232.

[79]Kotzbue, *Narrative of a Journey*, 169–70.

[80]Porter, *Travels in Georgia*, 1:253.

[81]Drouville, *Voyage en Perse*, 2:78.

difficulty Iranians experienced having to give up smoking during the month of fasting, and elaborated on Fraser's contention that no dispensation was given for addicted smokers by saying that many of the latter would often resort to the house of some European friend to indulge their habit, "for fear of scandalizing the more rigid observers of the law, and of letting loose against them the Mullahs."[82]

Just as in Safavid times, for the well-off traveling was no impediment to the enjoyment of tobacco. The Qajar elite never went without their smoking gear, not even during horseback riding trips. Travelers had a pair of large cases or drums suspended at the saddle-bow, one of them containing the water pipe and the other the tubes, tobacco, and other accoutrements, while a fire-pan or iron censer containing fire would be suspended by the chins from the cantle of the saddle.[83] The wealthy employed servants whose only task it was to clean and polish, light, and recharge their qalyans.[84] Nasir al-Din Shah even took his own *qalyan-dar* with him on his trips to Europe. When traveling, the very rich made use of a special travel *qalyan*, a copy of the glass reservoir normally used for smoking, "of a rather squat shape, in buffalo or rhinoceros hide . . . and usually covered with enameled plates of gold and silver, often encrusted with gems."[85] Riding with their *qalyan-dar* at their side, they employed special coils, called *marpich*, between fifteen and twenty feet long and made of elastic leather, so as to keep a certain distance between the horses.[86] Binning described this type of smoking as follows:

The Persians commonly smoke while riding along. The pipe, with all its apparatus, is carried by a servant, who bears, fixed in front of his saddle, (where the pistol holders would otherwise be) two oblong cases; like a pair of drums, made of wood or leather, one of which is stowed the principal potion of the pipe, the crystal vase with its upright stalk of carved wood; and in the other the other, the long snake-tube coiled up, the silver head and cover, and a provision of tobacco ready pounded and moistened. From the forepart of the saddle hang iron chains, sustaining on one side a small iron chafing disk filled with burning charcoal, which hangs below the rider's stirrup, but a little way above the ground; counterbalanced on the opposite flank by a metal aftâba full of water. With these aids, the kaleon is got ready with ease, whenever called for; and the servant hands his master the

---

[82]De Bode, *Travels in Luristan*, 2:301.

[83]Mitford, *Land March from England to Ceylon*, 1:329.

[84]AME, Paris, Mémoires et documents, 6, Rousseau, Tableau général de la Perse moderne, fols. 108v–109; Polak, *Persien*, 2:258; Lycklama a Nijeholt, *Voyage en Russie*, 2:244.

[85]Wills, *In the Land of the Lion and the Sun*, 30.

[86]Drouville, *Voyage en Perse*, 2:82; Flandin and Coste, *Voyage en Perse*, 1:123.

Master riding with his qalyan-carrier on his side, early Qajar period. G. Drouville, *Voyage en Perse, fait en 1812 et 1813*, 2 vols. (St. Petersburg, 1819–20).

end of the snake, through which he smokes, while the pipe bearer rides a little in the rear. In traveling it forms a part of his baggage, as indispensable as his wardrobe and his bed.[87]

The traveler who alighted at a caravanserai would be besieged by smoke-vendors who rented water pipes, carrying the coils slung around them, as well as provide him with tobacco bas and other paraphernalia.[88]

II. Etiquette and Hospitality

Tobacco was not just assimilated as a pleasurable consumable but also integrated into an elaborate tradition of ceremony, ritual, and hospitality. From the very beginning, smoking in Iran was not just a habit and an addiction but a social event, a habitus that quickly became interwoven with hospitality and conviviality. As one observer of Safavid Iran noted, the Iranians smoked tobacco as avidly as the Turks, but with them smoking involved much more ceremony.[89] This included the

---

[87]Binning, *Journal of Two Years' Travel*, 2:177–78. See also Feuvrier, *Trois ans à la cour de Perse*, 310; and Porter, *Travels in Georgia*, 1:253; the Russian envoy Griboyedov's observations about `Abbas Mirza, in Kelly, *Diplomacy and Murder in Tehran*, 63; and Armstrong, *Journal of Travels*, 115.

[88]Mitford, *Land March from England to Ceylon*, 1:343.

[89]Poullet, *Nouvelles relations*, 327–28.

elaborate ritual involved in the filling, *chaq kardan,* of the water pipe.[90] Tobacco and the water pipe, a device that lent itself to social gathering, early on had been turned into symbols of the strong tradition of hospitality and sociability in Iran. More than one seventeenth-century foreign visitor had remarked that as soon as a guest entered the house of an Iranian he would be offered a water pipe and coffee.[91] Tobacco, John Fryer noted, "is a general companion, and to give them their due, they are conversable good-Fellows, sparing no one his Bowl in their turn."[92] Reports from the Qajar period continue to suggest that smoking in Iran was not an individual pastime but a finely calibrated social ritual bespeaking a concern with decorum and reflecting issues of status and hierarchy. When people who knew each other met on the road, Polak noted, they would pause and smoke a *qalyan* together.[93] Family members were not supposed to smoke in front of the head of the household.[94] S. G. W. Benjamin, America's first ambassador to Iran, in 1882–83, drew attention to the social aspect when he said:

> The serving of refreshments is another important question regulated by undeviating custom. The nazir, or head-stewart of the household, enters in his stocking-feet, ushering a number of servants equal to the number to be served. If host and guest be of equal rank, the cup is presented to each exactly at the same moment; but if one outranks the other, he is first served. . . . The number and character of the refreshments depend on the rank, the hour, and the season. In the morning tea is served once. This is followed by the kaliân, or water pipe. When several persons of equal rank are to be served, it is the proper thing to bring an equal number of lighted pipes; but if one present outranks all the others, only one pipe is brought in, which is handed to him. . . . After the first kaliân, tea is served again, followed by a second pipe. After a proper interval, the length of which is regulated by the acceptability of the visit, coffee is served in tiny cups, followed in turn by the pipe. This is the signal that the limit of the entertainment has been reached. . . . These may seem trivial matters, but in Persia they have great weight; and not only is the taste of the host indicated by the quality and style of the refreshments, but the savoir-faire and the rank of the guest are weighed by his bearing on such occasions.[95]

---

[90]For details, see Floor, "Art of Smoking," 68.

[91]Du Mans, "'Estat de 1660,'" in Richard, *Raphaël du Mans,* 2:75, 81; Tavernier, *Les six voyages,* 1:714; De Bruyn, *Reizen over Moskovie,* 172.

[92]Fryer, *New Account,* 2:210.

[93]Polak, *Persien,* 2:258.

[94]Ibid.

[95]Benjamin, *Persia and the Persians,* 102–3, as quoted by Glünz, "Vorspiel zur Revolution," 148.

Polak confirms that not offering a water pipe to a visitor was tanta-mount to an insult and that handing the *qalyan* a third time to a guest was a sign that the visit was coming to an end and that the visitor was expected to leave.[96]

An even more suggestive passage by Benjamin is the following:

[I]f one present outranks all the others, only one pipe is brought in, which is handed to him. Before smoking, he makes a feint of offering it in turn to all present, but woe to him who incautiously accepts be-fore he of higher rank has smoked, for in that case he ill be made feel the withering scorn of which a Persian gentleman is capable. The Mestofi-Mamolek, the highest official in Persia after the King, has not smoked for forty years. He took a solemn resolution against tobacco, because, when a young man, the kaliân was on one occasion given in his presence to a man whom he considered of lower rank, before it was offered to him. When the pipe was presented to him he dashed it aside, and swore never to smoke again, in order to avoid the possibil-ity of being a second time subjected to such an affront.[97]

A similar observation concerning the etiquette involved in smoking comes from the pen of Edward Eastwick, British chargé d'affaires in Tehran from 1860 to 1863:

The pipe plays an important part at Persian visits. Until it is brought you can converse on the long ride you took yesterday, on the superior-ity of Arab horses to Turkuman, or *vice versa*, it mattering not a straw what your opinion may be, so that you say something. When the first pipe has been smoked you will enter on business, if you have any. The second pipe will arrive just when you are saying something which you do not wish to be known to the public, and you will conse-quently "shut up" with great speed; and the third pipe is you congé, and you will take yourself off.[98]

Wills, finally, echoed these remarks with his own keen observations:

When a visitor is offered a pipe, and there is not a second one to hand, it is at once taken to him by the host's servant. He then depre-catingly suggests that his host should smoke first; this is declined by a sweeping gesture. He now offers it to the other guests, if any, and on receiving a negative gesture, commences to inhale. Should, however, the host be much superior in position, the visitor will either refuse to

---

[96]Polak, *Persien*, 2:258.

[97]Benjamin, *Persia and the Persians*, 103, as quoted by Glünz, "Vorspiel der Revolu-tion," 149.

[98]Eastwick, *Journal of a Diplomat's Three Years' Residence*, 1:260.

smoke first, or, if he has the bad taste to do so, the host does not smoke at all, bust sends the pipe away. When there are many visitors and only one pipe, the greatest one smokes first, then the rest smoke in order of rank, previously paying the compliment of suggesting that some one else should precede them. These little punctilios are endless.[99]

Smoking in company entailed numerous other issues of etiquette— again reflecting a society that prized refined ways of social interaction. One was the rule that no water pipe should be passed on the next user without first making sure that the smoke had cleared from the bowl.[100] An extension of the elaborate hierarchical ritual that marked the enjoyment of the *qalyan* was the refusal on the part of some clerics to smoke a pipe owned by Europeans or to smoke from the same pipe with them. Foreigners usually circumvented this by bringing their own pipes. Alternatively, some Europeans carried their own mouthpiece so as to avoid embarrassing or unpleasant situations.[101]

In the mid-1880s it was estimated that $2\frac{1}{2}$ million Iranians out of a total population of circa 10 million were tobacco smokers.[102] Fars was the center of cultivation, though the tobacco from around Kazirun was not necessarily the best. One variety from the area was called *khushka* in Qajar times. Of inferior quality, it was sold in Arabia, Egypt and Turkey under the name of Shiraz tobacco.[103] The towns of Zarqan, also in Fars, and Jahrum, in Lar province, were known for their fine tobacco, with grades of a slightly lesser quality growing around Isfahan. Third-rate types, smoked by poorer people, came from Kashan and Yazd.[104] The best *tutun* came from Kirmanshah, and the environs of Urumiyah produced the largest quantity in Qajar times.[105] By the turn of the twentieth century, Shiraz was still known for producing choice tobacco, together with Kashan. Several sources also mention tobacco from Khurasan, which, being stronger, was less prized than the grades from Shiraz.[106]

---

[99]Wills, *In the Land of the Lion and the Sun*, 30–31.

[100]Drouville, *Voyage en Perse*, 2:81; O'Donovan, *Merv Oasis*, 2:20.

[101]Drouville, *Voyage en Perse*, 2:31–32; and Sykes, *Through Persia on a Side Saddle*, 18–19.

[102]I'timad al-Saltanah, "Kilid-i istita'at," 1198.

[103]Binning, *Journal of Two Years' Travel*, 1:176–77, 323–24.

[104]De Hagemeister, *Essai sur les ressources*, 32; Polak, *Persien*, 2:256; idem, "Beitrag zu den agrarischen Verhältnissen," 143; and Wills, *Land of the Lion and the Sun*, 30. In later times, tobacco from Hakan in Fars is said to have been the best. See Razpush, "Galyān," 262.

[105]Polak, *Persien*, 2:261; Wills, *In the Land of the Lion and the Sun*, 33.

[106]See Forster, *Journey from Bengal to England*, 2:158; De Hagemeister, *Essai sur les ressources*, 32; and Beyens, "Une mission en Perse," 22. De Hagemeister mentions that, despite its lesser quality, tobacco from Khurasan and Damghan had become popular at the court of Fath 'Ali Shah.

Tobacco cultivation, Rasht, Gilan, late Qajar period. H. R. D'Allemagne, *Du Khorassan au pays des Bachtiaris*, 4 vols. (Paris, 1911).

In the Qajar period the best tobacco from the environs of Shiraz was mainly consumed in Iran itself, and only the lesser quality, produced around Yazd and Kashan, was exported to Baghdad and Istanbul.[107]

By the mid-nineteenth century, tobacco had become one of Iran's leading export products, sent to India, the Ottoman Empire, and Russia. One observer, writing in the 1840s, claimed that, at that time, tobacco was Iran's leading export product. This seems a gross exaggeration, however; although tobacco was one of the country's significant agricultural export items, it constituted less than 4 percent of total visible exports in the late 1850s.[108] The Ottoman Empire especially became a major consumer of Iranian tobacco as of the 1840s.[109] By 1849, the annual output of Isfahan and the surrounding region was some forty thousand bales of twenty-two to twenty-four pounds each, twenty-four thousand of which were exported. Most exports went to the Ottoman Empire via Baghdad and Tabriz.[110] In the 1860s, the Isfahan area alone annually exported between seventeen hundred and nineteen hundred

---

[107]Polak, "Beitrag zu den agrarischen Verhältnissen," 143; Truilhier, *Mémoire descriptif*, 96. For export figures in the nineteenth century, see Natiq, *Iran dar rahyabi-yi farhangi*, 224–29.

[108]See Gilbar, "Persian Economy," 187.

[109]Natiq, *Bazarganan*, 77.

[110]AME, Nantes, Téhéran A, 21, Commerce d'importation et d'exportation de l'Europe avec la Perse, fols. 48–49.

tons of *tanbaku* via Bagdad.[111] By 1878 the total crop had increased to circa one million kilograms.[112]

The water pipe remained popular in Iran until the twentieth century, when it gradually fell out of favor, being replaced by cigarettes. Iran's acquaintance with cigarettes may go back to the 1860s, under Turkish and Russian influence, and by 1869 Tabriz is said to have had (a likely exaggerated) 350 cigarette sellers.[113] Indigenous cultivation was not long in coming. Cigarette tobacco was first cultivated in Gilan in 1876, the seeds having been brought in from Samsun on the Turkish Black Sea coast. Two years later, some was exported to Russia. Cigarettes, first smoked by a few foreign residents, were initially an affectation of sophisticated, Westernized Iranians. With indigenous tobacco becoming available, cigarette smoking soon spread, however, especially after Russian firms opened cigarette manufactories in Gilan.[114] By 1890 the typical merchant in the bazaar of Tehran could be seen with a cigarette in his mouth,[115] and by that time the practice had become so general that "even the lowest peasant now goes about with a cigarette case and cigarette paper and makes his own smokes."[116] The growing popularity of cigarettes came at the expense of especially the smoking of the *chupuq*, with those who wished to look Western, that is, modern and sophisticated, taking the lead.[117] But the new habit also led to the diminished popularity of *qalyan* smoking and by the turn of the century was fast on its way to replace the water pipe, leaving mullahs, tradition-minded Iranians, and people in rural areas to keep up the habit.[118] Cigars, imported from Switzerland and Russia in ca. 1860, were expensive at the time, and never really caught on in Iran.[119]

III. The Tobacco Protest

The *qalyan* would not definitively give way to cigarettes before it and the tobacco that fueled it had become a symbol of a different set of

---

[111]Rochechouart, "Le commerce et l'exploration de commerce," 60.

[112]PRO, FO60/482, Herbert, Report on the Present State of Persia, 7 May 1886, fol. 143.

[113]Floor, "Art of Smoking," 77.

[114]De Windt, *A Ride to India across Persia*, 46, 86.

[115]Ibid.

[116]*A&P*, 1893–94, vol. 95, Report on the Trade and Commerce of the Province of Gilan for the Year 1891, 4–5.

[117]Shahri, *Tarikh-i ijtima`i-yi Tihran*, 3:472.

[118]*A&P*, 1893–94, vol. 95, Report on the Trade and Commerce of the Province of Gilan for the Year 1891, 4–5.

[119]Gasteiger, *Handelverhältnisse Persiens*, 33. Also see Floor, "Art of Smoking," 82.

Tobacco shop, late Qajar period. H. R. D'Allemagne, *Du Khorassan au pays des Bachtiaris*, 4 vols. (Paris, 1911).

emotions. Given tobacco's economic importance, it is not surprising that the Qajar government attempted to bring this lucrative product under greater central control and harness its proceeds. In deference to religious sensibilities, the state forced tobacco shops to close their doors on Fridays. It is likely that this ordinance was passed sometime in the mid-1880s.[120] More drastic steps soon followed. In 1886 I'timad al-Saltanah wrote a tract, *Kilid-i istita`at* (*The Key to Power*), in which he argued that Iran's weakness was mainly because of its lack of governmental income and that one way of enhancing state revenue was to institute new forms of taxation. He singled out tobacco, a nonessential consumable as he called it, as a good candidate, claiming that 25,000 *tumans* per day went up in smoke in Iran, and advocated the establishment of a state tobacco monopoly in imitation of the Ottoman Tobacco Régie (which had been founded in 1884).[121] In the same year, Nasir al-Din Shah issued a *farman* that, in the guise of a state concerned to curb the negative effects of

[120]Natiq, *Bazarganan*, 74, letter Zill al-Sultan to Amin al-Zarb, 5 Shavval 1305/15 June 1888.
[121]I'timad al-Saltanah, "Kilid-i istita`at," 1194–95.

smoking on body and mind, sought to regulate the cultivation and consumption of tobacco and bring it under financial control. The text of the *farman* is as follows:[122]

> As the use of tobacco and tumbaka had no importance and was a luxury, the excessive use of it was a source of intoxication and the sources of physical weakness, therefore in order that the use of such a luxury should be brought within bounds we have ordered and ruled that from the beginning of this year [1304] and henceforth the guild of tobacco vendors of all Persia shall be under the direction of His Excellency the noble etc. Amin-us-Sultan, Minister of Finances, of the Court, etc. etc., so that through his enlightened capacity the number of tobacco and tumbaku vendors in all the towns, districts and villages throughout Persia should be determined according to the demands of those places; His Excellency will take the greatest pains in the extending of the planting of tobacco and its exportation, which is one of the most important items of commerce; he is also to prevent the adulterations of the leaf in order that it should not be rejected by the foreign buyers, that is to say without the strict and minute inspection of this article at the custom houses its exportation will be prohibited. A special certificate for exportation will be given free of charge. . . . From the above date no tumbaku vendor shall set up for himself without the sanction of the direction of the Regie.

This initial decree did not last, and in early 1887 the news broke that the project of establishing a tobacco regie had been abandoned, owing to "some departmental difficulties and intrigues."[123] Although the decree remained a dead letter, it served as a precursor to the infamous tobacco concession the shah in granted in 1890, whereby the corporation of the British Major Gerald F. Talbot was given the right to the sale, distribution and export of all Iranian tobacco for a period of fifty years. The concession galvanized popular resentment of long-standing government neglect and mismanagement and the selling out of national resources, sparking the famous Tobacco Protest of 1891–92. Leading merchants spearheaded opposition to the concession, with some setting fire to their tobacco stocks, but Iran's clerics made it into a truly popular issue.

Modern scholarship, especially that coming out of the Islamic Republic, has tended to portray the ulama as defenders of the people in the role they played in the Tobacco Revolt. This interpretation, however, requires further elaboration for, stated simply, it overlooks several aspects of their

---

[122]PRO, FO/60/480, enclosure in Nicholson, Tehran to London, 23 October 1886, fols. 199–202.

[123]PRO, FO60/485, Nicholson, Tehran to London, 1 February 1887, fol. 76.

participation in the movement. The first is that not all ulama were in favor of the boycott. In Isfahan, for instance, there was a division between those who supported Aqa Najafi, the fiery spokesman of local opposition to the concession who was instrumental in turning the movement into a nationwide one, and pro-government clerics around Mirza Hashim, who did not resist the government monopoly.[124] More important, far from simply acting as the protectors of the people, the ulama who opposed the concession did so in large part from economic self-interest. Tobacco grew on property they owned privately or on *vaqf* (religiously endowed) land.[125] What gave clerical activism the semblance of a stance for the people is a shared antigovernment and antiforeign position. The ulama were the leaders of the nation, *millat*, because they were the only opposition to the state, *dawlat*. They stood for faith and tradition, both of which were threatened by a state in collusion with foreign elements. The belief system of the ulama included a profound aversion to the presence and influence of foreigners in Iran and their perception of an attendant increase in immorality in the form of prostitution and drinking, by fears that mingling with foreigners would estrange people from Islam and open the door to Christian proselytizing, by their anxiety that the privacy of people's homes was in danger of being violated.

Tobacco was particularly sensitive in this regard, for the concession raised the specter of non-Muslims employing Muslims, and of tobacco, a product akin to food, being defiled by passing through infidel hands. Rasul Ja'fariyan has a point in disassociating the Tobacco Revolt from the Constitutional Revolution by arguing that the first was all about a struggle against foreign influence and intrusion, whereas the second was about reform, and by calling Fazl-Allah Nuri the only heir to the Tobacco Revolt in the constitutional struggle.[126] It is in their dream of a world purified of non-Shi'i elements that clerical interests converged with those of the common people, and it is through this convergence of interests that the ulama managed to rally people around a call for the abolition of the concession. In clamoring for protectionism they also appealed to a long-standing sensibility about foreign economic intrusion and self-sufficiency as an attainable ideal. This theme of boycotting foreign goods for the sake of autarky manifested itself in different forms, and just as its roots go back to the period before the Qajars, so it continued to reverberate long after their demise. Thus, in Isfahan, the resistance by the ulama played out against the larger backdrop of their desire to close and eliminate the Imperial Bank of Persia and to get rid of all

[124]Walcher, "In the Shadow of the King," 189.
[125]Keddie, *Religion and Rebellion in Iran*, 65.
[126]Karbala'i, *Tarikh-i dukhaniyah*, introd., 18–19.

foreign business.[127] Later on, it took the form of the establishment of a short-lived *shirkat-i islamiyah*, a company designed to encourage indigenous manufacturing. The people heeded the call because they, too, feared the growing presence of foreign interests but, more important, because in their general discontent and frustration about the state of affairs in the country they were desperate for leadership and guidance.[128]

It thus was a convergence of interests centering on a common dread of foreign intrusion and intervention and the fear that this would make prices go up, rather than a natural bond between the ulama and the masses that galvanized popular discontent and made the clerics into the champions of what quickly became a national cause. The result was that a nationwide protest movement got under way with the rallying cry "we are to be taxed for the benefit of foreigners."[129] The leading ulama of Karbala in Iraq, led by Mirza Hasan Shirazi, issued a ban that declared the handling and smoking of tobacco to be unlawful to the true believer. The boycott that followed was so successful that "raids were made upon suspected tea-shops by vigilance men, who smashed every water-pipe they could lay their hands on, and that foreigners had their cigars yanked from their mouths." Even the women in the shah's harem abandoned their water pipes, so that the shah had to smoke on the sly and was soon forced to repeal the concession.[130] The I'timad al-Saltanah experienced the reaction first-hand when he left the home of Dr. Feuvrier, the shah's personal physician, with a cigarette in his mouth and found himself cursed by passers-by.[131] Gordon vividly describes the gloomy atmosphere in Tehran following the boycott: "The shah was faced with the sight of silent and forsaken tea-shops as he passed through the streets of Tehran, and he saw the signs of the censuring strike in the rows of empty benches, on which his subjects used to sit at their simple enjoyment of pipes and tea."[132]

The tobacco revolt was one of the most momentous episodes in modern Iranian history. Tobacco cultivation was severely affected and took at least fifteen years to bounce back in Iran. Following the downfall of the Tobacco Régie, the ulama continued to inveigh against tobacco as a drug.

[127]Walcher, "In the Shadow of the King," 188.

[128]See the memorandum from Lascalles to Salisbury, Tehran, 22 December 1891, in Lambton, "Tobacco Régie," 249–50.

[129]Wilson, *Persian Life and Customs*, 290–92; and Sparroy, *Persian Children of the Royal Family*, 241.

[130]Sparroy, *Persian Children of the Royal Family*, 242; HHStA, XXVIII/11, Persien, Rosty, Berichte aus Teheran, 23 December 1891, fol. 158; Keddie, *Religion and Rebellion in Iran*; and Lambton, "Tobacco Régie."

[131]Bambad, *Sharh-i hal-i rijal-i Iran*, 2:405.

[132]Gordon, *Persia Revisited*, 26–27.

When the Qajar government made arrangements with the *Société du tombac*, the French company that, in imitation of the Iranian tobacco concession, had entered into an agreement with the Ottoman tobacco corporation in 1891 and that a year later entered into a largely secret agreement with the Qajar government that was more advantageous to Iranian merchants than the Talbot concession had been, some forbade people to sell to its agents. As a result, the entire crop of 1892 was left in the hands of the peasants and the villages that were dependent on tobacco were left in deep distress.[133] Pleas to the chief instigators of the boycott, Aqa Najafi and Shaykh Muhammad `Ali, were to no avail. They offered to purchase tobacco provided the peasants would agree not to sow any for two years, but as the price they offered was less than half of what the Régie had agreed to pay, no arrangement could be made. Even during the early days of the Constitutional Revolution the mullahs still argued against the cultivation of tobacco. Cotton, less labor intensive and less prone to damage, was a crop that enticed many peasants instead.[134]

Conclusion

In the Qajar period, people from all walks of life continued to consume both opium and tobacco in great quantity. Of the two, opium changed the most with the habit of smoking it sweeping the country in the late nineteenth century. This trend, which was apparently adopted by the upper classes even more than by laborers, had profound consequences. It made the use of opium into a recreational affair, turned it from an individual pursuit to a pastime of people sitting around a brazier, sharing a *vafur* and drinking tea together. But, inasmuch as smoking opium enhanced the incidence of addiction, it also turned the use of opium into a social problem where it had never been much of a social problem. The tremendous increase in cultivation diminished the amount of land given to the cultivation of cereals. This by itself did not cause the terrible famine of 1870, but it did bring about an imbalance in the domestic production of food and as such contributed to the famine.[135]

Tobacco saw more continuity from the Safavid period onward. Iranians remained avid smokers. The water pipe continued to be the medium of choice, with wealthy smokers owning expensive one made of precious

---

[133] *A&P* 1894, vol. 87, Report of a Journey Made to Yezd, Kerman and Shiraz, and on the Trade &c., of the Consular District of Ispahan, 46–47.

[134] AME, Brussels, 4265II, 3675, 't Serstevens, Exploration commerciale dans le sud de la Perse, 1907, 17–18.

[135] For the argument that the famine was not just caused by the switch from cereal to tobacco cultivation, see Okazaki, "The Great Persian Famine."

materials and employing cinder bearers, and poorer people smoking regular pipes. Only in the late nineteenth century did cigarettes become popular and begin to edge out the ubiquitous qalyan.

The economic importance of tobacco alone would have warranted the uproar caused by the shah's tampering with its cultivation and handling. Out of a total population of perhaps ten million in the late nineteenth century, some two hundred thousand people may have been employed in the cultivation and handling of tobacco. It is thus not surprising that the first protests against the concession arose in Shiraz, the principal center of cultivation, nor that the call for a boycott was heeded so massively.[136] But the Tobacco Revolt goes well beyond economic issues. An important aspect of the outcry and one of the main reasons why the ulama took the lead in it, was the notion that, by being relegated to foreigners, tobacco would become unclean, *najis*.[137] This fact should not be underestimated in a country that had long jealously cherished self-sufficiency as an ideal and where suspicion against imported goods goes back to Safavid times. Beyond that, inasmuch as tobacco smoking was intimate and private, the issue directly involved the privacy of the home. As one observer remarked, "The suggestion that the privacy of their homes was in danger of being violated sufficed to kindle the irrepressible vitality of the race."[138] The emotional nerve the tobacco concession touched and the vehement reaction against it become understandable in this light.

[136]Adamiyat, *Idi'uluzhi-yi nahzat*, 36–37.

[137]Karbala'i, *Tarikh-i dukhaniyah*, 105; and Feuvrier, *Trois ans à la cour de Perse*, 310.

[138]Sparroy, *Persian Children of the Royal Family*, 241.

CHAPTER 9

From Coffee to Tea: Shifting Patterns
of Consumption in Qajar Iran

> Tea is the customary treat, in exchanging calls, among the
> higher classes in Persia.
> Justin Perkins, *A Residence of Eight Years in Persia* (1843).

INTRODUCTION

Along with China, Japan, Russia, England, and some of the successor
states of the Ottoman Empire, most notably Turkey and Morocco, Iran
is one of the world's great tea-drinking nations. The commonality with
all but the first two countries goes beyond a current predilection for tea
and extends to the timing of the drink's introduction, the commercial
channels it followed, and its belated popularity. With the possible exception of its northeastern regions, Iran is likely to have become acquainted
with tea sometime in the sixteenth century. As in Russia, Iran's relative
proximity to China accounts for the original introduction of tea through
overland channels, but as in Morocco the activity of the European trading companies resulted in its importation via maritime trade routes as
well. Significantly, as in all other tea-drinking countries, with the exception of the original ones in East Asia, tea in Iran went through a long
period of gestation before it became the favored drink of the masses. As
in Russia, England, and Turkey, the real popularity of tea in Iran dates
from the nineteenth century. However, as far as the drink that tea replaced is concerned, Iran resembles not so much Russia, where tea competed mostly with distilled liquor for popularity, as some European
countries and most of the Ottoman Empire, where coffee was an early
contender for most favored status. England, which was among the first
western countries where coffee gained popularity in the seventeenth century, long favored this drink over tea. Introduced almost at the same
time, tea in England began to supersede coffee in popularity in the late
eighteenth century under the influence of factors that include cost,
sources of supply, working conditions, and changes in taste and fashion.[1]
Developments were more complex in the Ottoman Empire, where coffee

---

[1]Burnett, "Coffee in the British Diet," 35–52.

and tea became differentiated according to region, and in Germany and Holland, where religious affinities had an additional role in the choice between the two. The Arabic-speaking parts of the Ottoman state, Egypt, Syria, Iraq, and Libya and Algeria in the west, being among the first to become familiar with coffee after its spread from Yemen in the fifteenth century, have never switched to the other caffeinated drink. The exception is Morocco. There, tea, introduced by English and Dutch merchants in the sixteenth century, managed to become the more popular beverage.[2] At the other extreme, the diffusionist influence of Russian customs and taste caused Turkey to become a predominantly tea-consuming country as well, even if coffee remains highly valued by many until today.[3]

Iran over time similarly switched from coffee to tea, which since the late Qajar period has been the country's "national beverage." To chart that transformation will be the main aim of this chapter, following a preliminary discussion of the record of tea consumption in Iran prior to the nineteenth century.

I. Tea in the Safavid Period: Popularity and Spread

Although it is unclear exactly when tea was first introduced in Iran, there is no doubt that it was known at least in certain parts of the country prior to the Safavid period and thus precedes the entry of coffee into Iran. The supposedly oldest reference to tea in Europe involved an Iranian merchant, one Hajji Muhammad, who in the mid-sixteenth century informed the Venetian author and administrator Gianbattista Ramusio about tea in China.[4] But the Mongols may have introduced Iran to tea as early as the thirteenth century. Rashid al-Din (d. 1318), the famous Iranian historiographer-cum physician who served the Il-Khan ruler Ghazan Khan as chief minister, mentions tea as a Chinese drink with medicinal properties.[5] The word for tea in Persian, *chay*, indicates that it had traveled overland across Central Asia. It is not clear whether in those early times the tea consumed in Iran was or green Chinese tea or the black brick tea that nomadic peoples such as the Uzbegs, the Turkmen, and the Kalmyks drank with salt and butter fat.[6] By the late sixteenth

---

[2]Carlier, "Le café maure," 976–77.

[3]Tapper, "Blood, Wine and Water," 218–19.

[4]Ramusio, *Delle navigationi*, 2:15.

[5]Laufer, *Sino-Iranica*, 553–54.

[6]For Uzbegs and other northern nomads, tea was a form of nourishment in addition to being a beverage. Consumed with milk, butter, or fat from the sheep's tail, it contributed

century, it was known, although it had not yet become part of the Iranian pharmacological canon. In a treatise written in the late sixteenth century, Salik al-Din Muhammad Hamavi Yazdi noted that tea was an unknown drug not found in the well-known medical compendia.[7] A short reference to tea by 'Imad al-Din Shirazi, written in 1590–91, refers to tea prepared without sugar, thus pointing to green tea, and also suggests that it was as yet barely known in Iran. Shirazi mentions tea as a strange herb of medicinal value that came from China. A trustworthy person who had twice journeyed to China had informed him that there were several kinds, that some were so expensive that they sold for one silver *misqal* (4.25 gr.) per *man*, and that there was one exceptional variety of which a *misqal* in weight cost a *misqal* in silver. Among tea's health benefits he lists its effectiveness in providing relief for a bloated stomach, its digestive working, and its appetite enhancing function. Trying to assess its properties, he opines that it tends toward the hot and removes moistness from the stomach.[8] In seventeenth- and eighteenth-century medical compendia such as the *Tuhfah-i Hakim Mu'min*, the *Alfaz al-adviyah*, and the *Makhzan al-adviyah*, tea continues to be presented as a pharmaceutical substance that fortifies the heart, the brain, and the liver, increases the appetite, purifies the blood, and is effective against nausea, colic, and asthma. Made into an ointment, it was also said to be active as a cure against swelling and hemorrhoids.[9] Chardin, writing in the late seventeenth century, noted that in Iran, as in most places, tea counted as medicine more than as nourishment.[10]

Yet, by the early 1600s, black tea had made inroads and the drink's transition from medicinal substance to recreational beverage was already underway. Olearius, who visited Iran in the 1630s, claimed that tea came to Iran from China via Central Asia, carried overland by Uzbeg Tatars. He also asserted that Iranians put sugar in their tea, thus

---

significantly to a meager diet. See Elphinstone, *Account of the Kingdom of Caubul*, 470; and Fraser, *Narrative of a Journey into Khorasan*, 264, 283; and idem, *Winter's Journey*, 2:151, for tea among the Uzbegs. See Hommaire de Hell, *Les steppes de la mer Caspienne*, 2:104, for tea drinking among the Kalmyks. How important a part of daily life tea was among the Uzbegs is suggested by Connolly, who in the 1830s said that "The Oosbegs who live in a great measure upon tea, keep the leaves in their mouths to prevent thirst." See Conolly, *Journey to the North of India*, 1:54–55, as well as his contemporary Burnes, *Travels to Bokhara*, 1:221; 2:436–37, who averred that "nothing is done in this country without tea, which is handed round at all times and hours."

[7]Hamavi Yazdi, "De venenis celeberrimis," fol. 55.

[8]'Imad al-Din Shirazi, "Chay-i khata'i," fol. 71.

[9]Seligmann, ed., *Ueber drey höchst seltene persische Handschriften*, 40; and 'Aqili-Khurasani, *Makhzan al-adviyah*, 294.

[10]Chardin, *Du bon usage du thé*, 70.

suggesting the black tea that was to become Iran's national drink.[11] With his remark about the existence of "Chinese" teahouses, *chay khatay khanah*, Olearius testifies to the fact that, by this time, tea was already consumed as a regular beverage.[12] Fryer mentions the custom of serving the drink to customers of bathhouses and relates how in 1677 he had been entertained with tea (as well as coffee) by the officials of Bandar `Abbas.[13] Kaempfer was treated to tea in Shamakhi and Qazvin during his journey to Isfahan in 1683–84.[14] Villotte in the 1690s claimed that (wealthy) Iranians drank coffee for breakfast and that dinner was followed by "the water pipe, coffee, tea, and spirits." While Iranians never consumed coffee with sugar, he said, they took tea with candy sugar. Referring to a habit that persists until today in Iran, he claimed that people drank their tea while holding a lump of sugar in the mouth.[15] Chardin insisted that tea was neither rare nor expensive in Iran.[16] Yet it was apparently still precious and exotic enough to be part of royal gifts. A French embassy included tea in its offerings to Shah `Abbas II in 1664.[17] Shah Sulayman in 1683 received tea as part of a gift offered to him by the ambassador from Siam.[18] Tea was also included in the presents for Shah Sultan Husayn brought to Iran by the Russian envoy Artemii Volynskii in 1715–16.[19] The same ruler routinely served it—as well as coffee—to his guests.[20]

At least until the later seventeenth century, tea continued to be supplied overland from China. No references to tea are found in the literature on the Portuguese trade with Iran. It never became a hot commodity for the Dutch and the English either. The Persian Gulf records of the EIC do not mention it at all. Only the Dutch make various references to tea in the second half of the century, all of them to Chinese tea. These do not specify the kind imported by the VOC. Since the Dutch depended for supplies to their Asian headquarters in Batavia on the junk trade from China, which tended to furnish them with black Bohea tea, this is

---

[11]Olearius, *Vermehrte Newe Beschreibung*, 599.

[12]Ibid., 599–600.

[13]Fryer, *New Account*, 3:33–34; 2:162.

[14]Kaempfer, *Reisetagebücher*, 45, 69.

[15][Villotte], *Voyages d'un missionnaire*, 521, 525. Chardin, too, noted that in Iran tea was ingested with (cinnamon) sugar. See Chardin, *Du bon usage du thé*, 67.

[16]Ibid., 68.

[17]Chardin, *Voyages*, 3:193, 201–2.

[18]NA, VOC 1373, Van Heuvel, Gamron to Batavia, 19 April 1683, fol. 883v.

[19]Bell, *Travels*, 73; and Bushev, *Posol'stvo Artemiia Volynskogo*, 30.

[20]Valentyn, *Oud- en nieuw Oost-Indiën*, 5:277, 281; MAE, Paris, Corr. Pol., Perse, 5, Gardane, Isfahan to Paris, 31 October 1720, fol. 342; Dourry Efendy, *Relation de Dourry Efendy*, 19.

almost certainly the variety that found its way to Iran.[21] The VOC sources give various estimates about the extent of the demand for tea in Iran—reflecting the habitual market fluctuations—but on the whole suggest a rather modest consumption level. Thus, in 1643 the Dutch were left with some three hundred pounds of unsold tea in their warehouse in Bandar 'Abbas.[22] Seven years later, they stated that no Chinese tea had been imported for the last four years, and that the leaves were in great demand and would yield a handsome profit.[23] In 1694, by contrast, a missive from Bandar 'Abbas noted that the 12,045-pound consignment received had been transshipped to India for lack of demand in Iran.[24]

The uneven quality of source material renders a definitive conclusion about the relative popularity of tea in Safavid Iran impossible. Information on social and economic issues is particularly limited for Khurasan, where the drink may have been common.[25] Yet, it is clear that, with the possible exception of the northeast, tea in Safavid times was a distant second to coffee, and that neither matched *sharbat* (a fruit-flavored syrup diluted with water) in popularity.[26]

II. THE DECLINE IN COFFEE AND TEA CONSUMPTION

Regardless of the relative distribution of the two drinks in Safavid Iran, the popularity of neither survived the demise of the Safavids and the turmoil of the eighteenth century unscathed. Little is known about the fate of tea, which is rarely mentioned in the century following 1722. As for coffee, its consumption probably dropped off as well, although not necessarily as a result of the measures taken against coffeehouses in the late seventeenth century. It was seen earlier how, as a result, the Iranian coffeehouse lost its function as a venue for dubious forms of entertainment and subversive propaganda. Yet, the attendant increase in austerity did not affect the coffeehouse as such, especially not since the clerical debate over the nature of coffee had been won by those who argued for its religious permissibility. Even with restrictions imposed on them, coffeehouses continued to be public gathering places for people seeking company and

[21]For the Dutch role in the East Asian tea trade, see Ptak, "Die Rolle der Chinesen," 89–105.

[22]NA, VOC 1144, Gel. de Jongh, Gamron to Batavia, 14 May 1643, fol. 489.

[23]NA, VOC 1178, Sarcerius, Gamron to Batavia, 6 April 1650, fol. 803v.

[24]NA, VOC 1549, Verdonk, Gamron to Batavia, 24 October 1694, fol. 602r.

[25]While Safavid court chronicles yield much information on political and especially military events in Khurasan, it is not until the early nineteenth century that (European) eyewitness reports tell us more about social conditions and people's daily lives.

[26]Coolhaas, ed., *Generale Missiven, 1639–1655*, 30 November 1640, 115.

the enjoyment of a cup of coffee and a *qalyan*. Cornelis de Bruyn, visiting Iran a decade after Shah Sultan Husayn's enthronement, mentioned coffeehouses in Shamakhi and Kashan.[27] Isfahan had many coffeehouses, according to De Bruyn, who in particular noted the ones alongside the *Chahar Bagh*, where people were "to be found in great numbers smoking tobacco and drinking coffee, especially towards the evening."[28] The persistence of the coffeehouse is reflected as well in a *vaqfnamah* issued by Sultan Husayn in 1118/1706–07, which turned a great many ateliers, shops, and coffeehouses in Isfahan into religiously endowed property.[29]

It is not so much government intervention or clerical indictment as the dramatic political and economic convulsion caused by the Afghan overthrow of the Safavids that led to a decrease in coffee consumption. The Afghan occupation ushered in a protracted period of political instability and economic decline that would continue until well after the rise to power of the Qajars at the turn of the nineteenth century. The result, a disruption of trade routes and widespread impoverishment, caused prices to go up and the purchasing power of people to plummet. More importantly, the insecurity, violence and sheer destruction to which the country was subjected had a negative effect on public life. For more than a century, textual references to rural coffeehouses are exceedingly rare. A Persian-language source mentions the erection of a coffeehouse near Qandahar at the orders of Nadir Shah.[30] For the south we have a reference, dating from 1840, to a coffeehouse in the town of Bandar Daylam, situated north of Bushihr on the Persian Gulf coast, in "coffee-drinking" Arab territory.[31] Apparently more irrepressible than the coffeehouse, the tavern by this time had largely replaced the coffeehouse as a venue for oblivion and popular entertainment.[32] Coffeehouses continued to exist, to be sure, but they had changed in character. The Frenchman Olivier, visiting Iran in the closing years of the eighteenth century, compared the coffeehouses he saw with what he knew about the situation in Safavid times from reading the travelogues of Chardin and Tavernier. Whereas formerly coffeehouses had been spacious and elegant public establishments full of lively debate and entertainment, the ones he encountered

---

[27]De Bruyn, *Reizen over Moskovie*, 103, 131.

[28]Ibid., 150; and ARA, VOC 1856, Oets, Isfahan to Jacobsz., Gamron, 10 March 1714, fol. 685, which refers to a coffeehouse called *nazir*, and located "in a garden outside of Isfahan."

[29]Umidyani, "Nigarishi bar yik vaqfnamah," 23.

[30]Astarabadi, *Tarikh-i jahangusha-yi Nadiri*, 376.

[31]Al-i Davud, *Du safarnamah*, 85. The reference occurs in the first part, which is the account of a surveying trip undertaken by an anonymous government official in 1256/1840.

[32]Bélanger, *Voyage aux Indes-orientales*, 2/ii, 340–42. See the references in chapter 7.

were neither numerous nor well attended, nor indeed beautiful. His explanation for this was that during the civil wars the Iranians had ceased to go to these public places, where they could no longer converse in liberty, or even go without risking questioning and scrutiny with possibly nasty consequences. Whereas, he noted, in neighboring Turkey coffee consumption increased daily and everyone drank it at all hours of the day, Iranians offered sherbets and sweetmeats to their guests, and passed around the water pipe, but rarely presented coffee.[33]

Olivier's theory deserves serious consideration for its implication of a growing inward-looking tendency in Iranian society. Contrary to simultaneous developments in European societies, where a growing emphasis on the private sphere reflected an inexorable *embourgeoisement*, the Iranian situation has all the elements of extreme social and economic disruption leading to people's involuntary withdrawal into the confines of the private realm. Because little is known about the social history of the period between the demise of Safavid rule and the rise of the Qajars, we cannot tell much about the precise nature of this retrenchment. It is clear that the coffeehouse was not the only casualty. The polo game, too, disappeared in the eighteenth century. Polo, *gu-yi chugan*, had been played in Iran since time immemorial, and contemporary observers, Iranian and foreign alike, indicate that the game was one of the forms of public entertainment in the Safavid period as well. As in India, polo in Iran died out because of the foreign invasions and internal disorders of the early 1700s, only to be revived by the Englishman Percy Sykes in the last decade of the nineteenth century.[34]

Although direct contemporary corroboration of Olivier's thesis is lacking, circumstantial evidence supports his observation. For example, following the eclipse of the Safavid dynasty, the nature of refreshments offered in bathhouses appears to have changed. Whereas the seventeenth-century visitor to the *hammam* had enjoyed a veritable cornucopia of drinks, fruit, and sweets, a *qalyan* or water pipe was all he was offered on exiting the bath a century later, judging by observations to that effect by various eyewitnesses in the late eighteenth century.[35] Less anecdotally, none of the famous coffeehouses lining Isfahan's royal square survived the sack of 1722. The Italian missionary Leandro di S. Cecilia, who visited the city in 1738, does not mention coffeehouses in his description of the square.[36] In the early, nineteenth century, little had

---

[33]Olivier, *Voyage dans l'empire othoman*, 5:275–77.

[34]Sykes, *Ten Thousand Miles in Persia*, 334–44; and Sirjani, ed., *Vaqa'i`-i ittifaqiyah*, 548.

[35]Lerch, "Nachricht," 415; and Francklin, *Observations*, 29.

[36]Leandro di S. Cecilia, *Persia*, 186–87.

changed in the former capital. James Morier said of the houses that used to surround the square that they were "no longer inhabited," adding that "the very doors are all blocked up, so that there is now only a dead row of arches to be seen all around." The great market, he continued, "is now confined to one corner near the Nokara Khaneh. All the rest is quite empty; scarcely a person is seen to pass along."[37] Porter in 1818 conveyed exactly the same image when he noted that the "streets were everywhere in ruin, the bazars silent and abandoned, the caravanserais equally forsaken . . ."[38]

None of this means that coffee—or, for that matter, tea—disappeared altogether from the Iranian diet. Both continued to be imported in small quantities in the later 1700s, some from Russia, some from Yemen via Basra.[39] Aside from the odd references to a rural coffeehouse we have the testimony of English Russia Company agent James Spilman, who in 1739 was treated to coffee and tea by the vizier of "Languaon" (Lankuran?) in Gilan.[40] Throughout the nineteenth century, people of means, when traveling, would carry coffee in dried form with them in boxes, and would eat this like chocolate, mixed in with some honey, after cutting off chunks with a spoon.[41] Toward the end of the same century, William Francklin claimed that Iranians drank a cup of coffee without milk or sugar after eating breakfast.[42]

These examples, although suggesting a degree of continuity, do not invalidate Olivier's observation about the disruption of the public sphere. It is equally clear that this disruption went beyond the physical destruction that had befallen Isfahan and many other Iranian towns after 1722. Early-nineteenth-century observations by travelers who visited those parts of Iran that had either escaped ruin or were in the process of being rebuilt confirm and strengthen this impression. James Buckingham, who entered Iran from Baghdad in 1828, noted how Kirmanshah, the first town he visited, was in a state of (re)construction. Entering the town through a newly built wall, he went "through fine streets in every stage of their progress," where "all was like the bustle and activity of a perfectly new place." Furthermore, "there seemed an abundance of every thing to be desired, both necessaries and luxuries. The half-built streets

---

[37]Morier, *Journey through Persia*, 170. The *naqqarah khanah* was the music house.
[38]Porter, *Travels in Georgia, Persia*, 1:408.
[39]Iukht, *Torgovlia*, 42, 94; IOR, G/19/25, Report by Manesty and Jones on trade in the Persian Gulf, 15 August 1790, fols. 219, 255.
[40]Spilman, *Journey through Russia into Persia*, 18.
[41]Drouville, *Voyage en Perse*, 2:77–78; Dubeux, *La Perse*, 465; Polak, *Persien*, 2:267.
[42]Francklin, *Observations made on a Tour from Bengal*, 76.

and new bazars were thronged with people, all extremely busy, and intent on some important errand."[43] However, he did not find this bustling scene accompanied by the kind of leisurely and languid public life that he had witnessed in Ottoman lands. Everything, he noted, "offered a striking difference to the towns of Turkey and Arabia. There were no coffeehouses at which grave idlers were lounging over their pipes; no slow and solemn-paced passengers who moved as if for pleasure only; no fine flowing dresses or gay colours, compatible only with stately attitudes and the freedom from menial occupation."[44] Of Hamadan, the next town he visited on his way to Tehran, Buckingham similarly noted that it did not have one single coffeehouse.[45] Finally, in his comments on the meal he enjoyed at the residence of the governor of Isfahan during his stay in that city, he noted the absence of coffee, a beverage he claimed the Iranians did not usually drink either in public or in private.[46]

No early-nineteenth-century source contests or contradicts Buckingham's observations about public consumption of coffee. No foreign observer between 1800 and 1840 alludes to the existence of coffeehouses anywhere in Iran. As elsewhere in the Middle East, in Safavid Iran coffeehouses may never have existed outside the urban centers and beyond caravan routes.[47] In any case, rural coffeehouses were not common even in the mid-nineteenth century. The first clear reference to what seems like a revival comes from the Russian-French Orientalist Nicolas de Khanikoff, who, traveling in Khurasan between Nishapur and Mashhad in 1860, passed some villages that he called prosperous. What distinguished them from ordinary Iranian villages, he remarked, was the presence of numerous coffeehouses, on whose front porch a number of water pipes and yellow brass Russian samovars and German or English tea sets were arranged.[48]

III. The Distribution of Tea and Coffee

Buckingham's remark about the absence of coffee drinking even in the private sphere contradicts the experience of other travelers. Gaspard Drouville, writing in the 1810s, insisted that the "Persian taste for coffee borders on frenzy." He added that he did not believe there was one person in the country who did not consume the beverage several times a

---

[43]Buckingham, *Travels in Assyria*, 1:130.
[44]Ibid., 131.
[45]Ibid., 194.
[46]Ibid., 380.
[47]For the situation in Egypt, see Tuchscherer, "Café et cafés dans l'Egypte ottomane," 55.
[48]Khanikoff, *Mémoire sur la partie méridionale de l'Asie Centrale*, 96.

day, something that was all the easier, since coffee was very inexpensive. According to Drouville, travelers who were unable to drink as much of it as they desired carried some of it in ground form with them in a kind of tobacco pouch, so they could enjoy some, mixed in with some honey or opium, on the road.[49]

Clearly, we should treat generalizations by foreign travelers with circumspection. More specifically, contrasting or contradictory statements point up the important issue of geographical and societal distribution with regard to patterns of consumption. That different foreign travelers mention different beverages could be the result of their having visited different parts of the country and having taken their own observations and experience as typical of Iran and all Iranians. Thus, when we read Drouville's statement that coffee was both widely available and cheap, the question we should ask is which parts of Iran he visited, whether his journey took him to just the main cities and the roads connecting them or into rural and nomadic territory as well, in what company he traveled, and what his standards were for comparing prices.

When we take the three variables of geography, the urban-rural division, and social status coupled with financial means into account, the variety of observations becomes less bewildering, simple notions of coffee versus tea disappear, and a new, more varied picture emerges. What stands out most clearly from this picture is that the distribution and the consumption of coffee and tea in the first half of the nineteenth century was, first and foremost, a matter of financial means and affordability, and, beyond that, a question of geography. Outside the monied classes, tea was available mostly in the north, whereas coffee figured predominantly in the south.

Numerous travelers visiting Iran from the early to the mid-nineteenth-century report being offered coffee and tea at once, in places ranging from Zanjan and Tehran in the north to Shiraz and Bushihr in the south. Invariably, such references are to receptions and invitations by high officials, from the shah himself to local khans.[50] Some observers explicitly link these beverages to the well-off. One spoke of the "comfortable middle class" as offering the *qalyan*, tea, and coffee to their guests.[51] Another called coffee and tea "luxuries of ceremonious meetings," adding

---

[49]Drouville, *Voyage en Perse*, 1:78.

[50]See Jaubert, *Voyage en Arménie*, 206; Tancoigne, *Narrative of a Journey*, 101; Ouseley, *Travels in Various Countries*, 1:189, 267; Kotzbue, *Narrative of a Journey into Persia*, 167, 235, 294, 297; Stuart, *Journal of a Residence*, 156; Sheil, *Glimpses of Life and Manners in Persia*, 133; Serena, *Les hommes et les choses*, 67; Le Messurier, *From London to Bukhara*, 234.

[51]Flandin and Coste, *Voyage en Perse*, 2:55–56.

that "the lower classes ... live principally upon bread, fruits, and water."[52] A third claimed that the middling classes, which could not afford beverages, consumed "sugared water," (*sharbat*) or simply water mixed with honey, to which vinegar (*sirkanjibin*) was added.[53]

Whereas coffee and tea were regularly served by the wealthy and the powerful, their distribution among the less fortunate appears to have been more distinctly tied to market supply and thus to a combination of pricing and geography. The most telling observation with regard to the link between cost and consumption with regard to tea comes from Peter Gordon, who in 1820 claimed that tea was "very little used in Persia on account of its price."[54] Speaking about Khurasan in the 1820s, Edward Stirling noted that tea was brought via Bukhara from the northern parts of China, and was expensive at forty rupees per *man* (thirteen pounds).[55] A similar picture emerges from Gilan and Mazandaran, both separated from the rest of Iran by the high mountains, where Fraser noted the general absence of tea (as well as coffee) in the same period. In Mazandaran, he was able to procure a small quantity of tea only with great difficulty and at a high price.[56] William Richard Holmes, who traveled through Azerbaijan, Gilan, and Mazandaran twenty years later, repeatedly mentions receptions by local khans that included tea, but never once refers to tea being sold in the market or being available in the public sphere.[57] According to him, only a very small quantity of tea was brought from Russia to Astarabad, Iran's gateway from Turkistan.[58]

The failure of these travelers to find tea in the markets implies that, even in the north, common people did not consume tea. When Lady Sheil, entering Iran in late 1849, noted that "at every station, from Aras to Tehran, the first thing I beheld on entering the room was several pounds of tea, flanked by a suitable number of loaves of sugar," she refers to official lodging made available to the mission led by her husband, Colonel Sheil.[59] More specifically, Fraser's remarks about the eating habits of the Turkmen tribes of Khurasan suggest that the diet of the poorer nomadic population of the north did not include tea. The Turkmen, he noted, only consumed what they themselves produced, except for sugar. They drank a mixture of buttermilk and water (*dugh*) with their

[52]Porter, *Travels*, 2:41.
[53]Drouville, *Voyage en Perse*, 1:68–69.
[54]Gordon, *Fragment of the Journal*, 100.
[55]Stirling, *Journals*, 179.
[56]Fraser, *Travels and Adventures*, 105.
[57]Holmes, *Sketches on the Shores of the Caspian*, 61, 73, 268.
[58]Ibid., 282.
[59]Sheil, *Glimpses of Life and Manners*, 81.

meals.[60] This drink even accompanied the use of the water pipe, a role elsewhere invariably reserved for tea or coffee.[61]

Fraser draws our attention to geographical differentiation with his assertion that "there are many parts of Persia remote from the gulf or from the great marts, where this favourite oriental beverage [coffee] is to be had only in small quantities, or not at all."[62] Fraser had traveled thousands of miles throughout Iran, visiting urban areas as much as remote rural and tribal regions of the country, so his empirical observations deserve to be taken seriously. In northeastern Khurasan, he insisted, "coffee was seldom to be seen, and was given only in the house of the richest nobles." Tea, by contrast, was "always procurable, and was offered to guests in its place." Until he reached the Caspian province of Mazandaran, Fraser did not remember any place where "either the one or the other of these refreshments was not in occasional use, and to be purchased in the public market." When he asked local inhabitants of Mazandaran about coffee, he writes, they were ignorant of the name.[63]

Coffee, we may conclude, never really penetrated the northern part of Iran. As in neighboring Afghanistan, where it seems to have been all but unknown other than a medicine, coffee was especially rare in Khurasan. As far as Stirling knew, in Khurasan coffee was seldom offered for sale and not encountered in the market.[64] The Caspian provinces reveal the same picture. Tea, by contrast, was fairly common in the north. The term north, however, is too vague here, for within the northern parts of the country a great deal of variety existed. In Khurasan, for instance, the Uzbegs and other nomadic people had their brick tea, mixed in with bread and butter, to which salt was added. Green China tea, drunk with a great deal of sugar, was served to guests in urban centers such as Mashhad.[65] But, as Fraser observed, poor Turkmen did not consume tea. In the early nineteenth century, the drink does not seem to have been common in northwestern regions such as Armenia and Georgia, either. Caucasian peoples such as the Karatchai and the Ossetians certainly did not consume tea in this period.[66] Even the cities were not well served. The German M. Freygang, who visited Tabriz from Tiflis in 1812,

---

[60]Fraser, *Winter's Journey*, 2:151; idem, *Narrative of a Journey into Khorasan*, 264, 283.

[61]Fraser, *Narrative of a Journey into Khorasan*, 603.

[62]Fraser, *Travels and Adventures*, 105.

[63]Ibid.

[64]Stirling *Journals*, 179. For the situation in Afghanistan, see Bellew, *Journal of a Political Mission*, 30–31.

[65]Fraser, *Narrative of a Journey into Khorasan*, 489, 532.

[66]Klaproth, *Voyages au mont Caucase*, 1:299, 2:266.

claimed to speak for Iranians as such when he listed a diet that did not include tea of coffee. In reality, however, the perimeters of his itinerary limited the validity of his observations to Armenia and Azerbaijan.[67] Freygang's wife does not refer to coffee or tea either in her letters from Tiflis and other places in the Caucasus. The one in which she describes an elaborate dinner would surely have included a reference to tea had it been offered.[68]

There seems to be a clear correlation between geography and the degree of penetration and distribution of tea, with the examples of Gilan and Mazandaran suggesting the obstacles posed by inaccessible terrain. Until the mid-twentieth century, when much of demand could be met with domestically cultivated tea, the poor in the country's remote parts could not afford tea. In the nineteenth century, when all tea had to be imported, many more people must have been unable to afford it.

The south resembled the north in terms of the social distribution of caffeinated beverages. While traveling from Khuzistan in the southwest to Isfahan through Bakhtiari territory in 1831, the English journalist and writer Siddon noted that "the khans and Meerzas of Behbuhan are considerable consumers of coffee" (which, instead of drinking, they ate "in a powdered or roasted state"). The same author also claimed that the diet of the Bakhtiari tribes consisted of *mast* (yoghurt), goats' meat, goats' milk, and acorns.[69] The implication that the Bakhtiari did not drink either tea or coffee is reinforced by the same observer's remark that the traveler in these areas was bound to fast rather frequently during his journey, as "accident alone will bring him to a tenanted spot, where a little *mas* [*sic*] and milk will be obtained."[70] Baron de Bode's remark that the favored drink of the ones in the southwest was a mixture of sour milk, water, and salt confirms the impression that in the early to mid-nineteenth century neither coffee nor tea was common among Iran's pastoralists.[71]

Just as tea was far from common in the north, so coffee was not ubiquitous in the south. With this caveat, it still can be argued that tea was a "northern" drink, whereas coffee was mainly encountered in the south, the southwest, and the western regions bordering on Ottoman territory. We have reports of visitors being treated to coffee in Kirman, Shiraz, Bushihr, Sinnah in Kurdistan, and Dawraq and Bihbahan in Khuzistan, between 1800 and 1856, when elsewhere tea had begun to replace

[67]Freygang, "Account of a Journey to Tabriz," 341.
[68]Ibid., 132, 134–36; 163–65.
[69]Stocqeler, *Fifteen Months' Pilgrimage,* 1:99–100; 119
[70]Ibid., 121.
[71]De Bode, *Travels in Luristan,* 2:108.

coffee as the favored drink.[72] But important changes were underway in this period. As early as 1840, Mitford insisted that, "as soon as you cross the Persian frontier, coffee is no longer in use, the national beverage being black tea."[73] Some fifteen years later, Siddon was quite explicit about the relative rarity of coffee, even in southern Iran, as compared with the lands to the west and southwest, when he noted that "the moment a stranger enters the tent of the wildest Arab, or the hut of the poorest Osmanli, coffee and the chibouk are offered him; yet the instance he has crossed the frontier, and finds himself in Persia, he detects a change in the form of hospitality, and forgets the black and bitter stomachic in the refreshing draught of sherbet and the soothing qualities of the kaleeoun."[74]

IV. From Coffee to Tea

What of the supposed change from coffee to tea in Qajar Iran? The shift from coffee to tea in various countries, as well as the regional and religious differentiation between the two drinks, has thus far received little attention, no doubt because many see coffee and tea as being too similar to warrant much separate discussion. For example, the ramifications of the change in taste from coffee to tea in England have been downplayed by Schivelbusch, who called it "not drastically significant" because it occurred "*within* a culture of consumption first revolutionized by coffee."[75] Others have similarly minimized the differences between the two by drawing attention to the fact that both are nonfermented and caffeinated.[76] This view, however, perhaps focuses too narrowly on consumption and fails to take into account patterns of social, economic, and political life at the intersection of which stimulants tend to operate.

A survey of sources suggests that metropolitan Iran did witness, first, a gradual phasing out of coffee as a regularly consumed beverage and, second, an overall increase in tea consumption and a greater availability of tea throughout the country, including places where it had not previously been common. Iran thus resembles England in first taking to coffee and only turning to tea at a later period—a development exemplified

---

[72]Hollingbery, *A Journal of Observations*, 50; Waring, *A Tour to Sheeraz*, 8; Pottinger, *Travels to Beloochistan*, 210–11; Rich, *Narrative of a Residence*, 1:203; Stocqeler, *Fifteen Months' Pilgrimage*, 1:75, 99–100; Shepherd, *From Bombay to Bushire*, 135, 148.

[73]Mitford, *Land March from England to Ceylon*, 1:357.

[74]Shepherd, *From Bombay to Bushire*, 213–14.

[75]Schivelbusch, *Tastes of Paradise*, 83.

[76]Desmet, "Approche méthodologique," 35.

by the fact that the ubiquitous Iranian *qahvah-khanah*, or "coffee-house," has long served tea rather than coffee. Although Fraser had not been able to find tea in Mazandaran, Wilbraham was treated to an "excellent tea" in its capital Barfurush (modern Babul) in 1838.[77] The same traveler referred to tea in Tiflis where twenty years earlier Freygang's wife had failed to mention it.[78] Whereas Tancoigne and Porter in the early decades of the century had mentioned coffee in connection with breakfast, B. M. Binning in 1851 noted that breakfast was taken with tea.[79] A final example of the profound changes that took place in the early nineteenth century is found in the contrast between a passage on coffee written by John Malcolm in 1800 and one on tea written sixty years later by Lycklama a Nijeholt. Malcolm failed to mention tea but expressed astonishment at the ways in which the ritual of offering and consuming tobacco and coffee reflected the intricacies of social rank and intimacy in Iran.[80] The careful observer Lycklama a Nijeholt, by contrast, did not mention coffee as a common drink in Iran at all. Instead, he noted how "tea . . . forms the ordinary drink of the various inhabitants of Persia."[81]

It would be impossible to identify a precise moment for Iran's conversion from tea to coffee, which was evidently a gradual and long-term development rather than a sudden transformation. Contemporary accounts, to be sure, point to a specific moment in time, when the samovar supposedly reached Iran, to account for the surge in tea consumption. This moment is presented in more than one version. According to one story, told by Salim al-Mutabbib Qarabaghi in the late Qajar period, the first Russian samovar was given as a present to Muhammad Riza Mirza, governor of Rasht in Gilan, in 1820–21. Muhammad Riza is said to have donated the device, together with the harem girl who had learned how to prepare tea, to Fath `Ali Shah. The shah put the girl in charge of a coffee-house that was created especially to serve the monarch. Suggesting the novelty of the device and its function, Salim al-Mutabbib relates how one day when the shah felt like coffee, the slave girl happened not to be available. Because no one else knew how to prepare tea with a samovar, the shah had to forego his tea. A second samovar made its way to the royal court with the assistance of `Abbas Mirza, who ordered it from Russian merchants in Tabriz. For a while, the same source avers, these two

---

[77]Wilbraham, *Travels in the Transcaucasian Provinces of Russia*, 466.

[78]Ibid., 179.

[79]Tancoigne, *Narrative*, 175; Porter, *Travels*, 1:241; Binning, *Journal of Two Years' Travel*, 1:317.

[80][Malcolm], *Sketches of Persia*, 79–80.

[81]Lycklama a Nijeholt, *Voyage*, 2:105, 243.

samovars were the only ones in the royal palace.[82] The Austrian physician Jacob Polak, writing in the 1850s, offers a different version that is reminiscent of Olivier's about coffee, in which he claims that tea had fallen out of consumption following the civil wars of the eighteenth century. He continues by asserting that—according to Iranians—tea had been "reintroduced" when in the early 1830s crown prince `Abbas Mirza (d. 1833) received a few little packages of it as a gift.[83] The modern Iranian historian Firaydun Adamiyat, in a similar and oft-repeated claim, situates the story of the introduction of samovars at the time when Amir Kabir was grand vizier, that is, in the late 1840s.[84] While all these sources suggest that tea "returned" to Iran sometime between the 1820s and the 1850s, they also create the misleading impression that the popularization of tea was the outcome of a single official or event.

The completion of the process of popularization of tea is as difficult to situate as its beginning. One traveler in 1873 claimed that "tea is now served in Persia quite as often as coffee."[85] Twelve years later, the French traveler Houssay went even further by insisting that "all Persians, even the common people, drink it up to eight or ten times a day."[86] Yet the Iranian politician and author `Abd Allah Mustawfi, who was born in 1876, suggests in his autobiography how long it took for tea truly to become a household drink in Iran. He writes that in his early youth tea was not customary and that tea began to replace fruit juice only later.[87] And the *Tarikh-i Kashan*, which was written in 1870–71, distinguished between the wealthy and the middling classes by saying that whereas in the homes of the former, tea was served continuously, mornings and evenings, the latter consumed it more sparingly and only drank it to cool down their food in the summer.[88] Overall, it is safe to say that, although before 1880 tea was still a drink that the poor could not afford, the last part of the nineteenth century witnessed a rather sudden increase in the importation and consumption of tea. An anonymous Russian who in 1887 visited Iran as a member of a Russian delegation claimed that "some twenty years earlier all Iranians drank black aromatic coffee, but now the consumption of tea has reduced this completely."[89] I'timad

---

[82]This story occurs in Salim al-Mutabbib Qarabaghi, *Tafannunat-i salasah*, which appeared in 1898–99, and is recounted in Afshar, "Tarikh-i chay dar Iran." See also Afshar, "Gushah'i az tarikh-i chay," 768.

[83]Polak, *Persien*, 2:265.

[84]Adamiyat, *Amir Kabir va Iran*, 394–95.

[85]Baker, *Clouds in the East*, 187.

[86]Houssay, "Souvenirs d'un voyage," 860–61.

[87]Mustawfi, *Sharh-i zindigani-yi man*, 1:182.

[88]Darabi, *Tarikh-i Kashan*, 247.

[89]Anon., *Guzarish-i Iran*, 55.

al-Saltanah's *al-Ma'asir va al-asar* in the same decade claimed that, whereas formerly tea had been restricted to a small elite, it now was a "general drink," consumed by all, from urbanites to country dwellers, during breakfast and dinner. Specialty shops selling a variety of teas had been established by then.[90] The Frenchman Pellet, who in 1892 wrote a report on the manufacture of sugar in Iran, quotes a mason who had told him that the adults in his family each day drank three cups of tea, while the children consumed two.[91] Six years later, the Dutch estimated that tea consumption in Iran had risen to 1½ kilograms per person and that six million Iranians now drank it, so that the country's annual consumption was some nine million kilograms.[92] At half a cent per glass in a teahouse, tea was now within reach of all classes of the urban population.[93] Indeed, it had spread far beyond the country's urban areas. In the eastern half of the country, where Indian merchants imported large quantities of cheap, poor-quality tea, the drink was consumed in even remote places by the turn of the twentieth century.[94] Even some groups in society that formerly did not drink tea, such as nomads, Jews, and Parsis, had become avid consumers.[95] Further popularization in the country's rural areas was stimulated by the introduction of tea cultivation in Iran at this point and continued into recent times. As late as the 1960s the consumption of tea and sugar was still new and infrequent among poor families in remote areas.[96]

Numerous factors contributed to the "comeback" of tea and the shift from coffee to tea. One is the role played by opium. We saw how the late nineteenth century witnessed a dramatic rise in the cultivation of the poppy as a cash crop in Iran, and how more and more people took to smoking opium. The rise in opium consumption likely went together with an increase in tea consumption.[97] Opium, considered "cold" and "dry" in the traditional Galenic canon, balances tea, which is seen as "hot" and "humid." Polak hinted at this balance with his remark that Iranians drank two medium cups in the morning, and two in the evening with an opium pill.[98] Smoking opium actually leaves the mouth dry and it is therefore only natural that tea consumption went up considerably

---

[90]I'timad al-Saltanah, *al-Ma'asir va al-asar*, 101–2; and 172.

[91]NA, Legatie Perzië, 6, 1892, Pellet, "Rapport sur la fabrication du sucre."

[92]NA, Legatie Perzië, 26, Pater, Tehran to Bosschart, The Hague, 15 July 1898.

[93]Samuel Wilson in the 1890s noted that tea in a teahouse cost half a cent. See Wilson, *Persian Life and Customs*, 253.

[94]Yate, *Khurasan and Sistan*, 56 and 63.

[95]Gleadowe-Newcomen, Report on the Commercial Mission, 394.

[96]See Tapper, "Blood, Wine and Water," 218.

[97]This is suggested by Goushegir, "Le café en Iran," 104.

[98]Polak, *Persien*, 2:250, 265.

with the spread of opium smoking. As one observer said, "every person addicted to the opium habit drinks an abnormal quantity of tea."[99]

The role sugar played in the adoption of tea in Iran adds an intriguing element to the story. Iranians never took their coffee with sugar but drank sweetened tea long before the habit became customary in Europe. It remains unclear why that would have been the case, although we do know that sugar was generally used in abundance in Iran. In Safavid times, many a foreign traveler noted the sweet tooth of the Iranians. Sugar was used in great quantities by a court that regularly regaled its guests to a "sugar banquet," and great quantities of it were imported for use in the kitchens of the wealthy. The origins of this convergence between a traditional predilection for sweetened food and beverages, and a drink to which sugar appeared a natural additive, remain unclear, but it is entirely possible that, through the activities of the maritime companies, the Iranian habit was responsible for its adoption in England and Holland in the late 1600s.[100]

The question of the sweetened tea reminds us that changing taste tends to be a multifaceted process that is rarely induced by a single or a simple causal factor. The difficulty of establishing a precise causal framework for shifts in taste is illustrated by the complex story of the popularization of tea in early modern England and the Netherlands, societies that are far better documented than Iran. In England, consumer inclination toward tea was clearly stimulated by its elevation in the eighteenth century to the rank of high-brow beverage. Tea was hailed by publicists and social reformers as a fashionable and respectable drink, an antidote to alcohol and, in general, a wholesome beverage with salutary effects on physical discipline and moral vigilance. In the Netherlands, the spread of coffee and tea and the growing popularity of the latter followed changes in social relations, the transformation of people's diets, and questions of social status.

Nothing in the sources indicates that increased tea consumption in Iran was in any way associated with a clerical or governmental campaign against alcohol or coffee. The English (and Dutch) case might still illuminate the Iranian situation, for there are some clues that tea's growing popularity was linked to an increased status appeal similar to that in England and Holland. Although differing on the precise date of the "reintroduction" of tea, the conventional narratives initially associate it with the royal court. The best-known story, the one that links tea's introduction with Amir Kabir, relates that court ministers and nobles soon took to the use of samovars and that, gradually, the middling ranks

---

[99]Gleadowe-Newcomen, Report on the Commercial Mission, 394.

[100]For the introduction of the habit of sweetening tea in Europe, see Smith, "Complications of the Commonplace."

Tea vendor, late Qajar period. J. Bleibtreu, Persien. *Das Land der Sonne und des Löwen* (Freiburg im Breisgau, 1894).

of society followed suit. Independent sources confirm that tea was first served and consumed among the upper strata of society and that it then gained acceptance among larger groups of consumers who adopted the samovar as a common household good. R. Mignan in the 1830s noted that tea was becoming more fashionable, remarking that "all who can afford it are now in the habit of drinking tea throughout the day: it is even usual in Azerbaijan, for the people to greet their visitors with a cup of tea. The use of this beverage is becoming very general throughout the northern parts of Persia, although as yet it bears a high price."[101] The

[101]Mignan, *Winter Journey through Russia*, 1:175–76.

ascendancy of tea is further confirmed by b J. Perkins, whose observations, like Mignan's, are from the 1830s. He stated that "tea is the customary treat, in exchanging calls, among the higher classes in Persia. Sometimes both coffee and tea are brought forward; and a more formal attention still is tea, coffee and rose-water—the latter for scenting the beard—but neither coffee, nor rose-water, nor both together can properly supersede tea, where much respect is intended."[102]

Affordability is likely to have played the key role in the commodity's "downward" movement. In England, tea gained in popularity in the early eighteenth century in part because its price dropped relative to that of coffee following a fiscal system that favored tea.[103] For Qajar Iran, we do not have the extensive information on prices and taxes that is available for England, but we do know that by the late nineteenth century tea was getting cheaper. This was a slow process, and by 1880s tea was still more expensive than coffee. Wills at that time noted that "the prices are those of Europe for tea, but the best *Mocha* coffee is only a shilling a pound."[104] But, by the turn of the century, tea prices had fallen to the point where all urbanites could afford a glass.[105] Falling sugar prices may have been a factor, too. Sugar imports from Java rose steeply as of the 1840s, and France and later Russia became major suppliers as well.[106] In an ironic reversal, it was the wealthier Iranian who by this time still drank coffee.[107]

That people of different means also drank different kinds of tea is further proof that the dissemination of tea was a matter of a balance between status and affordability. The upper classes in the 1890s preferred Chinese tea, while everyone else drank much cheaper Indian (and some Java) tea.[108] It is especially unclear to what extent the "trickle-down" process extended to the impoverished rural parts of the country, where coffeehouses long remained rare and where for many the cost of tea and sugar remained prohibitive well into the twentieth century.[109]

The issue of price shifts the debate from demand factors to supply factors. Tea's popularization clearly was not simply a matter of diffusion from the court down. Whereas status appeal, rising standards of urban living, and cultural and social diffusion appear to have been chiefly

---

[102]Perkins, *Residence of Eight Years in Persia*, 270.

[103]Smith, "Accounting for Taste."

[104]Wills, *In the Land of the Lion and the Sun*, 298.

[105]Wilson, *Persian Life and Customs*, 253.

[106]PRO, FO 248/218, Mounson, Tehran to Alison, London, 3 February 1864. For the increase in sugar imports into Iran in the later nineteenth century, see also Seyf, "Production of Sugar."

[107]Anon., "Thee- and koffiehandel in Perzië," 109.

[108]Ibid., 108.

[109]Balland and Bazin, "Čāy," 103.

responsible for the spreading popularity of tea in Iran, greater demand combined with affordability would not have been possible without a matching increase in supply. Tea remained an import commodity until the onset of indigenous cultivation in the early twentieth century. It is therefore reasonable to look for further clues with regard to price and distribution in (changing) patterns of outside influence. The growing supply and popularization of tea in England was in part the result of the monopolization of the trade by the powerful East India Company. In contrast, the commerce in coffee remained in the hands of small independent merchants with less developed distribution networks.[110] Does Iran exhibit similar circumstances?

In the Safavid period all coffee consumed in Iran came from the Arabian Peninsula. In the early eighteenth century the VOC sought to use its control of the East Indian archipelago to turn the island of Java into the principal supplier of the beans. As far as Iran is concerned, its success in doing so was short-lived, in part because Iranians disliked Java coffee, preferring coffee from Ceylon instead.[111] The Dutch in the mid-eighteenth century imported small quantities from Java as well as Ceylon.[112] But as their commercial activities in the Persian Gulf faltered, Arabia resumed its role as the main provider of coffee, with local Arab and Iranian merchants acting as the main suppliers. Some coffee continued to be imported from Java and Ceylon, but Arabia supplied the bulk of Iran's coffee at the turn of the nineteenth century.[113] Most of it entered the country via the Persian Gulf ports, especially Bushihr. Table 5 shows that the English

TABLE 5
Coffee imports into Bushire in English ships, 1817–23, Value in Rupees

1817	115,489	1821	55,784
1818	52,206	1822	95,204
1819	166,397	1823	12,460
1820	61,835		

Source: PRO FO60/24, reports by E. G. Stannus, fols. 194–210.

[110]Schivelbusch, Tastes of Paradise, 79–85.

[111]Floor, Economy of Safavid Persia, 142; and NA, VOC 2511, Koenad, Gamron, to Batavia, 31 July 1740, fol. 60.

[112]NA, VOC 2511, list of goods sold in Gamron, 1738–39, fols. 1376; VOC 2584, price list 1741, fol. 2444; VOC 2680, list of goods sold in Gamron, 1742–43 season, fols. 70–71.

[113]Jaubert, Voyage, 286–87; Malcolm, "The Melville Papers," (1800), in Issawi, ed., Economic History of Iran, 264; Milburn, Oriental Commerce, 1:123, 129; and Fraser, Travels and Adventures, 371.

were involved in this trade, but a figure of 12,460 *rupees* carried by English ships in 1823 compared to 480 bales, equaling 74,500 *rupees* shipped by local bottoms, suggests that indigenous traders far outdid them in volume. Some of the coffee imported in this period was probably carried overland via the Baghdad route, which in the late eighteenth century was the principal commercial connection between Iran and the outside world.[114] The predominantly southern spread of coffee appears logical in light of the provenance of the beans and the main channels of importation.

Tea traditionally came from China, but in the 1800s it also arrived from Bengal and Coromandel. Khurasan in the northeast and the central parts of the country as far south as Kirman continued to receive their tea from Bukhara in Central Asia in the early years of the century.[115] Although the importation of tea from India to Bushihr is recorded as early as the turn of the nineteenth century,[116] the quantities involved for the time being were too small to affect the predominance of coffee in the south.

Until the nineteenth century these import patterns remained fairly stable. Change, when it came, occurred under the influence of several economic and political developments. The most important of these was a greatly increased volume of trade between Iran and the outside world, and the country's incorporation into the commercial and political sphere of influence of the two Western powers with wide-ranging Asian interests and ambitions, Russia and Great Britain. Taking advantage of Iran's weakness, the Russians between 1800 and 1828 annexed most of the territories between the Black and the Caspian Seas, thus initiating a process that would gradually integrate the Caucasus into their economy. Russia also forced Iran to open up to foreign merchants by instituting a (short-lived) tax-free transit trade to the country in 1821. A great volume of European goods began to be transported into Iran via the Russian Black Sea ports and through Tiflis and other points in Transcaucasia. Thus, the volume of goods imported into Iran through Russia increased from 397,000 rubles in 1825 to almost 2 million in 1829.[117] Eager to strengthen their commercial position in Central Asia as well, the Russians similarly began to extend trade lines across the Caspian Sea, to Orenburg and beyond. Following these developments, many Russian

---

[114]Issawi, ed., *Economic History of Iran*, 74. As late as the 1820s, Iran imported some coffee from Baghdad via Sulaymaniyah. See Rich, *Narrative of a Residence*, 1:305.

[115]Pottinger, *Travels in Beloochestan*, 226. Afghanistan, too, received its tea "in small lead boxes," from Central Asia in the early nineteenth century. See Perrin, *L'Afghanistan*, 193.

[116]Dupré, *Voyage en Perse*, 2:43.

[117]Kukanova, *Russko-iranskaia torgovlia*, 6–7.

trade representatives took up residence in cities like Tabriz, Rasht, Anzali, Ardabil, Astarabad, and Tehran. Iran, in turn, witnessed an exodus of people going to Russia in pursuit of trade and employment or, in the case of Armenians, of a more congenial religious environment. By 1862 at least fifty thousand Iranians are estimated to have lived in Transcaucasia.[118] When Russia allowed the export of specie to Central Asia and Iran in the 1830s, Iranian merchants also began to visit the annual summer fair of Nizhnii Novgorod, where Chinese tea was one of the main commodities.[119] They continued to do so until, in the 1880, they were said to be the largest group of Asian merchants visiting the fair.[120]

As a result of this change, Mignan in the late 1830s could claim that the Iranian tea trade was entirely monopolized by the Russians.[121] Conolly, too, observed how large tea imports coming in from Russia had edged out the traditional supply into northeastern Iran via Bukhara.[122] The main participants in the trade, however, were neither Russians nor Iranians, but Georgian and Armenian merchants, who in the 1830s began to import the leaves from Germany—where the annual fair of Leipzig became an important market—and later from England, which became a source for transshipment for tea destined for the Russian market as well. The term *chay nimsah*, German (literally Austrian) tea, in Iran for high-quality tea suggests that much of the early tea supply came via Germany.[123]

This enhanced interaction through labor migration and commercial ties contributed to a convergence in taste. The introduction and spread of the samovar in Iran was instrumental in this process. The first samovar used in Iran originated in the merchant community in Tabriz.[124] Around 1861, some three hundred Russians—mostly Armenians and merchants from Baku—visited Mazandaran annually, importing samovars, among other merchandise.[125] The British resident in Bushihr, Colonel Pelly, in the same year was struck "all along the route of North Persia with the unvarying presence of Russian lumbersome tea-urns (Samawar) brought

---

[118]The Italian zoologist De Filippi in 1862 estimated that at least fifty thousand Iranians lived in Transcaucasia, migrating there in search of work. See De Filippi, *Note di un viaggio*, 51.

[119]Kukanova, *Ocherki po istorii russko-iranskikh torgovykh otnoshenii*, 205; Bulmerincq, "Die Jahrmärkte Russlands"; and Fitzpatrick, *The Great Russian Fair*, 82, 91.

[120]Nassakin, "Von der Messe in Nishni-Nowgorod," 168.

[121]Mignan, *Winter Journey*, 175–76.

[122]Conolly, *Journey to the North of India*, 1:347.

[123]See Polak, *Persien*, 2:266; and Schlimmer, *Terminologie médico-pharmaceutique*, 542. Dr Iraj Afshar tells me that *chay nimsah* is also (incorrectly) pronounced *chay lamsah*.

[124]Afshar, "Gushah'i az tarikh-i chay," 768.

[125]Melgunov, *Das südliche Ufer des kaspischen Meeres*, 185.

from the great fairs beyond the Caspian."[126] The long-lasting effects of this Russian influence are reflected in terminology as well: not just the samovar became a thoroughly familiar device and a household term in Iran, but the tea glass became known under the Russian name of *istikan*.

The Russian transit route did not retain its "monopoly" for long. In 1831 St. Petersburg, concerned about foreign competition, imposed custom duties on the Transcaucasian transit trade. This measure did not stem the flow of goods; it merely prompted merchants to find different outlets for their commerce. Much of the international transit trade between Europe and Iran was transferred to the southern shores of the Black Sea in the 1830s, when the Ottoman government opened its ports to foreign shipping, thus allowing merchants to ship their wares to the port of Trabzon, whence they were transported overland to Iran.[127] Agents of Greek trading houses, Caucasian Armenians, Iranian, and Russian merchants thus transported tea from England via Istanbul, Trabzon and Erzurum to Tabriz.[128] Tabriz and Khuy, Iran's gateways in the northwestern province of Azerbaijan, became the busiest entrepôt markets for this transit trade.[129]

In 1846 the Russians lowered import tariffs on the Transcaucasian route in an attempt to regain their market share, but by that time the northern supply line had already begun to be challenged. Following the signing of the Anglo-Persian Commercial Treaty of 1841, which gave their merchants the same privileges as the Russians, the British managed to increase their share of trade with Iran, until they dominated the Iranian market with supplies of cheap tea from India, where they had set up cultivation with the aim of being able to compete with imports from China. So successful were the British that by the early twentieth century 83 percent of all tea consumed in Iran came from India.[130] Some tea, to be sure, continued to be supplied via Russia. By the 1870s, very small quantities still reached Iran via Tiflis, whereas an equally small volume was transported in transit via Astarabad, Mashhad, and Herat.[131] Yet, despite a continuing popular perception of Russia as the

[126]Pelly, "Remarks on the Tribes," 55; and *British Documents on Foreign Affairs*, Part I, Ser. B, *Persia, 1856–1885*, vol. 10, 197, Acting Political Resident and Consul-General in Persian Gulf to Chief Secretary to the Government of Bombay, Bushihr, 13 April 1863.

[127]A. S[epsis], "Perse. Du commerce de Tauris,"133–34.

[128]Bakulin, "Ocherk' vneshnei torgovli Azerbaidzhana," 220–21.

[129]See Wilbraham, *Travels*, p. 68 and, for recent analyses, Issawi, "The Tabriz-Trabzon Trade 1830–1900"; and Schneider, *Beiträge zur Wirtschaftsstruktur*.

[130]Gleadowe-Newcomen, Report on the Commercial Mission, 392.

[131]Bakulin, "Ocherk' vneshnei torgovli Azerbaidzhana"; and idem, "Ocherk' russkoi torgovli v' Mazandarane," 277, 289, 300, 302.

main source of tea consumed in the country, tea "from Moscow" was now "sold very little in Iran and at high prices."[132]

Cost advantage was an important aspect of this shift. Benefiting from vastly lower carriage expenses, the English were able to underbid the Russians to the point where Chinese tea shipped from Canton began to be smuggled into Russia from Western custom houses such as Hamburg and Leipzig (the official transshipment of Chinese wares via Europe being prohibited by the Russian government).[133] By the 1850s, tea had become cheaper in Iran than in Russia, and as Russian tariffs on Indian and English goods were exorbitant, Iranian merchants began to smuggle great quantities of it from Iran into Georgia, thus prompting the Russians to seek ways to set up their own cultivation in the Caucasus.[134] Most of the tea now entering the country was shipped from Bombay in British India, even Chinese tea destined for Central Asia. Black Indian tea had not only won over the people of Khurasan but had even begun to make inroads in Central Asia.[135] All this was part of a comprehensive long-term shift of Iran's commercial center of gravity away from the Caucasus and toward the Persian Gulf basin.[136]

Most of the growing volume of tea imported by Iran from India was carried via the maritime route. In the Persian Gulf Bushihr became the most important port of entry, distributing its wares to Muhammarah (Khurramshahr) on the Shatt al-'Arab. The rising figures for tea imports through this and other southern ports illustrate the trend involved. The annual supply via Bandar 'Abbas in circa 1850 is given as 1,500 to

[132]Anon., *Guzarish-i Iran*, 55.

[133]Petrov, "Foreign Trade of Russia and Britain," 630–31.

[134]See Polak, *Persien*, 2:266; and Blau, *Commerziele Zustände Persiens*, 143; as well as *British Documents on Foreign Affairs*, part I, Ser. A, vol. 1, *Russia, 1859–1880*, 8, Rawlinson, Report from Tabriz to the Secretary of State for India, 14 Nov. 1859. Tea imports into Russia doubled in the 1870s as compared to the previous decade. See Schütz, *Russlands Samowar*, 28. Russia had experimented with tea cultivation in the early nineteenth century and, as of 1853, undertook a series of attempts to stimulate the production of tea in the Black Sea region. Indigenous cultivation took off in the 1880s.

[135]In the 1860s, Indian tea began to challenge Chinese tea in Central Asia. High Russian toll tariffs notwithstanding, tea was increasingly carried to Turkistan by merchants from Kabul and Qandahar. See Vambéry, "Die Anglo-russische Theeconcurrenz," 106–7. In 1874 a British report claimed that six thousand loads worth three million rubles were annually carried into Central Asia from Afghanistan. See *British Documents on Foreign Affairs*, Part I, Ser. A., *Russia, 1859–1880*, vol. 1, 237, Report of Colonel Glukovsky, 14 June 1874. By 1890, one third of tea imported into Bukhara was said to be Indian and two thirds Chinese. See *A&P*, 1890, vol. 86, Maclean, Report on the Trade of Khorassan for the Year 1889–90, 2–3.

[136]PRO, FO/60483, enclosure to Abbott, Tabriz, 20 November 1886; and FO60/489, enclosures to Abbott, Tabriz, 8 November 1887.

2,000 cases of 474 *man* (6,162 lb.) each.[137] In 1863 tea in the amount of 80,000 *rupees* was imported from India to Iran via Bushihr.[138] Bandar `Abbas continued to serve the country's northeast. Most of the tea sold in Mashhad in the 1890s arrived from Bandar `Abbas via Kirman and Turbat-i Haydariyah. Indian merchants also pushed hard to supply Iran overland, via Sistan and Khurasan. Until the market became overstocked, Indian tea carried overland to Mashhad commanded higher prices than imports via Bandar `Abbas, in part because of higher transshipment and customs fees on seaborne tea, in part because of a stubborn popular belief that tea exposed to the warm sea air lost some of its aroma or would even be spoiled.[139]

By the late 1800s, the tea consumed by Iranians mostly consisted of Indian black tea. But as one English official cautioned, "it is important for Indian producers to bear in mind the fact that the taste of consumers varies in Persia, and that what pleases tea drinkers in the north, will not, of necessity, suit the people of the south, and *vice versa.*"[140] In the south, the demand was for a low-priced tea that was flowery or even leafy. Absolutely black teas were not much cared for and the demand for green teas was small. In the north, by contrast, leafy teas were not much in demand; people rather liked black tea, "wiry and even, with few tips." Some Russian tea was sold and even became fashionable in the northern towns.[141] Initially much of the tea consumed in Iran consisted of coarse black tea, called *chay-i siyah.* Indian traders "eager for big profits and quick returns," bought large quantities of the "cheapest and lowest grade tea they could find in Bombay and Calcutta" and imported it to Iran. This tea "of the vilest description," gradually fell out of favor, however. The worst kind, "of large leaf and ugly appearance, poor in fragrance and yielding a very strong dark liquor," disappeared from the Shiraz market by circa 1885, but seems to have lingered on in the northeast.[142]

---

[137]Amanat, ed., *Cities & Trade*, 91, 107, Trade Report by Consul Abbott in 1849–50.

[138]For the import figures from Russia in the latter part of the century, see Entner, *Russo-Persian Commercial Relations*, 10, 66, 70. Tea and coffee imports in 1863 are found in Pelly, "Remarks on the Tribes," 47. For figures of goods imported through the various entry points for the period 1878–82, see also Stolze and Andreas, "Die Handelsverhältnisse Persiens."

[139]A&B, 1895, vol. 91, Elias, Report on the Trade and Commerce of Khorassan, 1894–95, 6; Landor, *Across Coveted Lands*, 2:154–55.

[140]Gleadowe-Newcomen, Report on the Commercial Mission, 393.

[141]Ibid., 393–94.

[142]Ibid.; *A&P*, 1895, vol. 91, Elias, Report on the Trade and Commerce of Khorassan, 1894–95, 6.

TABLE 6
Value of Tea imports from England to Iran, 1878–87, in pounds sterling

1878	34,870	1883	43,928
1879	26,928	1884	65,440
1880	40,176	1885	81,120
1881	19,064	1886	75,200
1882	25,880	1887	96,600

Source: *British Documents on Foreign Affairs*, Part I, Ser. B, Vol. 13, *Persia, Britain and Russia 1886–1907*, Law, British Trade and Foreign Competition in North Persia, Constantinople, 6 December 1888, App. IV, 45.

The reputation of Indian tea damaged, those Iranians who could afford it reached for better teas, preferably in sealed boxes.[143] Of much higher quality were *chay-i nimsah*, what the British called *lamsar*, or Dutch tea, "a blend of Pekoe and Orange Pekoe with a good percentage of the tips," and so-called white tea, *chay-i sifid*, which in reality was "nothing but a common Pekoe with a sprinkling of the unfermented sun-dried tips thrown in." Both comprised China as well as Java teas. The former, "yielding a pale, straw-coloured liquor, and possessing a delicate flavour," was the preferred tea all over the country because it lent itself to stewing on the samovar. Heavily taxed, both were smuggled into the country, but nevertheless were well above the means of the common people. The latter variety in particular was exceedingly expense at 5 *tumans* per *man-i shiraz* (ca. 7½ lb.), so that it found much favor among the upper classes in the larger cities, especially during ceremonial visits.[144]

Table 6 shows the growing tea imports from England between 1878 and 1887.

By century's end, Russia managed to recapture its former position in trading with Iran, opening new transit routes connecting Batum with Julfa and Ashqabad, respectively.[145] This process was facilitated by the completion of the Caucasian railway—which reached Petrovsk in 1984 and Baku in 1900—competitive Russian railway and shipping charges, and heavy subsidies on Russia's export products. Anzali on the south shore of the Caspian Sea now became the port of entry for tea arriving from Russia and destined either for Iran or for the Trans-Caspian region

[143]Gleadowe-Newcomen, Report on the Commercial Mission, 393.

[144]Ibid., 391–93; *A&P*, 1895, vol. 91, Elias, Report on the Trade and Commerce of Khorassan, 1894–95, 12.

[145]Gleadowe-Newcomen, Report on the Commercial Mission, 390.

of Russian Turkistan.[146] The building of a cart road between Rasht and Qazvin—by a Russian company—facilitated distribution.[147] This trade revival is reflected in a near-40-percent Russian share in Iran's tea supply by 1910.[148] There was no fundamental change in the provenance of the leaves, however. Most of the tea now entering Iran, even consignments transshipped via Russia, continued to originate in British India.

This shift in commercial and political patterns reflects a secular change of global import: the extension of Western economic and political hegemony to parts of the world where Europeans had hitherto played a minor or at least a less than dominant role. Iran was one of those areas. Whereas Iran had been the object of European commercial penetration since the seventeenth century, it only became fully integrated into the expanding world market in the course of the nineteenth century, when it lost its economic independence and became incorporated into a European-dominated trading network that spanned the entire Asian continent. The main players in this network, England and Russia, had both become tea-consuming societies in the nineteenth century, in part because their commercial empires extended predominantly to regions where tea was or might be cultivated. The nature of their home market made both countries active in the tea trade, and by the mid-nineteenth century they imported large quantities of tea. The demand for tea in both cases led to efforts toward import substitution. England in the 1830s began to encourage tea production in its Indian dominions. In 1853 Russia had undertaken a series of attempts to stimulate the cultivation of tea in the Black Sea region, and indigenous cultivation took off in the 1880s.[149] Given these developments and the intensity of the interaction with Iran, it is only natural that, by way of commercial channels and cultural interaction, the external stimulus exerted on Iran fostered the consumption of tea rather than coffee.

CONCLUSION

Like coffee, Chinese green or black tea was known in Iran before the advent of European merchants to the shores of the Persian Gulf. As in early China and seventeenth-century Europe, tea in early modern Iran

---

[146]Gordon, *Persia Revisited*, 17.

[147]Ibid., 23–24.

[148]Entner, *Russo-Persian Commercial Relations*, 72. In Russia, cheaper seaborne tea was an important factor in its growing popularity in the same period.

[149]See Radde and Koenig, *Das Ostufer des Pontus*, 34–35.

was above all valued as a medicinal agent. Even as tea became a recreational beverage as well, coffee remained the more popular drink for the duration of the Safavid period. The demise of the Safavid state in the early eighteenth century greatly reduced the number of coffeehouses as well as the overall consumption of coffee. A function of the large-scale terror and destruction inflicted on the country in this period, this decrease was expressed as a retrenchment of public life.

Although neither tea nor coffee ever disappeared from the Iranian urban scene, both regained in visibility in the early nineteenth century, in part because of a greater abundance of sources from parts of the country that went unreported in the eighteenth century, and in part because a revival of trade and social life led to a substantial increase in the consumption of imported commodities. Coffee, however, had ceded its former predominance, and the picture that emerges from the sources in early Qajar times shows a clear distribution of the two drinks along lines of regional division and social stratification. The upper classes were in a position to serve both tea and coffee at their receptions, regardless of geography. Otherwise tea predominated in the north, whereas coffee was the drink of choice in the south. This division was in flux, however. Tea clearly made inroads into parts of Iran where it had not been customary before, until it began to edge out coffee even in the Persian Gulf region. Less dramatic than it appears at first sight—both, after all, are nonfermented beverages with the same addictive substance—this long-term change is above all interesting because of the larger social and economic context in which it occurred.

Tea's growing popularity involved issues of status and changing taste. The presentation of samovars to the royal court played a role in this. If the involvement of the shah's court did not literally "reintroduce" tea to Iran, it publicized the drink and its preparation and thus had a "trickle down effect" on its spread. Tea, moreover, was as expensive as the sugar that invariably accompanied it, so that both were initially affordable only to the elite. Over time, tea evolved from a luxury into a staple and a necessity. Demand-oriented causes do not suffice to explain this popularization. Given Iran's exposure to outside influence and its lack of internal economic dynamism, the market and, more specifically, the impact of changing international supply channels, played an equally important role. Iran in the 1800s was integrated into the world economy and began to interact commercially with the Asian continent under the aegis of its two superpowers, England and Russia. Russia at first dominated, and all indications are that tea-drinking Russia was mostly responsible for Iran's conversion to tea.

As far as tea is concerned, Russia's hegemony in Iran abated when merchants when Great Britain concluded a commercial treaty with Iran, and even more so when they established a direct, inexpensive link between producers in India and consumers in Iran. For Iran to be drawn into the Russian or the British sphere of influence made no difference as far as its changing taste in caffeinated beverages was concerned: in either case, the conversion to tea was a historical "inevitability."

CHAPTER 10

Drinking Tea in the *Qahvah-khanah*: The Politics of Consumption in Qajar Iran

> The samovar as a matter of course is not allowed ever to get cold in a Persian house, since even servants drink tea all the time.
>
> *Neue Freie Presse*, Vienna, 28 Feb. 1879

INTRODUCTION

The sources marshaled in the previous chapter suggest that in the course of the nineteenth century metropolitan Iran witnessed, first, an overall increase in tea consumption and a greater availability of tea throughout the country, including places where previously it had not been common, and, second, a gradual phasing out of coffee as a regular beverage, even in the southern parts of the country, until in the twentieth century it was observed that "Persians seldom serve coffee except at wakes."[1] It was seen that it would be impossible to identify a precise moment for the conversion. Just as the rate of conversion to tea was uneven, with different parts of the country taking to it sooner than others, the type of tea preferred by consumers was not all uniform throughout Iran either. Everyone wanted tea that was suitable to stewing on the samovar, but people in the south liked their tealeaves flowery and leafy, while consumers in the north preferred a wiry leaf. Many northerners continued to drink green tea.[2]

This final chapter further explores the changes that accompanied this switch in consumption patterns. The first part examines the revival of the coffeehouse as a venue where newly popular tea was consumed, and focuses on its origins and subsequent developments. The second part addresses issues of centralization and modernization in Qajar Iran. It looks at government involvement in economic life and attempts at control over public morality, and centers on the reaction of the authorities to the increased importation of tea in the late nineteenth century as well as to the proliferation of the locales where people consumed the drink.

---

[1] Koelz, *Persian Diary*, 32.
[2] Gleadowe-Newcomen, Report on the Commercial Mission, 392–93.

I. THE POPULARIZATION OF TEA AND THE REEMERGENCE
OF THE "COFFEEHOUSE"

The spread and popularization of tea must be seen as a gradual and long-term process rather than the outcome of a sudden transformation. Tea appears to have been fairly widespread at the time when, according to the conventional story, it was still restricted to court circles. After all, a well-informed survey of Iran's economic resources from 1839 states that, whereas the Turks consumed great amounts of coffee, in Iran tea had taken over, having become so common that shops in urban areas now sold it to passers-by.[3] In the same year Edward Conolly was treated to tea at the home of the governor of remote Farah in western Afghanistan.[4] A decade later, the value of annual tea imports into Iran had reached 8,500,000 rubles.[5] Tea continued its upward movement from there, until by 1875 it had become a fairly common beverage among the urban masses. At that time druggists and sugar vendors in the bazaar of Tabriz sold it "wrapped in coarse pink paper."[6] The *Jughrafiya-yi Isfahan*, referring to the same period, claimed that, in Isfahan, tea had not been customary and the profession of tea vendor nonexistent until recently. It was only in the last few years, Mirza Husayn Khan continued, that the drinking of tea had become more popular and that a number of coffeehouses had been established in town.[7]

Changes in the refreshments offered in bathhouses reflect the same development. G. Fowler, describing his visit to a *hammam* in Tabriz in the late 1830s, noted how on entering he had been "refreshed with coffee and pipes," whereas afterward "you are clothed in soft drappers, and coffee and pipes are again introduced to restore the inner man."[8] By the second half of the nineteenth century, coffee had clearly been replaced by tea as the favorite beverage for those who frequented the bathhouse, something that is reflected in the observation of the American James Bassett, who in the 1870s noted that a tea shop was usually kept near the Iranian bathhouse, and that the bath was commonly followed by tea drinking.[9]

The samovar played an important role in this development. Its spread and popularization were crucial to the emergence of the new

---

[3]Hagemeister, *Essai sur les ressources*, 168.

[4]Conolly, "Journal Kept while Travelling in Seistan," 323.

[5]MAE, Nantes, Téhéran A, 21, Commerce d'importation et d'exportation de l'Europe avec la Perse, fols. 43v–44.

[6]Bakulin, "Ocherk' vneshnei torgovli Azerbaidzhana," 220–21.

[7]Husayn Khan, *Jughrafiya-yi Isfahan*, 120–21.

[8]Fowler, *Three Years in Persia*, 1:270.

[9]Bassett, *Persia, the Land of the Imams*, 266.

coffeehouses. The anonymous Russian who came to Iran in 1887 claimed that Iranian tea consumption has been greatly aided by the Russian influence in the country, with people adopting Russian terms such as samovar and *istikan* (glass).[10] The Russian samovar naturally made inroads into the north before it spread to other parts of the country. Its growing penetration prompted Amir Kabir to commission Iranian artisans to copy Russian models and to grant an Iranian businessman a monopoly of their manufacture as part of his import-substitution economic policies.[11] Little more than a decade later, the samovar had become commonplace in the urban areas of the north and middle of the country. According to Polak "these days tea is so common in the cities that there is hardly a well-to-do family which does not own a Russian samovar . . ."[12] A representative of the Austrian military mission in Tehran in 1879 conveyed the same image: "The samovar as a matter of course is not allowed ever to get cold in a Persian house, since even servants drink tea all the time."[13] A decade later, samovars and the Russian way of brewing tea had penetrated deep into the interior. In 1889 the bazaar of Burujird in Luristan was well stocked with Russian samovars, tea glasses and tea trays.[14]

The increasingly common use of samovars hastened changes in taste but also may have contributed to the conversion of tea booths into the real sit-down establishments referred to by Gobineau, who in the mid-1850s averred that coffeehouses (*cafés*) were a recent invention in Iran.[15] Other sources confirm this assertion, if only by omission. Mitford, for instance, in 1840 called Iran a tea-drinking nation. But visiting Kirmanshah, he talked about cook-shops that, he said, served an excellent dinner of stews and kebabs as well as *sharbats*, but made no mention of *qahvah-khanah*s.[16] Little is known about the evolution of the new coffeehouses in the quarter century after Gobineau referred to them. Khanikoff's comments about the coffeehouses that he observed while traveling between Nishapur and Mashhad in 1860 and especially his claim that the villages where they existed differed from ordinary Iranian villages, suggest that, by that time, these new establishments were still limited to the north.[17] But they are not likely to have been ubiquitous

---

[10]Anon., *Guzarish-i Iran,* 55.

[11]For this, see Al-i Davud, *Namah'ha-yi Amir Kabir,* 309–12. See also Furughi, "Samavar sazi dar Iran"; and Adamiyat, *Amir Kabir,* 216–18.

[12]Polak, *Persien,* 2:265.

[13]*Neue Freie Presse,* Friday, 28 February 1879.

[14]Bird, *Journeys in Persia and Kurdistan,* 2:130.

[15]Gobineau, *Trois ans en Asie,* 359.

[16]Mitford, *Land March from England to Ceylon,* 343.

[17]Khanikoff, *Mémoire sur la partie méridionale de l'Asie Centrale,* 96.

even there. Mirza `Ali Rishtah-dar, passing through Zanjan in 1871, commented that its inhabitants used the gardens surrounding the town as leisure grounds where they consumed tea. He added that this was not the case everywhere. The inhabitants of Qazvin, which Rishtah-dar visited later during his trip and which he called ruined and filled with poor people, did not consume tea and lump sugar.[18]

By 1880 coffeehouses had become a common sight in urban areas. The Frenchman Orsolle, who was in Tehran in 1882–83, offers a vivid description of the atmosphere that would descend on its bazaar at noon:

> Towards noon, the alleys of the bazaar empty out as if by enchantment; the strollers go back home, only to return a bit later; in their shops, merchants, kneeling in the direction of Mecca, perform their prayers while touching a small disk made of sacred soil from Karbala or Qum, with their foreheads. From all sides little boys run around carrying fruit, some cheese wrapped in thin leaves of dough, grilled over red stones, which serve as bread; richer or more discriminating people surround the open kitchens, which display pots of soup or mutton, skewers of kebab and pyramids of pilaf with saffron. This is followed by the hour of *kif*, the hour of tea and water pipe, and from one end of the bazaar to the other, in the most elegant alleys and in the disreputable passageways where they sell rags, in all avenues and in each and every corner, one only hears the noise of samovars and the gurgling of water in the water pipes.[19]

In more rural areas, the number of new coffeehouses seems to have grown in the decades that followed. `Ali Akbar Mishkat al-Sultan traveled from Tabriz to Karbala in 1899–1900 and in the dairy that he kept of his journey he noted on several occasions the existence of "newly built" coffeehouses.[20]

But not all coffeehouses were alike. Orsolle and other eyewitnesses, as well as the occasional photograph, suggest a range of establishments, from the traditional and the seedy to the modern, from isolated, primitive stalls alongside caravan routes and corners in the bazaar where common people could repose after a day's labor, to chic and fashionable places catering to a clientele seeking leisure rather than a brief respite from hard work. In 1884 we hear of a coffeehouse named Hajji Muhammad Husayn Sarraf, located some three kilometers outside Shiraz, where a few ruffians, *ashrar va awbash*, had been caught holding a drinking

[18]Sar Rishtah-dar, *Safarnamah*, 144, 156.
[19]Orsolle, *Le Caucase et la Perse*, 237.
[20]Mishkat al-Sultan, "Mishkat al-musafirin," 27, 37, 48.

Coffeehouse in the Qum area, late Qajar period. H. R. D'Allemagne, *Du Khorassan au pays des Bachtiaris*, 4 vols. (Paris, 1911).

party.[21] Edward Stack, writing in 1881, alludes to a different kind, more upscale establishment in his description of the newly established coffee-houses in Tehran. The coffeehouses, he said, "are distinctly Persian. They open on gardens behind, and through the doors can be seen small round tables, samovars, teacups, and qalyans, arranged against a back-ground of green leaves and falling water." The same author drew atten-tion to a coffeehouse of European fashion, with elegant couches and mirrors, and a drinking-bar."[22] S.G.W. Benjamin concurred by saying "tea-houses abound on every side, of every quality of rank and degree of comfort, but all alike resorts for repose and entertainment."[23] Yet an-other foreigner, Brugsch, echoed these visitors by describing the coffee-house as a venue that combined the old and the traditional with the new and the fashionable:

> In the bazaars, too, the coffeehouse (*qahvah-khanah*) opens its doors invitingly with its wooden glass-paneled doors; the guests inside either sit on chairs like real Farangis, or prefer to take a seat on the long tall

[21]Sirjani, ed., *Vaqa'i'-i ittifaqiyah*, 225, 13 Zu'l-qa`dah 1301/4 September 1884.
[22]Stack, *Six Months in Persia*, 2:151–52.
[23]Benjamin, *Persia and the Persians*, 99–100.

Coffeehouse in Tehran, late Qajar period. Auguste Bricteux, *Au pays du lion et du soleil* (Brussels, 1908).

wooden bench with its carved banister to slurp their chay (tea), which the owner prepares in a Russian samovar according to the rules. . . . Flowers and colorful glass chandeliers with glittering festoons decorate the tearooms, whose walls dazzle the eye with unveiled women, sweet lovers, mute singers and wine drinkers who grin with contentment. Colorful birds sway on the trees. In sum, everything breathes love and lust in a Persian teahouse.[24]

The references to chairs suggest that the new coffeehouse was associated with modern taste and comportment and that the downward movement referred to in the previous chapter applies to the beverage as much as to the venues where it was consumed. Mirza Husayn Khan claimed that Istahan's local population considered it shameful (*qabih*) to drink tea in a coffeehouse. The business of tea, he insisted, was associated with foreigners and travelers.[25] The growing presence of foreigners in late-nineteenth-century Iran, most of them tea-drinking Englishmen and Russians, thus seems to have played a role in the status appeal of tea. The Russian influence on Iranian tea-drinking habits is reflected in the adoption of the samovar and of tea glasses. No comparable influence can be detected with regard to other European nationals residing in Iran. It is

[24]Brugsch, *Im Land der Sonne*, 146.
[25]Husayn Khan, *Jughrafiya-yi Isfahan*, 120–21.

Coffeehouse, late Qajar period. Credit: Rijksmuseum voor Volkenkunde, Leiden, no. 3268.

tempting, though, to ascribe at least part of the spread of tea beyond its initial highbrow status to the influx of Englishmen, who as of the 1870s began to visit the country and to take up residence in the main cities in large numbers. A tantalizingly vague reference by Hagemeister who in a report, written in 1839, noted that "the English have much contributed to spreading the taste for tea in Persia . . . ," suggests that such contagious diffusion began very early.[26] More concrete support for later developments is found in the Persian *Jughrafiya-yi Isfahan*, written between 1877 and 1891, which echoed Hagemeister in averring that tea was associated with foreigners and travelers.[27] By century's end, in the remoter parts of Iran tea had not yet lost it aura as a drink consumed by the elite as part of an outing. Walter Harris, visiting Sinnah (today's Sanandaj) in Kurdistan in the 1890s, tells us that the valley below the town was a charming spot much frequented by the townspeople, where "the dandies of the place come to drink tea in one of the many *cafés* . . ."[28]

The growing popularity of tea in this same period, and its appeal to the literate and educated segment of the population, finally, are reflected

[26]Hagemeister, *Essai sur les ressources*, 168.
[27]Husayn Khan, *Jughrafiya-yi Isfahan*, 120–21.
[28]Harris, *From Batum to Baghdad*, 243, 246.

as well in the coverage the beverage received in the press. The biweekly publication *Ittila'*, for example, in 1303–04/1885–86 published some ten articles on tea, arguing that the recent popularity of the drink neces-sitated a greater knowledge of its provenance and properties. Mostly translated from Turkish, the articles discuss practical questions such as the best way to prepare the drink, the perishable nature of tea, whether tea was wholesome or, if taken in excess, could do damage to the stom-ach, in addition to addressing issues such as the origins of the tea drunk in Iran and the problem of the drain on bullion the importation of tea constituted for countries that lacked indigenous cultivation.[29]

Tea had clearly become a staple of the Iranian diet by century's end. Just as the greater availability of tea and sugar might be taken as an index of rising living standards of urbanites after the turmoil of the "long" eighteenth century, so the "reappearance" of the coffeehouse in metropolitan Iran reflects a degree of political stability that had been ab-sent from the country for more than a century.

II. THE ROLE OF THE STATE

Among the most interesting aspects of the growing imports and the in-crease in consumption of tea in Iran is the role that the Qajar state played in this process. As early as the 1840s, the dominant position of foreign merchants in the Iranian tea trade was such that it caused the government to impose a ban on the sale, purchase and consumption of tea in Tehran and Tabriz. Noting that the ban was ostensibly instituted because the "Chinese mixed poison in their tea," the British consul in Iran surmised that its real motivation was a desire on the part of Iranian merchants to embarrass the "Russian Georgians" who had the "principal traffic in that article, whereas native merchants have none, by representing to the author-ities that numerous deaths have occurred in consequence of people drink-ing tea."[30] More specifically, the reference to poison points to a Chinese tendency in the nineteenth century to scent tea with Chloranthus as well as to add dye powder consisting of Prussian Blue and gypsum to tea meant for export, all in order to satisfy European consumers who expected finer teas to have a blue hue and an exotic aroma.[31]

---

[29]*Ittila'* 128 (12 Muharram 1303/24 October 1885), 4, "Dar haqiqat-i mahsul-i chay"; as well as 129 (24 Muharram 1303/2 November 1885); 133 (15 Rabi' al-avval 1303/22 December 1885); 135 (12 Rabi' al-sani 1303/18 January 1886); 136 (22 Rabi' al-sani 1303/28 January 1886).

[30]PRO, FO 60/82, E. W. Bonham to J. Bidwell, 13 March 1841.

[31]For this, see Evans, *Tea in China*, 129–30. The adulteration of tea was a problem in Europe as well. In eighteenth-century England, laws were passed four times to prevent the

People in Iran long appear to have held foreign tea merchants rather than (Chinese) producers responsible for this adulteration and its result, the presence of glazed and lied teas.[32] From the turn of the twentieth century we have the example of Indian tea disappearing from the market of Shiraz after Niyamat al-Saltanah Vazir-i Jang had found traces of *aznik*, or yellow arsenic, on burning the black tea that came from India. The popular scare this caused made the sale of Indian *chay-yi siyah* (black tea) plummet.[33]

The measures inspired by such popular perceptions were neither unique nor taken in a vacuum. Iranians had long harbored suspicions about the activities of the foreigners working and residing among them. More concretely, these measures must really be seen as a reaction to the increasingly dominant position of foreign merchants in the Iranian market, and specifically to the various trade agreements that Russia and England imposed on Iran at the time. The tariff system that came into being as a result of treaties with Russia in 1828 and with England in 1841 put Iranian merchants at a distinct disadvantage vis-à-vis their foreign competitors, who obtained the right to travel freely in Iran while their goods were subjected to a mere 5 percent *ad valorem* import and export duty.

The ban of the 1840s and the motives for issuing it also bespeak an attempt to try and protect domestic industries and to safeguard the country's balance of payments—both urgent concerns in the miserable economic circumstances following the war over Herat of 1837. There was nothing new about the preoccupation with the outflow of bullion and the response to it, protectionist measures: its antecedents can be traced to various Safavid attempts to engage in forms of import substitution. The early Qajar period, too, witnessed numerous initiatives designed to protect local industries. Fath `Ali Shah confined the use of cashmere shawls to people of high rank so as to stimulate the shawl manufactures of Kirman.[34] Muhammad Shah in 1835 encouraged the indigenous manufacture of chintz and the wearing of Iranian woolens for the same reasons.[35] Amir Kabir's import-substituting measures, and especially his granting of a monopoly on the making of samovars, "so that the Iranian people will not be deprived of such a device and will not

---

importation of so-called glazed teas (low-quality teas doctored to improve color), and "lie" teas (tea mixed with earthly substances), and two thirds of all tea sold in Britain in the second half of the century reportedly was either smuggled or counterfeit. See Smith, "Accounting for Taste," 207.

[32]*Ittila`* 147, 10 shavval 1303/13 July 1886), 4, "Chay-yi Chin."

[33]Gleadowe-Newcomen, Report on the Commercial Mission, 393.

[34]Brydges, *Account of the Transcations*, 101–2.

[35]Lambton, "Persian Trade under the Early Qājārs," 32; and Natiq, *Iran dar rahyabi-yi farhangi*, 214.

be forced to order it from foreign lands," fall into the same category.[36] In subsequent years Iranian merchants repeatedly petitioned the Qajar authorities to prohibit the import of European manufactures so as to save them from ruin. None of these campaigns proved successful.[37] In sum, anxieties about economic dependence on foreign powers and (unsuccessful) resistance against it were major themes in Iranian history long before the modern age. The reported reluctance of nomadic groups at the turn of the twentieth century to integrate tea into their diets for fear of becoming "tributary" to foreigners underscores that this reflex was not confined to the state.[38]

The aftermath of the 1840 episode—a lack of enforcement of the measure followed by its quiet death—is as characteristic of Qajar Iran as the cause. Already in his initial report the British consul expressed his opinion that he thought it unlikely that the prohibition could be permanently maintained. Less than six months later, the same official reported that "after a short time endeavouring to enforce the prohibition, the Persian authorities ceased to interfere or give further inconvenience to merchants on this account. The prohibition has not been formally withdrawn, but there is no probability of any further attempt being made to act upon it."[39]

The switch from import prohibition to encouragement of tea consumption on the part of the Qajar government might seem contradictory, but in its concern over the need to have imports and exports equalized we recognize a similar impulse. This involves the famous story of Amir Kabir's support for the establishment of an indigenous samovar industry. As the story is told, one day all locksmiths in the bazaar of Isfahan were called to the residence of the local governor. The governor selected the very best from their ranks and sent the most expert one to Tehran to have an audience with Amir Kabir. The Amir showed him a Russian samovar and asked him if he could make something similar. The locksmith answered in the affirmative, and proceeded to build a replica. He was next given 100 *tumans* to have a shop outfitted, and went to work under government protection. He had barely begun, however, when the news came of Amir Kabir's ouster. This proved the end of the experiment. The locksmith was forced to return the money. Pleas to wait so that he could set up his business, make a profit, and then repay the money went unheeded, and the poor man was beaten up so badly that he lost his eyesight and was left to beg for his livelihood.[40]

[36] Al-i Davud, *Risalah-i navadir al-Amir*, 309.
[37] Issawi, *Economic History of Iran*, 76.
[38] D'Allemagne, *Du Khorassan*, 4:181.
[39] PRO, FO 60/82, Bonham, Tehran, to Bidwell, London, 28 August 1841.
[40] Furughi, "Samavar sazi dar Iran."

A poem that recounts the same story suggests that Amir Kabir's intention was precisely the stimulation of domestic industry for which he is traditionally credited:

دست مریزاد و دلت شاد باد   خنده کنان گفت زهی اوستاد

خاطرم از غصه بپرداختی   هر چه دلم خواست همان ساختی

آتش و آبی به سماور بریز   بعد بفرمود یکی را که خیز

دم کن از چای و به هر کس که هست   ده که بنوشد شود از وجد مست

زمزمهٔ آب همی شد بلند   خادمی آتش به سماور فکند

غلغلش انداخت به ایوان خروش   گرم چو شد ز آتش و آمد به جوش

تا که کنم بر تو یکی راز فاش   چون همه رفتند مرا گفت: باش

زنده کنم صنعت ایرانیان   گر دهدم فرصتی این آسمان

ثروت این ملک فراوان شود   صادره و وارده یک سان شود

باید از ایران به اروپا برند   کاغذ و کبریت و حریر و پرند

دیو جهالت شود آخر زبون   هست امیدم که ز دار الفنون

صاحب علم شود و با فر و زور   ملک ایران شود از جهل دور

گفت که شب رفت، بیاور طعام...   این همه را گفت و سپس با غلام

He said laughing, well-done, master.
　You did everything my heart desired.
He then told someone to get up,
To let the tea stew and to offer it to all present,
　The servant lit a fire under the samovar.
When it turned hot from the fire and came to a boil,
　When all were gone, he told me, stay,
　When the heavens give me a chance,
So that exports and imports become equal,
　Paper and matches and silk and leather,
　It is my hope that the Dar al-Funun[41]
People leave ignorance behind,
　He said all this and then told his servant,

Good for you and let your heart be happy.
　You relieved my mind of sadness.
to light a fire and pour water into the samovar.
so they would become drunk with ecstasy.
　The bubbling of the water rose up.
its gurgling made a noise in the courtyard.
　for I want to tell you a secret.

I will revive the industry of the Iranians.
and this country's wealth becomes abundant
　all has to go from Iran to Europe.
　will weaken the spirit of ignorance.
to become masters of knowledge, with brilliance and force.
　the night is gone, bring me food . . .[42]

III. Closing the Coffeehouses

By 1850, public consumption of tea had increased to the point at which the Qajar authorities felt the need to take prohibitive measures against the newly established coffeehouses—which now served tea. Little is known about their motives. It is quite possible that the ulama had a hand in the policy. As was seen in chapter 6, from the moment that the beverage had gained currency in the seventeenth century, coffee had aroused suspicion among the religious leaders some of whom opposed it for having intoxicating properties similar to wine.[43] Coffee itself in time

---

[41]The *Dar al-Funun* refers to the first institute of higher learning of that name in Iran, founded in 1850 under the auspices of Amir Kabir.

[42]In Bastan-Parizi, *Azhdha-yi haftsar*, 42.

[43]See, for example, Hurr al-`Amili, *Wasa'il al-Shi`ah*, 307.

had gained acceptance in religious circles, and tea never seems to have run into religious objections, but the ulama are likely to have seen in the operation of coffeehouses the same threat to religious propriety that had led their predecessors in late Safavid times to lash out against lascivious and frivolous practices such as dancing and music-making that were associated with these establishments. Music-making continued to be frowned upon in Qajar times, as is demonstrated by the action of Muhammad Baqir Shafti, the most prominent cleric of the time, who in 1844 petitioned Muhammad Shah to have the *naqqarah-khanah* (music house) banned for being incompatible with Islam.[44] Several stories from Shiraz in the 1880s similarly illustrate the ongoing suspicions coffeehouses and the activities associated with them aroused among the ulama. Thus in 1882 mullahs forced the local authorities to make all coffeehouses inside and outside the city close their doors during Ramadan.[45] In a more elaborate example, recorded in June of 1884, a mullah by the name of Muhammad Husayn Mahallati walked past a coffeehouse and heard the sound of a reed flute inside. He sent his men inside to grab the flute player and in the scuffle that followed the flute was destroyed. Several men who came out of the coffeehouse to protect the flute player next beat up the mullah, who proceeded to complain with the authorities. The investigation that ensued showed that both the flute player and his defenders had been soldiers. The mullah was reprimanded and the soldiers were absolved and released.[46]

The specific context of the measures of 1850–51 may have been the unrest that gripped several parts of Iran following the death of Muhammad Shah in 1848. In part inspired by the stirrings of the millenarian Babi movement, this unrest expressed itself in uprisings in several cities. Regrettably, the available sources fail to make a direct connection with the excitement caused by the preaching of the charismatic Bab; they only speak of political considerations without mentioning specific circumstances. Nor is it possible to establish a link with the decree that Napoleon III, fearing political disorder and the rise of secret societies, issued against French cafés in the early 1850s.[47] The resemblance with the measures in France is striking, however. Comte de Gobineau, suggesting government fears of sedition and political unrest as the motivation, claimed that Amir Kabir had suppressed the coffeehouses because "people talked politics and engaged in too much opposition." Gobineau does not provide any more details but merely alludes to the existence of a connection between ambulant

---

[44]Arjomand, *Shadow of God*, 239.
[45]Sirjani, ed., *Vaqa'i'-i ittifaqiyah*, 166, 4 Ramazan 1299/25 July 1882.
[46]Ibid., 220–21, 28 Sha'ban 1301/23 June 1884.
[47]Barrows, "'Parliaments of the People'" 88.

storytellers and the spread of unwelcome political news and rumor, suggesting how the government had made efforts to isolate and channel their activities. These entertainers, he noted, now performed on the streets and in a "kind of hangar made of wood boards, open on all sides," which could accommodate two hundred to three hundred spectators, and with a stage, on which from morning to evening a succession of storytellers would entertain the audience with narrations from the "Thousand and One Nights," the "Secrets of Hamzah," funny anecdotes, and puns on mullahs and women, all of it interspersed with verse and singing.[48]

The coffeehouses had not been reestablished at the time when Gobineau resided in the country, from 1855 to 1858. If fear of sedition and a desire for control had been the primary motivation for the state to clamp down on coffeehouses in the 1850s, the hand of a government concerned with similar questions of control and regulation can be discerned in the second "reappearance" of the coffeehouse, thirty years later. The Frenchman E. Orsolle, whose observations date from the early 1880s, noted that cafés were novelties previously not tolerated by the government. Some, he said, had been permitted to open their doors after Nasir al-Din Shah came back from his second European trip (in 1879).[49] Rather than operating as purely private establishments, however, the "new" coffeehouses were brought under state control. They were subjected to supervision by the police department, which was reorganized and put under the command of the Count di Monteforte, an Italian from Sicily who served the Austrian Crown and who was one of the European advisors employed in Iran following the shah's trip to Europe in 1878. In his capacity as chief of police of Tehran, Monteforte proposed a range of measures designed to enhance the standards of orderliness, cleanliness, and efficiency, and to foster public security in the city. Coffeehouses, some of which by then were known to serve alcohol and had become hangouts for drug users and the scene of brawls, were deemed to fall short in all of those categories. An ordinance was thus issued to permit the operation of one coffeehouse per city quarter, with a lodging place, a library and a police station attached to it. Those found to create disturbances in a coffeehouse risked being put in jail for anywhere between 48 hours and one month, as well as being fined up to two *tumans*. Coffeehouse owners who did not notify the police in a timely fashion about irregularities in their establishments were liable to punishment as well.[50] That this kind of governmental supervision was not

---

[48]Gobineau, *Trois ans*, 359; and idem, "Voyage en Perse," 46.

[49]Orsolle, *Le Caucase et la Perse*, 222.

[50]Bigi, *Tihran-i qadim*, 302–05. For Count di Monteforte and the measures he proposed, see Piemontese, "Gli ufficiali italiani," 91–95; and Adamiyat and Natiq, *Afkar-ijtima`i*, 80–88.

confined to Tehran is suggested by a reference in the *Jughrafiya-yi Isfahan*, which notes that [in Isfahan] coffeehouses were not customary and that their existence was confined to only one, located along the old Chahar Bagh, which was "governmental" (*dawlati*).[51]

This type of governmental surveillance was short-lived. Before long the *qahvah-khanah* was targeted in more drastic fashion. On 11 Rabi` al-sani 1303/17 January 1886, a royal *farman*, distributed to all provincial governors, declared that all coffeehouses in the entire country should forthwith be closed and that no tea was to be sold surreptitiously in the back of coffeehouses either. This initial announcement does not seem to have had much effect, for on 19 Sha`ban 1303/23 May 1886, the order was repeated in the form of a more insistent decree that linked coffeehouses and tea-booths to "certain vices" that had become apparent and to whose harmful consequences many had attested. In Tehran, therefore, the decree continues, the order had been given to close all coffeehouses at the onset of Ramadan, and now the same measure was to be implemented throughout the country "without excuse or negligence."[52]

Even though it is left undefined, the term "vices," *mafasid*, in the directive points to a moral dimension. A threat to morality indeed seems to have a state concern with regard to the coffeehouses and it certainly provided the excuse for curbing their operation. A passage in I`timad al-Saltanah's diary from Wednesday 15 Jumadi al-sani 1302/1 April 1885, more than a year before the proclamation of the formal ban, illustrates this point. In it he notes that, on his return from Dushan Tappah, the royal retreat east of the capital, the shah had passed the coffeehouse of Barbar Abad whose owner had decorated his establishment with "meaningless" tableaux and paintings depicting, among other things, a royal welcoming ceremony, love-scenes of Solomon with the Queen of Sheba, and a dancing party, all for the visual entertainment of the customers. Seeing this, the shah had given orders to Monteforte to destroy the pictures. The latter, entering the coffeehouse on horseback, had ripped the paintings with his sword.[53] According to I`timad al-Saltanah, it was unclear what motivated the shah to issue this order. Yet, the subsequent developments, culminating in the formal ban, suggest that, more than representing a whim, the shah's actions were informed by a fear that coffeehouses were centers of frivolous and morally suspect entertainment, probably including pederasty, as well as places where men went to spend hard-earned money, to the detriment of the country's moral fiber as well as its precious resources.

---

[51]Husayn Khan, *Jughrafiya-yi Isfahan*, 120.

[52]Bayani, ed., *Panjah sal-i tarikh-i Iran*, 4:32.

[53]I`timad al-Saltanah, *Ruznamah-i khatirat*, 351–52.

A slightly more illuminating reference to the same issue and in particular the vices associated with coffeehouses is found in the diary, *Ruznamah*, of the I'timad al-Saltanah, who for 8 *Shawwal* 1303/10 July
1886 noted that the coffeehouses had been closed, suggesting that this
measure had been taken in the context of the unusually high incidence
of thievery in the city. What had triggered the order, he added, was a
coppersmith who had spoken harsh words in the *Majlis-i fava'id-i
`ammah*.[54] The initial task of this body, which had been created in 1871
as a ministry of public works, was to engage in urban development, but
over time various responsibilities were added to or withdrawn from it.
In 1886 the *Majlis* may have been charged with the affairs of the Tehran
municipality, which would have included the supervision of coffeehouses. It also occasionally heard public complaints and petitions. Its
reputation as a forum for fierce rivalry between various government
functionaries, who often accused each other of conspirational behavior
and violations of law and order in the capital, would explain the reference to thievery. The precise connection between this, the coppersmith's
intervention and the closure of the coffeehouses, however, remains un-
explained in I'timad al-Saltanah's entry.[55]

A more concrete explanation that puts the measure in a socioeconomic context and attributes it directly to royal initiative appears in the
Austro-Hungarian diplomatic reports. Representative Kosjek wrote on
15 July 1886:

> The impoverishment and discontent of the populace are steadily in-
> creasing, and I know of no serious governmental measures to combat
> the worsening of this situation. . . . The ruler of Persia all of a sudden
> found that one of the principal causes for the impoverishment was the
> frequent visits to the coffeehouses, and ordered all these establish-
> ments, in which mostly tea is consumed, closed. Since the revenue of
> these coffeehouses was used to help feed the teachers and students of
> public schools, those institutions had to be closed as well. The coffee-
> house owners, who had built up large sugar reserves, demanded com-
> pensation, and for days this question was the topic of some of the
> most important discussions in the council of ministers.[56]

The British scholar E. G. Browne, who was in Iran shortly after 1886,
in his well-known travel account refers to the issue by stating that most
of the coffeehouses "were closed some time ago by order of the shah."

[54]Ibid., 444.

[55]Thanks to Abbas Amanat for clarifying the role of this ministry to me.

[56]HHStA, P.A. XXVIII, 10, Persien, Rapports de Téhéran, Freiherr von Kosjek, Disashub, 15 July 1886, fols. 57v–58v.

Browne noted that this was mostly an urban phenomenon. Outside the towns some coffeehouses were still permitted to "continue their trade and provide the '*bona fide* traveller' with refreshment . . ."[57] He echoed Kosjek's claim by linking their closure to their supposed encouragement of "extravagance and idleness, or [. . .] evils of a more serious kind," the latter part perhaps in reference to sexual irregularities.

Further clarification of the episode in the Persian sources is furnished by the *al-Ma'asir va al-asar*, which corroborates the assertion of irregularities by saying that tea shops had only recently been brought under control and that previously there had been all kinds of dissent and disturbance (*ikhtilaf va ightishash*) associated with the trade.[58] These manifestations of dissent and disturbance were a direct result of the terrible conditions in Iran in the years 1885–87, when bad harvest led to price hikes that were exacerbated by bread rings organized by officials. Poorly informed about the true conditions in his realm and increasingly avaricious, the shah could hardly be counted on to make an ineffectual government take adequate measures to meet the demands of an exasperated populace.[59]

The terminology used here is interesting and significant as well. The term *ightishash*, disturbance or riot, was commonly employed for manifestations of female protest against increased food prices in times of scarcity and famine. Women indeed staged frequent protests against the frequent bread shortages and price increases in this very period—as they had done since time immemorial—but for a fuller explanation of the events in question we have to turn to C. J. Wills, the physician who lived in Iran for many years between 1866 and 1886. His words, written at the time of the events, deserve to be quoted in full:

> The women of Teheran went a few weeks ago in a body to the King's palace, and complained that the coffeeshops (of which an extraordinary number have been opened lately) took away their husbands from their work and their home duties, causing them to spend all their money in drink and smoke. After all, the drink was merely tea and coffee. The Shah sympathized with the wives of Teheran. He acted promptly, and, as the Commander of the Faithful is said to have done under similar circumstances, he ordered that all the coffee-houses in

---

[57]Browne, *A Year Amongst the Persians*, 89–90.

[58]I'timad al-Saltanah, *al-Ma'asir va al-asar*, 126.

[59]The harvests of 1885 and 1886 were bad ones in Iran, and both years witnessed bread riots in several cities, including Shiraz. See Archives des MAE, Perse 39, F. Souhay, Tehran, to M. de Freylinet, Paris, 6 October 1885, fol. 380; Perse 40, De Balloy, Tehran, to M. de Freylinet, Paris, 14 August 1886, fol. 59; id., 12 Nov. 1886, fols. 68v–69; and HHStA, P.A., 10, Persien, Rapports de Téhéran, Koshek, Disashub, 22 July 1886, fols. 61v–62.

the capital were to be closed. Closed they were; closed they remain. The next day the Royal edict went forth that all the provincial coffee-houses were to be closed. They, too, are all shut up [. . .] The women, of course, are in ecstasies; but the haunters of coffee-houses, who form by far the larger proportion of the male sex in the large Persian towns, are in despair.[60]

More than a typical manifestation of popular outrage about economic hardship, this expression of female disgruntlement with profligate male behavior conveys the same sentiment that arises from a contemporary polemic involving gender relations. No direct connection between the petition and the polemic can be established; yet the tone of both suggests a reaction arising from the same frustration. The first volley in the fascinating debate was a tract entitled *Disciplining Women* (*Ta'dib al-nisvan*), the author of which remains unknown. The text, a rather misogynous book of advice on female behavior and ways for men to deal with it, was apparently widely read and seems to have created quite a stir among women of the court. Written shortly before 1886, *Disciplining Women* may have contributed to the anger and frustration that led to the women's demonstration and the petition. Whatever its role in the protest movement, the text in 1894 elicited a satirical response in the form of a tract entitled *The Vices of Men* (*Ma'ayib al-rijal*). Written by Bibi Khanum Astarabadi, a woman in the entourage of the court, *The Vices of Men* includes several passages in which men are criticized for squandering their money and time in opium dens, gambling parlors, and coffeehouses.[61]

The association of coffee (and later tea) with male idleness and pointless gossip induced by stimulants such as opium and coffee, and of the coffeehouse with profligacy and moral degeneracy of course was not without historical precedent in Iran. We find it expressed in seventeenth-century Persian treatises and chronicles.[62] The association is further pursued in Safavid religious tracts that perceive a connection between coffeehouses, idle merriment, and the use of drugs.[63] One author even called the coffeehouses "schools of the devil," *madaris-i shayatin*.[64] The direct targeting of coffeehouses by women appears a rarity, however, notwithstanding many documented instances of obstreperous female

[60]Wills, *Persia as It Is*, 315.

[61]Najmabadi, *Ma'ayib al-rijal*, 80, 82; and Javadi, Mar'ashi and Shakarlou, *Ruyaru'i zan va mard*, 174, 177.

[62]Qazvini, "Dar mazarrat-i dukhaniyyat," 372–74; and Junabadi, *Rawzat al-safaviyah*, fol. 320r–320v.

[63]Ja'fariyan, *Din va siyasat*, 364.

[64]Jaza'iri, in Ja'fariyan, *'Ilal-i bar-uftadan-i Safaviyan*, 336.

behavior in Iranian history. For a similar initiative we have to turn to Restoration England, where women initiated a protest movement against coffeehouses for reasons that sound remarkably similar to those expressed by the women of Tehran. The women of London in 1673 submitted a "Women's Petition Against Coffee," in which they complained that coffee caused domestic disorder because their husbands, by frequenting the coffeehouses, spent too much idle time and money away from home.[65]

The persistence of the image of the *qahvah-khanah* as a domain of male irresponsibility is reflected in the fact that the name of one of Tehran's main coffeehouses in Qajar times, Qanbar, in popular parlance came to signify a gathering place for lazy and good-for-nothing people. The `Arsh coffeehouse, located on the Khiyaban-i Chiragh-i Barq, had a reputation for being a hangout for opium users.[66] Some coffeehouses in the 1880s also bore a striking resemblance to the ones in Safavid times in being venues of dubious forms of entertainment. In the words of Benjamin: "Here also are to be seen public dancers, who by law are compelled to be men, although women of questionable repute sometimes exhibit in the harems. The male dancers are brought up to their vocation from boyhood, and invariably wear long hair in imitation of women, and save their faces smooth."[67]

The coffeehouses indeed were not exclusively a male domain. By referring to female servants, *khadamah-i qahvah-khanah*, and *kaniz-i qahvah-khanah*, both I'timad al-Saltanah and `Ayn al-Saltanah suggested that women were attached to these establishments as well. In a piquant detail, the latter even insisted that the Nasir al-Din Shah regularly had sexual relations with such women.[68]

Nor did the image of wastefulness and dissolution disappear in the next few decades. In 1907, according to Ella Sykes, the "women of Meshed went in a body to the Governor of the city begging him to close the *tchai-khanas*, on the plea that their husbands spent all their earnings there."[69] The issue of coffeehouse as a threat to the moral fiber of the nation, first raised in the mid-seventeenth century, resurfaced in the

---

[65]See Ukers, *All about Coffee*, 66–67; Ellis, *Penny Universities*, 88. Pincus, "`Coffee Politicians Does Create'," 815, argues that there is no evidence that this, and two other female pamphlets circulated at the time, were actually written by women and that they reflect a high church viewpoint rather than a specifically female one.

[66]Bigi, *Tihran-i qadim*, 297, 302.

[67]Benjamin, *Persia and the Persians*, 100.

[68]I'timad al-Saltanah, *Ruznamah-i khatirat*, 816, Sunday, 9 Zu'l-qa'dah 1309; `Ayn al-Saltanah, *Ruznamah*, 1:738, 752.

[69]Sykes, *Persia and Its People*, 98.

1920s, when the municipality of Tehran banned the recitation of mythological poems and the representation on coffeehouse walls of mythical images from the *Shahnamah*.[70]

The *Vaqa'i`-i ittifaqiyah*, which recounted events and developments in southern Iran, confirms that the ordinance to close coffeehouses applied to the entire country by stating that a telegraphic message was sent to all provincial governors to the effect that all coffeehouses should be closed, adding that in Shiraz this had been put to effect.[71]

Police reports from Tehran from 1304/1887 indicate that the ban on coffeehouses was occasionally violated but also was enforced that year, at least in the capital. These reports typically note that someone had been caught operating a coffeehouse in a side alley or in his shop and that the policy had forcibly closed the establishment, whereas the person in question had been taken into custody. In one case, a certain Karbala'i Ibrahim had been found setting up a coffeehouse in a side alley and in his own stable. His establishment was wrecked when the police found out about it.[72] In another case, a greengrocer by the name of Asghar had turned his shop into a coffeehouse where he served tea. He was arrested.[73] More than a year later, a former coffeehouse that had been closed was found to have reopened in secret. The police moved in and destroyed the place.[74] A few days later another illegal coffeehouse was detected. It, too, was wrecked and the customers were forced to disperse.[75]

How far-reaching the measure was and how strictly it was enforced is further indicated by a complaint directed by Count di Monteforte to the shah about the intrusive behavior of state functionaries who had entered police headquarters one night to announce that the Vazir-i Nizam (Muhammad Ibrahim Khan, the minister of the Tehran government) wished to see the person who provided the officials in the building with coffee, tea, and qalyans. Later that same night, a troupe of fifty soldiers had entered the building and taken the man away. Thrown into prison, he was accused of having sold coffee, tea, and water pipes to the Police Department. Monteforte's defense in his letter was that the man had been his personal servant who received a salary from him and that the monarch should know that he, Monteforte, was not in the coffee, tea, and tobacco business.[76]

---

[70]M. Nurbakhsh, *Musafiran-i tarikh*, quoted by Goushegir, "Le café en Iran," 90.

[71]Sirjani, ed., *Vaqa`i-i ittifaqiyah*, 261.

[72]See Riza'i and Azari, eds. *Guzarish'ha-yi nazmiyah*, 341, Tuesday, 14 Jumadi al-ula 1304.

[73]Ibid., 417, Tuesday, 10 Rajab 1304.

[74]Ibid., 652, Wednesday, 11 Ramadan 1305.

[75]Ibid., 659, Friday, 13 Ramadan 1305.

[76]Letter from Count di Monteforte to Nasir al-Din Shah (1886), in Monteforte's memoirs, in possession of his granddaughter, Silvia Zengueneh di Monteforte.

In the same petition to the shah, Monteforte notes that in several parts of the city the Vazir-i Nizam had allowed cafes to open their doors and that tea was sold in all liberty in those establishments. This may be a reference to the decree issued by Nasir al-Din Shah in 1306/1889, which partially repealed the order that in 1886 had caused the closure of coffeehouses. Issued in a cable from Berlin, which the shah was visiting as part of his third European tour that year, it gave orders to reopen 20 of the reportedly 360 coffeehouses that had sprung into existence prior to their closure. `Ayn al-Saltanah, who reports this in his diary, added that the reopening was subject to certain conditions, but unfortunately does not elaborate.[77] It is therefore unclear what the immediate reaction was to the royal order. It remains equally unclear when and how the remainder of the coffeehouses resumed operation. In all likelihood, the coffeehouse owners gradually chose to disregard the ordinance. In its aftermath, this government measure was probably similar to the ban on tea consumption of 1841, which was never officially rescinded but fell into desuetude when after a few months the government stopped enforcing it. In this case, too, coffeehouses gradually reopened their doors in the years following the issuance of the proclamation.

The government's anticoffeehouse policy of the 1850s and the 1880s did nothing to stem Iran's growing craving for tea. On the contrary, the tremendous increase in tea consumption, reflected in the proliferation of coffeehouses, around the turn of the twentieth century once more resulted in state intervention, this time of a stimulating nature. In keeping with traditional concerns about loss of state revenue through imports, Iran followed the examples of England and Russia by initiating indigenous tea cultivation in the Caspian provinces. The idea itself was not new. In the mid-1870s the British consul in Rasht, Mr. Churchill, recognizing the similarity of the climate of Gilan and Mazandaran to that of the foothills of the Indian Himalayas, requested tea seeds from India. This first experiment came to naught, however, as a British national who approached the Qajar government with the idea of cultivating tea domestically left the country on account of ill health.[78] Further attempts by Iranians in the 1880s were equally as unsuccessful.[79] A breakthrough was only achieved when Kashif al-Saltanah, a Qajar official hailing from Gilan who in the 1890s served as Iran's consul-general in India, brought back a number of seedlings, and introduced tea cultivation in his home province in 1900, beginning with the planting of some three hundred

---

[77]`Ayn al-Saltanah, *Ruznamah*, 211.

[78]*A&P*, 1876, vol. 86, Churchill, Trade and Commerce of the Province of Ghilan and Asterabad for the Years 1874 and 1875, 1490.

[79]Balland and Bazin, "Čāy," 103.

thousand bushes near Lahijan. It would be an exaggeration to attribute the *introduction* of tea as an article of mass consumption to Kashif al-Saltanah, but it is nevertheless true that the growing affordability of the drink was due in part to this official's efforts.[80] Whereas by 1904, no domestically grown tea had yet reached the market, by 1920 the area set aside for tea cultivation was a mere one hundred hectares. A decade later this had expanded to eight hundred hectares.[81]

By the early twentieth century, tea had truly become a drink of the masses, even if it had yet to reach all layers of society in all areas of the country. In Sykes's words, "Tea is the national drink of Persia . . . and the tea-shop is the club of the middle and lower class Persian, where he can talk to his friends or listen to the song of a caged *bulbul*. Here the public story-teller finds an audience, and sometimes the *lutis* will give a performance of music and dancing."[82] The Belgian diplomat Bricteux at the same time asserted that the "Persian will deprive himself of meat, even boiled rice, his favorite food, but he will not give up pouring tea that is as sugary as syrup. In even the smallest village does one find a glass of drinkable tea."[83] All along caravan routes one would find structures made of loam where a sweet tea was served for a few *shahis*.[84]

Although the coffeehouse now served tea instead of coffee, in their appearance many were remarkably similar to their counterpart of the seventeenth century, including the raised platforms lining the walls of the room and the depictions of scenes from the *Shahnamah* on the walls.[85] On the panels of every café were "depicted in gaudy colours, if not this same story of Rustam and the Div Sefid, other human figures, both male and female, the wine-cup being no infrequent addition to the pictures."[86]

As was true of the coffeehouses of Istanbul, the clientele in Iran broke down along professional lines rather than according to class or religion.[87] Members of guilds frequented specific coffeehouses in Tehran. Thus, the carpenters and sawyers used the coffeehouse of Hajj Aqa `Ali

[80]Kazimi, *Hajji Muhammad Mirza*, 35, 41.

[81]Gleadowe-Newcomen, British Indian Commercial Mission, 394; and Ehlers, "Die Teelandschaft von Lahidjan/Nordiran," 233.

[82]Sykes, *Persia and Its People*, 98.

[83]Bricteux, *Au pays du lion et du soleil*, 159. This does not seem to have been true for all of Iran. Freya Stark, traveling in Luristan in the 1920s, met villagers who were so poor that they had "neither meat, nor fowl nor eggs, milk, rice, tea, nor sugar." See Stark, *Valley of the Assassins*, 80.

[84]Grothe, *Wanderungen in Persien*, 145.

[85]Wilson, *Persian Life and Customs*, 253; and Kalantari, "Le livre des rois," 141–58.

[86]O'Donovan, *Merv Oasis*, 1:180.

[87]Kırlı, "Struggle over Space," 95–96.

on the Khiyaban-i Chiragh-i Barq as their hangout, whereas the masons congregated in the Qanbar coffeehouse on the Khiyaban-i Nasir-i Khusraw. Coffeehouses, like caravanserais, even had a regional clientele. People from Arak in west-central Iran visiting Tehran found the comfort of a home away from home where they could meet others from their town in the Panjabashi coffeehouse, also located on the Khiyaban-i Nasir-i Khusraw. These venues served not just as meeting places for kindred spirits where people of the same background and profession could socialize and exchange gossip but also as employment offices, places where employers would recruit their workers, the unemployed came to be hired, and temporary laborers would collect their paycheck after a day's work.[88]

The enjoyment of consuming tea in an atmosphere of sociability was accompanied by entertainment in the form of music-making by itinerant musicians, dancing and recitals of poems and stories, legends and epics. During the Constitutional Revolution, the coffeehouse became a gathering place for political news as well. E. G. Browne noted how in many of the coffeehouses "professional readers [were] engaged, who, instead of reciting the legendary tales of the Shah-nama, now regale[d] their clients with political news."[89] The paintings that traditionally had decorated the coffeehouse walls changed in character as well around the Constitutional Revolution. Where previously tableaux inspired by the *Shahnamah* had been designed to please rulers and had adorned the pages of books, the battle scenes from Iran's national epic now adorned the walls of urban coffeehouses for the entertainment of the common man.[90]

Still the venue for "the gossip of the bazars and the Court," as well as the forum for dervish storytellers it had always been, the coffeehouse was now "only frequented by the men of the lower orders and the servants." The downward trend of tea completed, cafes thus presented an image that they would retain until the very recent past.[91] F. L. Bird described the ambience as follows at the end of the Qajar period:[92]

> The tea-house is the democratic institution Persian's political and social club, a splendid institution for which we have no adequate equivalent in America. It is everywhere—in the city, in the village, even along the desert caravan trail. Here the harassed business man or

---

[88]Mahjub, "Sukhanvari," in Meier, "Drei moderne Texte," 291.

[89]Browne, *Persian Revolution*, 143.

[90]Kalantari, "Le livre des rois," 141.

[91]De Lorey and Sladen, *Queer Things about Persia*, 78.

[92]Bird, "Modern Persia and Its Capital," 383–86.

weary traveller can refresh his careworn soul with a glass of tea, a leisurely cigarette or waterpipe, and a bit of light gossip or exchange of current news with fellow-being of kindred spirit. The tea-house may be in external appearance anything from an adobe hut with a few crude benches to the glorified cafes of Lalehzar, but it always possesses these unfailing essentials, a big, brass Russian samovar, an adequate collection of little tea-glasses, bright-colored saucers, and filigree spoons, a bubbling hubble-bubble or two for public use, and a genial atmosphere of camaraderie reminiscent, perhaps, of the obsolete American bar-room.

Conclusion

Although various sources suggest that as early as 1840 Iran had become a predominantly tea-drinking nation, it is clear that the popularization of tea involved a gradual and long-term transformation rather than a sudden change. This process, epitomized by the tea-purveying coffeehouse that emerged in the country's urban centers as of the 1850s, was accompanied by the "return" or at least the revitalization of the public sphere after an absence of more than a century.

By the 1880s coffeehouses had once again become a common sight in Iran's urban areas, and even in smaller towns in rural, fairly remote parts of the country these new establishments could be seen. Some of these new *qahavah-khanah*s were sophisticated and smart, airy and open, equipped with mirrors, couches, and chairs, patronized by an upscale clientele whose sense of leisure appears rather modern. Others remained primitive hovels lining the road, or dark and dank niches tucked away in the bazaar, where laborers would steal a moment of respite after a hard day's work.

The reemergence and the proliferation of coffeehouses created a public sphere that a government keen on preserving its authority by maintaining the established order came to see as a threat. As had happened in numerous occasions in countries as diverse as England, the Ottoman Empire, and China, soon after their proliferation in the mid-nineteenth century coffeehouses became the focus of attention of the Qajar state. The wider context for their occasional closure was familiar enough: a bureaucratic penchant for law and order, discipline, and control, and thus represents an intriguing chapter of state involvement in social life and, more generally, of the process of modernization and centralization. This time-honored reaction struck up a momentary alliance with female protest against male vice and wastefulness. The precise political context of the dissatisfaction of (upper-class) women remains unclear. Nor can a direct link be established between the references to the purported negative impact of coffeehouses on male behavior and the closure of coffeehouses in 1886. The two phenomena, however, seem to be too close in spirit and time for the simultaneity to be coincidental. At other times, the Qajar government tried to regulate coffeehouses by enhancing their standards of orderliness, cleanliness and efficiency. None of these measures was without precedent—the Safavids, too, had tried to establish control over public life—but the recurrent preoccupation of the Qajar authorities with the issue and the absence of religious argumentation reflect a newly emerging modernizing instinct on the part of the Qajar state.

The government's anticoffeehouse policy of the 1850s and the 1880s did nothing to stem Iran's growing craving for tea. Indeed, so strong was demand that at the turn of the twentieth century it triggered the time-honored reflex of state intervention, this time of a stimulating nature. In keeping with traditional concerns about loss of state revenue through imports, Iran followed the examples of England (in India) and Russia by initiating indigenous tea cultivation in the Caspian provinces. Here, too, the Qajar state showed itself a traditional state with modernizing impulses.

THIS STUDY has considered the vast landscape of drugs and stimulants in early modern Iran, integrating economics into issues of social significance and political implication, tying production and commerce together with distribution and consumption. Exploring both the intoxicants known since ancient times and the consumables introduced in the wake of Europe's exploration of the seas, from multiple angles, it has not just shown their importance in matters of everyday life in Safavid and Qajar Iran but also employed them as an entrée into a set of broader issues in these societies. To do so, it relied on a variety of sources, Persian ones whenever available, and external ones for added information. The latter sources proved indispensable because, short of excess, drugs excitants were too much embedded in the self-evident fabric of society and the routine of daily life to be noticed much by indigenous observers—mostly traditional annalists, who generally had entirely different concerns. Far from painting a lurid picture of a society wracked by rampant drug use, many foreign commentators stand out for their dispassionate observations and the thoughtful insight into daily life their reports and travelogues offer. Longtime residents of Safavid Iran such as Du Mans and Chardin, and astute observers of life in the Qajar period such as Polak and Wills paired their perspicacity to a sympathetic appreciation of the country and its ways.

Drugs and stimulants, all the evidence shows, were ubiquitous and readily available in premodern and early modern Iran, especially in urban areas. (Rural and especially tribal society remains much less well documented.) Religion proscribed the use of alcohol, yet wine, transmitted through a combination of pre-Islamic patterns and outside influence, was an integral part of court life, as well as consumed by the elite, including some clerics. Viewing its intoxicating quality as a symbol of their rapturous love for the divine, Sufis used it in great quantity and not just metaphorically in their poems. They were the exception, however, for unlike the situation in parts of early modern Europe, where alcohol supplemented the meager diet of ordinary people and had long accompanied religious and secular rites and festivities, commoners in Iran as a rule only drank water.

Opium use was even more widespread. Consumed by the rich and, unlike wine, by the poor as well, it was fully integrated into the practice of daily life. A rather moderate intake by the average user and the fact that little moral opprobrium was attached to it caused opium to receive little attention from contemporary observers, suggesting that it was much less of a social problem than, say, hard liquor was in parts of early modern Europe.

In the sixteenth century, the old substances were joined by new stimulants that were less severe in their physiological effect, though hardly so in terms of social import and outcome. The introduction and rapid spread of coffee and tobacco demonstrate that, far from retreating into isolation, nurturing its newly acquired Shi'i identity, Iran in the Safavid period embraced the world in unprecedented, vibrant, and accelerating ways[1]. The country's integration into a worldwide sphere of trade and consumption patterns is part and parcel of this development. The speed and eagerness with which Iranians adopted tobacco, their ingenuity in turning the water pipe into an aesthetically pleasing and highly efficient device, the rituals they wove around its use—all suggest a highly sophisticated society that was receptive of new consumables and ready to assimilate them into existing patterns of social practice.

It has been one of this book's arguments that culturally determined demand factors played a crucial role in the alacrity with which the Iranian elite drank wine and the enthusiasm with which all greeted tobacco and coffee, took to tea and massively succumbed to opium smoking at various points in time. This is not to dismiss material considerations or to negate the importance of supply factors involving geographical proximity to areas of cultivation, commercial patterns and price levels. Like people elsewhere, Iranians in the premodern era naturally sought relief in drugs from what were generally monotonous lives that lacked modern medication, but their specific involvement with opium has everything to do with the fact that Iran's climate lends itself to the cultivation of *papaver somniferum*. Economic forces and external influence were important factors in the rather sudden popularity of tea and the large-scale introduction of the opium poppy as a cash crop in the nineteenth century. Still, even if it can not always be identified as the primary cause, the cultural context—referring to an assembly of cultural traits such as social structures, customary behavior, ideas, words and material objects that made sense to contemporaries as elements of their world[2]—must count as the key to understanding the receptiveness of the country to specific drugs and stimulants.

This operates on different levels of historical transmission, elective affinity, complementarity and substitution. Its pivotal place in the eastern Mediterranean world and its ritual connotations enabled alcohol to survive the Arab conquest and to retain an important place in life in

---

[1]From concluding remarks by Edmund Herzig at the conference "Iran and the World in the Safarid Age," SOAS, London, 4–7 September 2002.

[2]Smith, "Complications of the Common Place," 261

Islamic Iran. Alcohol remained crucial to a tradition in which fighting and feasting were indissolubly linked. Sufis used wine as a metaphor for their intoxicating love of the divine. Inasmuch as Iran's Islamic milieu saw sexuality as part of the natural order of things, it embraced opium as a means to enhance and prolong its pleasures. Other aspects of the Iranian search for truth beyond the tangible world connect wine and opium. For the Sufi, the trance induced by a hallucinogenic like hashish, like the oblivion caused by sedatives such as opium and alcohol, symbolized the transportation of the user to a realm beyond physical existence and into the orbit of the divine. Medical wisdom and religious notions linked the two as well. A common belief held that the easiest way to wean oneself from opium was to turn to wine. Those who chose to abstain from alcohol out of piety might indulge in opium as an alternative— strong in its effect yet religiously licit, and as such producing pleasure without guilt.

Variants of the mutuality that existed between wine and opium are found in the combination of the newly introduced stimulants or in the symbiosis and synergy of old and new ones as well. Like wine and opium, coffee played a role in Sufi ritual, though for the opposite reason: it produced vigilance rather than hallucination. Although hashish long predated smoking, the prior use of *bang* may have been instrumental in the rapid spread and popularization of tobacco in the Safavid period, and the simultaneous use of tobacco and hashish possibly explains the emergence of the water pipe as the typical smoking implement in Iran. The rise of the coffeehouse in the early 1600s yoked tobacco and coffee together, and with those, opium and hashish. The nineteenth century saw the formation of another inseparable pair, opium and tea. It is arguable that the dramatic increase in tea consumption would not have been possible without the attendant rise in the consumption of opium in the nineteenth century.

Wherever they were introduced in the seventeenth century, the new excitants only acquired sociocultural significance by giving rise to new social rituals and cultural institutions, lifestyles, and business practices. In the Ottoman Empire the first truly urban culture is said to have come into existence not in the Tulip Period, in the early eighteenth century, but much earlier, in the 1600s, when coffeehouses became the venue for a culture of worldly pleasure.[3] Iran witnessed something similar in the same period. The consumption of not just alcohol, tobacco, coffee, and tea but even that of opium developed around and generated its own, patterns of sociability. Coffeehouses inspired new forms of social gathering, turning into venues of literary discourse and the exchange of rumor, gossip, and information.

[3]Kafadar, "Yeniceri-Esnaf Relations," 92.

We might even see them as contributors to the formation of a civil society if, following Habermas, we define it as a sphere of life where individuals and social classes interact to create organizations free of state control. To be sure, we must be careful not to push the analogy with developments in Europe too far. After all, the Safavid coffeehouse spawned no debates leading to treatises advocating social and political reform, nor did it contribute to the emergence of a modern press or a novel political consciousness, much less foreshadow "norms later associated with nineteenth-century liberalism and its attendant model of civil society."[4] But in a society where the theory of all-pervasive, absolute political and religious surveillance fell far short of a reality of loose control and connivance, one can perhaps speak of a public sphere by default, one that operated against the grain and in the interstices of officially sanctioned practice.

A significant part of this book has been concerned with the relationship between ideal and reality, between normative writing about life and the daily practice of life. Norm and practice are never separate categories but intertwined, often dialectically so. Islam demands from its adherents not so much belief—choosing to leave that judgment to God—as conformity. To belong to the community implies following its precepts in public.[5] Because public deviance affects fellow believers and ultimately undermines Islam itself as a communal faith, Islam requires its followers to comply with the rules of the public sphere as well a to be vigilant in their maintenance. Yet, its spokesmen have always been forced to make multiple concessions to reality in their pursuit of the perfect community. The existence of a private sphere of sorts, including a private refuge for thought and inner belief, or what Michael Cook calls a contingently private sphere—in reference to behavior that contravenes the Islamic law but that is tolerated as long as it does not entail harming others and remains indoors—has always made life livable in Muslim societies, allowing people to behave as they wished while maintaining the pretense that society continued to pursue the ideal.[6]

Hafiz's poetry reminds us that Iranians have long viewed minding one's own business as an individual right and a societal virtue. In Iran, the tension between outward conformity and private freedom has often taken the form, less of a dichotomy than of an ambiguous play between hedonistic and puritanical forces, fitting into what Roy Motahhedeh calls a "kaleidoscopic world of meaningful ambiguity."[7] For all their

---

[4] Melton, *Rise of the Public*, 247.
[5] Grunebaum, *Studien zum Kulturbild und Selbstverständis des Islams*, 16.
[6] Cook, *Commanding Right and Forbidding Wrong*, 594.
[7] Motahhedeh, *Mantle of the Prophet*, 164.

focus on spiritual essence, Iranians have always had a healthy appetite for life's earthly pleasures. The watchdogs of faith and morality were never in a position to eradicate this appetite; at most they managed to banish it to the private sphere. Religious arguments usually played a role in arguments against drugs. Yet, it would be an error to take such injunctions at face value.

If in early modern Western history we have perhaps paid too much attention to the "triumph" of secularism, in Middle Eastern history the prevailing popular and even scholarly perception surely leans too far in the direction of conflating outward religiosity with real life. In Iran, the religious hold over the public sphere was often more rhetorical than real. Hartford Jones Brydges's dictum that "religion, except in the performance of its outward ceremonies . . . sits very lightly on a Persian," must strike anyone familiar with Iran's Islamic past (and present) as apposite. The record of wine and, to a lesser extent, of tobacco and coffee shows that in pre-twentieth-century Iran, religion had to compete with other forms of legitimacy and authority. The outward religiosity of the late Safavid period did little to change that. The idea that at the time of Shah Sultan Husayn's accession a literalist version of Islam had become hegemonic, edging out a more tolerant variant, is largely predicated on a decree that, as the shah's own subsequent behavior demonstrated, was honored more in the breach than in the observance almost as soon as it was proclaimed. People always managed to defy and deflect royal or religious injunctions and to find or forge a social space where they could speak their minds and pursue the pleasure or oblivion of their choice. Despite the challenges it encountered, this space managed to survive, even thrive, as a realm that defied the transcendent moral vision of pure Islamic values envisioned in the writings of the ulama. What caused it (temporarily) to wither in the eighteenth century was less clerical disapprobation than the political turmoil that followed the collapse of the Safavid state.

A normative system ultimately remains embedded in the reality that it attempts to encode, encapsulate and emend. It is crucial to realize that the ulama did not stand apart from society but were fully engaged with and integrated into it. They might excoriate the existence of vice but that same vice served to validate their own existence and role as guardians of virtue. A deep-rooted conception of identity as being situated in changeable circumstances had important repercussions for attitudes as well.[8] Lomnitskii's story about the mullahs and the hats bespeaks a fluidity of identity that is not confined to the Qajar period. One could be a mullah one moment, and enjoy a drink the next, without experiencing this as a contradiction. This was more than facetiousness or cynicism.

[8]For this, analyzed for Morocco, see Rosen, *Culture of Islam*.

One was a mullah but that did not complete one's identity just as it did not set one apart from society; one could be a mullah and a politician, a mullah and a poet or, as the Constitutional Revolution was to show, a mullah and a freethinker.

Adaptability expressed itself in other ways as well. The ulama sought to achieve greater purity in life, but they knew better than to ran afoul of the society in which they operated and whose cooperation they needed. Representatives of a faith that was as diverse as it was decentralized, they were split amongst themselves, between those who adhered to a mystical intellectual tradition and those who advocated a strict interpretation of the faith. No fixed lines divided the ones who professed "orthodoxy" and those who engaged in esotericism, and it would be far too schematic to see them as two opposite camps. Even those with a reputation for strictness exhibited flexibility and pragmatism, with more than a touch of self-serving rationalization. There is an obvious link between Majlisi the avid smoker and Majlisi the supreme cleric who decided to countenance smoking. In Qajar times, inveterate opium users could get dispensation from the obligation to abstain during Ramadan by offering extra alms to the poor. Although tobacco was just as popular as opium, addicted smokers did not enjoy the same clemency, since the pipe was "not considered a necessity of life," and as a result often would steal away to the homes of European friends to indulgence their habit, carefully removing all traces of their transgression before returning to a Muslim environment.[9] At time when they could rationalize it, as they were able to do with prostitution—by arguing that it fulfilled a male need—the ulama might justify untoward behavior.[10] If it was impossible to adapt the holy law to reality, as in the case of wine, they chose to connive at it so long as it stayed indoors.

More than any drug or stimulant, wine exemplifies these tensions and contradictions and ways of dealing with them. Individual, activist clerics such as al-Karaki and Majlisi might get the shah on their side but only whenever an external logic in the form of military defeat, royal illness or natural disaster presented itself to support their cause, and even then their victory was invariably Pyrrhic. Wine continued to be a royal privilege; as no other consumable, it remained symbolic of royal ability to flout the tenets of Shi'i Islam that prescribe ritual purity, doubly so when the shah allowed non-Muslim guests to share the goblet with him. As Tavernier put it, the Iranians obeyed the laws of their prince more than they obeyed God's laws. Chardin completed the picture by stating that his subjects believed the shah to be despotic, indeed expected him to be

[9]Fraser, *Travels and Adventures*, 161.
[10]See Matthee, "Courtesans, Prostitutes and Dancing Girls."

despotic and oblivious to any laws and restraint.[11] Small wonder, then, that royal power usually trumped clerical power. Even when the ulama stepped into the political vacuum left by the demise of the Safavids, this did not fundamentally change. In the early years of the Qajar dynasty Harford Jones Brydges could still insist that, "in Persia the throne awes the priesthood," explaining that "the Shah may, if he so incline, hang the Mufti, and no one will care or think much about the matter."[12] Even as their autonomy, including their financial autonomy, grew in this very same period, the ulama mostly continued to defer to worldly rule, either from an implicit ideological conviction that even a shah who lacked proper religious credentials was the executer of God's will, or from a belief that the state was the ultimate guarantor of stability.

Varying with time and circumstance, the reaction of the state to drugs and stimulants was often marked by contradiction as well. Its motives for proscriptive or curbing measures ranged from royal whim to concerns about social unrest to momentary deference to clerical pressure at the accession of a new shah or in times of economic or military stress. With the exception of Shah Tahmasb, no Safavid shah definitively gave in to the exhortations of the ulama. Shah `Abbas II courted Sufis but also gave latitude to hardline clerics who sought to enforce the rules of the faith. Even Shah Sultan Husayn's initial firmness on vice quickly dissolved under pressure from the harem. Caught in between competing forces, the shah and his advisers engaged in "tacit bargaining" with society and tried to balance the various religious and secular constituencies to its own advantage, at any given time favoring one without eliminating the other.[13] Aware of the popularity of coffeehouses, it was unwilling to accommodate the hardline clerics and move full-force against these establishments, choosing instead to strip them of the more egregious manifestations of un-Islamic behavior. Though unacknowledged in the indigenous sources, in the end, the stiffest competitor to the inclination to ban on moral and disciplinarian grounds was often the need for tax revenue. The Iranian state was in good company here. The authorities of eighteenth-century China levied an excise tax on opium imports while punishing those who used it with execution, the whip, imprisonment or exile. The British in India found a different way to circumvent the dilemma between sin and profit: while proscribing the internal consumption of opium, they allowed it to be exported to China.[14]

[11]Chardin, *Voyages*, 5:219.

[12]Brydges, *Account of the Transactions*, 407.

[13]Eickleman, "Foreword: The Religious Public Sphere in Early Muslim Societies," in Hoexter et al., eds., *The Public Sphere in Muslim Societies*, 6.

[14]Booth, *Opium*, 109–12.

This book has sought to document processes of change alongside patterns of continuity as habit or as strategy designed to guarantee stability. Although the ambiguities inherent in wine were never solved—were impossible to solve—its place in society changed considerably in the course of the Safavid period. Where Shah Isma`il's drinking orgies had been flamboyant, highly visible affairs, later shahs wavered between indulgence and abstention, reflecting the evolution of Safavid rule from a steppe polity deeply influenced by pagan ritual to a sedentary state in outward conformity with the tenets of formal religion. Firmly anchored in the pre-Islamic world of divine kingship and the shamanistic milieu of the Central Asian steppes, wine was a natural accompaniment to the rituals of early Safavid Iran. Its evolution from assertive indulgence to surreptitious pleasure, punctuated by short-lived bans, mirrors the trajectory of the polity itself: a society whose Dionysian celebration of the sacral aura of a shah unfettered even by divine injunction soon ran up against the sobering reality of military defeat, and subsequently began to separate itself from its moorings to evolve on the path of greater outward conformity with the religious law.

The trend toward royal sobriety received a boost with the fall of Isfahan in 1722. Both the Afghans and the Afsharids derived their legitimacy in part from their appearance as robust and clean-living rulers in contrast to the feeble and degenerate later Safavids. Following the Zand period with its bon vivant image, the Qajar period exhibits further change. Lacking the divine legitimacy of the Safavids, and far removed from their exuberant millenarian creed, the Qajar rulers gave up on wine as public display and opted for different, sanitized forms of ceremony. If in distancing itself from traditional ritual the Qajar court pioneered a modernizing state, this did not spell overall societal transformation. Throughout the nineteenth century local magistrates, especially, it seems, those from rural areas such as Luristan and Kurdistan where the imprint of formal Islam was light at best, still unabashedly indulged in alcoholic excess.[15]

There were yet other modernizing impulses. A convergence of intruding European values and traditional Iranian skepticism—expressed as doubt about the verities of religion, about its exclusive claim to the truth—brought about a changing attitude toward drinking. The growing importation of European liquor and a desire to emulate Western life styles appear to have caused an increase in the incidence of alcohol consumption, and especially of that of arak, in elite circles, which in turn led to a shift in tone and emphasis in public calls for restriction and curtailment. In concerns about the social ills and health problems associated

---

[15]For the link between court ceremony and modernizing tendencies, see Elias, *Court Society*, 118.

with this perceived increase in drinking, published in newspapers, we see an incipient medicalization of the problem of drinking. This occurred in the context of a growing secularism. For some, this probably led to a loss of inhibition to drinking in public, as appears to have been the case in Ottoman cities. But, confronted with the growing assertiveness of the Shi'i clergy, it also joined forces with a deep strain in Iran's cultural consciousness to flaunt itself as unbelief at a new level of oppositional political emphasis. Persian Sufism, Leonard Lewisohn argues, especially in the twentieth century, increasingly aligned itself with the forces of the secularist intelligentsia, "no doubt in reaction to the vigorous persecution of Sufism by Iranian mujtahids in late Safavid and early Qajar times."[16] We might turn this around to say that Iranian secularism sought an alliance with Iranian Sufism in its "conscious opposition to the religious intolerance and exclusivism of the mullas," noting that this alliance, built on a long-standing Iranian tradition, goes back to early Qajar times.

Coffee and tea underwent change as well following the fall of Isfahan. The demise of a central state providing a minimum of security caused the public sphere that had emerged in Safavid times to contract, driving people into the privacy of their homes. Just as the polo game died out with Iran's descent into chaos, the coffeehouse took a beating, even if taverns seems to have emerged as a partial substitute. By definition furtive and semiclandestine, the tavern could not fully substitute as a public place. Responding to a continuing need of a populace living in wretched circumstances, it survived, however, allowing people momentarily to forget about their misery while enjoying the narration of stories, the sight of dancing boys, and the tunes of music.

Coffee and possibly tea were still consumed in the eighteenth and early nineteenth century, mostly, it seems, in the private sphere, but their distribution was uneven. Coffee prevailed in the south and in the regions bordering on Arab-speaking parts of the Ottoman Empire. Tea, by contrast, appears to have been more common in the north, and not just among the nomadic population of Khurasan where it had been part of people's diet for many centuries. Whereas coffee and tea were regularly served by the wealthy and the powerful, their distribution among the lower classes was more distinctly tied to market supply and thus to geography and pricing.

When caffeinated drinks regained their visibility in the Qajar period, tea rapidly gained the upper hand, until in the twentieth century coffee had all but disappeared from the repertoire of Iranian beverages. No single official or event accounts for the introduction of tea, and it is impossible to identify a precise moment for Iran's conversion from tea to coffee. Gobineau's reference to the "reemergence" of coffeehouses in

---

[16]Lewisohn, "Introduction to the History of Modern Persian Sufism," 1:439.

Iran's urban centers suggests that tea had "returned" by 1850s, but true popularization was a long-term process that involved supply factors as well as issues of status appeal and fashion.

This entire shift in commercial patterns reflects a secular change of global import: the extension of western economic hegemony to parts of the world where Europeans had hitherto played a subordinate commercial role. For Iran, this development went hand in hand with the country's incorporation into a European-dominated trading network that spanned the entire Asian continent. The main players in this network, England and Russia, had both become tea-consuming societies in the course of the eighteenth and nineteenth centuries, in part because their commercial empires extended to regions where the cultivation of tea originated or was introduced. Given this interest and involvement, it is only natural that the external stimulus exerted on Iran favored tea rather than coffee.

The newly emerging "coffeehouses" of the later nineteenth century served tea rather than coffee, but otherwise retained a strong link with the past. Like their counterparts in the Safavid period, many offered popular entertainment in the form of storytelling and dancing by boys dressed up as women. Some were seedy haunts serving opium and liquor in addition to tea, where hoodlums congregated and violence was not uncommon. But the new coffeehouse, and the tea associated with it, also heralded something new. Tew carried a whiff of sophistication and betokened modernity. The Qajar court had a role in its introduction and spread. Expensive at first, tea originally was mostly an elite drink, and there is some evidence that it was initially associated with foreigners. Many of the establishments that offered it were traditional, hole-in-the-wall-type establishments tucked away in the bazaar or hovels lining caravan routes, but some clearly appealed to a new, more upscale clientele, with their chairs, couches, and mirrors, and their feel of airiness.

The authorities reacted to the emerging public sphere exemplified by these new "coffeehouses" by attempting to bring it under their control—through surveillance, curbing measures, and closings. The terms used to justify these methods, idleness and dissipation, resonated with wives who saw their household money frittered away in establishments they could not enter. Yet such moral language ultimately reflected deeper anxieties on the part of a state that saw the specter of social unrest and sedition in behavior associated with some of these establishments, ranging from drug use and hooliganism to sexual deviance and political discourse. In their preoccupation with discipline and social order, Qajar rulers were little different from their Safavid predecessors. What lent the measures they took a modernizing touch is less the actual arguments made to justify them than the less overtly religious tone employed and the drastic surveillance and enforcement techniques applied by someone like the Count di Monteforte.

The Qajar period registered yet other changes. However we assess its immediate impact, the extraordinary popularity of smoking in Safavid Iran did lay the groundwork for a craze that became so pervasive, economically important and socially sensitive that two centuries later it would spark Iran's famous Tobacco Protest. Opium underwent an important shift when many people began smoking rather than ingesting it as of the later nineteenth century. The origins of this transformation are to be found in China but it remains unclear which channels of transmission are involved. What is clear, however, is that opium became a problem where it had hardly been a problem before. The land area given to the cultivation of the poppy expanded to the point of making the country vulnerable to famine, and the number of opium addicts and the attendant social ills grew manifold as well, so that by the end of the nineteenth century Iran took the first steps on the road to opium's criminalization.

This study suggests that Qajar society, in spite of its modernizing impulses, retained many premodern features and showed few signs of being an incipient consumerist society—with consumerism going beyond an accelerated consumption of goods and foods but representing a complex set of patterns of consumption in which a lust for novelty and fashion generates a self-generating process that counteracts and subverts the dominant value system and that ends up being a value in itself and a marker of identity, edging out other, primordial ones, such as security.[17] None of the social processes documented in this book's pages fundamentally altered the live and let live attitude that characterized Iran's traditional society. The surge in opium addiction created anxieties that led to calls for restrictive legislation. State officials harbored suspicions about the connection between the newly emerging coffeehouses and social and political unrest. These establishments also retained the age-old link between the coffeehouse and the use of drugs, questionable forms of entertainment, and dubious sexual practices. Yet, any measures taken remained as haphazard and short-lived as they had been in the Safavid period. Qajar society remained a traditional society, with its patterns of undisciplined pastimes and work settings.[18] The onset of the modern age, bureaucratized, mechanized, and characterized by a growing wariness with drugs in the context of their incompatibility with the dreams of the modern world, had to wait until the twentieth century and more specifically until the reign of Reza Shah (1921–41). But, even before modern times would bring structural transformation, Iranian society underwent plenty of change.

[17]Stearns, *Consumerism in World History*, 1–24.
[18]Courtwright, *Forces of Habit*, 178.

Bibliography

ARCHIVAL SOURCES

Netherlands

The Hague. Nationaal Archief (NA). Eerste afdeling.
  Records of the Verenigde Oostindische Compagnie (VOC).
  Overgekomen Brieven en papieren, vols. 1106–2584 (1133–1741).
  Uitgaande brieven, vols. 882, 926.
  Copiebrieven, vols. 317, 323, 325.
  Resoluties Heren XVII, vols. 110–13.
  Collectie Gelyenssen de Jongh, vols. 97a, 157a, 158.
Nationaal Archief (NA). Tweede afdeling.
  Legatie Perzië, 6 and 26.
Leiden University Library.
  Hamavi Yazdi, Salik al-Din Muhammad. Untitled treatise on coffee, tea etc.,
    "De venenis celeberrimis, quae quam plurimus," Ms. Or. 945.
  al-Qusuni, Badr al-Din al-Hakim. "Fi bayan ahwal al-qahwah wa khasiyatiha
    wa manafi`iha." Ms. Or 945, fol. 58.

England

London. British Library.
  Shamlu, Vali Quli. "Qisas al-khaqani." Ms. Or. 7656.
India Office Records (IOR). Records of the English East India Company (EIC).
  Letters from Persia, Original Correspondence, vols. E/3/6, E/3/52, G/36/106,
    G/37/107, G/36/87.
London. Public Record Office, vol. 60.
Cambridge University. Christ's College:
  Khuzani Isfahani, Fazli. "Afzal al-tavarikh." Or. Ms. Dd.5.6.

Austria

Vienna. HHStA. Haus-, Hof- und Staatsarchiv. Persien, vol. XXVIII.

France

Nantes. Archives du Ministère des Affaires Etrangères (AME). Téhéran, A. 21.
Paris. Archives du Ministère des Affaires Etrangères (AME). Corr. Pol. Perse 21;
  Mémoires et documents 6.

Belgium

Brussels, Archives du Ministère des Affaires Etrangères de Belge (AME).
  Perse, vol. 4265II.

Iran

Tehran. Kitabkhanah-i Majlis
'Imad al-Din Shirazi. "Afiyuniyah." Ms Or. 352, fols. 1–70.
"Chay-i khata'i." Ms Or. 352, fol. 71.

United States

Minneapolis. University of Minnesota. James Ford Bell Library:
Bembo, Ambrosio. "Viaggio e giornale per parte dell'Asia di Quattro anni
incirc fatto da me Ambrosio Bembo Nob. Veneto."

COLLECTIONS OF DOCUMENTS, NEWSPAPERS, AND REFERENCE WORKS

Accounts and Papers. (A&P). Reports from British consuls and presented to the
Parliament.
Agha Buzurg al-Tihrani, Muhammad Muhsin, ed. *al-Dhari`ah ila tasanif al-
Shi`ah.* Najaf, 1936–.
Amanat, Abbas, ed. *Cities & Trade: Consul Abbott on the Economy and Soci-
ety of Iran 1847–1866.* London, 1983.
Bayani, Khanbaba, ed. *Panjah sal dar dawrah-i Nasiri mustanad bih asnad-i
tarikhi va arshivi.* 6 vols. Tehran, 1375/1996.
*British Documents on Foreign Affairs: Reports and Papers from the Foreign
Office Confidential Print.* Part I, Series A, Vol. 1, *Russia, 1859–1880*; Part I,
Series B, Vol. 10, *Persia, 1856–1885*; Part I, Series B, Vol. 13, *Persia, Britain
and Russia 1886–1907.* Frederick, MD, 1985.
Bruce, John. *Annals of the Honourable East India Company, 1600–1708.*
3 vols. London, 1810; repr. 1968.
Busse, Heribert. *Untersuchungen zum islamischen Kanzleiwesen an Hand turk-
menischer und safawidischer Urkunden.* Cairo, 1959.
Chijs, J. A. van der, ed. *Dagh-Register gehouden int Casteel Batavia Anno
1661.* Batavia/The Hague, 1890.
Coolhaas, W. Ph., ed. *Generale missiven van Gouverneurs Generaal en Raden
aan Heren XVII der Verenigde Oostindische Compagnie,* vols. 2–7,
1639–1725. The Hague, 1964–79.
Dunlop, H., ed. *Bronnen tot de geschiedenis der Oostindische Compagnie in
Perzië, 1630–38.* The Hague, 1930.
Fihrist-i nuskha'ha-yi khatti-yi kitabkhanah-i Malik. Ed. Iraj Afshar and
Muhammad Taqi Danishpazhuh. Vol. 8. Tehran 1369/1990.
Foster, William, ed. *The English Factories in India,* 1618–21, 1622–23,
1651–54. Oxford, 1900–15.
Iran. Newspaper, Tehran.
Ittila`. Newspaper, Tehran.
Nava'i, `Abd al-Husayn, ed. *Shah `Abbas. Majmu`ah-i asnad va muktibat-i
tarikhi.* 3 vols. Tehran, 2nd edn., 1366/1987.
———, ed. *Shah Tahmasb-i Safavid. Majmu`ah-i asnad va mukatibat-i tarikhi
hamrah ba yaddashtha-yi tafsili.* Tehran, 2nd edn., 1368/1989.
Neue Freie Presse. Newspaper, Vienna, 1879.

Riza'i, Ansiyah Shaykh, and Shahl Azari, eds. *Guzarish'ha-yi nazmiyah az mahallat-i Tihran. Rapurt-i vaqa'i`-i mukhtalifah-i mahallat-i Dar al-Khilafah (1303–1305 h.q.)*. Tehran, 1377/1999.

Ruznamah-i Vaqa'i`-i-ittifaqiyah. Newspaper, Tehran.

Sainsbury, Noel W., ed. *Calendar of State Papers, Colonial Series, East Indies, China and Persia, 1625–1629*. London, 1884.

Schlimmer, Johann. *Terminologie médico-pharmaceutique et anthropologique français-persane*. Tehran, 1874.

Yule, Henry and A. C. Burnell. *Hobson-Jobson. A Glossary of Colloquial Ango-Indian Words and Phrases*. London, 1886; new edn., Delhi, 1994.

OTHER PUBLISHED PRIMARY SOURCES

Abbé Carré. *The Tavels of the Abbé Carré in India and the Near East 1672 to 1674*. Trans. Lady Fawcett and ed. Sir Charles Fawcett. 3 vols. London, 1948.

Afshar, Iraj. "Tarikh-i chay dar Iran." In idem, *Savad va biyaz: Majmu`ah-i maqalat*, 2 vols. Tehran, 1349/1970, 2:498–99.

Afushtah Natanzi, Muhammad b. Hidayat Allah. *Nuqavat al-asar fi zikr al-akhyar*. Ed. Ihsan Ishraqi. Tehran, 2nd edn., 1373/1994.

Al-i Davud, Sayyid `Ali, ed. *Du safarnamah az junub-i Iran dar salha-yi 1256h.q.-1307h.q.* Tehran, 1368/1989.

———. ed. *Namah'ha-yi Amir Kabir bih inzimam-i risalah-i navadir al-Amir*. Tehran, 1371/1992.

Alpinus, Prosper. *De plantis Aegypti liber*. Venice, 1592.

al-`Amili, Muhammad Baha al-Din. *Jami`-i `Abbasi*. Bombay, 1329/1911.

Alonso, P. Carlos OSA. "Due lettere riguardanti i primi tempi delle missione agostine in Persia." *Analecta Augustiniana* 24 (1961): 152–201.

Ange de Saint-Joseph. *Souvenirs de la Perse safavide et autres lieux de l'Orient (1664–1678)*. Trans. and annotated Michel Bastiaensen. Brussels, 1985.

Anon. `*Alam-ara-yi Shah Tahmasb. Zindigani-dastani-yi divvumin padishah-i dawrah-i Safavi*. Ed. Iraj Afshar. Tehran, 1370/1991.

Anon. [Ritter von Riederer]. *Aus Persien. Aufzeichnungen eines Oesterreichers der 40 Monate im Reiche der Sonne gelebt und gewirkt hat*. Vienna, 1882.

Anon. [Chick], ed. *A Chronicle of the Carmelites in Persia and the Papal Mission of the XVIIth and XVIIIth Centuries*. 2 vols. London, 1939.

Anon. *Guzarish-i Iran bih sal-i 1305h.q./1887 miladi az yik sayyah-i Rus*. Trans. Sayyid `Abd Allah; ed. Muhammad Riza Nasiri. Tehran, 1363/1984.

Anon. "Opium in Persia." *The Journal of the Anthropological Institute of Great Britain and Ireland* 23 (1894): 199–200.

Anon. "Thee- and koffiehandel in Perzië." *De Indische Gids* 19, no. 1 (1897): 108–9.

Anon. *The Travels of a Merchant in Persia*. In Charles Grey, ed., *A Narrative of Italian Travels in Persia in the 15th and 16th Centuries*, 141–207. London, 1873.

`Aqili Khurasani. *Makhzan al-adviyah*. Tehran, 2535/1976.

Armstrong, T. B. *Journal of Travels in the Seat of War during the Last Two Campaigns of Russia and Turkey*. London, 1831.

Astarabadi, Mirza Mihdi Khan. *Tarikh-i jahangusha-yi Nadiri*. Tehran, 1368/1989.

`Ayn al-Saltanah. *Ruznamah-i khatirat-i `Ayn al-Saltanah (Qahraman-i Mirza Salvar)*, vol. 1, *Ruzgar-i padishah-i Nasir al-Din Shah*. Ed. Mas`ud Lalvar and Iraj Afshar Tehran, 1374/1995.

`Azud al-Dawlah, Sultan Ahmad Mirza. *Tarikh-i `Azudi*. Ed. `Abd al-Husayn Nava'i. Tehran, 2535/1976.

Baiao, Antonio, ed. *Itinerarios da India a Portugal por terra*. Coimbra, 1923.

Baker, Valentine. *Clouds in the East. Travels and Adventures on the Perso-Turkoman Frontier*. London, 1876.

Bakulin, F. "Ocherk' russkoi torgovli v' Mazandarane." *Vostichniy Sbornik* 1 (1877): 269–327.

———. "Ocherk' vneshnei torgovli Azerbaidzhana za 1870–71 g." *Vostochniy Sbornik* 1 (1877): 205–66.

Barbosa, Duarte. *The Book of Duarte Barbosa*. Ed. and trans. Mansel Longworth Dames, 2 vols. London, 1918.

Bassett, James. *Persia, the Land of the Imams: A Narrative of Travel and Residence*. New York, 1886.

Bastami, Muhammad Tahir. *Futuhat-i firayduniyah (Sharh-i jangha-yi Firaydun Khan charkas amir al-umara-yi Shah `Abbas-i avval)*. Ed. Sayyid Sa`id Mir Muhammad Sadiq and Muhammad Nadir Nasiri Muqaddam. Tehran, 1380/2001.

Bedik, Bedros. *Chehil sutun, seu explicatio utriusque celeberrimi, ac pretiosissimi theatri quadraginta columnarum in Perside orientis, cum adjecta fusiori narratione de religione, moribus . . .* Vienna, 1678.

Bélanger, C. *Voyage aux Indes-orientales par le nord de l'Europe, les provinces du Caucase, la Géorgie, l'Arménie et la Perse pendant les années 1825 à 1829*, 3 vols. Paris, 1838.

Bell of Antermony, John. *Travels from St. Petersburgh in Russia to Various Parts of Asia*. Edinburgh; new edn. in one vol., 1805.

Bellew, Henry Walter. *From the Indus to the Tigris. A Narrative of a Journey through the Countries of Balochistan, Afghanistan, Khorasan and Iran, in 1872*. London, 1874; repr. Karachi, 1977.

———. *Journal of a Political Mission to Afghanistan in 1857*. London, 1862.

Beneveni, Florio. *Poslannik Petra I na Vostoke. Posol'stvo Florio Beneveni v Persiiu i Bukhari va 1718–1725 godakh*. Ed. M. L. Vais et al., Moscow, 1986.

Benjamin, S.G.W. *Persia and the Persians*. London, 1887.

Berezin, I. N. *Puteshestvie po severnoi Persii*. Kazan, 1852.

Bernardino, Frei Gaspar de S. *Itinerário da Índia por terra até à ilha de Chipre*. Ed. Augusto Reis Machado. Lisbon, 1953.

Bernier, François. *Travels in the Mogul Empire A.D. 1656–1668*, Trans. Archibald Constable. London, 1916.

Beyens, Baron. "Une mission en Perse, 1896–1898." *Revue Générale* 177 (Brussels, 1927): 19–47, 157–82, 318–50, 461–71.

Binning, Robert B. M. *A Journal of Two Years' Travel in Persia, Ceylon*, 2 vols. London, 1859.

Bird, F. L. "Modern Persia and Its Capital." *National Geographic Magazine* 39, no. 4 (April 1921): 383–86.

Bird, Isabella. *Journeys in Persia and Kurdistan*, 2 vols. London, 1891.

Blau, Otto. *Commerziele Zustände Persiens, Aus den Erfahrungen einer Reise im Sommer 1857 dargestellt*. Berlin, 1858.

Bleibtreu, I. *Persien, das Land der Sonne und des Löwen*. Freiburg, 1894.

Bricteux, Auguste. *Au pays du lion et du soleil*. Brussels, 1908.

Brosset, M.-F., trans and ed. *Histoire de la Géorgie depuis l'antiquité jusqu'au XIXe siècle*. 2 vols. St. Petersburg, 1856.

———. *Collection d'historiens arméniens*, 2 vols. St. Petersburg, 1874.

———. *Des historiens arméniens des XVIIe et XVIIIe siècles: Arakel de Tauriz, régistre chronologique*. St. Petersburg, 1873.

Browne, Edward Granville. *The Persian Revolution of 1905–1909*. London, new edn., 1966

———. *A Year Amongst the Persians*. London, 3rd edn., 1950.

Brugsch, Heinnrich. *Im Lande der Sonne. Wanderungen in Persien*. Berlin, 2nd edn., 1886.

Brydges, Harford Jones. *An Account of the Transactions of his Majesty's Mission to the Court of Persia in the Years 1807–11*. London, 1834.

Buckingham, J. S. *Travels in Assyria, Media, and Persia*, 2 vols. London, 1830.

Budaq Qazvini, Munshi. *Javahir al-akhbar*. Ed. Muhsin Behramnizhad. Tehran, 1378/1999.

Bulmerincq, M. v. "Die Jahrmärkte Russlands, insbesondere jener von Nischni-Nowgorod." *Globus. Illustrierte Zeitschrift für Länder- und Völkerkunde* 6 (1864): 298–301.

Burgess, C. and E. Burgess. *Letters from Persia, 1828–1855*. Ed. B. Schwartz. New York, 1942.

Burnes, Lieut. Alexander. *Travels to Bokhara, being an Account of a Journey from India to Cabool, Tartary, and Persia . . . in the Years 1831, 1832, and 1833*, 3 vols. London, 1834.

Chardin, Jean. *Du bon usage de thé et des épices en Asie. Réponses à Monsieur Cabart de Villarmont*. Ed. Ina Baghhdiantz McCabe. Paris, 2002.

———. *Voyages du chevalier Chardin en Perse et en autres lieux de l'Orient*. Ed. L. Langlès, 10 vols. and atlas. Paris, 1810–11.

Cheref-ou'ddîne (Sharaf al-Din). *Chèref-nâmeh ou fastes de la nation kourde*, 2 vols. Ed. François Bernard Charmoy. St. Petersburg, 1873.

Chinon, Gabriel de. *Relations nouvelles du Levant ou traités de la religion du gouvernement et des coûtumes des Perses, des Arméniens et des Gaures*. Paris, 1671.

Collins, E. Treacher. *In the Kingdom of the Shah*. London, 1896.

Conolly, Arthur. *Journey to the North of India overland from England through Russia, Persia, and Affghaunistan*, 2 vols. London, 1834.

Conolly, Edward. "Journal Kept while Travelling in Seistan." *Journal of the Asiatic Society of Bengal* 10 (1841): 319–40.

Curzon, George N. *Persia and the Persian Question*. London, 1892; repr. 1966.

Dahlavi, Sahba'i. *Shar-i Mina Bazar*. Kanpur, 1903.

D'Allemagne, H. R. *Du Khorassan au pays des Backhtiaris*, 4 vols. Paris, 1911.

Darabi, `Abd al-Rahim Kalantar. *Tarikh-i Kashan*. Ed. Iraj Afshar. Tehran, 2nd edn., 1341/1962.

Daulier Deslandes, A. *Les beautez de la Perse ou la description de ce qu'il ya de plus curieux dans ce royaume*. Paris, 1673.

Dawlatabadi, Yahya. *Hayat-i Yahya*, 4 vols. Tehran, 4th edn., 1362/1983.

De Bode, Baron C. *Travels in Luristan and Arabistan*, 2 vols. London, 1845.

De Bruyn, Cornelis. *Reizen over Moskovie, door Persie en Indie*. Amsterdam, 2nd edn., 1714.

De Filippi, F. *Note di un viaggio in Persia nel 1862*. Milan, 1865.

Della Valle, Pietro. *Viaggi di Pietro della Valle, il pellegrino*, 2 vols. Ed. Gancia. Brighton, 1843.

De Lorey, Eustache, and Douglas Sladen. *Queer Things about Persia*. Philadelphia, 1907.

De Windt, Harry. *A Ride to India across Persia and Baluchistan*. London, 1891.

Dodson, G. Everard. "The Opium Habit in Persia." *The Moslem World* 17 (1927): 261–5.

Don Juan of Persia. *Don Juan of Persia: A Shi`ah Catholic 1560–1604*. Ed. Guy le Strange. London, 1926.

Dourry Efendy, Ahmad. *Relation de Dourry Efendy, ambassadeur de la Porte Othomane auprès du Roi de Perse*. Ed. L. Langlès. Paris, 1810.

Drouville, Gaspar. *Voyage en Perse fait en 1812 et 1813*, 2 vols. in one tome, and atlas. St. Petersburg, 1819–20.

Dubeux, M. Louis. *La Perse*. Paris, 1841.

Dufour, Philippe Sylvestre. *Traitez nouveaux et curieux du Café, du Thé, et du chocolate*. Lyons, 1685.

Dupré, A. *Voyage en Perse fait dans les années 1807, 1808, 1809*, 2 vols. Paris, 1819.

Eastwick, Edward B. *Journal of a Diplomat's Three Years' Residence in Persia*, 2 vols. London, 1864.

Efendi, Evliya (Chelebi). *Narrative of Travels in Asia, Africa, and Europe in the Seventeeenth Century*, 2 vols. Trans. from the Turkish. London, 1834.

Elphinstone, M. *An Account of the Kingdom of Caubul and its Dependencies in Persia, Tartary, and India*, 2 vols. London, 1815; repr. Graz, 1969.

Fasa'i, Hajj Mirza Hasan Husayni. *Farsnamah-i Nasiri*, 2 vols. paginated as one. Ed. Mansur Rastigar Fasa'i. Tehran, 1367/1988.

Fasa'i, Hasan. *History of Persia under Qājār Rule*. Trans. from the Persian by Heribert Busse. New York and London, 1972.

Ferrier, J. P. *Caravan Journeys and Wanderings in Persia, Afghanistan, Kurdestan and Belochistan*. London, 1857.

Feuvrier, J. B. *Trois ans à la cour de Perse*. Paris, 1899.

Flandin, E., and P. Coste. *Voyage en Perse de M. M. Eugène Flandin, peintre, et Pascal Coste, architecte, 1840–41*, 2 vols. Paris, 1850–54.

Florencio des Niño Jesús, P. Fr. Biblioteca Carmelitano-Teresiana de Misiones, vol. 2, *A Persia (1604–1609). Peripecias de una embajada pontificia que fué a Persia a principios del siglo XVII.* Pamplona, 1929.

Forster, George. *A Journey from Bengal to England through the Northern Part of India, Kashmire, Afghanistan, and Persia, into Russia, by the Caspian Sea,* 2 vols. London, 1798.

Foster, William, ed. *The Embassy of Sir Thomas Roe to India, 1615–19.* London, 1926.

Fowler, G. *Three Years in Persia with Traveling Adventures in Koordistan,* 2 vols. London, 1841.

Francklin, Wiliam. *Observations Made on a Tour from Bengal to Persia in the Year 1786–87.* London, 1790.

Fraser, James Baillie. *Narrative of a Journey into Khorasan in the Years 1821 and 1822.* London, 1825; 2nd edn., Delhi, 1984.

———. *Travels and Adventures in the Persian Provinces of the Southern Banks of the Caspian Sea.* London, 1826.

———. *A Winter's Journey from Constantinople to Tehran,* 2 vols. London, 1838.

Freygang, M. "Account of a Journey to Tabriz." In idem and F. K. Freygang, *Letters from the Caucasus and Georgia.* Trans. from the French. London, 1823.

Fryer, John A. *A New Account of East India and Persia, Being Nine Years' Travels, 1672–1681,* 3 vols. Ed. W. Crooke. London, 1909–15.

Gasteiger, Albert Ritter von. *Die Handelverhältnisse Persiens in Bezug auf die Absatzfähigkeit österrreichischer Waaren.* Vienna, 1862.

———. *Von Teheran nach Beludschistan. Reis-Skitzzen.* Innsbruck, 1881.

Gemelli Careri, Giovanni Francisco. *Giro del mondo del dottor D. Gio. Francesco Gemelli Careri,* 6 vols. Naples, 1699–1700.

Ghaffari Qazvini, Qazi Ahmad. *Tarikh-i jahan-ara.* Tehran, 1343/1964.

Gleadowe-Newcomen, A. H. "Report on the British Indian Commercial Mission to South-Eastern Persia during 1904–1905." In *British Documents on Foreign Affairs,* Part 1, From the Mid-Nineteenth Century to the First World War. Series B: the Near and Middle East 1856–1914, vol. 13: Persia, Britain and Russia, 1886–1907. London, 1985.

Gobineau, Joseph Arthur de. *Correspondance entre le Comte de Gobineau et le Comte de Prokesch-Osten (1854–1876).* Ed. Clément Serpeille de Gobineau. Paris, 1933.

———. "Les religions et les philosophies dans l'Asie centrale." In *Œuvres,* vol. 2, 405–809. Paris, 1983.

———. "Trois ans en Asie." In *Œuvres,* vol. 2, 29–401. Paris, 1983.

———. "Voyage en Perse, fragments." *Le Tour du Monde* 2me semestre (1860): 34–48.

Goldsmid, Sir Frederic John. *Eastern Persia. An Account of the Journey of the Persian Boundary Commission 1870–71–72,* vol. 1, *The Geography with Narratives by Majors St. John, Lovett, and Euan Smith.* London, 1876.

———. "Journey from Bandar Abbas to Mash-had by Sistan, with some Account of the Last-named Province." *JRGS* 43 (1873): 63–83.

Gordon, Peter. *Fragment of the Journal of a Tour through Persia in 1820.* London, 1833.

Gordon, Sir Thomas Edward. *Persia Revisited (1895), with Remarks on H.I.M. Mozuffer-ed-Din Shah, and the Present Situation in Persia.* London and New York, 1896.

Gouvea, Antonio de. *Relation des grandes guerres et victoires obtenues par le roy de Perse.* Trans. A. de Meneses. Rouen, 1646.

Grothe, Hugo. *Wanderungen in Persien. Erlebtes und Erschautes.* Berlin, 1910.

Gulbenkian, Roberto, ed. *L'ambassade en Perse de Luis Pereira de Lacerda et des Pères Portugais de l'Ordre de Saint-Augustin, Belchior dos Anjos et Guilherme de Santo Agostinho 1604–1605.* Lisbon, 1972.

Hagemeister de, Jules. *Essai sur les ressources territoriales et commerciales de l'Asie occidentale, le charactère des habitants, leur industrie et leur organisation municipale.* Vol. 3 of K. E. von Baer and Gr. von Helmersen, eds., *Beiträge zur Kenntnis des russisschen Reichs und der angränzenden Länder Asiens.* 9 vols. St. Petersburg, 1839; new edn., Osnabrück, 1968.

Hakluyt, Richard, ed. *The Principal Navigations Voyages Traffiques & Discoveries of the English Nation,* 12 vols. Glasgow, 1903–5.

Hamavi, Muhammad b. Ishaq. *Anis al-Mu'minin.* Ed. Mir Hashim Muhaddis. Tehran, 1363/1984.

Hanway, Jonas. *An Historical Account of the British Trade over the Caspian Sea,* 3 vols. London, 1753.

Harris, Walter B. *From Batum to Baghdad via Tiflis, Tabriz, and Persian Kurdistan.* Edinburgh and London, 1896.

Hedin, Sven. *Verwehrte Spuren. Orientfahrten des Reise-Bengt und anderer Reisenden im 17. Jahrhundert.* Leipzig, 1923.

Herbert, Thomas. *Some Years Travel into Divers parts of Asia and Afrique.* London, 1638.

———. *Travels in Persia 1627–29.* Abridged and ed. William Foster. London, 1928.

Hollingbery, W. *A Journal of Observations made during the British Embassy to the Court of Persia in the Years 1799–1801.* Calcutta, 1814.

Holmes, William Richard. *Sketches on the Shores of the Caspian.* London, 1845.

Hommaire de Hell, Xavier. *Les steppes de la mer Caspienne,* 3 vols. and atlas. Paris, 1843.

Horn, Paul, ed. and trans. *Die Denckwürdigkeiten Schâh Tahmâsp's des Ersten von Persien (1515–1576).* Strassbourg, 1891.

Houssay, F. "Souvenirs d'un voyage en Perse," part 2. *Revue des Deux Mondes* 79 (1887): 367–91; 856–83.

Houtum Schindler, A. "Reisen im südlichen Persien." *Zeitschrift der Gesellschaft für Erdkunde zu Berlin* 14 (1879): 38–67.

al-Hurr al-`Amili, Shaykh Muhammad b. al-Hasan. *Wasa'il al-Shi`ah ila tahsil masa'il al-shari`ah,* vol. 17. Tehran, 1388/1968–69.

Husayn Khan, Mirza. *Jughrafiya-yi Isfahan.* Ed. Manuchihr Situdah. Tehran, 1342/1963.

Isfahani, Mirza Muhammad Sadiq Musavi Nami. *Tarikh-i giti-gusha.* Ed. Sa`id Nafisi. Tehran, 2nd edn., 1363/1984.

al-Isfahani, Muhammad Mihdi b. Muhammad Riza. *Nisf-i jahan fi ta`rif al-Isfahan.* Ed. Manuchihr Situdah. Tehran, 2nd edn., 1368/1989.

Isfahani, Muhammad Ma`sum b. Khajigi. *Khulasat al-siyar. Tarikh-i ruzgar-i Shah Safi Safavi.* Ed. Iraj Afshar. Tehran 1368/1989.

Ishraqi, Ihsan. "Shah Sultan Husayn dar Tuhfat al-`alam." *Tarikh. Nashriyah-i Guruh-i Amuzishi-yi Tarikh. Zamimah-i Majallah-i Danishkadah-i Adabiyat va `Ulum-i Insani-yi Danishgah-i Tihran* 1:1 (2535/1976): 74–102.

I`timad al-Saltanah, Muhammad Hasan Khan. "Kilid-i istita`at." Tehran 1303/1886. In Mahmud Mahmud, *Tarikh-i ravabit-i siyasi–yi Iran va Inglis dar qarn-i nuzdahum-i miladi,* 4th edn., 1193–1200. Tehran, 1330/1951.

———. *al-Ma'asir va al-asar.* Ed. Iraj Afshar. Tehran, 1363/1984.

———. *Ruznamah-i khatirat-i I`timad al-Saltanah.* Ed. Iraj Afshar. Tehran, 1345sh./1966; 4th edn., 1377/1998.

———. *Tarikh-i muntazam-i Nasiri,* 3 vols. Ed. Muhammad Isma`il Rizvani. Tehran, 1367/1988.

Ives, Edward. *A Voyage from England to India in the Year MDCCLIV and a Narrative of the Operations of the Squadron and Army in India.* London, 1773.

Ja`fariyan, Rasul. "Risalah fi bayan hukm shurb al-tutun va'l qahvah." In Ja`fariyan, ed., *MII,* 7:81–92. Qum, 1377/1998.

———. "Sih risalah dar barah-i Abu Muslim va Abu Muslimnamah'ha." In Ja`faryan, ed., *MII,* 2:247–301. Qum, 1374/1995.

Jahangir. *The Tūzuk-i Jahāngīrī or Memoirs of Jahāngīr,* 2 vols in one tome. Trans. Alexander Rogers; ed. Henry Beveridge. Delhi, 2nd edn. 1968.

Jaubert, P. Amédée. *Voyage en Arménie et en Perse fait dans les années 1805 et 1806.* Paris, 1821.

Javadi, Hasan, Manjeh Mar`ashi and Simin Shakarlou, eds. *Ruyaru'i zan va mard dar `asr-i qajar: Ta'dib al-nisvan va Ma`ayib al-rijal.* Washington, D.C., 1992.

al-Jaza'iri, Sayyid Ni`mat Allah al-Musavi. *al-Anwar al-nu`maniyah.* 4 vols. Tabriz, 1959–62.

Jourdain, John. *The Journal of John Jourdain 1608–1617, Describing His Experiences in Arabia, India and the Malay Archipelago.* Ed. William Foster. London, 1905.

Junabadi, Mirza Bayg ibn Hasan. *Rawzat al-Safaviyah.* Ed. Ghulamriza Tabataba'i Majd. Tehran, 1378/1999.

Jurjani, Sayyid Isma`il. *Zakhirah-i Khvarazmshahi.* Ed. Sa`idi Sirjani. Tehran, 2535/1976.

Kaempfer, Engelbert. *Am Hofe des persischen Grosskönigs, 1684–1685.* Ed. Walther Hinz, Tübingen and Basel, 1977.

———. *Amoenitatum exicotarum politico-physico-medicarum, faciculi V.* Lemgo, 1712.

———. *Die Reisetagebücher Engelbert Kaempfers.* Ed. Karl Meier-Lemgo. Wiesbaden, 1968.

Kalantar-i Fars, Mirza Muhammad. *Ruznamah-i Mirza Muhammad Kalantar-i Fars.* Ed. `Abbas Iqbal Ashtiyani. Tehran, 1362/1983.

Karbala'i, Shaykh Hasan Isfahani. *Tarikh-i dukhaniyah ya tarikh-i vaqa'i`-i tahrim-i tanbaku.* Ed. Rasul Ja`fariyan. Qum, 1377/1998.

al-Karmi, Shaykh Mar'i b. Yusuf. *Tahqiq al-burhan fi sha'n al-dukhan.* Ed. Muhammad Jamil al. Shita. Damascus, 1341/1922–23.

Kashani, Mirza Taqi Tabib. "Dar bayan-i ikhtilal-i nizam-i `alam *bih-vasitah-i musakkirat.*" *Iran* (10 Safar 1289/29 April 1872).

Khami, Abu'l Qasim Shihab al-Din Ahmad. *Mansha' al-insha.* Tehran, 1357/1978.

Khanikoff de, Nicolas. *Mémoire sur la partie méridionale de l'Asie Centrale.* Paris, 1862.

Khandamir, Amir Mahmud. *Habib al-siyar fi akhbar afrad bashar.* 4 vols. Ed. Muhammad Dabirsiyaqi. Tehran, 3rd edn., 1362/1983.

———. *Tarikh-i Shah Isma`il va Shah Tahmasb-i Safavi (Zayl-i tarikh-i habib al-siyar).* Ed. Muhammad `Ali Jarrahi. Tehran, 1370/1991.

Khatunabadi, Sayyd `Abd al-Husayn. *Vaqa'i` al-sannin va'l a`vam.* Ed. Muhammad Baqir Bahudi. Tehran, 1352/1973.

Khurshah b. Qubad al-Husayni. *Tarikh-i Ilchi-yi Nizam Shah.* Ed. and annotated M. R. Nasiri and Koichi Haneda. Tehran, 1379/2000.

Klaproth, Jules. *Voyage au Mont Caucase et en Géorgie,* 2 vols. Paris, 1823.

Korf, Baron Feodor. *Vospominaniia o Persii 1834-1835.* St. Petersburg, 1838.

Kotov, Fedot. *Khozhenie kuptsa Fedota Koshova vi Persiiu.* Ed. A. A. Kuznetsov. Moscow, 1958.

Kotzbue, M von. *Narrative of a Journey into Persia in the Suite of the Imperial Russian Embassy in the Year 1817.* London, 1819.

Kroell, Anne, ed. *Nouvelles d'Ispahan 1665–1695.* Paris, 1979.

Krusinski, Father. *The History of the Late Revolutions of Persia,* 2 vols. Trans. Father du Cerceau. London, 2nd edn., 1733.

Lafont, F.D., and H. L. Rabino. "Culture de la gourde à ghaliân en Guilan et en Mazandaran (Perse)." *RMM* 28 (1914): 232–36.

Lamberti, Archange. "Relation de la Colchide ou Mengrellie." In M. Thévenot, *Relation de divers voyages curieux, qui n'ont point estée publiées, ou qui ont esté traduites d'Haclyt, de Purchas & d'autres voyageurs,* 4 vols. in two tomes. Paris, 1663–72.

Landor, A. Henry Savage. *Across Coveted lands or a Journey from Flushing (Holland) to Calcutta, Overland,* 2 vols. New York, 1903.

Lawhi, Sayyid Muhammad b. Muhammad Mir. "Salvat al-Shi`ah va quvvat al-shari`ah." In Rasul Ja'fariyan, ed., *MII,* 2:337–59. Qum, 1374/1995.

Layard, Sir Henry. *Early Adventures in Persia, Susiana, and Babylonia including a Residence among the Bakhtiyari and Other Wild Tribes before the Discovery of Nineveh,* 2 vols. London, 1887.

Leandro di S. Cecilia, F. *Persia, o sia secondo viaggio.* Rome, 1753.

Le Messurier, Colonel A. A. *From London to Bukhara and a Ride through Persia.* London, 1889.

Lerch, Johann Jacob. "Nachricht von der zweiten Reise nach Persien welche der kaiserl. russische Collegienrath Herr D. Johann Jacob Lerch von 1745 bis 1747 gethan hat." *Magazin für die neue Historie und Geographie* 10 (1776): 365–476.

Lettres édifiantes et curieuses, écrites des missions étrangères, 8 vols. Toulouse; new edn., 1810.

Loftus, William Kenneth. *Travels and Researches in Chaldea and Susiana.* London, 1857.

Lomnitskii, S. *Persiia i Persy.* St. Petersburg, 1902.

Lucas, G. "Memorandum on the Cultivation and Exportation of Opium in Persia." *Annual Report on the Adminstration of the Persian Gulf Residency from the Year 1874–75*, 26–30.

Lycklama a Nijeholt, T. M. *Voyage en Russie, au Caucase, et en Perse*, 4 vols. Paris, 1872–75.

Macdonald, Robert. *Personal Narrative of Military Travel and Adventure in Turkey and Persia*. Edinburgh, 1859.

MacGregor, C. M. *Narrative of a Journey through the Province of Khorasan and the Northwest Frontier of Afghanistan in 1875*, 2 vols. London, 1879.

Machado, Augusto Reis, ed. *Itinerário da Índia por terra até à ilha de Chipre por Frei Gaspar de S. Bernardino*. Lisbon, 1953.

Mahdavi, Asghar, and Iraj Afhar, eds., *Yazd dar asnad-i Amin al-Zarb*. Tehran, 1380/2001.

Majlisi, Muhammad Taqi. "Kitab al-mas'ulat," ed. Abu'l Fazl Hafiziyan Babuli. In R. Ja`fariyan, ed., *MII*, 3:687–705. Tehran, 1375/1997.

Malcolm, Napier. *Five Years in a Persian Town*. London, 1905.

Malcolm, Sir John. *History of Persia*, 2 vols. London, 1815.

———. "The Melville Papers." In Issawi, ed., *The Economic History of Iran*, 262–67.

[———]. *Sketches of Persia from the Journals of a Traveller in the East*, 2 vols. London, 1828.

Mandelslo, Johann Albrecht von. *Morgenländische Reyse-Beschreibung* Schleswig, 1658.

Manucci, Nicolao. *Storia do Mogor or Mugul India 1653–1708*, 2 vols. Trans. William Irvine. London, 1907.

Mar`ashi Safavi, Mirza Muhammad Khalil. *Majma` al-tavarikh dar tarikh-i inqiraz-i Safaviyah va vaqa'i`-i ba`d ta sal-i 1207 h.q.* Ed. `Abbas Iqbal Ashtiyani. Tehran, 1363/1983.

Marvi, Muhammad Kazim. `Alam-ara-yi Nadiri*. 3 vols. Ed. Muhammad Amin Riyahi. Tehran, 2nd edn., 1369/1991.

Mashizi (Bardsiri), Mir Muhammad Sa`id. *Tazkirah-i Safaviyah-i Kirman*, Ed. Muhammad Bastani-Parizi. Tehran, 1369/1990.

Meier, Fritz, trans. "Drei moderne Texte zum persischen 'Wettreden'." *Zeitschrift der Deutschen Morgenländischen Gesellschaft* 114 (1961): 289–327.

Melgunov, G. *Das südliche Ufer des kaspischen Meeres oder die Nordprovinzen Persiens*. Trans. from the Russian. Leipzig, 1868.

Membré, Michele. *Mission to the Lord Sophy of of Persia (1539–1542)*. Trans. and ed. A. H. Morton. London, 1993.

Mignan, R. *A Winter's Journey through Russia, the Caucasian Alps, and Georgia*, 2 vols. London, 1839.

Milburn, William. *Oriental Commerce*, 2 vols. London, 1813.

Minorsky, Vladimir, ed. and trans. *Tadhkirat al-Mulūk. A Manual of Safavid Administration*. Cambridge, 1943; repr. 1980.

Mishkat al-Sultan, `Ali Akbar. "Mishkat al-musafirin." Ed. Mir Hashim Muhaddis. *MII* 5: 11–118. Qum, 1376/1977.

Mitford, Edward Ledwich. *A Land March from England to Ceylon Forty Years Ago*, 2 vols. London, 1884.

Morgan, E. Delmar, and C. H. Coote, eds. *Early Voyages and Travels to Russia and Persia*, 2 vols. London, 1886.

Morier, James. *A Journey through Persia, Armenia, and Asia Minor to Constantinople in the Years 1808 and 1809*. London, 1812.

Mu`ayyir al-Mamalik, Dust `Ali Khan. *Yaddashtha-i az zindigani-yi khususi-yi Nasir al-Din Shah*. Tehran, 3rd edn., 1372/1993.

Mudarrisi Tabataba'i, ed. *Turbat-i pakan*, 2 vols. 2535/1976.

Mulla Kamal. *Tarikh-i Mulla Kamal*. In Ibrahim Dihgan, ed., *Tarikh-i Safaviyan Khulasat al-tavarikh-Tarikh-i Mulla Kamal*. Arak 1334/1955.

Munajjim Yazdi, Mulla Jalal al-Din. *Tarikh-i `Abbasi ya ruzgar-i Mulla Jalal*. Tehran, 1366/1987.

Musävi, Mämäd Tagi, ed. *Orta äsr Azärbajān tarichinä dari fars dilindä jazilmyš sänädlar*. Baku, 1965.

Mustawfi, `Abd Allah. *Sharh-i zindigani-yi man ya tarikh-i ijtima`i va idari-yi dawrah-i Qajar*, 3 vols. Tehran, 3rd edn., 1360/1981.

Mustawfi, Muhammad Muhsin. *Zubdat al-tavarikh*. Ed. Bihruz Gudarzi. Tehran, 1375/1996.

Mustawfi Bafqi, Muhammad Mufid. *Jami`-i Mufidi ya tarikh-i Yazd ta ibtida-yi saltanat-i Shah Isma`il-i avval*. Tehran 1342/1963.

Najmabadi, Afsaneh, ed. *Ma`ayib al-rijal dar pasukh bih ta'dib al-nisvan*. Chicago, 1992.

Najm al-Mulk, Hajj `Abd al-Ghaffar. *Safarnamah-i Khuzistan*. Ed. Muhammad Dabirsiyaqi. Tehran, 1341/1962.

Nakhchavani, Haj Husayn. "Masjid-i Jami`-i Tabriz va sharh-i katibah'ha-yi an." *Nashriyah-i Danishkadah-i Adabiyat-i Tabriz* 6:1 (1333/1954): 36–38.

Nasiri, Muhammad Ibrahim b. Zayn al-`Abidin. *Dastur-e shahriyaran*. Ed. Muhammad Nadir Nasiri Muqaddam. Tehran, 1373/1994.

Nasrabadi, Muhammad Tahir. *Tazkirah-i Nasrabadi. Tazkirat al-shu`ara*. Ed. Muhsin Naji Nasrabadi, 2 vols. paginated as one. Tehran, 1378/1999.

Nassakin, Nicolaus von. "Von der Messe in Nishni-Nowgorod." *OMO* 12 (1886): 168.

Neander, Johann. *Tabacologia medico-cheirurgico pharmaceutica*. Leiden, 1622.

Niebuhr, Carsten. *Reisebeschreibung*, 2 vols. 1778.

———. *Travels through Arabia and Other Countries in the* East, 2 vols. Edinburgh, 1792.

O'Donovan, Edmond. *The Merv Oasis: Travels and Adventures East of the Caspian During the Years 1879–80–81 Including Five Months' Residence among the Tekkés of Merv*, 2 vols. London, 1882.

Olearius, Adam. *Vermehrte newe Beschreibung der Muscowitischen und Persischen Reyse*. Schleswig, 1656; facsimile repr. Ed. Dieter Lohmeier. Tübingen, 1971.

Olivier, G. A. *Voyage dans l'Empire Othoman, l'Egypte et la Perse*, 6 vols. Paris, 1807.

Orsolle, E. *Le Caucase et la Perse*. Paris, 1885.

Ouseley, Sir William. *Travels in Various Countries of the East, More Particularly Persia*, 2 vols. London, 1819–21.

Ovington, John. *A Voyage to Suratt In the Year 1689*. London, 1696.

Pelly, Lieut. Col. Lewis. "A Brief Account of the Province of Fars." *TBGS* 8 (1865): 175–85.

———. "Remarks on the Tribes, Trade and Resources around the Shore Line of the Persian Gulf." *TBGS* 17 (1863–64): 32–112.

Perkins, J. *A Residence of Eight Years in Persia, Among the Nestorian Christians with Notices of the Muhammedans.* Andover, 1843.

Perrin, Narcisse. *L'Afghanistan ou description gégraphique du pays théatre de la guerre.* Paris, 1842.

Petis de la Croix, François. *Extrait du journal du sieur Petis, Fils, Professeur en Arabe, et secrétaire interprète entretenu en la marine renfermant tout ce qu'il a vu en fait en Orient.* In Doury Efendy, *Relation de Dourry Efendy,* 73–174.

Pires, Tomé. *The Suma Oriental of Tomé Pires (1512–1515).* Ed. Armando Cortesão, 2 vols. London, 1944.

Polak, Jacob Eduard."Beitrag zu den agrarischen Verhältnissen in Persien." *Mittheilungen der Kaiserlich-Königlichen Geographischen Gesellsschaft* 6 (1862): 107–43.

———. "Das persische Opium." *OMO* 9 (1883): 124–5.

———. *Persien, das Land und seine Bewohner,* 2 vols. Leipzig, 1865; repr. Hildesheim, 1976.

Porter, Robert Ker. *Travels in Georgia, Persia, Armenia, Ancient Babylonia &c. &c. During the Years 1817, 1818, 1819, and 1820,* 2 vols. London, 1821.

Poser, Heinrich von. *Tage Buch Seiner Reise von Kon stantinopel aus durch Bulgarey, Armenien, Persien und Indien.* Jena, 1675.

Pottinger, Henry. *Travels in Beloochistan and Sinde.* London, 1816; repr. Karachi, 1976.

Poullet, Sr. *Nouvelles relations du Levant . . . Avec une exacte description . . . du royaume de Perse,* 2 vols. Paris, 1668.

Preece, J. R. "Journey from Shiraz to Jashk, via Darab, Forg, and Minar." *JRGS,* Suppl. Paper 1 (1885): 403–41.

Qazi Ahmad b. Sharaf al-Din al-Husayn al-Husayni Qummi. *Khulasat al-tavarikh.* Ed. Ishraqi. Tehran, 1359/1980.

Qazvini, A. "Dar mazarrat-i dukhaniyyat va qahvah va afyun." *Sukhan* 17 (1346/1967): 372–4.

Qazvini, Abu'l Hasan. *Fava'id al-Safaviyah.* Ed. Maryam Mir Ahmadi. Tehran, 1367/1988.

Qazvini, Muhammad Shafi`. *Qanun-i Qazvini. Intiqad-i awza`-i ijtima`i-yi Iran-i dawrah-i Nasiri.* Ed. Iraj Afshar. Tehran, 1370/1991.

Qazvini, Mulla `Abd al-Nabi Fakhr al-Zamani. *Tazkirah-i maykhanah.* Ed. Ahmad Gulchin Ma`ani. Tehran, 1340/1961.

Rabino, H.–L. "Les anciens sports au Guilan." *RMM* 14 (1914): 97–110.

Radde. G., and E. Koenig. "Das Ostufer des Pontus und seine kulturelle Entwicklung im Verlaufe der letzten dreissig Jahre." *Ergänzungsheft No. 112 zu "Petermanns Mittheilungen"* (Gotha, 1894): 34–35.

Rafi`a, Mirza. *Dastur al-Muluk.* In Iraj Afshar, ed., *Daftar-i tarikh,* vol. 1, 475–651. Tehran, 1380/2001.

Ramusio, Giovanni Battista. *Navigationi e viaggi,* 2 vols. Turin, 1979.

————. *Delle navigationi e viaggi raccolte da M. Gio. Battista Ramusio*, 3 vols Venice, 1559; new edn., 1606.

Rauwolf, Leonhard. *Aigentliche Beschreibung der Raiss . . . inn die Morgenländer.* Laugingen, 1582; repr. Graz, 1971.

Rebelo, Nicolao de Orta. *Un voyageur portugais en perse au début du XVIIe siècle. Nicolao de Orta Rebelo.* Ed. And trans. Serrão, Joaquim Veríssimo. Lisbon, 1972.

Rich, Claudius. *Narrative of a Residence in Koordistan*, 2 vols. London, 1836.

Richard, Francis, ed. *Raphaël du Mans missionnaire en Perse au XVIIe s.*, 2 vols. Paris, 1995.

Rivadeneyra, D. Adolfo. *Viaje al interior de Persia*, 3 vols. Madrid, 1880.

Rochechouart de, J. "Le commerce et l'exploration de la Perse et ses fabriques d'armes." *Annales de voyages* 1 (1867): 50–80.

Ross, Sir Denison E., ed. *The Journal of Robert Stodart, Being an Account of His Experiences as a Member of Sir Dodmore Cotton's Mission in Persia in 1628–29.* London, 1935.

Rumlu, Hasan Bayg. *Ahsan al-tavarikh.* Ed. `Abd al-Husayn Nava'i. Tehran, 1357/1978.

Rustam al-Hukama (Asif, Muhammad Hashim). *Rustam al-tavarikh.* Ed. Muhammad Mushiri, 2nd edn. Tehran, 1352/1973. Trans. into German as *Persische Geschichte 1694–1835 erlebt, erinnert und erfunden. Das Rustam, at-tawarih in deutscher Bearbeitung*, 2 vols. Trans. and ed. Birgitt Hoffmann. Bamberg, 1986.

Rycaut, Paul. *The History of the Turkish Empire from the Year 1623 to the Year 1677*, 2 vols. London, 1680.

Sabzavari, Mulla Muhammad Baqir. *Rawzat al-anwar-i `Abbasi (dar akhlaq va shivah-i kishvardari).* Ed. Isma`il Changizi Ardaha'i. Tehran, 1377/1998.

Sam Mirza Safavi. *Tuhfah-i Sami.* Ed. Rukn al-Din Humayunfarrukh. Tehran, n. d.

Sanson, N. *Voyage ou relation de l'estat présent du royaume de Perse.* Paris, 1694.

Sar Rishtah-dar, Muhammad `Ali. "Safarnamah-i Sar Rishtah-dar. Tabriz bih Tihran (1288)." In Iraj Afshar, ed., *Daftar-i tarikh*, vol. 1, 137–66. Tehran, 1380/2001.

Schuyler, Eugene. Turkistan. *Notes of a Journey in Russian Turkistan, Khokand, Bukhara, and Kulja*, 2 vols. New York, 1876.

Seligmann, K., ed. *Ueber drey höchst seltene persische Handschriften. Ein Beytrag zur Litteratur der orientalischen Arzneymittellehre.* Vienna, 1833.

Sepsis, A. "Perse. Quelques mots sur l'état réligieux actuel de la Perse." *Revue de l'Orient* 3, nos. 11–12 (1844): 97–114.

Serena, Carla. *Les hommes et les choses en Perse.* Paris, 1883.

Sheil, Lady. *Glimpses of Life and Manners in Persia.* London, 1856.

Shepherd, William Ashton. *From Bombay to Bushire and Bussora, including an Account of the Present State of Persia and Notes on the Persian War.* London, 1857.

Sherley, Sir Anthony. *His Anthony Sherley His Relation of his Travels into Persia.* London, 1613; repr. Westmead, U.K., 1972.

Shirazi, `Abdi Bayg. *Takmilat al-akhbar. (Tarikh-i Safaviyah az aghaz ta 987 h.q.).* Ed. `Abd al-Husayn Nava'i. Tehran, 1369/1990.

Silva y Figueroa, Don Garcia de. *Comentarios de D. Garcia de Silva y Figueroa de la embajada que de parte del rey de España Don Felipe III hizo al rey Xa Abas de Persia*, 2 vols. Madrid, 1903.

Sipihr, Muhammad Taqi (Lisan al-Mulk). *Nasikh al-tavarikh*, 2 vols. Ed. Jamshid Kiyanfar. Tehran, 1377/1998.

Sirjani, Sa`idi, ed. *Vaqa'i'-i ittifaqiyah. Majmu`ah-i guzarish'ha-yi khufyah-nivisan-i Inglisi dar vilayat-i junubi-yi Iran az sal-i 1291 ta 1322 qamari.* Tehran, 1361/1983.

Sparroy, Wilfirid. *Persian children of the Royal Family. The Narrative of an English Tutor at the Court of H.I.H. Zillu's-Sultán, G.C.S.I.* London and New York, 1902.

Speelman, Cornelis. *Journaal der reis van den gezant der O.I. Compagnie Joan Cunaeus naar Perzië in 1651–1652.* Ed. A. Hotz. Amsterdam, 1907.

Spilman, James A. *Journey through Russia into Persia in the Year 1739.* London, 1742.

Stack, Edward. *Six Months in Persia.* New York, 1882.

Stark, Freya. *The Valley of the Assassins and Other Persian Travels.* London, 1936.

Stern, Henry A. *Dawnings of Light in the East: With Biblical, Historical, and Statistical Notices of Persons and Places Visited during a Mission to the Jews, in Persia, Coordistan, and Mesopotamia.* London, 1854.

Stirling, Edward. *The Journals of Edward Stirling in Persia and Afghanistan 1828–1829.* Ed. and intro. Jonathan L. Lee. Naples, 1991.

Stocqeler, H. H. (pseud. for J.H. Siddon). *Fifteen Months Pilgrimage through Untrodden Tracts of Khuzistan and Persia*, 2 vols. London, 1832.

Stolze, F., and. F. C. Andreas. "Die Handelsverhältnisse Persiens, mit besonderer Berücksichtigung der deutschen Interessen." *Ergänzungsheft 77 zu "Petermanns Mittheilungen."* (Gotha, 1885): 69–83.

Stuart, Lieutenant-Colonel Charles. *Journal of a Residence in Northern Persia and the Adjacent Provinces of Turkey.* London, 1854.

Sykes, Ella C. *Persia and Its People.* London, 1910.

———. *Through Persia on a Side Saddle.* London, 1898.

Sykes, Major Percy Molesworth. *Ten Thousand Miles in Persia or Eight Years in Iran.* London, 1902.

Tabrizi, Muhammad Husayn b. Khalaf (Burhan). *Burhan-i qati`*, 5 vols. Ed. Muhammad Mu`in. Tehran, 2nd edn., 1342/1963.

Tahmasb, Shah b. Isma`il b. Haydari al-Safavi. *Tazkirah-i Shah Tahmasb.* Ed. Amr Allah Sifri. Tehran, 1363/1984.

Tancoigne, J. M. *A Narrative of a Journey into Persia.* Trans. from the French. London, 1820.

Taqizadah, Sayyid Hasan. *Zindigi-yi tufani (Khatirat). Tarikh-i Iran-siyasat-madaran-i Iran.* Ed. `Aziz Allah `Alizadah. Tehran, 1379/2000.

Tavernier, Jean-Babtiste. *Les six voyages de Jean-Bapt. Tavernier en Turquie, en Perse et aux Indes*, 2 vols. Utrecht, 1712.

Tectander, Georg. *Eine abenteuerliche Reise durch Russland nach Persien 1602–1604.* Ed. Dorothea Müller-Ott. Tulln, 1978.

Teixeira, Pedro de. *The Travels of Pedro de Teixeira*. Trans and annotated W. Sinclair and D. Ferguson. London, 1902.

Tenreiro, António. "Itinerário de António Tenreiro." In António Baião, ed., *Itinerários da Índia a Portugal por terra*. Coimbra, 1923.

Thevenot, Jean de. *Relation d'un voyage fait au Levant*. Vol. 2, *Suite du voyage de Levant*. Paris, 1674.

———. *Voyage Mr. de Thevenot au Levant*. Paris, 1689.

———. The Travels of Monsieur de Thevenot into the Levant, 3 vols. London, 1687.

Tournefort, J. Pitton de. *Relation d'un voyage du Levant*, 2 vols. Paris, 1717.

Truilhier, M. *Mémoire descriptif de la route de Téhran a Meched et de Meched à Iezd, reconnue en 1807*. Paris, 1841.

Tucci, Ugo. "Una Relazione di Giovan Battista Vecchietti sulla Persia e sul regno di Hormuz (1587)." *Oriente Moderno* 35 (1955): 149–60.

Tunakabuni, Hakim Mu'min Husayni. *Tuhfah-i Hakim Mu'min*. Tehran, new edn., 1360/1981.

Turkaman, Iskandar Bayg (Munshi). *Tarikh-i `alam-ara-yi `Abbasi*, 2 vols. Ed. Iraj Afshar. Tehran, 2nd edn., 1350/1971.

———. *zayl-i Tarikh-i alam-ara-yi `Abbasi*. Ed. Suhayli Khansari. Tehran, 1317/1938.

Umidyani, Sayyid Hasan. "Nigarishi bar yik vaqfnamah-i tarikhi az dawrah-i Safaviyah." *Ganjinah-i Asnad* 21–22 (1375/1996): 20–27.

Ussher, John. *A Journey from London to Persepolis; Including Wanderings in Dagehstan, Georgia, Armenia, Kurdistan, Mesopotamia, and Persia*. London, 1865.

Vahid Qazvini, Mirza Muhammad Tahir. `Abbasnamah*. Ed. Dihqan. Arak, 1329/1951.

Valah Qazvini Isfahani, Muhammad Yusuf. *Khuld-i barin (Iran dar ruzgar-i Safaviyan)*. Ed. Mir Hashim Muhaddis. Tehran, 1372/1993.

———. *Iran dar zaman-i Shah Safi va Shah `Abbas-i divvum (Khuld-i barin, rawzah 6, hadiqah 6–7)*. Ed. Muhammad Riza Nasiri. Tehran, 1380/2001.

Valentyn, François. *Oud- en nieuw Oost-Indien*, 8 vols, vol. 5, *Keurlyke beschryving van Choromandel, Pegu, Arakan, Bengale, Mocha, van 't Nederlandsch Comptoir in Persien* . . . Dordrecht-Amsterdam, 1726.

Vámbéry, H. "Die anglo-russische Theeconcurrenz in Turkestan." *OMO* 2 (1876): 106–7.

———. *Meine Wanderungen und Erlebnisse in Persien*. Pest; facs. repr. Nuremberg, 1979.

Verberkmoes, Johan, and Eddy Stolds, ed. *Aziatische omzwervingen. Het levensverhaal van Jacques de Coutre, een Brugs diamanthandelaar, 1591–1617*. Berchem, 1988.

[Villotte], Père Jacques, S. J. (attributed to), *Voyages d'un missionnaire de la Compagnie de Jésus en Turquie, en Perse, en Arabie et en Barbarie*. Paris, 1730.

Waring, Scott. *A Tour to Sheeraz*. London, 1807.

Watson, Robert Grant. *A History of Persia from the Beginning of the Nineteenth Century to the Year 1858, with a Review of the Pincipal Events that Led to the Establishment of the Kajar Dynasty*. London, 1866.

Wilbraham, Richard. *Travels in the Transcaucasian Provinces of Russia.* London, 1839.

Wills, C. J. *In the Land of the Lion and the Sun or Modern Persia. Being Experiences of Life in Persia from 1866 and 1881.* London, 1883; repr. London, 1891.

———. *Persia as It Is.* London, 1886.

Wilson, Sir Arnold T. *SW. Persia: A Political Officer's Diary 1907–1914.* London, 1941.

Wilson, S. G. *Persian Life and Customs.* New York, 3rd edn., 1900.

Yate, C. E. *Khurasan and Sistan.* Edinburgh and London, 1900.

Zak`aria of Agulis, *The Journals of Zak`aria of Agulis.* Ed. and trans. George A. Bournoutian. Costa Mesa, 2003.

MODERN STUDIES

Abisaab, Rula Jurdi. *Converting Persia: Religion and Power in the Safavid Empire.* London and New York, 2004.

Adamiyat, Firaydun. *Amir Kabir va Iran.* Tehran, 4th edn., 1354/1975.

———. *Idi'uluzhi-yi nahzat-i mashrutiyat-i Iran.* Tehran, 2535/1976.

Adamiyat, Firaydun, and Huma Natiq, *Afkar-ijtima`i va siyasi va iqtisadi dar asar-i muntashir nashudah-i Qajar.* Tehran, 1356/1977.

Adshead, S. A. M. *Material Culture in Europe and China, 1400–1800: The Rise of Consumerism.* London and New York, 1997.

Afshar, Iraj. "Gushah'i az tarikh-i chay." *Ayandeh* 17 (1370/1991): 765–7.

———. "Tarikh-i chay dar Iran." In idem, ed., *Savad va biyaz. Majmu`ah-i maqalat,* 2 vols., 2: 498–99. Tehran, 1349/1970.

———. "Tazah'ha va parah'ha-yi iranshinasi." *Bukhara* 28 (1381/1992): 77.

Agnew, Jean-Christophe. "Coming Up for Air: Consumer Culture in Historical Perspective." In John Brewer and Roy Porter, eds., *Consumption and the World of Goods,* 19–39. London, 1993.

Ajudani, Masha'Allah. *Mashrutah-i Irani va pish-zaminah'ha-yi nazariyah-i "vilayat-i faqih."* London, 1997.

Akyeampong, Emmanuel Kwaku. *Drink, Power, and Cultural Change: A Social History of Alcohol in Ghana, c. 1800 to Recent Times.* Portsmouth, N.H., 1996.

Albrecht, Peter. "Coffee-Drinking as a Symbol of Social Change in Continental Europe in the Seventeenth and Eighteenth Centuries." *Studies in Eighteenth-Century Culture* 18 (1988): 91–103.

Āl-e Dāvūd, `Ālī. "Coffee." *EIr.* 5 (1992): 893–6.

Algar, Hamid. *Religion and State in Iran 1785–1906: The Role of the Ulama in the Qajar Period.* Berkeley, 1969.

Allsen, Thomas T. *Culture and Conquest in Mongol Eurasia.* Cambridge, 2001.

———. "Ever Closer Encounters: The Appropriation of Culture and the Apportionment of Peoples in the Mongol Empire." *Journal of Early Modern History* 1 (1997): 2–23.

Alonso, Carlos O.S.A. "El P. Antonio de Gouvea O.S.A. y la embajada persa de Denzig Beg (1609–1612)." *Analecta Augustiniana* 38 (1975): 63–94.

———. "La embajada persa de Denguiz-Beg y Antonio de Gouvea, osa, a la luz de nuevos documentos." *Archivo Agustiniano* 64 (1980): 49–115

———. "Embajadores de Persia en las Cortes de Praga, Roma y Valladolid (1600–1601)." *Anthologica Annua* 36 (1989): 11–271.

Amanat, Abbas. *Resurrection and Renewal: The Making of the Babi Movement in Iran, 1844–1850*. Ithaca, N.Y., and London, 1989.

And, Metin. *Istanbul in the 16th Century: The City, the Palace and Daily Life*. Istanbul, 1994.

Arendonk, C van. "Kahwa." *EI²* 4 (1978), 449–53.

Arjomand, Said Amir. "The Mujtahid of the Age and the Mullā-bāshī: An Intermediate Stage in the Institutionalization of Religious Authority in Shi`ite Iran." In idem, ed., *Authority and Political Culture in Shi`ism*, 80–99. Albany, 1988.

———. *The Shadow of God and the Hidden Imam*. Chicago, 1984.

Aubin, Jean. "L'avènement des Safavides reconsideré." *MOOI* 5 (1988): 1–130.

———. "Le royaume d'Ormuz au début du XVIe siècle." *Mare Luso-Indicum* 2 (1973): 77–179.

———. "Révolution chiite et conservatisme. Les Soufis de Lâhejân, 1500–1514." *MOOI* 1 (1984):1–40.

Babaie, Sussan. "Shah `Abbas II, the Conquest of Qandahar, the Chihil Sutun, and Its Wall Paintings." *Muqarnas* 11 (1994): 125–42.

Babayan, Kathryn. *Mystics, Monarchs and Messiahs: Cultural Landscapes of Early Modern Iran*. Cambridge, Mass., 2003.

———. "The Safavid Synthesis: From Qizilbash Islam to Imamite Shi`ism." *IS* 27 (1994): 135–61.

———. "Sufis, Dervishes and Mullas: the Controversy over Spiritual and Temporal Dominion in Seventeenth-Century Iran," in Melville, ed., *Safavid Persia*, 117–38.

———. "The Waning of the Qizilbash." Ph.D. Dissertation, Princeton University, 1993.

Bacqué-Grammont, Jean-Louis. *Les Ottomans, les Safavides et leurs voisins. Contribution à l'histoire des relations internationales dans l'Orient islamique de 1514 à 1524*. Istanbul, 1987.

Bakhash, Shaul. *Iran: Monarchy, Bureaucracy and Reform under the Qajars: 1858–1896*. London, 1978.

Balabanova, Svetlana. "Tabak in Europa vor Kolumbus." *Antike Welt* 25 (1994): 282–5.

Baland, Daniel, and Marcel Bazin. "Çāy." *EIr.* 5 (1992), 103–7.

Bamdad, Mihdi. *Sharh-i hal-i rijal-i Iran dar qarn-i 12, 13, 14 hijri*, 6 vols. Tehran, 4th edn., 1371/1992.

Barendse, J. R. "Trade and State in the Arabian Seas: A Survey from the Fifteenth to the Eighteenth Century." *JWH* 11 (2000): 173–224.

Barrows, Susanna. "`Parliaments of the People': The Political Culture of Cafés in the Early Third Republic." In Susanna Barrows and Robin Room, eds, *Drinking: Behavior and Belief in Modern History*, 87–97. Berkeley, 1991.

Bastan-Parizi, Muhammad Ibrahim. *Azhd'ha-yi haftsar: Majma`ah-i maqalat*. Tehran, 1352/1974.

Bazin, M. "Angur." *EIr.* 2 (1987), 70–72.

Becker, Lotherd. "Zur Ethnologie der Tabakspfeife." In Sergius Golowin, ed., *Kult und Brauch der Krauterpfeife in Europa*, 5–25. Allmendingen, 1982.

Berger, Lutz. "Ein Hertz wie ein trockner Schwamm. Laqānis und Nābulusis Schriften über den Tabakrauch." *Der Islam* 78 (2001): 249–93.

Bigi, Hasan. *Tihran-i qadim*. Tehran, 3rd edn.,1373/1994.

Birnbaum, E. "Vice Triumphant: The Spread of Coffee and Tobacco in Turkey." *Durham University Journal* 49:1 (1956): 21–27.

Bleibtreu, I. *Persien, das Land der Sonne und des Löwen*. Freiburg, 1894.

Booth, Martin. *Opium: A History*. New York, 1999.

Bouchon, Geneviève. "Notes on the Opium Trade in Southern Asia during the Pre-Colonial Period." In Roderich Ptak and Dietmar Rothermund, eds., *Emporia, Commodities and Entrepreneurs in Asian Maritime Trade*, c. 1400–1750, 95–106. Stuttgart, 1991.

Bouhdiba, Abdelwahab. *La sexualité en Islam*. Paris, 1975.

Briant, Pierre. *Histoire de l'Empire perse de Cyrus à Alexandre*. Paris, 1996.

Brongers, G. A. *Pijpen en tabak*. Bussum, 1964.

Brookshaw, Dominic P. "Palaces, Pavilions and Pleasure-gardens: The Context and Setting of the Medieval *Majlis*," *Middle Eastern Literatures* 6 (2003): 199–223

Brouwer, C. G. "Al-Mukha as a Coffee Port in the Early Decades of the Seventeenth Century According to Dutch Sources." In Tuchscherer, ed., *Le commerce du café*, 271–95.

———. *Cauwa ende comptanten: De Verenigde Oostindische Compagnie in Jemen 1614–1655/Cowa and Cash: The Dutch East India Company in Yemen, 1614–1655*. Amsterdam, 1988.

Brunel, René. *Le monachisme errant dans l'Islam. Sīdi Heddi et les Heddāwa*. Paris, 1955.

Burnett, John. "Coffee in the British Diet, 1650–1990." In D. U. Ball, ed., *Kaffee im Spiegel europäischer Trinksitten*, 35–52. Zurich, 1991.

Bushev, P. P. *Istoriia posol'stv i diplomaticheskikh otnoshenii russkogo i iranskogo gosudarstv v 1586–1612 gg.* Moscow, 1976.

———. *Istoriia posol'stv i diplomaticheskikh otnoshenii russkogo i iranskogo gosudarstv v 1586–1612 gg.* Moscow, 1987.

———. *Posol'stvo Artemiia Volynskogo v Iran v 1715–1718 gg.* Moscow, 1978.

———. "Posol'stvo V. G. Korobina i A. Kubshinova v Iran v 1621–1624 gg." In *Iran. Ekonomika, Istoriia, Istoriografiia, Literatura (Sbornik statei)*, 124–55. Moscow, 1976.

Calder, Norman. "Legitimacy and Accommodation in Safavid Iran: The Juristic Theory of Muhammad Bāqir al-Sabzavārī (d. 1090/1679)." *Iran* 25 (1987): 91–106.

Carlier, Omar. "Le café maure. Sociabilité masculine et effervescence citoyenne (Algérie XVIIe–XXe siècles)." *Annales E.S.C.* 45 (1990): 975–1003.

Carnoy, Dominique. *Représentations de l'Islam dans la France de XVIIe siècle. La ville des tentations*. Paris, 1998.

Chaudhuri, K. N. "Kahwa, Trade with Europe" *EI*² 4 (1978).

———. *The Trading World of Asia and the English East India Company 1660–1760*. Cambridge, 1978.

Christensen, Arthur. *L'Iran sous les Sassanides*. Copenhagen, 1944.

Comes, O. *Histoire, Géographie, statistique du tabac*. Naples, 1900.

Cook, Michael. *Commanding Right and Forbidding Wrong in Islamic Thought*. Cambridge, 2001.

Corti, E. C. *A History of Smoking*. Trans. Paul England. London, 1931.

Courtwright, David, T. *Forces of Habit: Drugs and the Making of the Modern World*. Cambridge, Mass., 2001.

Dale, Stephen. *The Garden of the Eight Paradises: Babur and the Culture of Empire in Central Asia, Afghanistan and India (1483–1530)*. Leiden, 2004.

Danishpazhuh, Muhammad Taqi. "Yik pardah az zindigani-yi shah Tahmasb-i Safavi." *Majallah-i Danishkadah-i Adabiyat va `Ulum-i Insani-yi Mashhad* 7:4 (1350/1971): 915–97.

Darhuhaniyan, Harutun. *Tarikh-i Julfa-yi Isfahan*. Trans. L. G. Minasian and Musavi Firaydani. Isfahan, 1379/2000.

Das Gupta, Ashin. *Indian Merchants and the Decline of Surat c. 1700–1750*. Wiesbaden, 1979.

Davenport-Hines, Richard. *The Pursuit of Oblivion: A Global History of Narcotics 1500–2000*. London, 2001.

De Bruijn, J. T. P. *Of Piety and Poetry: The Interaction of Religion and Literature in The Life and work of Hakim Sana'i of Ghazna*. Leiden, 1983.

Desmet, Hélène, "Approche méthodologique pour l'étude des cafés dans les sociétés du Proche et Moyen Orient." In idem, ed., *Contributions*, 27–51.

———. ed. *Contributions au thème du et des cafés dans les sociétés du Proche Orient*. Aix-en-Provence, 1991.

Desmet-Grégoire, Hélène. *Le divan magique. L'Orient turc en France au XVIIIe siècle*. Paris, 1994.

Desmet-Grégoire, Hélène, and François Georgeon, eds. *Cafés d'Orient revisités*. Paris, 1997.

Di Borgomale, Rabino. *Mazandaran and Astarabad*. London, 1928.

Dikötter, Frank, Lars Laamann, Zhou Xun. *Narcotic Culture: A History of Drugs in China*. Chicago, 2004.

Eberhard, Elke. *Osmanische Polemik gegen die Safawiden im 16. Jahrhundert nach arabischen Handschriften*. Freiburg im Breisgau, 1970.

Ehlers, Eckart. "Die Teelandschaft von Lahidjan/Nordiran. In H. Wilhelmy et al., eds., *Beiträge zur Geographie der Tropen und Subtropen, Festschrift für Herbert Wilhelmy*, 229–42. Tübingen, 1970.

Elgood, Cyril. *A Medical History of Persia and the Eastern Caliphate*. Cambridge; repr. Amsterdam, 1979.

———. *Safavid Medical Practice or the Practice of Medicine, Surgery and Gynaecology in Persia between 1500 A.D. and 1750 A.D.* London, 1970.

Ellis, Aytoun. *The Penny Universities: A History of the Coffee-Houses*. London, 1956.

Entner, Marvin. *Russo-Persian Commercial Relations, 1828–1914*. Gainesville, FL, 1965.

Epinette, M. "Le thème du vin dans la poéesie lyrique persane des Xe et XIe siècles." Thèse, Université de Paris, 1986.

Evans, John C. *Tea in China: The History of China's National Drink.*
New York, 1992.

Fahey, David M. "'I'll Drink to That!': The Social History of Alcohol." *Choice*
(Dec. 2000): 637–45.

Falsafi, Nasrullah. "Sar-guzasht-i 'Saru Taqi' Makhdum al-umara va khadim
al-fuqara." In idem, ed., *Chand maqalah-i tarikhi va adabi*, 287–309. Tehran,
1342/1963.

———. *Zindigani-yi Shah `Abbas-i avval*, 5 vols. in 3 tomes. Tehran, 4th edn.,
1369/1990.

Faroqhi, Suraiya. "Coffee and Spices: Official Ottoman Reactions to Egyptian
Trade in the later Sixteenth Century," *Wiener Zeitschrift für die Kunde des
Morgenlandes, Festschrift für Andreas Tietze* 76 (1986): 87–93.

———. *Subjects of the Sultan: Culture and Daily Life in the Ottoman Empire.*
London and New York, 2000.

Fekhner, M. V. *Torgovlia russkogo gosudarstvo so stranami vostoka v XVI veke*
Moscow, 1956.

Ferrier, Ronald. "An English View of Persian Trade in 1618—Reports from the
Merchants Edward Pettus and Thomas Barker." *JESHO* 19 (1976): 182–214.

Fitzpatrick, Anne Lincoln. *The Great Russian Fair. Nizhnii Novgorod,
1840–90.* Basingstoke, 1990.

Floor, Willem. "The Art of Smoking in Iran and Other Uses of Tobacco." *IS* 35
(2002): 47–86.

———. "Change and Development in the Judicial system of Qajar Iran
(1800–1925)." In Edmund Bosworth and Carole Hillenbrand, eds., *Qajar Iran:
Political, Social and Cultural Change 1800–1925*, 113–47. Edinburgh, 1983.

———. "The Lūtīs—A Social Phenomenon in Qājār Persia." *WI* 13 (1971):
103–20.

———. "The Office of Muhtasib in Iran." *IS* 18 (1985): 53–74.

———. "The Secular Judicial System in Safavid Persia." *Stud. Ir.* 29 (2000): 9–60.

Fouchécour, Charles-Henri de. *Moralia. Les notions morales dans la littérature
persane du 3e/9e au 7e/13e siècle.* Paris, 1986.

Furughi, Abu'l Hasan. "Samavar sazi dar Iran." *Yaghma* 20 (1346/1967):
477–79.

Gaube, Heinz, and E. Wirth. *Der Bazar von Isfahan.* Wiesbaden, 1978.

Gelpke, Rudolf. *Vom Rausch im Orient und Okzident.* Stuttgart, 1966.

Georgeon, François. "Les cafés à Istanbul à la fin de l'Empire Ottoman." In
Desmet-Grégoire and Georgeon, eds., *Cafés d'Orient revisités*, 39–78.

———. "Ottomans and Drinkers: The Consumption of Alcohol in Istanbul in
the Nineteenth Century." In Eugene Rogan, ed., *Outside In: On the Margins
of the Modern Middle East*, 7–30. London and New York, 2002.

Gignoux, Philippe. "Matériaux pour une histoire du vin dans l'Iran ancien." In
Rika Gyselen and Maria Szuppe, eds., *Matériaux pour l'histoire économique
de monde iranien*, 35–50. Paris, 1999.

Gilbar, Gad G. "Persian Agriculture in the the Qājār Period, 1860–1906: Some
Economic and Social Aspects." *Asian and African Studies* 12 (1978): 312–65.

———. "The Persian Economy in the Mid-19th Century." *WI* 19 (1979):
177–211.

Gladwell, Malcolm. "Java Man: How Caffeine Created the Modern World," *The New Yorker* (July 30, 2001), 76–80.

Glamann, Kristoff. *Dutch-Asiatic Trade 1620–1740*. Copenhagen and The Hague, 1958.

Glassen, Erika. "Schah Isma`il und die Theologen seiner Zeit." *Der Islam* 48 (1972): 254–68.

Glünz, Michael. "Das Vorspiel zur Revolution. Der iranische Tabakboycott von 1891/92 und der historische Kontext des Rauchens in Iran." In Thomas Hengartner and Christoph Maria Merki, eds., *Tabakfragen. Rauchen aus kulturwissenschaftlicher Sicht*, 139–50. Zurich, 1996.

Gnoli, G. "Bang" (in ancient Iran). *EIr.* 3 (1989), 689–90.

Gokhale, B. G. "Tobacco in Seventeenth-Century India," *Agricultural History* 48 (1974): 484–92.

Goldstone, Jack. "The Problem of the 'Early Modern' World." *JESHO* 41 (1998): 249–84.

Goodman, Jordan. *Tobacco in History*. London, 1993.

Gopal, Surendra. *Indians in Russia in the 17th and 18th Centuries*. Calcutta, 1988.

Goushegir, Aladin. "Forme et évolution sémantique de quelques noms arabo-persans relatifs au <<café>> depuis la période médiévalé à nos jours." Thèse de doctorat, Universite de Paris III, 1996.

———. "Le café et les cafés en Iran, des Safavides a l'époque actuelle." In Desmet-Grégoire and Georgeon, eds., *Cafés d'Orient revisités*, 141–76.

Gronke, Monika. *Derwische im Vorhof der Macht. Sozial- und Wirtschafsgeschichte Nordwestirans im 13. und 14. Jahrhundert*. Stuttgart, 1993.

———. "La religion populaire en Iran mongol." In Denise Aigle, ed., *L'Iran face à la domination mongole*, 205–20. Tehran, 1997.

Gutas, "Avicenna; Mysticism." *EIr.* 3 (1989), 79–83.

Hanaway, W. "Blood and Wine: Sacrife and Celebration in Manuchihri's Wine Poetry." *Iran* 26 (1988): 69–80.

Hartwich, Carl. *Die menschliche Genussmittel*. Leipzig, 1911.

Hattox, Ralph S. *Coffee and Coffeehouses: The Origins of a Social Beverage in the Medieval Near East*. Seattle, 1985.

Hedin, Sven. *Verwehte Spuren. Orientfahrten des Reise-Bengt und anderer Reisenden im 17. Jahrhundert*. Leipzig, 1923.

Heine, Peter. *Weinstudien. Untersuchungen zu Anbau, Produktion und Konsum des Weins im arabisch-islamischen Mittelalter*. Wiesbaden, 1982.

Herbette, Maurice. *Une ambassade persane sous Louis XIV*. Paris, 1907.

Herzig, Edmund. "The Armenian Merchants of New Julfa, Isfahan: A Study in Pre-Modern Asian Trade." Ph.D. dissertation. University of Oxford, 1991.

Hinz, Walther. "Schah Esma`il II. Ein Beitrag zur Geschichte der Safaviden." *Mitteilungen des Seminars für Orientalische Sprachen zu Berlin. Westasiatsiche Studien* 36 (1933): 19–99.

Hoexter, Miriam, Shmuel N. Eisenstadt and Nehemia Levtzion, eds. *The Public Sphere in Muslim Societies*. Albany, 2002.

Höllmann, Thomas O. *Tabak in Südostasien. Ein Ethnographisch-historischer Überblick*. Berlin, 1988.

Horn, Paul, ed. and trans. *Die Denckwürdigkeiten Schâh Tahmâsp's des Ersten von Persien (1515–1576)*. Strassbourg, 1891.

Ishraqi, Ihsan. "Shah Sultan Husayn dar Tuhfat al-`alam." *Tarikh* 1, vol. 1 (2535/1976): 90–91.

Islam, Riazul. *Indo-Persian Relations: A Study of the Political and Diplomatic Relations between the Mughul Empire and Iran*. Teheran, 1970.

Issawi, Charles, ed. *The Economic History of Iran 1800–1914*. Chicago, 1971.

———. "The Tabriz-Trabzon Trade 1830–1900." *IJMES* 1 (1970): 18–27.

Iukht, A. I. *Torgovlia s vostochnymi stranami i vnutrennii rynok Rossii (20-60-e gody XVIII veka)*. Moscow, 1994.

Ja`fariyan, Rasul. "Andishah'ha-yi yik `alim-i Shi`i dar dawlat-i Safavi (Ayat Allah `Ali Naqi Kamarah'i)." *Hukumat-i Islami* 5 (1376/1997): 108–40.

———. *Din va siyasat dar dawrah-i safavi*. Tehran, 1370/1991.

———. *`Ilal-i bar uftadan-i Safaviyan: Mukafat-namah*. Tehran, 1372/1993.

———, ed. *MII*, 10 vols. Qum, 1374/1995.

———. *Safaviyah dar `arsah-i din, farhang va siyasat*. 3 vols. Qum, 1379/2000.

———. *Tarjumah-i anajil-i arba`ah*. Tehran, 1375/1996.

Józefowicz, Z. "Z dziejów stosunków Polsko-Perskich," *Przegląd Orientalistyczny* 44 (1962): 329–38

Kafadar, Cemal. "Yeniçeri-Esnaf Relations: Solidarity and Conflict." MA Thesis, McGill University, 1981.

Kalantari, Manucher. "Le livre des rois et les peintures des maisons de thé." *Objets et Mondes* 11:1 (1971): 141–58.

Karamati, Yunis. "Abu'l Fath Gilani." *Da'irat al-ma`arif-i buzurg-i islami* 6 (Tehran, 1373/1994): 106–9.

Karamustafa, Ahmet T. *God's Unruly Friends. Dervish Groups in the Islamic Later Middle Period 1200–1550*. Salt Lake City, 1994.

Kazimi, Suraya. *Hajji Muhammad Mirza Kashif al-Saltanah, pidar-i chay*. Tehran, 1372/1993.

Keall, Edward J. "One Man's Mede is Another Man's Persian; One Man's Coconut is Another Man's Grenade." *Muqarnas* 10 (1993): 275–85.

Keddie, Nikki R. *Religion and Rebellion in Iran: The Iranian Tobacco Protest of 1891–1892*. London, 1966.

Kelly, J. B. *Britain and the Persian Gulf 1795–1880*. Oxford, 1968.

Kelly, Laurence. *Diplomacy and Murder in Tehran: Alexander Griboyedov and Imperial Russia's Mission to the Shah of Persia*. London, 2002.

Keyvani, Mehdi. *Artisans and Guilds Life in the Later Safavid Period: Contributions to the Social-Economic History of Persia*. Berlin, 1982.

Kiernan, V. G. *Tobacco: A History*. London, 1991.

Kırlı, Cengiz. "The Struggle over Space: Coffeehouses of Ottoman Istanbul." Ph.D. Dissertation, SUNY Binghamton, 2000.

Kissling, Hans Joachim. "Zur Geschichte der Rausch- und Genussgifte im osmanischen Reiche." *Südostforschungen* 16 (1957): 342–56.

Klein-Franke, Felix. "No Smoking in Paradise: The Habit of Tobacco Smoking Judged by Muslim Law." *Le Muséon* 106 (1993): 155–83.

Knaap, G. J. "Coffee for Cash: The Dutch East India Company and the Expansion of Coffee Cultivation in Java, Ambon and Ceylon 1700–1730." In J. van Goor, ed., *Trading Companies in Asia 1600–1830*, 33–50. Utrecht, 1986.

Koelz, Walter N. *Persian Diary, 1939–1941*. Ann Arbor, 1983.

Kueny, Kathryn. *The Rhetoric of Sobriety: Wine in Early Islam*. Albany, 2001.

Kuhi-Kirmani, H. *Tarikh-i taryak va taryaki dar Iran*. Tehran, 1324/1945.

Kukanova, N.G. *Ocherki po istorii russko-iranskikh torgovykh otnoshenii v XVII- pervoi polovinie XIX veka*. Saransk, 1977.

———. *Russko-iranskaia torgovlia 30-50-e gody XIX veka (Sbornik dokumentov)*. Moscow, 1984.

Lambton, Ann K. S. *Continuity and Change in Medieval Persia. Aspects of Administrative, Economic and Social History, 11th–14th Century*. New York, 1988.

———. "Persian Trade under the Early Qājārs." In eadem, *Qājār Persia: Eleven Studies*, 108–39. Austin, 1988.

———. "The Tobacco Régie: Prelude to Revolution." *SI* 22 (1966): 71–90.

Lane, George. *Early Mongol Rule in Thirteenth-Century Iran: A Persian Renaissance*. London and New York, 2003.

Latifi-Niya, Mashhid. "Taryak va iqdamat-i anjuman-i mubarizah ba taryak va alkul." *Ganjinah-i Asnad* 7–8 (1371/1992): 110–29.

Laufer, Berthold. *Sino-Iranica: Chinese Contributions to the History of Civilization in Ancient Iran with Special Reference to the History of Cultivated Plants and Products*. Chicago, 1919.

———. *Tobacco and Its Use in Asia*. Chicago, 1924.

Laufer, Berthold, Wilfrid D. Hambly, and Ralph Linton, *Tobacco and Its Use in Africa*. Chicago, 1930.

Lefèvre, R. "Su un ambasciata persiana a Roma nel 1601." *Studi Romani* 35 (1987): 359–73.

Lewisohn, Leonard. "An Introduction to the History of Modern Persian Sufism; part 1, The Ni`matullāhī Order: Persecution, Revival and Schism." *BSOAS* 61 (1998): 437–64.

Losensky, Paul E. *Welcoming Fighānī: Imitation and Poetic Individuality in the Safavid-Mughal Ghazal*. Costa Mesa, Calif., 1998.

Lowry, Heath W. "Impropriety and Impiety among the Early Ottoman Sultans (1351–1451)." *The Turkish Studies Association Journal* 26, vol. 2 (2002): 29–38.

MacLaren, Donald. "Opium Eating and Smoking." *The Medical Brief* 35 (1907): 505–08; 592–95.

Macro, Eric. *Yemen and the Western World Since 1571*. New York, 1968.

Magelhães-Godinho, Vitorino. *L'Economie de l'empire portugais aux XVe et XVIe siècles*. Paris, 1969.

Mahdavi, Sayyid Muslih al-Din. *Zindiginamah-i `Allamah Majlisi*, 2 vols. Tehran, 1378/2000.

Mahjub, Muhammad Ja`far. "Sukhanvari." *Sukhan* 9:6 (1357/1958): 530–35; 9:7 (1358/1958): 631–37; and 9:8 (1337/1958): 779–86; trans. in Meier, "Drei moderne Texte."

Malecka, Anna. "The Muslim Bon Vivant: Drinking Customs of Bābūr, the Emperor of Hindustan." *Der Islam* 78 (2001): 310–27.

Martin, A. Lynn. *Alcohol, Sex, and Gender in Late Medieval and Early Modern Europe*. New York, 2001.

Martin, Vanessa. "An Evaluation of Reform and Development of the State in the Early Qajar Period." *WI* 36 (1996): 1–24.

Matthee, Rudi (Rudolph) "Administrative Stabiliy and Change in Late 17th-Century Iran: The Case of Shaykh ʿAli Khan Zanganah (1669–1689)." *IJMES* 26 (1994): 77–98.

———. "Blinded by Power: The Rise and Fall of Fatḥ ʿAlī Khān Dāghestānī, Grand Vizier under Shāh Solṭān Ḥosayn Ṣafavī (1127/1715–1133/1720)." *Stud. Ir.* 33 (2004): 179–219.

———. "The Career of Mohammad Beg, Grand Vizier of Shah ʿAbbas II (r. 1642–1666)." *IS* 24 (1991): 17–36.

———. "Coffee in Safavid Iran: Commerce and Consumption," *JESHO* 37 (1994): 1–32.

———. "Courtesans, Prostitutes and Dancing Girls: Women Entertainers in Safavid Iran." In Rudi Matthee and Beth Baron, eds., *Iran and Beyond: Essays in Middle Eastern History in Honor of Nikki R. Keddie*, 121–50. Costa Mesa, Calif., 2000.

———. "Exotic Substances: The Introduction and Global Spread of Tobacco, Coffee, Tea, Cocoa, and Distilled Liquor, 16th–18th Centuries." In Roy Porter and Mikulas Teich, eds., *Drugs and Narcotics in History*, 24–51. Cambridge, 1985.

———. "From Coffee to Tea: Shifting Patterns of Consumption in Qajar Iran." *JWH* 6 (1996): 199–230.

———. "Mint Consolidation and the Worsening of the Late Safavid Coinage: The Mint of Huwayza." *JESHO* 44 (2001): 505–39.

———. "Politics and Trade in Late Safavid Iran: Commercial Crisis and Government Reaction under Shah Solayman (1666–1694)." Ph.D. Dissertation., University of California, Los Angeles, 1991.

McAuliffe, J. D. "The Wines of Earth and Paradise: Qur'anic Proscriptions and Promises." *Logos Islamikos* 6 (1984): 159–74.

McChesney, Robert D. "The Anthology of Poets: *Muzakkir al-Ashab* as a Source for the History of Seventeenth-Century Central Asia." In Michel M. Mazzaoui and Vera B. Moreen, eds., *Intellectual Studies on Islam*, 57–84. Utah, 1990.

McGovern, Patrick E. *Ancient Wine: The Search for the Origins of Viniculture*. Princeton, 2003.

Melikian-Chirvani, A. S. "From the Royal Boat to the Beggar's Bowl." *Islamic Art* 5 (1990–91): 3–106.

———. "The Iranian Bazm in Early Persian Sources." In R. Gyselen, ed., *Banquets d'Orient*, 95–118. Bures s/Yvette, 1992.

———. "The Iranian Wine Leg from Prehistory to Mongol Times." *Bulletin of the Asia Institute*, new ser. 11 (1997): 65–91.

———. *Islamic Metalwork from the Iranian World 8th–18th Centuries*. London, 1982.

———. "Les taureaux à vin et les cornes à boire de l'Iran islamique." In Paul Bernard and Frantz Grenet, eds., *Histoire des cultes de l'Asie Centrale préislamique*, 101–25. Paris, 1991.

————. "The Wine Bull and the Magian Master." In Philippe Gignoux, ed., *Recurrent Patterns in Religion: From Mazdaism to Sufism*, 101–34. Paris, 1992.

Melton, James van Horn. *The Rise of the Public in Enlightenment Europe.* Cambridge, 2001.

Melville, Charles. "'The Year of the Elephant': Mamluk-Mongol Rivalry in the Hejaz in the Reign of Abū Saʿīd (1317–1335)." *Stud. Ir.* 21 (1992): 197–214.

Mintz, Sidney W. *Sweetness and Power: The Place of Sugar in Modern History.* New York, 1985.

Mitchell, Colin Paul. "The Sword and the Pen: Diplomacy in Early Safavid Iran, 1501–1555." Ph.D. Dissertation, University of Toronto, 2002.

Mordtmann, J. H. "Sunnistisch-schiitische Polemik im 17. Jahrhundert." *Mitteilungen des Seminars für Orientalische Sprachen* 29 (1926): 116–19.

Moreen, Vera Basch. "The Persecution of Iranian Jews during the Reign of Shah ʿAbbas II." *Hebrew Union College Annual* 52 (1981): 275–309.

Morgan, David. *The Mongols.* Oxford, 1986.

Motahhedeh, Roy. *The Mantle of the Prophet: Religion and Politics in Iran.* New York, 1985.

Muʿtazid, Khusraw. *Hajj Amin al-Zarb. Tarikh-i tijarat-i sarmaguzari-yi sanʿati dar Iran.* Tehran, 1366/1987.

Natiq, Huma. *Bazarganan dar dad u sitad ba bank-i shahi va rizhi-yi tanbaku.* Tehran, 1373/1994.

————. *Iran dar rahyabi-yi farhangi, 1834–1848.* Paris, 1368/1990.

Necipoğlu, Gülru. "Framing the Gaze in Ottoman, Safavid, and Mughal Palaces." *Ars Orientalia* 23 (1993): 303–42.

Neligan, A. R. *The Opium Question, with Special Reference to Persia.* London, 1927.

Newman, Andrew J. "Clerical Perceptions of Sufi Practices in late Seventeenth-Century Persia: Arguments over the Permissibility of Singing (*Ghinā'*)." In Leonard Lewisohn and David Morgan, eds., *The Heritage of Sufism, vol. III, Late Classical Persianate Sufism (1501–1750)*, 135–64. Oxford, 1999.

————. "Fayd al-Kashani and the Rejection of the Clergy/State Alliance: Friday Prayers as Politics in the Safavid Period." In Linda S. Walbridge, ed., *The Most Learned of the Shiʿa: The Institution of the Marjaʿ Taqlid*, 34–52. Oxford, 2000.

————. "The Myth of the Clerical Migration to Safawid Iran: Arab Shiite Opposition to ʿAlī al-Karakī and Safawid Shiism." *WI* 33 (1993): 66–112.

————. "Sufism and Anti-Sufism in Safavid Iran: The Authorship of the Hadīqat al-Shīʿa Revisited." *Iran* 37 (1999): 95–108.

Newman, R. K. "Opium Smoking in Late Imperial China: A Reconsideration." *MAS* 29 (1995): 765–94.

Okazaki, Shoko. "The Great Persian Famine of 1870–71." *BSOAS* 49 (1986): 183–92.

Olson, Roger T. "Persian Gulf Trade and the Agricultural Economy of Southern Iran in the Nineteenth Century." In Michael E. Bonine and Nikki Keddie, eds., *Continuity and Change in Modern Iran*, 143–59. Albany, 1981.

Pampus, Heinz. "Die theologische Enzyklopädie Bihār al-Anwār des Muhammad Bāqir al-Maǧlisī (1037–1110 A.H. = 1627–1699 A.D.). Ein Beitrag zur Literaturgeschichte der Šī`a in der Safawidenzeit." Dissertation, Friedrich Wilhelm Universität, Bonn, 1970.

Parsadust, Manuchihr. *Shah Tahmasb-i avval*. Tehran, 1377/1998.

Parvin, Manuchehr, and Maurie Sommer. "Production and Trade of Persian Opium: Economics and Law in Retrospect." *Orient* 28 (1987): 244–60.

Perry, John. *Karim Khan Zand. A History of Iran, 1747–1779*. Chicago, 1979.

Petrov, A. M. "Foreign Trade of Russia and Britain with Asia in the Seventeenth to Nineteenth Centuries." *MAS* 21 (1987): 625–37.

Petrushevsky, I. P. "The Socio-Economic Condition of Iran under the Il-Khans." *Cambridge History of Iran* 5 (1968), 483–537.

Piemontese, Angelo Michele. "Gli ufficiali italiani al servizio della Persia nel XIX secolo" In G. Borsa and P. Beonio Brocchieri, eds., *Garibaldi, Mazzini e il Risorgimento nel risveglio dell-Asia e dell-Africa*, 65–130. Milan, 1984.

Pincus, Steve. "`Coffee Politicians Does Create': Coffeehouses and Restoration Political Culture." *The Journal of Modern History* 67 (1995): 807–34.

Price, Jacob M. "The Tobacco Adventure to Russia: Enterprise, Politics, and Diplomacy in the Quest for a Northern Market for English Colonial Tobacco, 1676–1722." *Transactions of the American Philosophical Society*, new ser. 51 (1961): 1–120.

Ptak, Roderich. "Die Rolle der Chinesen, Portugiesen und Holländer im Teehandel zwischen China und Südostasien (ca. 1600–1750)." *Jahrbuch für Wirtschaftsgeschichte* (1994/1): 89–105.

Pur-i Davud, Ibrahim. *Hurmazdnamah*. Tehran, 1331/1952.

Qaziha, Fatimah, ed. *Marasim-i darbar-i Nasiri (Jashn-i ashpazan (1285–1313 h.q.)*. Tehran, 1382/2003.

Quataert, Donald. ed. *Consumption Studies and the History of the Ottoman Empire 1550–1922. An Introduction*. Albany, 2000.

Quinn, Sholeh A. "Rewriting Ni`matu'llāhī History in Safavid Chronicles." In Leonard Lewisohn and David Morgan, eds., *The Heritage of Sufism: late Classical Persianate Sufism (1501–1750)*, 201–24. London, 1999.

Rafeq, Abdul-Karim. "The Socioeconomic and Political Implications of the Introduction of Coffee into Syria, 16th–18th Centuries." In Tuchscherer, ed., *Le commerce du café*, 127–41.

Ravandi, Murtaza. *Tarikh-i ijtima`i-yi Iran. Manazir az hayat-i ijtima`i, hunari va san`ati-yi Iraniyan ba`d az Islam*, vol. 7. Tehran, 3rd edn. 1369/1990.

Raymond, André. *Artisans et commerçants au Caire au XVIIIe siècle*, 2 vols. Damascus, 1973.

Razpush, Shahnaz & EIr. "Galyān." *EIr*. 10 (2000), 261–65.

Rival, Ned. *Tabac, Miroir du temps*. Paris, 1982.

Rogers, J. M., ed. and trans., *The Topkapı Saray Museum: The Albums and Illustrated Manuscripts*. London, 1986.

Röhrborn, Klaus Michael. *Provinzen und Zentralgewalt Persiens im 16. und 17. Jahrhundert*. Berlin, 1966.

Rosen, Lawrence. *The Culture of Islam: Changing Aspects of Contemporary Muslim Life*. Chicago, 2002.

Rosenthal, Franz. *The Herb. Hashish versus Medieval Muslim Society.* Leiden, 1971.

Ruotsala, Anntii. *Europeans and Mongols in the Middle of the Thirteenth Century: Encountering the Other.* Helsinki, 2001.

Ruymbeke, Christine van. "Le vin, interdiction et licence, dans la poésie persane." *Acta Orientalia Belgica* 10 (1997): 173–86.

Salati, Mario. *I viaggi in Oriente di Sayyid `Abbâs b. `Alî al-Makkî letterato e cortigiano (1718–1729).* Venice, 1995.

Sandgruber, Roman. *Bittersüsse Genüsse.* Vienna, Cologne, Graz, 1986.

Sangar, S. P. "Intoxicants in Mughal India." *Indian Journal of History of Science* 16 (1981): 202–14.

Santen, H. W. van. *De Verenigde Oost-Indische Compagnie in Gujarat en Hindustan, 1620–1660.* Meppel, 1982.

Saraçgil, A. "Generi voluttuari e ragion di stato. Politiche repressive del consumo di vino, caffè e tabacco nell' impero ottomano nei secc. XVI e XVII." *Turcica* 28 (1996): 163–94.

Saraçgil, A. "L'introduction du café à Istanbul (XVIe–XVIIe s.)." In Desmet-Grégoire and Georgeon, eds., *Cafés d'Orient revisités*, 25–38.

Satow, Ernest M. "The Introduction of Tobacco into Japan" *Transactions of the Asiatic Society of Japan* 6 (1878): 68–84.

Sayf, Hadi. *Naqqashi-yi qahvah-khanah.* Tehran, 1369/1990.

Scarsborough, John. "The Opium Poppy in Hellenistic and Roman Medicine." In Roy Porter and Mikuláš Teich, eds., *Drugs and Narcotics in History*, 4–23. Cambridge, 1995.

Schivelbusch, Wolfgang. "Die trockene Trunkenheit des Tabaks." In Völger, ed., *Rausch und Realität*, 1:216–23. *Drogen im Kulturvergleich*, Cologne, 1981.

———. *Tastes of Paradise: A Social History of Spices, Stimulants, and Intoxicants.* New York, 1992.

Schneider, Manfred. *Beiträge zur Wirtschaftsstruktur und Wirtschaftsentwicklung Persiens 1850–1900.* Stuttgart, 1990.

Schopen, Armin. "Tabak in Jemen," in Völger, ed., *Rausch und Realität. Drogen im Kulturvergleich*, 1:244–47. Cologne, 1981.

Schütz, Joseph. *Russlands Samowar und russischer Tee. Kulturgeschichtlicher Aufriss.* Regensburg, 1986.

Seyf, A. "Commercialization of Agriculture: Production and Trade of Opium in Persia, 1850–1906." *IJMES* 16 (1984): 233–50.

———. "Production of Sugar in Iran in the Nineteenth Century." *Iran* 32 (1994): 139–43.

Shahnavaz, S. "Afyūn." *EIr.* 1 (1985), 594–98.

Shahri, Ja`far. *Tarikh-i ijtima`i-yi Tihran dar qarn-i sizdahum. Zindigi, kasb u kar*, 6 vols. Tehran, 1378/1999.

Sherrat, Stephen. "Alcohol and Its Alternatives: Symbol and Substance in Pre-Industrial Cultures." In Jordan Goodman, Paul E. Lovejoy, and Andrew Sherrat, eds., *Consuming Habits: Drugs in History and Anthropology*, 11–46. London, 1995.

Siddiqi, M. Z. "The Muhtasib under Auranzeb." *Medieval India Quarterly* 5 (1963): 113–19.

Simsar, Hasan. "Nazari bih paydayish-i qalyan va chupuq dar Iran." *Hunar va Mardum* 17 (1342/1963): 14–25.

———. "L'apparition du narghileh et de la chibouque." *Objets et Mondes* 11 (1971): 83–94.

Smith, John Masson Jr. "Dietary Decadence and Dynastic Decline in the Mongol Empire." *Journal of Asian History* 34 (2000): 35–52.

Smith, R.E.F., and David Christian. *Bread and Salt: A Social and Economic History of Russia.* Cambridge, 1984.

Smith, S. D. "Accounting for Taste: British Coffee Consumption in Historical Perspective." *The Journal of Interdisciplinary History* 27 (196): 183–214.

———. "The Early Diffusion of Coffee Drinking in England." In Michel Tuchscherer, ed., *Le commerce du café*, 245–70.

Smith, Woodruff D. "Complications of the Commonplace: Tea, Sugar, and Imperialism," *The Journal of Interdisciplinary History* 23 (1992): 259–78.

———. *Consumption and the Making of Respectability 1600–1800.* New York and London, 2002.

Sohrweide, Hanna. "Der Sieg der Safaviden in Persien und seine Rückwirkungen auf die Schiiten Anatoliens im 16. Jahrhundert." *Der Islam* 41 (1965): 95–223.

Soudavar, Abolala. "Between the Safavids and the Mughals: Art and Artists in Transition." *Iran* 37 (1999): 49–66.

———. "The Early Safavids and their Cultural Interaction with Surrounding States." In Nikki R. Keddie and Rudi Matthee, eds., *Iran and the Surrounding World: Interactions in Culture and Cultural Politics*, 89–120. Seattle, 2002.

Spence, Jonathan. "Opium Smoking in Ch'ing China." In Frederic Wakeman and Carolyn Grant, eds., *Conflict and Control in Late Imperial China*, 143–73. Berkeley, 1975.

Stahl, Günther. "Zur Frage des Ursprungs des Tabaksrauchens." *Anthropos* 26 (1931): 569–82.

Stearns, Peter N. *Consumerism in World History: The Global Transformation of Desire.* London and New York, 2001.

Stewart, Devin. "The First *Shaykh al-Islām* of the Safavid Capital Qazvin." *JAOS* 116 (1996): 387–405.

Tajbakhsh, Ahmad. *Tarikh-i Safaviyah.* Shiraz, 1373/1994.

Tanner, Jakob. "Rauchzeichen. Zur Geschichte von Tabak und Hanf." In Thomas Hengartner and Christoph Maria Merki, eds., *Tabakfragen: Rauchen aus kulturwissenschaftlicher Sicht*, 15–42. Zurich, 1996.

Tapper, Richard. "Blood, Wine and Water: Social and Symbolic Aspects of Drinks and Drinking in the Islamic Middle East." In Sami Zubaida and Richard Tapper, eds., *A Taste of Thyme: Culinary Cultures of the Middle East*, 215–32. London, 1994.

Tiedemann, Friedrich. *Geschichte des Tabaks und ander ähnlicher Genussmittle.* Frankfurt am Main, 1854.

Tomaschek, W. "Zur historischen Topographie von Persien." In *Sitzungsberichte der philosophischen, historischen Classe der Kais. Akademie der Wissenschaften zu Wien* 102 (Vienna, repr. Osnabrück, 1972): 145–231.

Tsadik, Daniel. "Foreign Intervention, Majority, and Minority: The Status of the Jews during the Latter part of Nineteenth-Century Iran (1848–1896)." Ph.D. Dissertation, Yale University, 2002.

Tuchscherer, Michel. "Commerce et production du café en Mer Rouge au XVIe siècle." In Tuchscherer, Le commerce du café, 69–90.

Tuchscherer, Michel, ed. Le commerce du café avant l'ère des plantations coloniales. Cahiers des annales islamologiques 20 (2001).

Ukers, William H. All about Coffee. New York, 1935.

Van der Merwe, Nikolaas J. "Cannabis Smoking in 13th–14th Century Ethiopia: Chemical Evidence." In Vera Rubin, ed., Cannabis and Culture, 77–80. The Hague and Paris, 1975.

Von Grunebaum, Gustav E. Studien zum Kulturbild und Selbstverständis des Islams. Zürich and Stuttgart, 1969.

Waines, David. "Al-Balkhi on the Nature of Forbidden Drink." In Manuella Marin and David Waines, eds., La alimentacion en las culturas islamicas, 111–26. Madrid, 1994.

Walcher, Heidi. "In the Shadow of the King: Politics and Society in Qājār Isfahān, 1874–1907." Ph.D. Dissertation, Yale University, 1999.

Weinberg, Bennet Alan, and Bonnie K. Bealer. The World of Caffeine: The Science and Culture of the World's Most Popular Drug. New York, 2001.

Wensinck, A. J. "Khamr." EI² 4 (1978), 994–97.

Werner, Christoph. An Iranian Town in Transition: A Social and Economic History of the Elites of Tabriz, 1747–1848. Wiesbaden, 2000.

Wiener, Leo. Africa and the Discovery of America, 3 vols. Philadelphia, 1920–22.

Wood, Barry David. "The Shahnama-i Isma`il: Art and Cultural Memory in Sixteenth-Century Iran." Ph.D. Dissertation, Harvard University, 2002.

Yarshater, Ehsan. "The Theme of Wine Drinking and the Concept of the Beloved in Early Persian Poetry." SI 13 (1960): 43–54.

Zarinebaf-Shahr, Fariba. "Tabriz under Ottoman Rule (1725–1731)." Ph.D. Dissertation, University of Chicago, 1991.

Zarrinkub, `Abd al-Husayn. Justiju dar tasavvuf-i Iran. Tehran, 1357/1978.

Zheng, Yangwen. "The Social Life of Opium in China, 1483–1999." MAS 37 (2003): 1–39.

Zilfi, Madeleine C. "The Kadizadelis: Discordant Revivalism in Seventeenth-Century Istanbul." Journal of Near Eastern Studies 4 (1986): 251–69.

———. The Politics of Piety: the Ottoman Ulema in the Postclassical Age (1600–1800). Minneapolis, 1988.

Zolli, Paolo. "Il caffè di Pietro della Valle." Lingua Nostra 50:2–3 (1989): 64–65.

Zubaida, Sami. Law and Power in the Islamic World. London and New York, 2003.

Index